THE
BROADWAY
MUSICAL
QUIZ
BOOK

THE
BROADWAY
MUSICAL
QUIZ
BOOK

Laura Frankos

APPLAUSE
THEATRE & CINEMA BOOKS

An Imprint of Hal Leonard Corporation
New York

Published in 2010 by Applause Theatre & Cinema Books
An Imprint of Hal Leonard Corporation
7777 West Bluemound Road
Milwaukee, WI 53213

Trade Book Division Editorial Offices
19 West 21st Street, New York, NY 10010

Printed in the United States of America

Book design by Lynn Bergesen
Typography by UB Communications

Library of Congress Cataloging-in-Publication Data

Frankos, Laura.
   The Broadway musical quiz book / Laura Frankos.
      p. cm.
   ISBN 978-1-4234-9275-7 (pbk.)
   1. Musicals—New York (State)—New York—Miscellanea. I. Title.
   ML1711.8.N3F73 2010
   782.1'4097471—dc22
                                        2010022711

www.applausepub.com

To my own Broadway babies—Alison, Rachel,
and Rebecca—who grew up speaking
fluent Sondheim

Contents

Act Two

Foreword

Warning: This is not a book for someone who can't tell *The Girl Who Came to Supper* from *The Man Who Came to Dinner*.

If you don't know Broadway musicals from *The Act* to *The Zulu and the Zayda*, close this book right now. Go visit your grandmother. Take a job, for heaven's sake, with my papa in his business.

But if you're a true Broadway baby, here's the ultimate way to test your knowledge. Beware, though. Once you delve in, you'll soon feel like Pippin: "Trapped, but happy." Don't be surprised if you feel your head swimming—or feel over your head—as much as the chorus boys and girls who inhabited the swimming pool in *Wish You Were Here*.

But much of the time, you'll be as proud as William Barfée (pronounced Bar-FAY) for recalling what you know—if it only takes a moment, or even if it takes considerably longer. For, as the boys in *All American* taught us, it's fun to think. You'll soon experience that delicious feeling of reading a lyric, suddenly jerking your head up from the book, staring straight ahead, and squinting, softly singing the line to yourself, repeating it while nodding in rhythm—until—Pow! Bam! Zonk!—you break into a big smile when you get it—if you get it. Good, you've got it—as it travels from the tip of your tongue to your Broadway-saturated brain.

Of course, in addition to the good times, there will be bum times when you'll be humbled by how much you don't know. Here, Laura Frankos shows that she's right up there with Maria Von Trapp. "Come! I'll make it easier for you!" she seems to say, exhibiting the quality of mercy by offering a number of helpful hints. And wasn't she as sweet as pie, and not tough as leather, to make many questions multiple choice so that the answer is right there in front of us?

But even if you know an answer outright, don't skip the multiple-choice items. Laura often includes one utterly absurd answer in order to reward savants with a good laugh. My favorite follows the question "What did producer Ken Harper do that dramatically boosted ticket sales for *The Wiz*?" Believe me, the answer is not that he "had the winged monkeys make appearances singing Cole Porter's 'Please Don't Monkey with Broadway.'"

Some are less obvious—and make more sense—than that. When Laura asks who took over for Hepburn in *Coco*, she offers Rosalind Russell as one of her choices. Well, that could have happened, given that Russell was married to Frederick Brisson, the show's lead producer. So looking through Laura's wrong answers can be as much fun as scouring for Ninas in Hirschfelds.

All of us who have enjoyed Q & A books have had the sad feeling of turning a page only to find that the Q section has concluded, and now the boring old A section has arrived. Laura knows that, too, so she's taken the most extraordinary pains to make her answer section as entertaining as the question section. And unlike other quiz masters who simply give the correct answer, Laura lets us see the careful consideration she gave the three or four duds. Her putting "Laurence Harvey" as one of the choices for "Who played Harry Bogen in *I Can Get It for You Wholesale*?" wasn't arbitrary; he came darned close to playing the part.

Of course, reading the answers you missed will make you occasionally smite your forehead with the same force that Arthur Laurents did when Stephen Sondheim asked him "Who's doing the lyrics to *West Side Story*?" Other times you'll feel your eyebrows rise as you learn what you never knew. Why did Alan Jay Lerner call the wind Maria and not Shirley? Laura will explain. And has anyone ever given a more complete list of musical adaptations from Shakespeare's plays?

So you'll soon feel, as Julius Caesar sang in *Her First Roman* (at least before a certain song was cut in Boston), "I had a wonderful time." That's also because the love that Laura has for this wondrous art form permeates the book. She could have asked dozens of questions about *42nd Street*, but you knew she'd choose "What does Julian Marsh tell Peggy Sawyer are the most beautiful words in the English language?" Long before you get to a reference to the obscure 1956 musical *Mr. Wonderful*, you'll be convinced that where musical theatre is concerned, Laura Frankos is Ms. Wonderful.

Peter Filichia

Preface

Willkommen, Bienvenue, Welcome

This book is for you if you—

- Get people to speak up by telling them, "Sing out, Louise!"
- Know the difference between *No, No, Nanette, Yes, Yes, Yvette,* and *La, La, Lucille*
- Spend too much time pondering the merits and demerits of songs cut from musicals, discussing original casts versus revivals, and reading about Broadway folk from Abbott (George) to Ziegfeld (Flo)
- Have an iPod stuffed with show tunes, show tunes, and more show tunes
- Know what Jerome Kern said about Irving Berlin's place in American music
- Celebrate Eliza Doolittle Day on May 20
- Find song cues for Broadway lyrics occurring anywhere, anytime in your daily life, thereby embarrassing or annoying children, significant others, friends, neighbors, and coworkers (example: do you find it impossible to refrain from singing a certain number from *1776* when entering a stuffy room?).

But don't fret if you don't do any of those things. This book is also for folks with a more casual (okay, less obsessive) interest in the American musical. Stick around, kids, you may learn something. You hold in your hands a collection of quizzes on practically every aspect of Broadway history, including different eras; themes and subject matter; lyrics, song titles, characters, and plots; notable songwriters, stars, directors, choreographers, and producers; theatres; famous quotes and anecdotes; and anything else I could think of. The questions, which number over twelve hundred, will range in difficulty from the easy (assuming the aforementioned casual familiarity with musicals) to fiendishly hard. While I've tried to include varying levels of difficulty within each quiz, I've marked a few that are particularly challenging. I hope the novices will be encouraged to look up the answers to questions that flummox them, and that the diehard musical nuts will not groan "That's too easy!" when encountering the simpler questions.

I've included details and commentary in the answer section which I hope will amuse, inform, or infuriate you. Also scattered throughout these pages are a number of "Broadway Bonus" questions that cover things particularly weird and obscure. If you can answer a good number of these, you can award yourself a virtual Tony for Excellence in Broadway Musical Trivia.

What shows are included? Well, anything goes, so to speak, from the turn of the previous century to the present, with a greater emphasis on the period from the thirties onward. In other words, there's more William Finn than Victor Herbert, and you should be more familiar with "I'm an Ordinary Man" (Lerner and Loewe, 1956) than "Yama Yama Man" (Hoschna and Harbach, 1908—trust me, it was a huge hit a century ago). Notable off-Broadway shows, British shows, and famous flops that closed on the road or had very short runs are also covered. I've given more attention to original shows over revivals, since many of the quizzes focus on the shows' creators and less to productions adapted from movie musicals. Over 700 shows, from 1866's *The Black Crook* to 2010's *Catch Me If You Can*, are mentioned in the text, commentary, and quiz questions, so if your favorite show was omitted, it wasn't from lack of effort.

Given a project like this, the author's personal choices play a role, but I have tried to include shows I dislike, knowing there are readers whose tastes differ. Still, I suspect you'll deduce where my passions lie (what, more Sondheim?) because it was easier to write quiz questions about shows I liked than those I didn't. Sometimes I couldn't help myself and, like Claire de Loone in *On the Town*, got carried away and wrote mini-quizzes on specific shows.

Most of the quizzes are multiple choice in format; wherever possible, I have tried to make the "distracters" (that's quiz speak for the incorrect answers) as challenging as I could. Some quizzes will require filling in the blanks or short answers, some matching terms, and some feature true or false questions.

The organization of the quizzes follows a theatrical playbill, beginning with setiing (musicals in France, imaginary places, addresses, etc.) and time (Broadway by the decades from 1900 to the present). The decade quizzes cover shows not mentioned elsewhere; e.g., there's no Rodgers and Hammerstein in the 1950s quiz because they rightly merit their own quiz. Act One includes quizzes on famous Broadway figures, followed by an intermission in which one can check out food and drink in musicals. Thematic quizzes (sports, literature, U.S. history, etc.) comprise Act Two. But the reader should feel free to skip around and answer them in any sequence.

The research material for this book included several hundred libretti, memoirs, biographies, chronicles, yearbooks, summaries, and histories, as well as countless cast albums. I can't include a full bibliography, but I would be remiss not to pay tribute to the contributions of Gerald Bordman, Ken Mandelbaum, Ethan Mordden, Richard C. Norton, John Stewart, and Steven Suskin. My heroes, all of them. Any errors, of course, are my own.

I would also like to acknowledge the assistance of my fellow musical fanatics, Mike Resnick, Len Wein, and P. J. Macari. If I can stump them, I'll have done something right.

Special thanks to Peter Filichia, whose work is constant inspiration to me, for the best introduction this side of the Inevitable Roscoe.

Finally, I would like to thank my husband, Harry Turtledove, and my three daughters, Alison, Rachel, and Rebecca, for their constant love, support, and encouragement. To say nothing of their patience in the face of obsession!

Oh, and in case you were wondering: Jerome Kern, when asked what he thought about Irving Berlin's place in American music, replied, "Irving Berlin has no place in American music. Irving Berlin *is* American music."

QUIZZES

Setting

Ah, Paris!

Musicals set in France

Oo la la! Following New York City, the most popular setting for musicals is France. And why not? France is the land of romance, music, infidelity, revolutions, and cheese: all qualities one can find in many musicals. So put on your beret, take this quiz book to your nearest sidewalk cafe and pretend you're on the Left Bank of the Seine. All of the following questions concern musicals (including a few that never made it to Broadway) set or partially set in France.

1. True or false: *Les Misérables* is set during the French Revolution.
2. You are an aging, but wealthy, sailmaker in Marseilles, eager for a son to carry on your name. Who are you and what show are you in?
3. What happens on the island of La Grande Jatte, c. 1884?
4. How much does Irma la Douce charge?
5. The odd events at the Paris Opera House have led manager M. Lefevre to seek less-stressful work. Who are his successors?
6. In which French city could you enroll in Madame Dubonnet's Finishing School for young ladies?
7. *Candide* (1956, music by Leonard Bernstein, lyrics by Richard Wilbur et al.) covers a lot of ground, from Westphalia to the New World, but in which song does Cunegonde specifically note that she's in Paris?
8. This celebrated Frenchwoman is eighty years old at the start of this show, but her ancient face peels away, revealing a vibrant teenager. Who is she and what is the show?
9. It's 1918. The Germans have placed bombs in the village of Du Temps. You are the American soldier sent in to defuse them. What do you find besides bombs (and what show—which bombed itself—are you in)?
10. This Boublil and Schönberg show, set in a sixteenth-century French village torn apart by religious conflict, won awards in its British run, but the revised version folded during its U.S. tryout.
11. In which French city would you find Georges and Albin's nightclub?
12. Maud lives in Surrey. Bobo lives in Paris. Though neither knows it, they have Henry in common. In what show are these maritally mixed-up characters found?
13. This 1951 flop is largely forgotten today save for Gower Champion's astonishing ballets, including one set in a Parisian department store.
14. In this operetta, King Louis XI lets the poet-outlaw Villon escape the hangman and be king for a day, assuming he can defeat the forces of the nasty Duke of Burgundy, then besieging Paris.

15. Who says, "Fetchez la vache!"?
16. The leads in this show sing a lovely ballad while in a balloon in the skies above Paris.
17. The idea for this show came to librettist Robert Sherwood while watching the faces of soldiers bidding farewell to the Statue of Liberty as they were shipped off to war.
18. Cole Porter lived in France for years and it rubbed off on him, since he wrote seven musicals with French settings. His first smash book musical was 1929's *Fifty Million Frenchmen*. Tour guide Peter takes some American tourists to various sights in "Do You Want to See Paris?" Which is *not* among them?
    A. the Arc de Triomphe
    B. the Eiffel Tower
    C. the Moulin Rouge
    D. Madame Du Barry's bedroom
    E. the Champs Elysées
19. According to Pistache, what does Paris do in the summer?
20. In this unassuming show, the lives of a prostitute, a news vendor, and a painter are improved by the Robin Hood–style aid of M. Passepartout, an ordinary guy who has developed the ability to walk through walls.
21. Where would you find Madeleine, Mathilde, Frieda, and Fannette?
22. This show, set in a French village, never made it to Broadway despite a lovely score. It was also the last show for which legendary designer Jo Mielziner created the sets.
23. Who intends to count "chickens" at the Folies Bergère?
24. *Les Miz* is not the only musical with a scene set in the sewers of Paris. What's the other?
25. This fabled Frenchwoman reveals at the end of act I that she wanted a red communion dress when she was eight.
26. The principals in this show did a lot of traveling. There are scenes set in Paris, Honfleur, Deauville, and St. Tropez, but it's the attitudes in one American state that had them concerned.
27. The original source material for this musical is so good, at least six attempts have been made to turn it into a musical. The first three failed to get to Broadway. The fourth did, though it didn't last long. Its impressive lead actor, however, picked up a Tony for playing the role he had done two years before in the nonmusical version. What was the show and who was the actor?
28. It's set in a Parisian dress shop... inherited by an American football player.
29. Aunt Alicia has specific requirements Gaston's representatives must meet in "The Contract." How many rooms does she insist must be in Gigi's new home?
30. True, it was the result of a Mickey Finn–inspired dream, but Ethel Merman once played Madame Du Barry. Who was her Louis XV?
31. Where would you find the girls (girls! girls!) of "Maxim's"?
32. Joan of Arc didn't want to burn, but she did. She also had a musical written about her, although the focus of the show was on the Dauphin, later Charles VII. What was it?
33. A lesson in French grammar or an award-winning, laugh-filled revue?
34. Great literature does not necessarily make great musicals. This show about Americans in 1906 Paris was based on a Henry James novel, but lasted a mere handful of performances.
35. Where is Freddy Benson hoping to find some great big stuff?

36. Maury Yeston tackled this classic French novel and did so in a most intelligent fashion, but difficulties involving copyright laws meant somebody else produced a successful musical on the same subject first. (Now there's an understatement.)

37. This show concerns two men—distinct opposites—who must travel through occupied France to meet a man with a flower in his lapel at Papa Clairon's cafe.

38. Where does Marguerite St. Just perform?

39. Who enjoys "Paris by Night"?

40. Cole Porter's first Broadway offering, *See America First* (1916) barely lasted two weeks, and he spent most of the next decade abroad, occasionally writing songs for British and French shows and revues. When he got back to Broadway in 1928, what was the title of his first hit?

41. What American miss from Mississippi became so Frenchified she could no longer say "yes," only "oui"?

42. Most of this Cole Porter hit was set in Russia (and, in fact, needed to be revised the following year after Stalin—whose character did a little dance in the original version—made a pact with Hitler), but the action began in Paris.

43. If the show mentioned in the last question had Americans going from Paris to Russia, this show had imperial Russian refugees working for rich Americans in Paris.

44. Harry is in Monte Carlo (yeah, I know it's not *France*, but it's close enough), trying to fulfill the complicated terms of his uncle's will. While there, he gets a lesson in "Speaking French." What's the show?

45. The original title for this musical, based on the life and death of an historical figure, was *Facade*. In the decades since its disastrous tryout, it has been revised and renamed *Ballad for a Firing Squad*. What was it called when it hastily closed in Washington, D.C.?

46. The inhabitants of a castle put on an extravagant production number to show their hospitality to their guest (who, in fact, is being held against her will). Their leader explains they act this way simply because they are in France, though the musical never specifies where or when (no, it's not a Rodgers and Hart show). What show is it?

47. Take three of the biggest musical names ever to come out of France: Michel Legrand, Alain Boublil, and Claude-Michel Schönberg. Have them update Dumas' *The Lady of the Camellias* to Nazi-occupied France. Put Ruthie Henshall in the lead role, and stage it in London in 2008. What have you got?

48. Although most of this show is set in Colorado, our heroine spends part of act II in Paris and Monte Carlo, and even takes a shot at a language lesson.

49. There are vampires running around "In Paris," but they didn't run long on Broadway.

50. One city was London. One city was Paris. And things got very revolting in many ways.

❧ ❧

BROADWAY BONUS: Which Cole Porter musical set in Paris was *not* mentioned in this quiz? Hint: it was not one of his successes, hence my listing it as a bonus, and Porter regarded it as "my worst show."

❧ ❧

Answers on page 193.

How Are Things in Glocca Morra?

Imaginary places

Well, there's Oz and Brigadoon and Urinetown... You could plan an extensive trip to the imaginary places where musicals are set. Fill in the blanks with the names of the shows for these locales not found in any gazetteer. A few of these places are not the locations of musicals but figure as the homelands of characters or are mentioned in some significant way.

1. Lichtenburg _____
2. Rumson (Town), California _____
3. The Kingdom of Romanza _____
4. The Jungle of Nool _____
5. Bali Hai _____
6. Bottleneck _____
7. Concorde, France _____
8. Czechogovina _____
9. Dogpatch, U.S.A. _____
10. Rainbow Valley, Missitucky _____
11. Sweet Apple, Ohio _____
12. Steeltown, U.S.A. _____
13. Custerville, Arizona _____
14. Ruritania _____
15. Bird-in-Hand, Pennsylvania _____
16. Mira _____
17. Never-Never Land _____
18. D'hum _____
19. Brunswick, Iowa _____
20. Rodney, Mississippi Territory _____
21. Katwyk-ann-Zee, Holland _____
22. River City, Iowa _____
23. Marsovia _____
24. Angel's Roost and Rhododendron, Washington _____
25. Joy City _____
26. Stoneyhead, Vermont _____
27. St. Pierre, Quebec _____
28. Carpathia _____
29. Three Point, Texas _____
30. Samolo _____

Answers on page 196.

Large Monopolizing Corporations
Workplaces

Good drama is all about conflict, and where do most of us find conflict? In the workplace, of course! If you had to punch a time clock at each of the following places of employment, where would you be?

1. Harriman Munitions Factory_____
2. Sleep-Tite Pajama Factory _____
3. Horace J. Fletcher Chocolate Works _____
4. Henry Ford's factory _____
5. a parachute factory in the South _____
6. World Wide Wickets Company _____
7. B. G. Bigelow, Inc. _____
8. Apex Modes, Inc. _____
9. Consolidated Life _____
10. the U.G.C. _____
11. Sincere Trust Insurance Company _____
12. World Wide Pictures _____
13. Shalford's Drapery Emporium _____
14. F.F.F. Studios _____

Answers on page 197.

Typically English
British shows

Although the British have influenced the American musical stage since before 1900, this quiz will focus largely on shows from the last quarter of the twentieth century, especially the "British Invasion" of the 1980s. Sir Andrew Lloyd Webber's shows, a large part of that phenomenon, are discussed elsewhere, but there is plenty still to ponder.

1. *The Rocky Horror Show*, an affectionate tribute to science-fiction movies, debuted in London in 1973 and became a cult hit. It came to New York in 1975, transforming the Belasco into a cabaret setting, but American audiences didn't take to it. Despite the pans, it was filmed the following year with many of the original London cast, including Tim Curry as Dr. Frank N. Furter. The film developed a cult following, and the musical did much better in its 2000 revival. The versatile Richard O'Brien was responsible for nearly everything in the original *Rocky Horror*. He did all of the following *except:*
   A. the book
   B. the music
   C. play the role of Riff Raff
   D. the lyrics
   E. direct

2. *Side by Side by Sondheim* was a British revue of songs by Stephen Sondheim performed by David Kernan, Millicent Martin, and Julia McKenzie, with Ned Sherrin as a narrator. The intimate show debuted at the Mermaid Theatre in 1976 and was one of producer Cameron Mackintosh's early successes. It moved to the West End and later the entire cast transferred to Broadway as a Harold Prince-Ruth Mitchell production. Sondheim, when approached by the person who had the initial idea, gave his blessing, but said, "I can't think of a more boring evening, unless it be a reading of the Book of Kells." Whose idea was it?

    A. David Kernan
    B. Ned Sherrin
    C. Julia McKenzie
    D. Millicent Martin
    E. Cameron Mackintosh

BROADWAY BONUS: What show did Cameron Mackintosh see as a child that convinced him he wanted a career in theatre?

3. Noel Gay's musical *Me and My Girl* was a hit back in 1937 in London, was filmed, and had three successful revivals in the forties. In the eighties, Gay's son Richard Armitage, Stephen Fry, and Mike Ockrent revised the show, adding six Gay songs from other shows. The result was a feel-good smash on both sides of the Atlantic. Robert Lindsay played the cockney chap unexpectedly in line for an earldom in both versions, nabbing a Tony for Best Actor. The production also won for choreography. What was the showstopping hit dance called?

4. A pair of Frenchmen, Alain Boublil and Claude-Michel Schönberg, were fans of British musicals, especially *Jesus Christ Superstar* and *Oliver!* As Bart had done with England's Dickens, they hoped to do with France's most beloved novelist, Victor Hugo. *Les Misérables* began as a concept album and then a presentation in Paris. Cameron Mackintosh gambled on it after hearing the album, despite not knowing any French. (James Fenton and Herbert Kretzmer would work on the English translations.) Marshaling the talents of Trevor Nunn, John Caird, and the Royal Shakespeare Company, Mackintosh produced one of the biggest blockbusters in musical history. *Les Miz* would become the longest-running show in West End history, and the Broadway version tagged 6,680 shows, from 1987 to 2003. Millions have seen it in thirty-eight different countries, but how many saw it during that New York run?

    A. 2.6 million
    B. 3 million
    C. 7.1 million
    D. 9.2 million
    E. 14.9 million

5. Tim Rice and ABBA's Benny Andersson and Bjorn Ulvaeus teamed up for *Chess*, which debuted in London in 1986 after a successful concept album. Rice had been tinkering for years on this Cold War analogy, using chess as a metaphor for political and romantic conflict. The original director was Michael Bennett, but his illness led to Trevor Nunn taking the helm. The show underwent countless redesigns and rewrites—something that hasn't stopped to this day. The London and Broadway versions differed dramatically (it closed on Broadway in 1988 after sixty-eight performances), and each subsequent major production seems to have some changes. Perhaps it is because *Chess* has tasty meat hidden within it, but no one can settle on the best way to prepare the entire meal.

Chess' American and Russian protagonists do their share of traveling. What city is *not* mentioned in the lyrics?

    A. Budapest
    B. Bangkok
    C. Constantinople
    D. Berlin
    E. Warsaw

6. Boublil and Schönberg, working with Richard Maltby, Jr., returned to the heights with *Miss Saigon* (London, 1989; New York, 1991), their modernization of *Madame Butterfly*. They set the show during the Vietnam War and its aftermath, focusing on the tragic love story between a U.S. soldier and a young Vietnamese girl. The Broadway production ran for over four thousand performances. Which of the following statements about *Miss Saigon* is *not* true?

    A. Michael Bennett's former assistant, Baayork Lee, did the choreography
    B. the famous helicopter was a three-quarter-size model that weighed 8,700 pounds
    C. Lea Salonga was only seventeen when she was discovered in Manila and cast as Kim
    D. Actors Equity protested Jonathan Pryce's casting as the Eurasian Engineer and only backed down when Cameron Mackintosh announced he would cancel the show
    E. Boublil and Schönberg were inspired to write the show after seeing a photo of a Vietnamese woman bidding her half-American child farewell at an airport

7. Willy Russell's *Blood Brothers* was a long-running hit in London (the revised version ran from 1988 to 2005) that took some time to cross the Atlantic. Several members of the British cast came over for the 1993 Broadway production in an exchange program with British Equity. The tale of twin brothers separated at birth, one raised in poverty, the other in riches, ran for 839 outings. What real-life pair of siblings came in as replacements and attracted plenty of publicity?

    A. David and Shaun Cassidy
    B. Ralph and Joseph Fiennes
    C. Alec and Daniel Baldwin
    D. Donnie and Mark Wahlberg
    E. Hunter and Sutton Foster

8. As the nineties progressed, the steam seemed to have run out of the so-called invasion. *Les Miz* and *Miss Saigon* continued their long runs, but Boublil and Schönberg's next efforts failed. *Martin Guerre*, a tale of mistaken identity in war-torn sixteenth-century

France, closed during its U.S. tryout in early 2000. *The Pirate Queen,* set in the Elizabethan era, ran briefly and expensively in 2007.

Andrew Lloyd Webber's later offerings also have struggled. His production company, the Really Useful Theatre Company, produced *Bombay Dreams* (book by Meera Syal, music by A. A. Rahman, lyrics by Don Black and David Yazbek), which earned out in Britain, but the 2004 Broadway version couldn't find an audience. The plot concerned relationships between wannabes and the movers and shakers in the Indian film industry. What was the name of one of the films in production in the show?

  A. *Love's Never Easy*
  B. *The Journey Home*
  C. *Diamond in the Rough*
  D. *Hurray for Bollywood*
  E. *Slumdog Millionaire*

9. In 2005, London saw the arrival of the most expensive show in history, *Chitty Chitty Bang Bang,* based on the 1960s children's film, with a score by Richard and Robert Sherman. The flying car soared over Broadway audiences for less than a year, but that didn't stop another attempt at a stage version of a 1960s children's film with a score by the Sherman brothers. Cameron Mackintosh and Disney Theatricals put their formidable powers behind 2006's *Mary Poppins,* filling out the film score with numbers by George Stiles and Anthony Drewe, and using a book by Julian Fellowes closer in tone to the P. L. Travers original series. Richard Eyre directed, with choreography by Matthew Bourne. Songwriters Stiles and Drewe had worked with Mackintosh before on a musical version of a classic children's book. What noted author was the source for their earlier effort?

  A. Beatrix Potter
  B. Rudyard Kipling
  C. A. A. Milne
  D. E. Nesbit
  E. Lewis Carroll

10. The Brits were back on top with the phenomenal success of *Billy Elliot*, picking up ten awards at the 2009 Tonys. Based on the film about a working-class family in 1980s Britain with a son who longs to dance, the show captured the hearts of audiences both in London and New York. Stephen Daldry directed, with book and lyrics by Lee Hall, music by Elton John, and choreography by Peter Darling. The trio of boys alternating in the lead role—David Alvarez (15), Trent Kowalik (14), and Kiril Kulish (15) became the youngest winners for the Best Actor Tony, and the first joint recipients. Which actor performed the incandescent "Angry Dance" to huge applause at the Tony ceremony?

Answers on page 198.

Groundhog! Groundhog!

Colleges

Institutions of higher learning can also be institutions of higher musical fun. Match the colleges and universities with the shows in which they take place or are mentioned.

1. Tait College
2. Knickerbocker University
3. Southern Baptist Institute of Technology
4. Harrison University, New York
5. University of Heidelberg
6. Pottawattomie College, New Mexico
7. Santa Rosa Junior College
8. Texas A&M
9. Rutgers University
10. St. Olde's College, Oxford
11. Haverhill College
12. University of Minnesota (Alpha Cholera Fraternity)
13. Metropolis Institute of Technology (MIT)
14. Harvard University
15. Atwater College
16. Shiz University

A. *The Student Prince*
B. *High Button Shoes*
C. *Wicked*
D. *The Day Before Spring*
E. *Barefoot Boy with Cheek*
F. *Leave It to Jane*
G. *All American*
H. *Smile*
I. *Where's Charley?*
J. *Too Many Girls*
K. *The Best Little Whorehouse in Texas*
L. *Roberta*
M. *It's a Bird . . . It's a Plane . . . It's Superman*
N. *On Your Toes*
O. *Good News*
P. *Legally Blonde*

There haven't been nearly so many, er, high-school musicals as collegiate ones, but see if you can name the schools the teens in these shows attend.

17. *Grease*
18. *High School Musical*
19. *Sarafina!*
20. *Hairspray*

❧ ❧

BROADWAY BONUS: A chance to show off your academic knowledge in a big way! Where did Wreck gain fame by demonstrating he could pass the football ? Where did Miss Marmelstein go to school and what was her major? Who will play Tait College in the Big Game? Who is Atwater College's big rival? What are the school colors of Joseph Taylor, Jr.? For which university did George and Ira Gershwin write a special version of "Strike Up the Band"? Where did Liza Elliott go to high school?

❧ ❧

Answers on page 199.

Be Italian

Musicals Set in Italy

There have been many musicals set in Italy. Not surprising, given that Italians are a musical and romantic people. What is surprising is that many of these shows flopped, while those set in France had more success.

1. What's the name of the spa where Guido and Luisa stay?
2. Name the cities in which a certain troupe of strolling players tour.
3. Giorgio and Clara fall in love in a park in this city.
4. Where does Leona stay in Venice?
5. Fabrizio works in a tie shop next to _____
6. *The Firebrand of Florence* is about noted Renaissance artist _____
7. A huge hit in Italy, this show came to Broadway and retained its Italian libretto and lyrics.
8. The characters in *Aspects of Love* have affairs all over the map of Europe, from the Pyrenees to Paree. In which Italian city is Giulietta's studio?
9. This show featured two rival restaurants in Rome and a secret tunnel between them.
10. *Mamma Mia!*, set in Greece, has a plot similar to this show set in the southern Italian town of San Forino.
11. This off-Broadway effort by Ahrens and Flaherty told the tale of a commedia dell'arte troupe in sixteenth-century Italy.
12. This fabled flop featured an Italian duke who races cars; his granddaughter, who is a witch; and Guido, who was "the Devil's Emissary."
13. The Roman author Plautus' plays formed the basis of this musical, set on a street in ancient Rome.
14. Barbara Cook was in a number of flops shows that are now fondly remembered. This show, which had a family moving from Long Island to Portofino, wasn't one of them.
15. This burlesque-style flop from 1955 had the action start in Sicily and then move out to sea. Which is where all of the investors were, unfortunately.
16. Valentine thinks life in Verona is dull. Where does this gentleman want to go?

Answers on page 200.

The Only Lobby I Know Is the Martin Beck

Theatres

Broadway theatres have long and rich histories. Over the decades, those that survived have often changed names, either to honor theatre greats or to reflect a change of ownership. Match the old names of theatres with the names currently in use. Some of the theatres have had multiple names.

1. the Alvin Theatre
2. the Guild/the ANTA/the Virginia Theatre
3. the 46th Street Theatre
4. the National/the Billy Rose Theatre
5. the Uris Theatre
6. the Forrest/the Coronet Theatre
7. the Richard Mansfield Theatre

8. the Selwyn Theatre
9. the Globe Theatre
10. the Little Theatre

11. the Ritz/the RFK Children's Theatre
12. the Martin Beck Theatre
13. the Theatre Masque
14. Erlanger's Theatre
15. Colony Theatre (vaudeville/films)
16. the Stuyvesant Theatre
17. the Republic/the Belasco /Minsky's/ Victory Theatre (films)
18. the Plymouth Theatre
19. the Golden Theatre/CBS Radio Theatre/the Royale Theatre
20. Henry Miller's Theatre
21. the Gallo Opera House/the New Yorker Theatre/the Palladium Theatre/Federal Music Theatre/CBS Studio*

A. the Eugene O'Neill Theatre
B. the American Airlines Theatre

C. the St. James Theatre
D. the New Victory Theatre
E. the Bernard Jacobs Theatre
F. the Brooks Atkinson Theatre
G. the Belasco Theatre (second of that name)
H. the John Golden Theatre
I. the Richard Rodgers Theatre
J. the Helen Hayes (second of that name)
K. the August Wilson Theatre
L. the Nederlander Theatre
M. the Stephen Sondheim Theatre
N. the Lunt-Fontanne Theatre
O. the Neil Simon Theatre
P. Studio 54
Q. the Gerald Schoenfeld Theatre

R. the Al Hirschfeld Theatre
S. the Walter Kerr Theatre

T. the Broadway Theatre
U. the George Gershwin Theatre

*This theatre was a nightclub twice in its history—I omitted those names.

❧ ❧

BROADWAY BONUS: What happened to the Lyric and the Apollo theatres, built in 1903 and 1910, respectively? What happened to the fabled Mark Hellinger Theatre?

❧ ❧

Answers on page 200.

On the Street Where You Live

Addresses

It's time for the Broadway mail to be delivered, and it's up to you to match the addresses with the characters. The addresses are all mentioned in lyrics or libretti from different shows.

1. 27-A Wimpole Street, London
2. Christopher Street, Greenwich Village
3. 23 Rue St. Vincent, Paris
4. Kearney's Lane, London
5. 17 Cherry Tree Lane, London
6. Sussex Arms Hotel, New York
7. 221-B Baker Street, London
8. Broadview Avenue, New Rochelle
9. Catfish Row, Charleston, South Carolina
10. 3 Beekman Place, New York
11. 5135 Kensington Avenue, St. Louis
12. a mansion, 5th Avenue and 82nd Street, New York
13. Quality Hill, Hackensack, New Jersey
14. 1617 Broadway, New York
15. 65 Skelmersdale Lane
16. 12 Ocean Drive
17. 7 Elm Street, Trenton, New Jersey
18. 125 East Lake Street, Winston-Salem, North Carolina
19. Misselthwaite Manor
20. Casa Rosada, Buenos Aires
21. 9 West 67th Street, New York (2nd floor front)
22. 24 Henry Street, New York

A. Alvin and Cleo
B. Archibald and Colin Craven
C. Mame Dennis
D. Noble Eggleston
E. Rita Racine
F. Mrs. Johnstone and Mickey
G. Clara Johnson and her mom
H. Fanny Brice and her mom
I. the Smith family

J. Ruth and Eileen Sherwood
K. Ida, Harry, Gert, Eunice, etc.
L. Mother, Father, Younger Brother, Edgar, and Grandfather
M. Marcel Dusoleil

N. Chuck Baxter
O. Porgy and Bess
P. Rita and Hal
S. Sherlock Holmes
T. Johanna and Judge Turpin

R. Daddy Warbucks
U. Juan and Eva Peron
V. the Banks family

W. Henry Higgins

❧ ❧

BROADWAY BONUS: What hometown do Peggy Sawyer and Rose Grant have in common? Oh, that's too easy for a Broadway Bonus! This one's better: what room does Kringelein have at the Grand Hotel, Berlin?

❧ ❧

Answers on page 201.

Time

The 1900s

Since I'm a historian by training, I thought it might be fun to take a look at Broadway history by the decades. In these quizzes, I'll try to focus on shows not covered in other parts of the book. The quizzes on the early years of Broadway are more difficult, given that few of these shows are performed today and their scores are not well known, but I hope readers will give them a try.

The first decade of the twentieth century saw the American musical taking shape. Extravaganzas, vaudeville and variety shows, revues, English comic operas (especially Gilbert and Sullivan), French opéra bouffe, and Viennese operettas all competed for audiences, along with musical comedies with a distinctly nationalistic flavor.

1. Joe Weber and Lew Fields, like Harrigan and Hart before them, got their start in vaudeville as comics targeting immigrants for their humor. They were known as "Dutch comics" (from *Deutsch*, German, or, more accurately, Yiddish), always performing in broad, over-the-top style. "Don't poosh me, Meyer," the smaller, rotund Weber would wail as the much taller Fields shoved him onstage. By 1900, their act, which consisted of a musical comedy and a burlesque—a takeoff of a popular show—was tops in New York. Some shows reportedly paid Weber and Fields to spoof them. (Has someone told this to Gerard Alessandrini?) Lew Fields would later have a notable record as a producer with his son Herbert, and his daughter Dorothy was one of our finest lyricists. What classic routine is attributed to Weber and Fields?
    A. "The Belt in the Back" (a.k.a. the Tailor sketch)
    B. "Slowly I Turn..." (a.k.a. "Niagara Falls")
    C. "Half of everything I own is yours."
    D. "Waiter, there's a fly in my soup."
    E. "That was no lady. That was my wife."

2. One of the smash hits of the decade was *Florodora* (1900), a British import by Paul Reubens and Leslie Stuart, that ran for 505 performances in an era when one hundred was considered outstanding. The show's highlight was not performed by the leads, but by a double sextet of men and gorgeous women, "Tell Me, Pretty Maiden." The Florodora Sextette became notoriously popular, and rumors abounded that they all wed millionaires. Those rumors were still in vogue by 1920, when the Shuberts revived the show, only to have Fanny Brice satirize it with "I Was a *Florodora* Baby," a *Ziegfeld Follies* number in which she claimed to have been the only member of the sextette to wed for love! Who or what was "Florodora"?
    A. the lead female role; the owner of a Philippine island and the perfume made there
    B. the leader of the sextette
    C. Leslie Stuart's wife's name
    D. the name of the island and its perfume
    E. a goddess in the Pacific island tradition

3. A century before Elphaba flew, *The Wizard of Oz* (1903) was a hit on Broadway, with book and lyrics by creator L. Frank Baum, and music by Paul Tietjens and A. Baldwin Stone (plus various interpolations, as was common then). It differed significantly from the novel, although a cyclone still blew Dorothy to Oz, where the Scarecrow, Tin Man, and a good witch help her find the Wizard for her return trip. The cyclone scene, designed by director Julian Mitchell, was allegedly so breathtaking, the producers warned the public in their ads not to be late. The other huge draw was the comic duo of Fred Stone and Dave Montgomery as the Scarecrow and Tin Man. Stone was an accomplished acrobat and employed many stunts while covered in greasepaint matching the original W. W. Denslow drawings from the novel. Who else went to Oz with Dorothy in this version?

  A. Billina, the talking chicken
  B. Imogene, the dancing cow
  C. Button Bright, a blissfully naive boy
  D. the nine tiny piglets
  E. Polychrome, the Rainbow's daughter

4. One of the masters of this era was composer Victor Herbert. Born in Ireland, raised in England and Germany, he helped originate and refine the American musical. One of his greatest successes was *Babes in Toyland* (1903), designed and produced by many of the same people who worked on *The Wizard of Oz*. Unlike that show, *Babes in Toyland* had a lovely and memorable score to match its spectacle. "March of the Toys" and "Toyland" are still performed at Christmas. What other Herbert hit came from *Babes in Toyland*?

  A. "Tramp! Tramp! Tramp!"
  B. "Go to Sleep, Slumber Deep"
  C. "The Streets of New York"
  D. "Ah, Sweet Mystery of Life"
  E. "Moonbeams"

❀ ❀

BROADWAY BONUS: What did Victor Herbert have to do with the Supreme Court?

❀ ❀

5. *In Dahomey* (1903) is notable as the first Broadway musical entirely created and performed by African Americans. The show had a brief run, went to London for a smash seven months, then returned for another Broadway engagement. It combined elements of vaudeville, minstrel shows, ragtime, and musical comedy, and starred one of the greatest comics of all time, Bert Williams. Williams played the harmless rube, Shylock Homestead. His partner, George Walker, played the con man, Rareback Pinkerton. Will Marion Cook did the music, but which highly lauded black author wrote most of the lyrics?

  A. Langston Hughes
  B. Countee Cullen
  C. Paul Laurence Dunbar
  D. Jean Toomer
  E. Zora Neale Hurston

6. One of Broadway's early giants was 5' 6" George M. Cohan. Born into a vaudeville family and tackling lead roles by the age of thirteen, Cohan was brash, arrogant, slangy, cocky, patriotic...and so were his shows. Critics scoffed, but the public adored the eleven musicals he staged between 1901 and 1911. "The Yankee Doodle Boy," "Give My Regards to Broadway," "So Long, Mary," "Mary's a Grand Old Name," and "You're a Grand Old Flag" are just a few of his songs that became standards. Cohan did it all: performing, writing, composing, managing, and producing. Anecdotes about him are legion. Which of these statements about him and his work is *not* true?

   A. the original title for the hit song from *George Washington, Jr.* (1906) was "You're a Grand Old Rag"

   B. "The Yankee Doodle Boy" goes to London to ride the ponies because the character in *Little Johnny Jones* (1904) was a jockey

   C. "Harrigan" in *Fifty Miles from Boston* (1908) was written in tribute to Cohan's idol, Ned Harrigan

   D. *45 Minutes from Broadway* (1906) created a real estate boom in New Rochelle, which expanded so much it became thirty minutes from Broadway.

   E. in 1919, when the actors went on strike, Cohan sided with the producers and swore if the actors won, he'd quit show business and drive a taxi

7. Victor Herbert had the monster hit of 1906 with *The Red Mill*, which went on to play in London and Australia and had numerous revivals. The plot featured the typical "thwarted romance," in which the Burgomaster of Katwky-ann-Zee wants his daughter Gretchen to wed the elderly (but randy) Governor of Zeeland instead of her handsome sea captain. But the standard romance was a mere backdrop for the antics of Fred Stone and Dave Montgomery, formerly seen in *The Wizard of Oz*. Here they played two penniless Americans touring Europe: the acrobatic Stone made his entrance sliding backward down a huge ladder, trying unsuccessfully to escape a hotel bill. He ended the first act by whisking the imprisoned Gretchen from the red windmill, gliding to safety on one on its vanes. Along the way, the duo impersonated Italian musicians and Holmes and Watson.

   True or false: Producer Charles Dillingham built a gigantic electric-powered windmill outside the theatre and covered it with lights, creating the first moving, illuminated sign on Broadway.

8. The arrival of Franz Lehár's *The Merry Widow* (1907) set off a craze for Merry Widow hats, Merry Widow dresses, and the entire nation danced to "The Merry Widow Waltz." It also heralded roughly a decade of other imported Viennese operettas and countless imitation Viennese operettas, ending only when the outbreak of World War I made all things Germanic distasteful or suspicious. But in 1907, that was all yet to come. *The Merry Widow* was so popular, it needed six road companies. After the war, it regained its appeal and has been revived twenty-eight times. It may have had more worldwide productions than any other musical, but perhaps some of Cameron Mackintosh's shows are catching up. Handsome tenor Donald Brian played the lead, Prince Danilo, in New York. The father of which famous Broadway composer played the same role in Berlin and in the first U.S. tour?

A. Kurt Weill
B. Frederick Loewe
C. Arthur Schwartz
D. Vernon Duke
E. Frank Loesser

9. Florenz Ziegfeld, the master showman, began his *Follies* in 1907. While later shows had more star turns (the main highlights of the early shows were Anna Held—Mrs. Ziegfeld—and Nora Bayes) and better scores, the *Follies* still started well with Joseph Urban sets, Julian Mitchell (and others) directing, and, of course, the Girls. In the *Follies of 1907, 1908,* and *1909*, the Girls (originally the Anna Held Girls, but that didn't last) appeared dressed as all of the following except:

    A. cavegirls with dinosaur headdresses modeled on Rudolph Zallinger's "Age of Reptiles" dinosaur murals at Yale's Peabody Museum
    B. jurors at the trial of Enrico Caruso
    C. mosquitoes in the New Jersey marshlands
    D. representatives from each state, each wearing a battleship on her head with functional searchlights
    E. taxi cabs with headlights that shone into the audience

10. One of the most popular Viennese operettas after *The Merry Widow* was *The Chocolate Soldier* (1909), based on a George Bernard Shaw play about a soldier who would rather carry chocolate in his holster than a gun. After all, you can eat chocolate. Oscar Straus provided the music and it ran for a terrific 296 performances. The public loved it, but Shaw loathed it and was reluctant to allow other works of his to be adapted into musicals. Fortunately for us, Lerner and Loewe were able to tackle *Pygmalion*, but Shaw didn't live to see it. What Shavian piece is the basis of *The Chocolate Soldier*?

    A. *The Devil's Disciple*
    B. *The Admirable Bashville*
    C. *The Man of Destiny*
    D. *Captain Brasshound's Conversion*
    E. *Arms and the Man*

Answers on page 202.

The 1910s

The musical soared in the teens. The mania for Viennese operettas ended with America's entry in the war. Ragtime peaked and was replaced by jazz, as even more syncopated rhythms found their way into Broadway scores. Jerome Kern and Irving Berlin were well established; see their individual quizzes for more on their work in this period. Youngsters like Porter, Gershwin, and Rodgers were starting to be heard. The overall quality of shows improved (oh, those influential Princess shows!), and revues became even more opulent and stunning. There were more theatres than ever before as Broadway entered a building boom.

1. Ziegfeld produced an edition of his *Follies* every year in this decade; the *Follies of 1919* generally is regarded as the pinnacle of the series. Throughout the period, comics

Fanny Brice, Leon Errol, Ed Wynn, W. C. Fields, and Eddie Cantor joined Bert Williams in *Follies* fun. Lillian Lorraine, Bessie McCoy, Marilyn Miller, and Frank Carter all headlined. Composers Berlin, Kern, Hirsch, Herbert, Smith and Levi filled Flo's stable. The *Follies* were the highlight of each season.

Possibly the greatest Follies star was Fanny Brice, who debuted in the 1910 edition. Brice could do it all, from outrageous dialect comedy to torch songs. The 1916 *Follies* had quite a lot of spoofing. Fans familiar with the film version of *Funny Girl* will know Brice parodied Pavlova in "The Dying Swan." But what other "belly" (ballet) star got targeted by Miss Brice in a skit that also featured W. C. Fields and Bert Williams? And wouldn't you have loved seeing all three of them onstage at the same time?

- **A.** Marie Taglioni
- **B.** Augusta Maywood
- **C.** Fanny Essler
- **D.** Agrippina Vaganova
- **E.** Vaslav Nijinsky

2. One of the decade's greatest musicals, Victor Herbert's *Naughty Marietta*, opened late in 1910. Many regard it as Herbert's masterpiece, with songs well integrated into the book and providing background on the locale (1780s New Orleans) and characters. *Naughty Marietta* set the standard for American operettas as later practiced by Romberg and Friml. The plot featured Countess Marietta coming to New Orleans to escape an unwanted suitor and vowing only to wed the man who can complete the melody she heard in a dream. Captain Dick and the dread pirate Bras-Príque vie for her attention, but only the captain knows that sweet mystery of life. Why did producer Oscar Hammerstein (grandfather of lyricist-librettist Oscar II) fill his cast with opera stars, including leads Emma Trentini and Orville Harrold?

3. The Shubert brothers surely rank among Broadway's greatest producers. During the 1910s, they established a series of revues, *The Passing Shows*, to rival Ziegfeld's Follies. There were twelve *Passing Shows* between 1912 and 1924 (missing only 1920) and many future stars got their starts in them. Who among the following was *not* featured in any of the *Passing Shows*? Some of them proved so popular, Ziegfeld promptly lured them away!

- **A.** Fred and Adele Astaire
- **B.** Will Rogers
- **C.** Marilyn(n) Miller (she later dropped the second "n")
- **D.** Fred Allen
- **E.** Ed Wynn

4. Belgian immigrant Ivan Caryll had some monster hits in the decade, but is now largely forgotten. *The Pink Lady* (1911) and *Oh! Oh! Delphine* (1912), both adapted from French farces, had astonishing runs of 320 and 248 performances. Who or what kept calling the name, "Oh! Oh! Delphine!"?

- **A.** her interfering niece
- **B.** her French cousin
- **C.** her soldier husband's commanding officer, who has the hots for her
- **D.** her parrot, which she takes everywhere
- **E.** an elephant named Toodle-Doo, who waved "Oh! Oh! Delphine!" in semaphore

5. Caryll followed these comedies with *Chin-Chin* (1914), a fantasy spectacular about Aladdin (here in love with the daughter of a rich American) and his lamp. The "Chinese" slaves of the lamp were played by the comic pair of Montgomery and Stone, once again doing stunts and wearing silly disguises while journeying to exotic locales like Paris and Holland. It ran for 295 performances, but the smash song from the score was an interpolation, not one of Caryll's. What was it? Hint: it was originally written for a Jolson show and became an international hit.
  A. "Alexander's Ragtime Band"
  B. "They Didn't Believe Me"
  C. "Peg o' My Heart"
  D. "It's a Long, Long Way to Tipperary"
  E. "A Little Girl at Home"

6. One of the next great names in musical theatre was Rudolf Friml, whose first hit was 1912's *The Firefly*, with lyrics by Otto Harbach. The story told of an Italian immigrant street singer, who escapes her abusive home by stowing away on a yacht to Bermuda while disguised as a boy and winning over the wealthy guy, much to the dismay of the fellow's snooty, upper-crust girlfriend. The show was produced by Arthur Hammerstein and featured a number of holdovers from Oscar Hammerstein's *Naughty Marietta*, including lead soprano and diva Emma Trentini. In fact, *Marietta*'s composer, Victor Herbert, was supposed to have written the score. Why did young Friml end up with the job?
  A. Trentini wouldn't perform an encore Herbert requested at a gala performance of *Naughty Marietta* and he swore he'd never work with her again
  B. Herbert got a gig writing for the *Ziegfeld Follies*
  C. Arthur Hammerstein preferred Friml over his dad's choice, Herbert
  D. Herbert was too busy founding ASCAP
  E. Trentini was having an affair with Friml and insisted on having him as composer

7. Sharing the mantle of American operetta with Friml was Sigmund Romberg, a Hungarian-born composer who first came to prominence writing interpolations for Shubert revues. In 1917, he convinced the brothers to give him a crack at writing a show his way. Rida Johnson Young and Cyrus Wood adapted a multigenerational Viennese story, keeping the Germanic origin hidden due to wartime sentiment. The result was *Maytime*, a bittersweet saga spanning sixty years and two families in New York. The doomed lovers of different social classes could never be together, but their grandchildren could fall in love by the withered remains of the apple tree planted by the original duo. *Maytime* proved hugely popular with soldiers departing for war, as *Oklahoma!* and *On the Town* would be in the next great conflict. True or false: *Maytime* was so popular, the Shuberts opened a second theatre across the street to accommodate everyone who wanted tickets.

8. Over in the Jerome Kern quiz, we'll look at the highly influential Princess Theatre Shows in the late teens. Louis Hirsch and Otto Harbach's *Going Up* (1917) showed the Princess style in its contemporary setting (including that modern mode of transport, aviation), its bouncy score and deft musical comedy. But most remember *Going Up* because of its hit dance. What was it?

A. the Gaby Glide
B. the Toddle
C. the Monkey Doodle Doo
D. the Syncopated Walk
E. the Tickle Toe

9. One of the biggest stars of this decade was Al Jolson, who got his start in vaudeville and burlesque. He hit the big time in the Shuberts' Winter Garden revue, *La Belle Paree* (1911), with "Paris Is a Paradise for Coons." He usually performed in blackface, with much eye-rolling and thigh-slapping, but there's no doubt he knew how to win over an audience. Which of these hits was *not* associated with Jolson?
   A. "Where Did Robinson Crusoe Go with Friday on Saturday Night?"
   B. "Swanee"
   C. "I Want to See a Minstrel Show"
   D. "Sister Susie's Sewing Shirts for Soldiers"
   E. "My Mammy"

10. The decade ended with one of the all-time successes, *Irene*, by Joseph McCarthy and Harry Tierney. The rags-to-riches tale ran for 675 performances and had seventeen touring companies. It boasted the standard "Alice Blue Gown," sung by the heroine, Edith Day. Who was the Alice mentioned in the title?
    A. Alice Roosevelt Longfellow, Teddy's daughter
    B. Alice Liddell, the inspiration for Carroll's *Alice in Wonderland*
    C. Alice B. Toklas
    D. Alice Paul, famous suffragette
    E. Alice J. Shaw, the world's greatest professional whistler

Answers on page 204.

The 1920s

The twenties roared for America, and Broadway was no exception for much of the decade. Revues continued to be hugely popular, with ongoing series like *George White's Scandals*, the *Music Box Revues*, the *Greenwich Village Follies* and others competing with Ziegfeld. Operettas set in exotic locales from the Canadian Rockies (*Rose-Marie*) to Morocco (*The Desert Song*) to medieval France (*The Vagabond King*) transported audiences. The new sound of jazz permeated scores, especially in smart and sassy musical comedies. It was an era of not just big-name stars but huge-name stars: Al Jolson, Eddie Cantor, Ed Wynn, Bobby Clark, Marilyn Miller, and Beatrice Lillie, to list just a few. Kern and Berlin continued their amazing output, joined by young songwriters like Rodgers and Hart, the Gershwins, Cole Porter, DeSylva, Henderson and Brown, and Dietz and Schwartz. Many of the plots of the twenties shows lacked depth, but a single offering from Kern and Hammerstein at the end of 1927, *Show Boat*, tackled serious themes and spanned generations in its complex plot.

1. The decade kicked off with another Cinderella story like the previous season's *Irene*. *Mary*, with a score by *Going Up*'s Otto Harbach and Louis Hirsch, and George M. Cohan at the helm as producer/director, was a huge hit. It gave us the standard, "The

Love Nest," later immortalized as the theme to *The Burns and Allen Show*. What were the "love nests" that the hero, Jack, hoped to build?

   A. shooting-boxes in Scotland
   B. bungalows in Quogue
   C. cottages in Cape Cod
   D. mobile homes in Kansas
   E. flats in Flatbush

2. The undisputed star of 1920s musicals was Marilyn Miller. She began in vaudeville at the age of five, was discovered by the Shuberts, but Ziegfeld made her a star. She headlined three of the long-run champions: *Sally* (1920, 570 performances), *Sunny* (1925, 517 performances), and *Rosalie* (1928, 335 performances). An excellent dancer but only an adequate singer, she nonetheless had the power to mesmerize audiences. In *Sally*, her character began as a dishwasher, but ended up:

   A. a Ziegfeld girl and married to a millionaire
   B. engaged to the prince of Romanza
   C. a circus performer
   D. married to a bootlegging English lord
   E. married to a transatlantic aviator

3. In 1921, *Shuffle Along*, with a score by Eubie Blake and Noble Sissel, and book by actors Flournoy Miller and Aubrey Lyles, packed in the audiences for 504 performances. This pioneering show paved the way for later black musicals and revues, as well as straight plays with black casts. During its long run, many future stars performed in it. Who was *not* among them?

   A. Jules Bledsoe
   B. Adelaide Hall
   C. Josephine Baker
   D. Florence Mills
   E. Paul Robeson

4. The Shuberts produced the big hit of 1921, *Blossom Time*, with book and lyrics by Dorothy Donnelly and music by Sigmund Romburg. It was a highly fictitious piece based on the life and alleged love of composer Franz Schubert. *Blossom Time* ran for 592 performances and spawned endless and increasingly tacky road companies. In the show, Schubert composes his B-minor symphony as a "Song of Love" for his beloved, who has (alas!) fallen for another man. His unrequited flame was one of a trio of maids. What were their names?

   A. Hannerl, Heiderl, and Hederl
   B. Sally, Irene, and Mary
   C. Kitzi, Fritzi, and Mitzi
   D. Betty, Winnie, and Flora
   E. Annette, Jeanette, and Nanette

5. One of the decade's top comics was Eddie Cantor, who got his start in vaudeville and as a singing waiter in his teens before coming to Ziegfeld's attention. Cantor and Ziegfeld had a tempestuous relationship, but there's no doubt they were good for each other. Cantor starred in many editions of the *Follies*, as well as two

successful musical comedies produced by Ziegfeld, *Kid Boots* (1923) and *Whoopee* (1928). His comic persona tended to be the same whether he worked in blackface or not—the timid, cringing "nervous wreck" who somehow manages to come out on top. In *Whoopee*, perhaps the quintessential twenties musical, given its sketchy plot, pointless ballets, parades of Ziegfeld girls, and a score full of interpolations, Cantor is out West, surrounded by swaggering cowpokes, Indians, and a nasty sheriff. Who played the nurse who ended up with Cantor's hypochondriac at the end? Hint: she would close her career singing Sondheim over four decades later.

- **A.** Frances Upton
- **B.** Ruth Etting
- **C.** Mary Eaton
- **D.** Jobyna Howard
- **E.** Ethel Shutta

6. The monster hit in 1924 was Harbach-Hammerstein-Friml's *Rose-Marie*, the highest-grossing show of the decade. Set in the Canadian Rockies and featuring the classic "Indian Love Call," *Rose-Marie* blended romance, thrills (such as an onstage murder done in mime), and spectacle. The costliest number included forty-five girls . . .

- **A.** dressed as Mounties
- **B.** masquerading as moose
- **C.** dressed as totem poles
- **D.** re-creating an Indian village
- **E.** going on sleigh rides through the forest

7. The most successful musical comedy in the twenties was *No, No, Nanette*, chock-full of flappers and fun. The Vincent Youmans hit, with book and lyrics by Otto Harbach and Irving Caesar, ran for 321 performances and had actually toured for a year before ever reaching Broadway. The character Lucille sings the little ditty about the importance of landing a husband, "Too Many Rings Around Rosie." In the song, she alludes to her childhood pals and how none of them became her beau since she tried to please all of them. Which of these fellows was *not* among her candy-munching playmates?

- **A.** Andy
- **B.** Joe
- **C.** Tommy
- **D.** Billy
- **E.** Harold

8. Producer George White was one of Ziegfeld's chief rivals and, in fact, got his start as a *Follies* dancer. He established his own series of revues, *George White's Scandals*, in 1919, which ran for twenty years. The *Scandals* weren't as flashy as the *Follies*, but with George Gershwin and later, DeSylva, Brown, and Henderson writing scores, they were hits. White also produced a black musical comedy, *Runnin' Wild*, in 1923, starring writer-actors Flournoy Miller and Audrey Lyles from *Shuffle Along*. What was so memorable about *Runnin' Wild*?

A. it introduced the dance sensation "The Black Bottom"

B. it featured Gershwin's twenty-five-minute jazz opera, "Blue Monday Blues"

C. it introduced the dance sensation "The Charleston"

D. it featured "The Birth of the Blues," pitting classical and modern music

E. it introduced Gershwin's "Somebody Loves Me"

9. Otto Harbach and Oscar Hammerstein II recaptured their operetta magic in 1926's *The Desert Song*. Sigmund Romburg did the music and Frank Mandel helped out on the libretto. The exotic locale here was French Morocco, where young Margot is attracted to Pierre Birabeau, the son of the governor. Unfortunately, Pierre's something-of a wuss. Margot wishes he were more like the leader of the Moroccan Riffs, the rebels currently fighting against the French. Now there's a real man! Of course, the leader is Pierre in disguise. What is his alter ego's name?

   A. the Scarlet Pimpernel

   B. the Red Shadow

   C. the Black Fox

   D. the Kinkajou

   E. the Sheik

10. DeSylva, Brown, and Henderson were the team behind 1927's *Good News*, the rollicking collegiate football musical. The entire nation learned how to do "The Varsity Drag," and discovered that "The Best Things in Life Are Free." What among the following list was *not* among those "free" things?

    A. spring flowers

    B. the moon

    C. robins

    D. sunbeams

    E. blue skies

Answers on page 205.

The 1930s

The Depression, combined with increased competition from Hollywood talkies, greatly hurt Broadway in the thirties. Many producers went bankrupt, including Dillingham, Arthur Hammerstein, Ziegfeld, and the Shuberts, though the Shuberts managed to reorganize. Shows declined in number and had shorter runs. Dance and swing characterized the era, and there were some memorable satiric gems disproving Kaufman's dictum about satire closing on Saturday night. Harold Rome, Ethel Merman, Vernon Duke, Harold Arlen, Mary Martin, and Alfred Drake all made their debuts, and there were hits from established pros like Cole Porter, Rodgers and Hart, the Gershwins, and Irving Berlin. The Street survived, and better days returned.

1. The hit of 1930 was *Flying High* with comic Bert Lahr reuniting with songwriters DeSylva, Henderson, and Brown from their 1928 success, *Hold Everything*. The show ran for 357 performances, a terrific run given the economy. Kate Smith starred opposite Lahr, whose character was:

A. a newspaper vendor who prefers fairy tales to the depressing news and dreams of having a picnic in the woods with a giant frog

B. a mechanic who sets an aviation record because he can't land the plane

C. a flimflam man promoting a cross-country race for unemployed actors going to Hollywood

D. a convict who really wants to go back to jail where he was on the polo team

E. the son of the Grand Eunuch who wants to inherit his dad's post without the necessary qualifications

2. Revues remained popular in the thirties. One of the best was Arthur Schwartz and Howard Dietz' *The Band Wagon* (1931), featuring such hits as "I Love Louisa," "New Sun in the Sky," and "Dancing in the Dark." It featured plenty of dances, including a dream ballet (a dozen years before *Oklahoma!*), and sketches by Dietz and George Kaufman. It also made extensive use of the revolving stage in its design. The cast was glorious. Who was *not* in this landmark show?

   A. Fred and Adele Astaire

   B. William Gaxton

   C. Tilly Losch

   D. Helen Broderick

   E. Frank Morgan

3. Nowhere near as classy as *The Band Wagon* but just as popular, the 1931 edition of the *Earl Carroll Vanities* ran for 278 performances. This production inaugurated Carroll's new enormous (3,000 seats) theatre. What was the highlight of the show?

   A. a 46'-tall fire-breathing dinosaur

   B. a revolving barricade built by revolutionary students

   C. the heroine's entrance on a giant movie camera crane

   D. a built-in swimming pool onstage

   E. a jungle scene with an actress entering on a live ostrich

4. Jerome Kern has a separate quiz, but his output was so huge and important, I couldn't resist slipping another of his shows in here. He wrote an updated operetta with Otto Harbach about the conflict between classical music and pop and jazz that continued many of the lessons from *Show Boat*, using underscoring for effect and integrating songs into the action. This successful show included the hit "Try to Forget." What was it?

   A. *Roberta*

   B. *Very Warm for May*

   C. *The Cat and the Fiddle*

   D. *Music in the Air*

   E. *On Your Toes*

5. J. P. McEvoy produced the revue *Americana* in 1932, using a talented stable of song-writers: Harold Arlen, Vernon Duke, Jay Gorney, Yip Harburg, Burton Lane, and Johnny Mercer. The show lasted only a few months, but gave the nation which Depression anthem?

   A. "Brother, Can You Spare a Dime?"

   B. "Let's Have Another Cup of Coffee"

   C. "I've Got Five Dollars"

D. "We're in the Money"

E. "We'd Like to Thank You, Herbert Hoover"

6. Opulent operettas were on the decline in the thirties, but *The Great Waltz* (1934) was a hit. The Rockefellers still had money, and they spent it on a cast of 180, a fifty-three-piece orchestra, and hydraulic set designs. The directorial genius behind the show and creator of its numerous special effects was Hassard Short, who pioneered the use of the double turntable, elevators, and modern lighting design. *The Great Waltz* was an adaptation of Strauss' *Walzer aus Wien* (*Waltzes from Vienna*). Who revised the book? (Hint: this was not the kind of material usually associated with this librettist.)

A. Otto Harbach

B. George Abbott

C. Oscar Hammerstein II

D. Herbert Fields

E. Moss Hart

7. The stock market crash hit Flo Ziegfeld badly, and he produced his last *Follies* in 1931, dying the following year. Working with Ziegfeld's widow, Billie Burke, the Shuberts staged *Ziegfeld Follies* in 1934 and 1936. The 1936 edition looked to be a hit, but star Fanny Brice became ill and by the time she recovered, the other cast members (emcee Bob Hope, Eve Arden, Josephine Baker) had scattered. What standard did Hope and Arden introduce in this show?

A. "It's De-Lovely"

B. "I Can't Get Started with You"

C. "You're Devastating"

D. "Thanks for the Memory"

E. "Don't Tell Me It's Bad"

8. Who would believe that a bunch of union workers, who initially could only perform on weekends, could star in one of the biggest hits (1,108 performances!) of the decade? The members of the International Ladies Garment Workers Union (ILGWU) took the "Labor Stage" for 1937's revue *Pins and Needles*, with a brilliant score by Harold Rome. Many of the songs became hits: "Chain Store Daisy," "Better with a Union Man," "Doin' the Reactionary," and "Nobody Makes a Pass at Me," but perhaps "Sing Me a Song of Social Significance" was most characteristic. In this number, the girls sing that they don't expect their fellows to croon romantically, but they do require the boys to be familiar with all of the following *except:*

A. FDR's attempt to pack the Supreme Court

B. strikes

C. wars

D. breadlines

E. front page news

9. The musical that set records with 1,404 performances was 1938's *Hellzapoppin*. Where *Pins and Needles* was topical, *Hellzapoppin* was just plain silly. Ole Olsen and Chic Johnson wrote and starred in the goofy mayhem. Which of the following was not true about *Hellzapoppin*?

A. it was heavily promoted by Walter Winchell
B. workmen would carry ladders through rows of house seats
C. a delivery man kept trying to deliver a potted plant, which was larger with each subsequent appearance
D. a gorilla dragged a screaming lady from her seat
E. Eddie Cantor headed the national tour

10. *Hellzapoppin*'s audience plants also included a scalper selling tickets to another 1938 show, Rodgers and Hart's *I Married an Angel*. This was supposed to be a film, but Rodgers and Hart got the rights and wrote the libretto themselves. Joshua Logan directed, with George Balanchine doing the choreography in a dance-heavy production. The stars were Walter Slezak, Dennis King, Vera Zorina (Mrs. Balanchine), and Vivienne Segal. It wasn't a large score, but "Spring Is Here" became a classic. The angel (Zorina) needs to learn about the human world, and much of her education comes through dance. There's a first-act ballet depicting the honeymoon, and a madcap second-act ballet set in New York…which makes perfect sense for a show set in Hungary, right? Which New York locale was the site for the ballet?
    A. the garment district
    B. the Automat
    C. the Arcade of the NBC Building, Radio City
    D. Central Park
    E. Roxy Music Hall

Answers on page 206.

The 1940s

The 1940s saw the American musical enter what many regard as its Golden Age, with Rodgers and Hammerstein's *Oklahoma!* seen as a line of demarcation. It was an era of giants—Lerner and Loewe, Jule Styne, Frank Loesser, and Comden, Green, and Bernstein got their first shows produced; Kurt Weill turned in six stunningly different shows before his untimely death; Porter and Berlin created their most enduring works; and Kern and Lorenz Hart wrote their final musicals. All these songwriters are covered in greater detail elsewhere in this book, but that's not to say there weren't other interesting things happening on the Great White Way in the forties. There were old standbys like leggy girl shows and operettas; there were patriotic revues, jaunty comedies, and daring experimental pieces.

1. One of those terrific experiments was 1940's *Cabin in the Sky* (book by Lynn Roux; songs by Vernon Duke and John Latouche). *Cabin* was the first black book musical (unless you want to argue that *Porgy and Bess* was a book musical and not an opera, which I don't; I mean, Gershwin himself called it a "folk opera"), a fantasy about the battle between the forces of heaven and hell for the soul of an ordinary man, Little Joe (Dooley Wilson). Joe's long-suffering wife, Petunia (Ethel Waters), helps him squeak past the pearly gates on a technicality. The score was one of Duke's finest; the characters were strong, appealing, and marvelously cast; young Boris Aronson designed the sets; and George Balanchine directed. Shortly before the opening, Duke added a song he had previously written with lyricist Ted Fetter. Latouche revised the

lyrics and it proved a hit. What was it? Give yourself a Broadway bonus point if you also know the original title.

   A. "Love Turned the Light Out"
   B. "Honey in the Honeycomb"
   C. "Taking a Chance on Love"
   D. "Happiness Is (Just) a Thing Called Joe"
   E. "Love Me Tomorrow"

2. George Abbott, skilled at spotting new talent, worked with young songwriters Hugh Martin and Ralph Blane and fresh-faced actors Gil Stratton, Jr., Maureen Cannon, Nancy Walker, and June Allyson in the prep-school show *Best Foot Forward* (1941). Who did Abbott and co-producer Richard Rodgers hire as dance director?

   A. Gene Kelly
   B. Stanley Donen
   C. Robert Alton
   D. Agnes de Mille
   E. Danny Daniels

3. Another daring show was the 503-performance blockbuster *Carmen Jones* (1943). Oscar Hammerstein II had hoped to stage or film his Americanization of Bizet's opera for nearly a decade, but no producer was willing to risk a black show with such an unusual background. But after Hammerstein scored with *Oklahoma!*, showman Billy Rose took the plunge, and the result was an enormous success. Hammerstein remained faithful to the opera's libretto, resetting the scene in a Southern parachute factory. Robert Russell Bennett scaled down the orchestrations for a Broadway pit. Which of the following Hammerstein songs is *incorrectly* paired with an original *Carmen* title?

   A. "Dis Flower"—"The Flower Song"
   B. "Dere's a Café on de Corner"—"Seguidilla"
   C. "Dat's Love"—"Habanera"
   D. "My Joe"—"Micaela's Air"
   E. "Stan' Up and Fight (Until You Hear de Bell)"—"Gypsy Song"

4. True or false: *Oklahoma!* had the first cast album of a musical.

5. Robert Wright and George Forrest made a smash debut by adapting Edvard Greig's music in 1944's *Song of Norway*. The operetta, loaded with luscious melodies and deliciously overripe dialogue, was a largely fictitious account of Grieg's life. Its popularity (860 performances!) was helped by the theme of Norwegian patriotism in a time when that country was occupied by the Nazis. Lawrence Brooks, Helen Bliss, and Robert Shafer played the love triangle, with Irra Petina as the Italian diva who lures Grieg to the wickedness of Rome. But on the cast album, Decca Records used one of their own sopranos in place of Petina. Who was it? Hint: her husband was in show business, too.

   A. Ruby Mercer
   B. Kitty Carlisle
   C. Barbara Scully

D. Marta Eggerth

E. Ann Andre

6. Rivaling *Oklahoma!* as long-running champs of the decade was *Follow the Girls*, a self-billed "burlesque musical." The story—such as it was—centered on Bubbles (Gertrude Niesen), a stripper at a stage door canteen, and her 4-F fiancé (Jackie Gleason), who attempts various disguises to sneak into the club since he's a civilian. The comedy was low, the girls were leggy, and the energy was high. No wonder departing GIs packed the houses! What was the catch phrase Gleason repeated numerous times throughout the show?

    A. "Follow those gals!"

    B. "She's the spy!"

    C. "But I'm a W.A.V.E.!"

    D. "Oh! Oh! Delphine!"

    E. "What the hell!"

7. Nancy Walker was one of our greatest comic actresses, often cast as wacky, offbeat characters—and often, alas, in shows unworthy of her skills. She was in five shows in the forties. Which of these roles was *not* played by Walker? What role did she play in that show?

    A. the blind date

    B. Yetta Samovar, student radical

    C. Lily Malloy, brewery heiress and underwriter of a ballet company

    D. Claire de Loone, enthusiastic anthropologist

    E. a perfume clerk, a poison victim, and a gal mad at Freud, among other sketch characters

8. *Call Me Mister* (1946), a revue that satirized military life and the difficulties of demobilization, was created and performed entirely by former servicemen and women and U.S.O. personnel. Harold Rome handled the songs and Arnold Auerbach wrote the sketches. It cemented the star power of Betty Garrett and Jules Munshin (both Donaldson winners) and boasted a smash song in "South America, Take It Away!" (a spoof of the insanely popular samba dances). Naturally, with Rome involved, there was "social significance" among the fun. Which song acknowledged the contributions of blacks in the Normandy campaign while pointing out their difficulties finding postwar work because of discrimination?

    A. "The Red Ball Express"

    B. "The Face on the Dime"

    C. "Call Me Mister"

    D. "Going Home Train"

    E. "Surplus Blues"

9. *Billion Dollar Baby* (1947) tried to create a nostalgia for the crazy 1920s, with flappers, gangsters, silent movies, and Follies-style revues. *Gentlemen Prefer Blondes*, just two years later, would do a better job. Still, *Baby* had a fine cast, headed by Joan McCracken and Mitzi Green, and managed a modest run. Interestingly, it reunited the entire creative team from 1944's *On the Town* with one exception. Who of these *On the Town* alumni did *not* work on *Billion Dollar Baby*?

A. Betty Comden and Adolph Green
B. Leonard Bernstein
C. Jerome Robbins
D. George Abbott
E. Oliver Smith

10. One of the era's most popular funny men was Bobby Clark, who teamed with fellow comic Paul McCullough when both were teens in 1905. They worked together in vaudeville, minstrel shows, revues, and musical comedies (including the Gershwins' *Strike Up the Band*) until McCullough's death in 1936. Thereafter, Clark worked alone. His character remained essentially unchanged, no matter the show—a likable, lecherous rogue, wearing painted-on glasses and armed with a cane and cigar. His four shows in the forties included two Michael Todd burlesque musicals, *Stars and Garters* (1942) and *As the Girls Go* (1948); the Cole Porter hit *Mexican Hayride* (1944); and a revival of Victor Herbert's *Sweethearts*, with the comic role rebuilt for his antic talents. *As the Girls Go* was his last show as an actor and it was one of the most expensive to date, with glamorous, revealing costumes by Oleg Cassini. (I think he's real good.) What was Clark's role in the show (not that plot mattered much!)? Extra credit if you can name the four comics who originated these other silly characters and the shows they're from.
   A. a washroom attendant who is slipped a Mickey Finn
   B. a wacky scientist who invents a poison gas
   C. a greeting-card salesman who gets tips on horse racing from the horses in his dreams
   D. First Husband to the first female president
   E. a swishy photographer for a prominent magazine

Answers on page 207.

The 1950s

The 1950s continued the Golden Age of the musical. Lerner and Loewe created *My Fair Lady*, which would dethrone *Oklahoma!* as the longest-running musical; new stars emerged (Gwen Verdon, Barbara Cook); choreographers became ever more important, with many taking over directing roles; established songwriters like Loesser, Rodgers and Hammerstein, and Comden and Green continued to turn out gems, while new talents emerged, including Stephen Sondheim, Bock and Harnick, Adler and Ross, and Meredith Willson. Fortunately for those of us who came along later, cast albums were big business, and even many flops got recorded, preserving a glimpse of what those shows were like. But, oh, do I long for a time machine!

1. 1951's *A Tree Grows in Brooklyn* had one of Arthur Schwartz and Dorothy Fields' finest scores, a book by Betty Smith (who wrote the novel) and George Abbott (who also directed), and outstanding choreography by Herbert Ross. It also boasted fabulous performances by Johnny Johnston, Shirley Booth, and Marcia Van Dyke. So why did it only run 267 showings? Perhaps it was too much star power from

Booth, whose comic portrayal of sister Cissy overwhelmed Van Dyke's somber Katie, married to the tragic, alcoholic Johnny Nolan (Johnston). Booth stopped the show with her numbers, "He Had Refinement" and "Love Is the Reason." Maybe such lightheartedness detracted too much from the struggles of the Nolans. Cissy says love is all of the following things *except* one:

A. a trip to the moon
B. palming an ace
C. lumpy mashed potatoes
D. a blow below the belt
E. a shot in the arm

2. Kurt Weill and Bertolt Brecht's *The Threepenny Opera* flopped in its first American production in 1933, but the composer always wanted to try again. After Weill's death, a new translation by Marc Blitzstein—with Weill's widow, Lotte Lenya, reprising her role as Jenny—had a record run off-Broadway. This version originally premiered at Brandeis College, with Leonard Bernstein conducting, but at which theatre did it run for over 2,700 performances?

A. the Sullivan Theatre
B. the Phoenix Theatre
C. the Theatre de Lys
D. the Theatre 80 St. Marks
E. the Cherry Lane Theatre

3. The year 1954 saw the first successful British import to Broadway since the 1920s. Coincidentally, the show was *about* the twenties: Sandy Wilson's *The Boy Friend*. Producers Cy Feuer and Ernest Martin bought the rights and invited Wilson and director Vida Hope over, too. Then—and here stories vary—conflicts arose, and the producers locked Wilson and Hope out of rehearsals, even hiring private detectives. Wilson may have been miffed, but his bank account was happy. With eighteen-year-old star Julie Andrews in the lead, *The Boy Friend* was a smash on Broadway, and three years later, had an amazing off-Broadway run as well. The simple tale based on a Mary Eaton–type twenties comedy saw a well-off, noble, English boy falling for a girl of similar status while both were posing as poor, working-class folk. What job does Tony pretend to have?

A. gendarme
B. waiter
C. teacher
D. delivery boy
E. grocer

4. *The Golden Apple* (1954) is a favorite cult show for many Broadway buffs. This imaginative retelling of *The Iliad* and *The Odyssey* in Washington State just after the Spanish-American War in 1900 had music by Jerome Moross and lyrics by John Latouche. It began off-Broadway at the Phoenix, became the critics' darling, but couldn't catch on with the general public. Either audiences were too dumb to understand how brilliantly Latouche—another genius who died too young—had adapted Homer or they were taken aback by the lack of dialogue (the work was through-sung) or the many dances or Moross' versatile score, which included everything from

vaudeville ditties to Hawaiian themes. An example of their cleverness: Paris' abduction of Helen helps spark the Trojan Way in Homer's original. He still runs off with her in *The Golden Apple*, but Moross and Latouche have recast him as a traveling salesman (a breed known to have a way with the ladies!) who performs entirely in mime and dance. He makes a fateful decision between the baked goods of Lovey Mars (Aphrodite/Venus), Miss Minerva (Athena), and Mrs. Juniper (Hera/Juno). How does Paris arrive in Angels' Roost?

    A. he sneaks back with Ulysses and the boys
    B. in a Model T
    C. by train
    D. in a balloon
    E. in the Wells Fargo wagon

5. The young songwriting team of Richard Adler and Jerry Ross worked with veteran co-directors George Abbott and Jerome Robbins for 1954's hit *The Pajama Game*. John Raitt, Janis Paige, Carol Haney, and Eddie Foy headed the cast in the lively comedy about a labor-management dispute in a pajama factory. Bob Fosse, fresh from MGM Studios, handled most of the dances, though Robbins staged the following number(s):

    A. "Racing with the Clock"
    B. "Steam Heat"
    C. "Seven and a Half Cents" and "There Once Was a Man"
    D. "Once a Year Day" and "Hernando's Hideaway"
    E. "Her Is" and "The Jealousy Ballet"

6. *Li'l Abner* (1956), with music by Gene dePaul, lyrics by Johnny Mercer, and book by Melvin Frank and Norman Panama (who both co-produced, along with choreographer-director Michael Kidd), was a musical comedy delight. Based on the Al Capp comic strip of the hillbilly adventures in Dogpatch, U.S.A., the show beautifully captured the silliness and satire of the source material. True or false: Elvis Presley was considered for the lead role of Li'l Abner.

7. Meredith Willson worked on the book, music, and lyrics for *The Music Man* for years before it finally made it to Broadway in 1957, and he was hailed as an overnight success. Drawing on his experiences in small-town Iowa, he created the community of River City, which encounters a fellow named Harold Hill in the summer of 1912. A fellow who wants to start a boys' band, or so it seems. After actors ranging from Danny Kaye to Phil Harris to Jackie Gleason turned down the role, veteran film actor Robert Preston auditioned, nailing the part. Barbara Cook played Marian Paroo, the suspicious librarian who ends up falling for the con man, and the show ran an amazing 1,378 performances.

When Harold teaches the boys his "think system," what musical piece are they supposed to be thinking about?

    A. the "Minuet in G"
    B. the "1812 Overture"
    C. the "Ode to Joy"
    D. the "Brandenburg Concerto #3"
    E. the "Stars and Stripes Forever"

8. One of 1959's hits was *Once Upon a Mattress*, with music by Mary Rodgers, lyrics by Marshall Barer, and libretto by Bruce Jay Thompson and Dean Fuller. *Mattress* retold the classic story of "The Princess and the Pea" with warmth, humor, and verve. It helped make Carol Burnett a star in the role of Princess Winifred of Farfalot. Jack Gilford played the mute king who would only regain speech when:

    A. his son, the prince, would wed a true princess

    B. a princess passed the queen's test

    C. the alligator of the swamp crested the mountain

    D. the mouse would devour the hawk

    E. the kingdom recovered from the Spanish panic

9. *Take Me Along* (1959) marked the second adaptation of a Eugene O'Neill play in the decade. (For more on *New Girl in Town*, see the Gwen Verdon quiz.) Bob Merrill (music and lyrics), and Joe Stein and Robert Russell (book) turned *Ah, Wilderness!* into the musical tale of the Miller family of Centerville, Ohio, circa 1910. The score was a delight, as was the cast, with Walter Pidgeon making his Broadway debut as the patriarch, Robert Morse as the love-struck juvenile lead, and Jackie Gleason stealing scenes as the ne'er-do-well brother-in-law. Morse sings of meeting his love, but when?

    A. "Nine O'clock"

    B. "Tonight at Eight"

    C. "Tomorrow"

    D. "About a Quarter to Nine"

    E. "Sunday Morning, Breakfast Time"

10. Another success off-Broadway was 1959's *Little Mary Sunshine*, which ran at the Orpheum Theatre for over a thousand performances. Rick Besoyan handled the book, music, and lyrics for this spoof of 1920s operettas, with loving digs at Princess Theatre shows, *Florodora*, and *The Firefly*, for good measure. As with all good operettas, it had an distinctive locale. Where was *Little Mary Sunshine* set?

    A. Vienna

    B. Canada

    C. Colorado

    D. the Essenzook Zee

    E. New Rochelle

Answers on page 208.

The 1960s

The 1960s saw the end of what many regard as the Golden Age of Broadway. Frank Loesser, Irving Berlin, Noel Coward, and the teams of Lerner and Loewe and Bock and Harnick had their last shows produced, with varying degrees of success. Oscar Hammerstein died, and Richard Rodgers ventured out on his own and with other lyricists. Jerry Herman arrived with his Big Lady big hits, and Broadway heard the music of Stephen Sondheim that went along with his sterling lyrics. David Merrick produced nearly everything under the sun, and tweaked the noses of the critics while doing it. By the end of the decade, musicals were presenting subject matter, staging, and types of music never seen or heard before on the Great White Way.

1. Gower Champion was at his creative best in the staging for 1961's *Carnival*, the musical version of the film *Lili*, itself adapted from even darker fiction by Paul Gallico. The story concerns a simple, naive girl, Lili (Anna Maria Albreghetti), who captures the heart of the crippled, bitter puppet master, Paul (Jerry Orbach), while working in a small circus in postwar Europe. Bob Merrill wrote the lovely score, and the show ran for 719 performances. Where had the circus last played before arriving in an unnamed town when the show opens?
   A. Paris
   B. Vienna
   C. Barcelona
   D. Monte Carlo
   E. Padua

2. When Oscar Hammerstein died in 1960, Richard Rodgers was left without a partner. He had written lyrics to his own music before, usually when Lorenz Hart was too drunk to do his job. Rodgers took on the sole lyric-writing credit for 1962's *No Strings*. The show featured innovative staging by Joe Layton, including seamless scene transitions, actresses onstage portraying models in dazzling costumes, and an onstage orchestra as well. (Rodgers had been wanting to get musicians out of the pit for years.) Dianne Carroll played the lead, an acclaimed model who enters into a romance with writer Richard Kiley. The interracial romance was controversial, and the show ended on a bittersweet note. Rodgers had pegged Carroll as a potential star long before and had hoped to cast her in which of the following musicals?
   A. *The Happy Time*
   B. *Flower Drum Song*
   C. *Pipe Dream*
   D. the film remake of *State Fair*
   E. the TV production of *Cinderella*

3. The year 1962 also saw Harold Rome and Jerome Weidman's *I Can Get It for You Wholesale*, based on Weidman's novel set in the garment district during the Depression. The show is best remembered today as the debut of nineteen-year-old Barbra Streisand, who sang the comic complaint "Miss Marmelstein." The show's lead character was a ruthless, conniving fellow whose schemes ultimately failed. Who played gotta-get-ahead-at-any-cost Harry Bogen?
   A. Lawrence Harvey
   B. Robert Morse
   C. Bob Fosse
   D. Elliott Gould
   E. Larry Kert

4. *Pal Joey* was based on a series of stories that first ran in *The New Yorker*. So was *Wonderful Town*. And so was a 1964 flop starring Chita Rivera (dancing up a storm) and Nancy Dussault (making strange animal noises) called *Bajour*. Dussault played

an anthropologist looking in New York and New Jersey for a tribe of Gypsies to study for her Ph.D. thesis. *Bajour*, with book by Ernest Kinoy and songs by Walter Marks, didn't have much going for it, but limped along for 232 performances and got a cast recording. Some Broadway buffs regard the album as a guilty pleasure, while others think it's radioactive.

What does "bajour" mean?

A. "good day" in Haitian Creole
B. tribal slang for "bosom"
C. "swindle" in Romany
D. "flahooley" in Romanian
E. a cry of dismay, as uttered by *Bajour*'s investors

5. Shows that run only nine performances are usually mere blips in musical history. But when the score is by Stephen Sondheim and the show is the unconventional satire *Anyone Can Whistle*, it becomes a cult favorite (and hundreds can lie about having been at those nine performances!). Set in a bankrupt town that manufactures a moneymaking miracle, *Whistle* had a stellar cast, including Angela Lansbury, Lee Remick, and Harry Guardino. Guardino played J. Bowden Hapgood, who announces he will use logic to separate the escaped inmates from the local insane asylum from the townsfolk. What does Hapgood call the two divisions?

~ ~

BROADWAY BONUS: What is the real name of the insane asylum popularly known as "the Cookie Jar"?

~ ~

6. Sondheim did the lyrics to Rodgers' music in *Do I Hear a Waltz?*, the 1965 adaptation of Arthur Laurents' *The Time of the Cuckoo*. The tryouts were troubled, with much ill will on many sides, but we're left with a lovely score today. American tourist Leona (Elizabeth Allen) comes to Venice, where she meets a handsome Italian (Sergio Franchi). Leona stays at the Pensione Fioria, where the owner seems pleased that her guests are "This Week, Americans." Her place is popular with other tourists. Who among the following are *not* guests or prospective guests at the Pensione?

A. Parisians
B. Brazilians
C. Germans
D. English
E. Dutch

7. I was going to ask what famous comedian had a small, non-singing role in the 1965 British import *Half a Sixpence*, but that's the one bit of trivia that everyone associates with this show. (Oh, all right, it was John Cleese.) But can you explain the significance of the "half a sixpence" that is the title of this rags-to-riches-to-(happy) rags tale?

A. Kipps (Tommy Steele) tosses it off Big Ben, where it hits young Walsingham and sends him to the hospital
B. it's the key to Kipps' inheritance
C. it's enough to buy one and a half bags of crumbs to feed the birds

D. it's a rare coin, so Kipps starts a numismatic shop with it

E. it's Kipps' love token to Ann

8. The blockbuster in 1965 was *Man of La Mancha*, with score by Mitch Leigh and Joe Darien and book by Dale Wasserman. Richard Kiley had his most famous role as Cervantes/Don Quixote, but during the long run (2,329 performances), other fine actors put on the Golden Helmet of Mambrino. Who was *not* among them?

A. Hal Holbrook

B. Michael Redgrave

C. Keith Michell

D. John Cullum

E. Jose Ferrer

9. The landmark rock musical *Hair* began at the New York Shakespeare Festival. "The American Tribal Love-Rock Musical" had music by Galt MacDermot and lyrics by James Rado and Gerome Ragni, who played Claude and Berger, respectively, when the show moved to the Biltmore in 1968. *Hair* addressed key issues of the day, from war and racism to attitudes about sex and drugs and free speech. It was daring, startling, and influential. The show added many songs, cut some others, and rewrote the book before the Broadway opening. Who was a co-lyricist for two added songs in act II?

A. Galt MacDermot

B. Joseph Papp

C. Mick Jagger

D. William Shakespeare

E. Abraham Lincoln

10. The play *1776* (1969) was the unlikely hit about the creation of the Declaration of Independence by songwriter and former history teacher Sherman Edwards, with a book by Peter Stone and Tony-winning direction by Peter Hunt. William Daniels was brilliant as the irascible and complex John Adams, and thankfully, his performance—along with many of his onstage colleagues—was preserved in the film version. Why did Daniels refuse his Tony nomination?

Answers on page 209.

The 1970s

The 1970s marked an era of change on Broadway. Dominating the period in the creative sense was the partnership between Stephen Sondheim and Hal Prince. Their work was not always commercially successful—a key feature of the seventies was soaring production costs—but it broke boundaries and set artistic standards few could match. Because of costs, longer runs were needed to pay off, so the decade saw numerous assaults on longest-run records. Producers seeking safer work turned more often to revivals, which grew in popularity. Different sounds came from the street as well, with shows featuring rock, country, and rhythm and blues scores. Andrew Lloyd Webber's work crossed the Atlantic for the first time, setting up the "British Invasion" of the eighties. (The Brits merit a quiz of their own elsewhere.)

1. *Two by Two* in 1970 marked Danny Kaye's return to Broadway after nearly thirty years, and was Richard Rodgers' thirty-eighth musical. Rodgers' lyricist was Martin Charnin, and Peter Stone adapted the book from Clifford Oddest's *The Flowering Peach*. Kaye played Noah, and as most Broadway buffs know, injured his leg early in the run. After missing two weeks, he returned in a wheelchair and proceeded to make an ass out of himself by maltreating his fellow actors, ad-libbing vaudeville bits, and yakking up the audience. What did *Two by Two* have in common with 1969's *Coco*, besides a huge-name star and a not-very-good show?

2. *Purlie* (1970) was the story of a black preacher (Cleavon Little) who battles to buy a church from Ol' Cap'n, the segregationist owner. With the help of the Cap'n's more liberal son, Purlie gets the church as well as the girl, played by a rousing Melba Moore. *Purlie*'s music and lyrics were by Gary Geld and Peter Udell. The book was co-authored by Udell, producer Philip Rose, and the talented actor-writer who wrote the straight play *Purlie Victorious* (and played its lead!). Who was it?
    A. James Earl Jones
    B. Roscoe Lee Browne
    C. Sidney Poitier
    D. Ossie Davis
    E. Emmett "Babe" Wallace

3. *Two Gentlemen of Verona* was the feel-good hit of 1971, winning the Tony for Best Musical. It began at Joseph Papp's New York Shakespeare Festival, with music by *Hair*'s Galt MacDermot and lyrics by John Guare, who adapted Shakespeare's play with director Mel Shapiro. The talented cast was ethnically diverse, with Clifton David, Raul Julia, Diana Davila, and Jonelle Allen in the leads. What among the following does Proteus *not* pack for his journey?
    A. his quiver and bow
    B. one thousand love letters
    C. sweet mints
    D. roses
    E. a toothbrush

4. *Grease* (1972) helped usher in the nostalgia craze for the fifties. With book and songs by Jim Jacobs and Warren Casey, the high-school love story of greaser Danny and sweet Sandy launched the careers of countless stars, from Barry Bostwick and Carole Demas to Kathi Moss and Adrienne Barbeau. It ran a record 3,388 performances, passing *Fiddler*, but eventually surpassed by *A Chorus Line*. Jacobs and Casey had a fun time spoofing fifties' pop culture. Which of these fifties' icons was *not* mentioned in "Look at Me, I'm Sandra Dee"?
    A. Doris Day
    B. Rock Hudson
    C. Annette Funicello
    D. Bobby Rydell
    E. Troy Donahue

5. Producer Ken Harper and songwriter Charlie Small were responsible for 1975's *The Wiz*, a retelling of *The Wizard of Oz* with an all-black cast and an eclectic score,

ranging from blues to gospel-tinged numbers. *The Wiz* was sassy, vigorous, and best of all, not afraid to laugh at itself. The cast was first-rate, with Ted Ross (the Lion) and Dee Dee Bridgewater (Glinda) nailing Featured Performer Tonys, and young Stephanie Mills solidifying the craziness with her very believable Dorothy. What did Ken Harper do that dramatically boosted Broadway sales?

> **A.** hired a publicist to help bring in black church groups
> **B.** ran ads on TV and R & B radio stations playing "Ease on Down the Road"
> **C.** had Shubert Alley by the Majestic Theatre paved with "yellow bricks"
> **D.** changed Dorothy's outfit from blue jeans to a pretty white dress
> **E.** had the winged monkeys make appearances singing Cole Porter's "Don't Monkey with Old Broadway"

✧ ✧

BROADWAY BONUS: Who was supposed to play the Queen of the Mice in *The Wiz*, but her role was cut in tryouts?

✧ ✧

6. The team that brought us *Purlie*—Gary Geld, Peter Udell, and Philip Rose—reunited in 1975 to adapt the film *Shenandoah* into a musical. Though billed as a family show, the tale of the pacifist father trying to keep farm and family intact throughout the Civil War was shockingly dark. Tony winner John Cullum was the glue that held the show together as patriarch Charlie Anderson. Cullum's eleven o'clock number took place at the graveside of Charlie's wife. What was this unseen character named?

> **A.** Jenny
> **B.** Martha
> **C.** Anne
> **D.** Evelina
> **E.** Sarah

7. *A Chorus Line* (1975). The Pulitzer Prize for Drama. The New York Drama Critics' Circle Winner. Nine Tonys. A record-shattering 6,137 performances. To many, the Best Musical Ever. Well, what more can I say? Most Broadway fans know the origins of this landmark show telling the tale of gypsies desperate to get cast, revealing their pasts, hopes, and dreams to the director in whose hands their fate lies. It began as a series of meetings between Michael Bennett and nineteen dancers, who recounted their own pasts, hopes, and dreams into a cassette recorder. That material was then worked up into the songs (music by Marvin Hamlisch, lyrics by Ed Kleban) and book (Dante and Kirkwood). How much were each of the original dancers paid for their stories?

> **A.** $1.00
> **B.** $88.00
> **C.** $100.00
> **D.** $1000.00
> **E.** $650.00

8. *Ain't Misbehavin'* (1978) was a revue based on the music of jazzman Fats Waller, Jr. Richard Maltby, Jr., Luther Henderson, and Murray Hewitt made it a point to cast

for personalities that fit their material, not just on vocal ability. They ended up with the amazing ensemble of Nell Carter, Andre de Shields, Ken Page, Armelia McQueen, and Charlaine Woodard. Henderson strove for authenticity in the arrangements and orchestrations. How did this lead to some musicians playing poker and smoking cigars in the basement during every performance?

9. Texans Carol Hill (score), Larry King (book), Peter Masterson (book/direction), and Tommy Tune (direction/choreography) combined to create the country-and-western-flavored *The Best Little Whorehouse in Texas* (1978). The story focused on the Chicken Ranch, its madam (Carlin Glynn), and the forces out to shut down the operation. Where did the source material come from?
   A. *Miss Mona's Memoirs*
   B. it's a Texan hybrid of *Irma la Douce* and *Can-Can*
   C. the Dolly Parton movie
   D. Larry King got the idea from the legalized prostitution houses in Nevada
   E. King wrote an article for *Playboy* about the real Chicken Ranch

10. *They're Playing Our Song* in 1979 told the tale of the collaboration and attraction between neurotic composer Vernon (Robert Klein) and wacky lyricist Sonia (Lucie Arnaz). The plot was inspired by the real-life relationship between composer Martin Hamlisch and lyricist Carole Bayer Sager. Neil Simon handled the laugh-filled libretto. Arnaz got good notices as Sonia, but wasn't the first choice for the role. Who was?
   A. Stockard Channing
   B. Ellen Greene
   C. Judy Kaye
   D. Meryl Streep
   E. Joanna Gleason

Answers on page 210.

The 1980s

The eighties were tough times for Broadway. Costs soared and the number of productions decreased. Some years, there were barely enough musicals to qualify for the Tonys, and certain categories were eliminated for lack of award-worthy performances. Still, Sondheim, Coleman, and Herman turned out some wheat among the chaff; Maury Yeston debuted; Michael Bennett directed his last stunner even while *A Chorus Line* ran on and on; the British invaded in a big way, but despite the general mania for spectacle, a few unassuming little shows ended up doing quite well.

1. *A Day in Hollywood/A Night in the Ukraine* (1980) was one little show that hit it big. With music by Frank Lazarus and book and lyrics by Dick Vosburgh (with some swell interpolations by Jerry Herman), *Day/Night* was a two-part show. Act one took place in the lobby of Grauman's Chinese Theatre and was a cabaret revue celebrating Hollywood, complete with the cast dressed as ushers. Act two was a retelling of Chekhov's *The Bear*—as performed by the Marx Brothers. With Tommy Tune at the

helm and Thommie Walsh as Tune's co-choreographer, the show was heavy on dance. The most memorable number may have been "Famous Feet," showing the lower limbs of some instantly recognizable film icons. Who was *not* among them?

A. Roy Rogers
B. Judy Garland
C. Sonja Henie
D. Dracula
E. Mickey and Minnie Mouse

2. Following 1978's *Ain't Misbehavin'* and *Eubie!*, revues that celebrated the work of Fats Waller and Eubie Blake, came 1981's *Sophisticated Ladies*. This show paid homage to Duke Ellington, featuring thirty-five of his hits in a gorgeously produced setting with phenomenal star power. Gregory Hines led the pack, ably backed up Judith Jamison, Phyllis Hyman, and Hinton Battle, among others. What happened to Hines in the show's Washington, D.C., tryout?

3. Perhaps one of the most innovative examples of staging in Broadway history was 1981's *Dreamgirls*, the story of a Motown girls' group hitting the big time—and all the highs and lows along the way there. With a score by Tom Eyen and Henry Krieger and featuring the blow-the-roof-off debut of Tony winner Jennifer Holliday, *Dreamgirls* was a show in constant movement. Five giant computer-controlled towers and multiple catwalks kept scenes shifting and allowed cinematic-like cuts and dissolves, contributing to the show's claim to be the most expensive musical ever at $3.5 million. Yet the production's beginnings were more modest—in workshops at the New York Shakespeare Festival. Who was the original director?

A. Tom Eyen
B. Michael Bennett
C. Michael Peters
D. Bob Avian
E. Tony Stevens

4. Maury Yeston's *Nine*, adapted from Fellini's film *8 1/2*, about a famed film director facing a midlife crisis and writer's block, took nearly a decade to get to Broadway. Once there, it cleaned up with five Tonys and 732 performances. Raul Julia played Guido Contini, surrounded by the twenty-one women in his life, including Karen Akers, Anita Morris, Kathi Moss, and Liliane Montevecchi. Tommy Tune staged the show in a glaringly white tiled spa, with the performers dressed in contrasting black. Yeston's score was intelligent and creative, ranging from penetrating character pieces to pull-out-the-stops production numbers for Guido's "Casanova" movie set. The score sounded even better since it was in the hands of master orchestrator:

A. Robert Russell Bennett
B. Jonathan Tunick
C. Irwin Kostal
D. William D. Brohn
E. Michael Starobin

5. In 1982, Gerard Alessandrini created the first *Forbidden Broadway* revue, mercilessly skewering Broadway shows, stars, and conventions. Twenty-seven years, eighteen

different editions, ten albums, more than 9,000 worldwide performances, one Tony Award for excellence, and a million belly laughs later, *Forbidden Broadway Goes to Rehab* closed on March 1, 2009. Those of us who loved the way *FB* lambasted LuPone, mocked Merman, and satirized Sondheim hope it won't be long before it returns. Over the years, the revue had many talented comic actors singing those nasty lyrics. Who was *not* among them?

    A. Brad Oscar
    B. Christine Pedi
    C. Bryan Batt
    D. Norma Mae Lyng
    E. Nathan Lane

6. *My One and Only* (1983) began as a planned revival of the Gershwins' *Funny Face*, starring Tommy Tune and Twiggy. By the time it opened, the original plot (typical goofy twenties' froth about stolen jewels) had vanished in favor of Tune's pilot attempting a distance record and romancing Twiggy, an English Channel swimmer. Some of *Funny Face*'s songs disappeared, too, replaced by songs from other Gershwin shows and movies. "Funny Face" was one title that remained, as were four of the five songs below. Which was *not* in *Funny Face*?

    A. "My One and Only"
    B. "High Hat"
    C. "He Loves and She Loves"
    D. "S'Wonderful"
    E. "Sweet and Low Down"

7. One of the finest scores from the eighties came from a show that had trouble finding an audience. *Baby* (1983), with book by Sybille Pearson, music by David Shire, and lyrics by Richard Maltby, Jr., only managed 241 performances. Set on a college campus, it examines how pregnancy affects the relationships of three couples. The show was revised after its closing, with one of the cut songs reinstated, and it has done well in regional and amateur productions. Which cut song was restored? (Hint: it is on the cast album, and all five of the songs below can be heard in the Maltby-Shire revue *Closer than Ever*.)

    A. "Father of Fathers"
    B. "I Wouldn't Go Back"
    C. "Like a Baby"
    D. "Patterns"
    E. "The Bear, the Tiger, the Hamster, the Mole"

8. Country music singer-songwriter Roger Miller didn't have any theatrical experience, but producer Rocco and Heidi Landesman gambled he was the right man to do the score for *Big River* (1985), the musical version of *Huckleberry Finn*. William Hauptman adapted Twain's novel and the show garnered a Tony, chalking up over a thousand performances. Huck meets the Duke and the King, two con men who bamboozle some locals into paying a dollar each to see the fantastical Nonesuch. Which of the following does *not* apply to the Nonesuch?

    A. it has ears like a hound dog
    B. it is nearly naked

C. it can smoke a cigarette

D. it has one breast

E. it is not a son of Adam or a daughter of Eve (i.e., not human)

9. Rupert Holmes was a quadruple-threat in 1985, creating the book, music, lyrics, and orchestrations for *The Mystery of Edwin Drood*, one of the truly original offerings of the decade. Based on the unfinished novel by Dickens, *Drood* took the form of a show put on by a British musical hall troupe in 1873, with Betty Buckley as "Miss Alice Nutting," the "principal boy," who plays the title character. Since no one knows how Dickens intended to end the tale, the company polled the audience for their choice of detective, murderer, and a romantic pairing. Holmes created musical solutions to fit every possible combination. One of the more colorful characters was Princess Puffer, enthusiastically portrayed by Cleo Laine. What's the story behind this character?

   A. she has a tobacco shop

   B. she's from Ceylon, but is keeping it secret

   C. she runs an opium den

   D. she's fond of fugu

   E. she owns the music hall in which the company plays

10. *Grand Hotel* (1989) had an unusual history. It began as *At the Grand*, a 1958 adaptation of Vicky Baum's novel and the MGM movie, with songs by Robert Wright and George Forrest and book by Luther Davis. *At the Grand* never got past the West Coast, but decades later, Tommy Tune reinvented it. Using a nonlinear structure, seamless staging, and a rewritten book (an uncredited Peter Stone), Tune gave us a theatrical mosaic in which all the myriad parts created a fascinating whole. Tune also brought in Maury Yeston to revise songs and create new ones more in keeping with the original novel than the movie. Liliane Montevecchi created the role of aging ballerina Grushinskaya. What movie musical star made her Broadway debut as a replacement for this part?

   A. Cyd Charisse

   B. Rita Moreno

   C. Taina Elg

   D. Leslie Caron

   E. Debbie Reynolds

Answers on page 211.

The 1990s

The 1990s were dominated by the arrival of Disney on Broadway, which staged enormous productions of *Beauty and the Beast*, *The Lion King*, and *Aida*. A host of musicals adapted from popular movies debuted, including *My Favorite Year*, *The Goodbye Girl*, *Footloose*, *Big*, and *Saturday Night Fever*. (Insert quote here from *[title of show]* if you are feeling snarky.) Dance shows like *Swing* and *Fosse* were hits and there were revues aplenty. And everywhere you looked, there were revivals. Some were successes—*Show Boat*, *A Funny Thing Happened on the Way to the Forum*, *Guys and Dolls*, *Carousel*, and particularly, Kander and Ebb's *Cabaret*, as reimagined by Sam Mendes, and *Chicago*, which would become the longest-running revival ever. Some were flops—*Company*, *Gentlemen Prefer Blondes*, *1776*, and *Annie*. We saw the first work of Ahrens and Flaherty, William Finn, Frank Wildhorn, Michael John LaChiusa, Jason Robert Brown, Andrew Lippa, Adam Guettel, and Jonathan Larson, who tragically died just before the opening of his landmark show, *Rent*.

1. One of the hits of 1991 was *The Secret Garden*, with music by Lucy Simon and book and lyrics by Marsha Norman, adapting Frances Hodges Burnett's classic novel. Norman altered the original, bringing in choruses of ghosts and heightening the dramatic tension. By the show's end, the dead garden is reborn, the ghosts are laid to rest, and the Cravens, who had been damaged in either spirit or body, are now "wick." (Except for Uncle Neville, but he's primarily there for that dramatic tension.)

   Daisy Eagan drew raves for her portrayal of Mary, becoming the youngest girl to win a Tony. How old was she?
   A. nine
   B. ten
   C. eleven
   D. twelve
   E. thirteen

2. When Disney released the 1991 Howard Ashman–Alan Menken animated film, *Beauty and the Beast*, *Variety* called it "the most appealing musical comedy score in years." No wonder, with Broadway vets Paige O'Hara, Angela Lansbury, and Jerry Orbach voicing the characters and proven songwriters Ashman and Menken (*Little Shop of Horrors*) providing the material. Disney CEO Michael Eisner saw possibilities in a theatrical version, and in 1994, ushered in the Disney era of stage musicals, though some have dubbed it the "Mousification" of Broadway. *Beauty and the Beast* ran for thirteen years and 5,464 performances, the sixth longest-running show in history. Which of the following is *not* true about *B&B*?
   A. Hugh Jackman played Gaston in the Australian production
   B. Belle's ball gown weighed over forty pounds
   C. Kristin Chenoweth was a replacement Belle on Broadway
   D. Susan Egan regularly had to pick "fur" off Terrance Mann's tongue since his makeup shed and his hands were encased in rubber gloves
   E. Disney, in order to save money, radically downsized the cast in 1999

3. *Ain't Misbehavin'* and *Sophisticated Ladies* had success in the late seventies and early eighties celebrating the works of Fats Waller and Duke Ellington, and in the nineties, revues honoring specific composers became quite popular. The champion was *Smokey Joe's Cafe* (1995, 2,036 performances), featuring the creations of songwriters Lieber and Stoller. (*Jelly's Last Jam*, which used the music of Jelly Roll Morton—and also was a smash in the nineties—actually was a book show, not a revue.) Which of the following songmen did *not* have a revue showcasing their work on Broadway in the decade?
   A. Louis Jordan
   B. Johnny Mercer

C. Johnny Burke

D. the Gershwins

E. Frank Loesser

4. What can be said about *Rent* (1996) that hasn't been said? It fused rock and true theatrical book and character numbers with a classical theme (an updating of *La Boheme*); it launched the careers of a host of young stars; it stands as a monument to its creator, Jonathan Larson, who died just before its opening; it brought young people into the theatre in droves; and it frankly addressed issues of homosexuality, AIDS, and intolerance. One of the more attractive aspects of the show was the way Larson never underestimated the intelligence of his audience. I have wondered how many young "Rentheads" caught all the cultural references in the lyrics, but I hope they were looking up the ones they didn't get. Which of the following is *not* mentioned in Larson's lyrics?

    A. Heidegger

    B. Thelma and Louise

    C. the Magna Carta

    D. Ted Koppel

    E. Stephen Sondheim

5. One of the finest scores of the decade came from the 1996 off-Broadway production of *Floyd Collins*, a compelling mixture of bluegrass, folk music, soaring ballads, and even a vaudeville-styled showstopper. Christopher Innvar starred as the real-life Kentucky man, Floyd Collins, who was an expert cave explorer, but became trapped deep underground in 1925. As his family (Jason Danieley and Theresa McCarthy) pray for his rescue, reporters descend on their small town in one of the century's first gigantic media frenzies. *Floyd Collins* won the Lucille Lortel award for Outstanding Musical.

Tina Landau directed and wrote a portion of the lyrics, but which able newcomer created this memorable score?

    A. Andrew Lippa

    B. William Finn

    C. Jimmy Roberts

    D. Laurence O'Keefe

    E. Adam Guettel

6. If you want to hear some fantastic Broadway choral singing, pick up the cast album of 1997's Tony winner, *Titanic*. With a varied and complex score by Maury Yeston (brilliantly orchestrated by Jonathan Tunick), a solid book by Peter Stone, and ably directed by Richard Jones, *Titanic* told the story of the mighty ocean liner's fateful voyage. Stone and Yeston developed over forty characters, nearly all of them based on real passengers or crew members, each with his or her own story and relationships with the others. And oh, could that huge cast sing! Which of these phenomenally talented performers was *not* present when *Titanic* launched on Broadway?

    A. Kevin Gray

    B. Victoria Clark

    C. Michael Ceveris

    D. David Garrison

    E. Brian D'Arcy James

7. *The Scarlet Pimpernel* (music by Frank Wildhorn, lyrics by Nan Knighton) took years to go from concept album to Broadway in late 1997, and once there, continued to evolve into three separate versions. (Four, if you count the revised sets on the national tour.) Still, it was frothy romantic fun, with Douglas Sills, Terrance Mann, and Christine Andreas admirably filling those larger-than-life roles. Throughout the revisions, one thing stayed the same: the crucial scene in which Percy learns Marguerite is not Chauvelin's willing accomplice, but another of his victims. Where does this scene take place?

    A. the Comédie Française
    B. the Bastille
    C. the ballroom at the palace
    D. the footbridge in the garden
    E. the library at the Blakeney estate

8. *Side Show* (1997) couldn't find its audience and flopped. Its publicity director admitted that too many people thought it was a real "freak show," rather than a surprisingly intimate tale of the Hilton sisters, a pair of conjoined twins from the 1920s. Henry Krieger did the music, Bill Russell provided the book and lyrics, while Robert Longbottom directed. Alice Ripley and Emily Skinner deftly portrayed Violet and Daisy merely by standing side by side. For dramatic effect, Daisy appears in one number without her twin. Which was it?

    A. "Private Conversation"
    B. "The Devil You Know"
    C. "You Should Be Loved"
    D. "More than We Bargained For"
    E. "Feelings You've Got to Hide"

9. Having struck musical gold with *Beauty and the Beast*, Disney Theatrical tried again and hit the mother lode with *The Lion King* (1997). Based on the 1994 animated film with songs by Elton John and Tim Rice, the stage version added more numbers by South African musician Lebo M and Mark Mancina, Jay Rifkin, Hans Zimmer, and Julie Taymor. Taymor was busy in a few other areas—directing and designing, including the stunning masks and over 230 puppets. *The Lion King* was a visual experience like no other musical, but it wasn't simply making Broadway history, it was conserving it. How did Disney and *The Lion King* help preserve Broadway's past?

10. *Parade* (1998), with songs by newcomer Jason Robert Brown and direction by Hal Prince, was based on events in 1913 Georgia, where a thirteen-year-old factory girl was raped and murdered. The anti-Semitic jury convicted the Jewish factory manager, Leo Frank, and when his sentence was converted to life, a lynch mob broke into the jail and hanged Frank. Brown's score was rich and varied, and the cast, led by Brent Carver, was superb. But perhaps the material was too bleak to catch on in a big way, a fate shared by 1999's *Marie Christine*, Michael John LaChiusa's retelling of Medea. Who helped bring Jason Robert Brown and Hal Prince together?

    A. Daisy Prince
    B. Alfred Uhry
    C. Evan Pappas

D. Carolee Carmello

E. Andrew Lippa

Answers on page 212.

The 2000s

The twenty-first century came to Broadway, continuing a number of the trends from the previous decade—lots of revivals, big, splashy shows, and adaptations from pop movies. Perhaps in a response to tough times, camp became king, so much so that *Forbidden Broadway* devoted an entire number to campy musicals...and had to add verses later when a new batch of camp premiered. Jukebox musicals multiplied—a few smash hits, more total disasters (they have their own quiz section). Still, there were some delightful surprises, including twenty-something puppets finding their purpose, John Doyle's new takes on Sondheim performed by actor-musicians, competing *Wild Partys*, and a revival of *Big River* performed by hearing and deaf actors in song and sign language. As in the past, new songwriters and librettists emerged and new stars took their places onstage to interpret their work. Broadway may be the fabulous invalid and we may wring our hands over costs and subject matter and why people send text messages while they're at a show, but musicals endure.

1. Mel Brooks' first work on Broadway included sketches for *New Faces of 1952*. Nearly a half century later, he became the "King of Broadway," adapting his 1968 film *The Producers* (2001) into the biggest smash the Street had seen in years. Nathan Lane and Matthew Broderick wowed audiences as Max Bialystock and Leo Bloom, putting on their intentional flop, *Springtime for Hitler*. *The Producers* set records at the Tonys. How many did it win?
    A. 11
    B. 12
    C. 13
    D. 14
    E. 15

2. If *The Producers* was the behemoth, *Urinetown* was the Little Show with the Unlikely Title That Could. The concept arose when librettist-lyricist Greg Kotis was in Paris, and dwindling funds forced him to choose between pay toilets and a meal. Kotis and composer Mark Hollman created a show set in a drought-stricken world where an evil corporation controls all toilets. *Urinetown* was the hit at the International Fringe Festival, and made it to Broadway, where it picked up three Tonys (editorial aside: but not Best Musical, dammit!). The show deliciously satirized musical traditions (especially Weill and Blitzstein, but also Yip Harburg's anti-capitalism, *West Side Story*, and *Gantry*, to name a few). The outstanding cast included Hunter Foster, Nancy Opel, John Cullum, and Jeff McCarthy as Officer Lockstock, who describes what happens to those who break the laws about peeing. Who among the following characters did *not* take a trip to Urinetown (the place, not the musical)?
    A. Julie Cassidy
    B. Joseph "Old Man" Strong

C. Little Becky Two Shoes
D. Roger Roosevelt
E. Jacob Rosenbloom

3. The blockbuster of 2002 was *Hairspray*, which had as its source the 1988 John Waters film. Thomas Meehan and Mark O'Donnell wrote the book, and Marc Shaiman and Scott Wittman handled the score. Marissa Jaret Winokur took home the Tony for her portrayal of Tracy Turnblad, the plucky schoolgirl with big dreams. Harvey Fierstein, in a size-54EEE bra, also nabbed a Tony for his rendering of Edna, Tracy's mom. Much of *Hairspray*'s charm came from its looks, with costumes by William Ivey Long, wigs by Paul Huntley (aspiring to "Versailles on speed"), and David Rockwell's conceptual, almost abstract sets. Which of the following was *not* an influence on the design elements for *Hairspray*?
   A. the "Lite Brite" toy
   B. Peter Maxx' artwork
   C. Necco wafers
   D. Boris Aronson's set designs for *Do Re Mi*
   E. Formstone—a type of faux stone exterior siding

～～～～～～～～～～～～～～～～～～～～～～～～～～～～～～～～～～

BROADWAY BONUS: This one requires you to know obscure facts about two shows! The designers for *Hairspray* tried using something onstage that corresponded to a lyric in "Good Morning, Baltimore" that was ultimately cut before opening because it looked "too Disney." Hal Prince tried and also rejected the same element—though in a different format—in *The Phantom of the Opera*. What was it?

～～～～～～～～～～～～～～～～～～～～～～～～～～～～～～～～～～

4. A musical using a cast half comprised of puppets and done in the style of children's educational television, but focusing on the very adult subjects of finding purpose in life, sex, dating and commitment, homosexuality, racism, and Internet porn as well? And it's funny, too? Sounds impossible, but that's the premise behind 2003's Tony winner, *Avenue Q*, the brainchild of songwriters Jeff Marx and Robert Lopez, with libretto by Jeff Whitty. Two of the puppet characters, Nicky and Rod, are roommates (and clearly inspired by *Sesame Street*'s Ernie and Bert). Rod is reading about Broadway musicals of the 1940s when Nicky interrupts him. Which two 1940s shows does Rod mention?

5. The film *Monty Python and the Holy Grail* already had a hilarious premise and a few good tunes. Python Eric Idle transformed King Arthur's quest into a big Broadway bonanza, complete with singing, dancing knights, and peasants, and the luscious chorus of the Lady of the Lake (and her Laker Girls). *Monty Python's Spamalot* (2005) took home the Best Musical Tony, and director Mike Nichols and "Lady" Sara Ramirez also nabbed hardware. Tim Curry was Arthur and Chris Sieber was handsome Sir Galahad. What gorgeous guy was originally slated for Galahad during *Spamalot*'s tryout run in Chicago, but had to bow out?
   A. Raúl Esparza
   B. Brian D'Arcy James
   C. Cheyenne Jackson

D. Jason Danieley

E. Douglas Sills

6. *The Light in the Piazza* (2005) was a luminous production (music and lyrics by Adam Guettel, book by Craig Lucas, direction by Bartlett Sher) about a young American girl, Clara (Kelli O'Hara), and her mother visiting Italy in the 1950s. Guettel's complex score took home the Tony, and Victoria Clark was honored for her portrayal of Clara's mother. Clara falls for a young Italian, Fabrizio (Matthew Morrison), who complains to his father that he wishes he were more like an American movie star. Which one?

   A. Farley Granger

   B. Gary Cooper

   C. Van Johnson

   D. Gregory Peck

   E. John Wayne

7. *The Drowsy Chaperone* (2006) introduced us to Man in Chair, a theatre lover who describes—in glorious detail—the plot of his favorite show, a 1920s comedy. As Man plays the record for us (yes, record), his shabby apartment turns into the set and the actors pop out of his fridge, closets, and Murphy bed. This delightful concept was devised by songwriters Lisa Lambert and Greg Morrison with librettist Bob Martin, who also originated Man in Chair. Casey Nicolaw handled the direction and choreography for the talented ensemble, which included Sutton Foster as the stage star who didn't want to "Show Off" any more. Why did Foster choose to do a one-handed cartwheel among the other stunts she performs in that showstopper?

8. Christine Ebersole gave what many regarded as the performance of a generation, playing the dual roles of Big Edith and Little Edie Bouvier Beale in 2006's *Grey Gardens*. The show was inspired by the lives of two eccentric relatives of Jackie Kennedy, and the cult documentary that preserved their reclusive ways. Scott Frankel and Michael Korie handled the music and lyrics, and Doug Wright wrote the libretto. Korie and Wright deftly worked many of the Beales' comments from the documentary into the show, and Frankel's score encompassed a wide variety of styles. The show began off-Broadway and underwent changes before reaching the Walter Kerr Theatre. (Thankfully, both versions were recorded. Blessings to those at PS Classics!) Which song was *not* in the off-Broadway edition?

   A. "Another Winter in a Summer Town"

   B. "Drift Away"

   C. "Revolutionary Costume"

   D. "Goin' Places"

   E. "Will You?"

9. *Spring Awakening* (2006), a rock musical based on an 1890 German play about teenagers and their personal conflicts, dominated the Tonys that season. Among those honored were Steven Sater (book and lyrics), Duncan Sheik (music), John Gallagher, Jr. (featured actor), and Michael Mayer (director). *Spring Awakening*, like *Rent* before it, attracted the teen and young adult crowds. Director Mayer staged the

show so that some members of the audience were allowed to sit on the stage, in the midst of the action. What was the explanation behind this?

A. they thought they were in line for the *Rent* lottery
B. they represent adult authority
C. they represent the spirit of life
D. they represent community
E. they're on the wait list for Herr Professor Knockenbruch's Latin class

❧ ❧

BONUS BROADWAY BONUS: What did John Gallagher, Jr., do with his handheld mike during "The Bitch of Living" on *Spring Awakening*'s opening night at the Eugene O'Neill?

❧ ❧

10. *In the Heights* (2008) blended rap, hip-hip, and Latino flavors with true musical theatre songs. Lin-Manuel Miranda created the show and played the role of Usnavi, who runs the local convenience store in a largely immigrant community in Washington Heights. Nina is the first in her family to go to college, but she fears facing everyone's disappointment after returning home, unable to balance academics and work. Where was she a student?

A. UCLA
B. Stanford
C. Cal Tech
D. UC Santa Barbara
E. Tait College

Answers on page 213.

Act One: Scene One

Richard Rodgers and Oscar Hammerstein II

When Richard Rodgers and Oscar Hammerstein teamed up in 1943, both men were well established in musical theatre. Rodgers had been with Lorenz Hart for over two decades, creating many fast-paced musical comedies. Hammerstein, born into a theatrical family, had worked with several composers, notably Jerome Kern and Sigmund Romberg, and wrote shows ranging from operettas like *Rose-Marie* to the groundbreaking *Show Boat*. Given their different temperaments, most show folk were surprised to learn that the pair were trying to musicalize Lynn Riggs' *Green Grow the Lilacs*, a project Rodgers had initially offered Hart. The resulting partnership would revolutionize Broadway.

1. What is there to say about *Oklahoma!* (1943)? It marked a watershed in musical theatre history. Even poor souls who know next to nothing about musicals have heard of it. Richard Rodgers' folksy melodies and Oscar Hammerstein's easy, conversational lyrics helped give this tale of cowboys and farmers its naturalistic feel. Which of the following critters is *not* found in *Oklahoma!* (the show, not the state)?
    A. a hawk
    B. a lark
    C. rams and ewes
    D. a field mouse
    E. a little brown maverick

2. The duo followed *Oklahoma!*'s triumph with another success, 1945's *Carousel*, based on Ferenc Molnár's *Liliom*. Fortunately for Rodgers and Hammerstein (and musical lovers everywhere), Molnár approved many changes to his play, including a drastically softened ending and its relocation from Hungary to New England. During the Boston tryouts, Hammerstein (or director Reuben Mamoulian, depending on which source you read) came up with a new concept for the deity figure: he became "the Starkeeper," perched on his ladder, polishing the stars. How was this character previously depicted?
    A. as a calm sea captain in a celestial boat
    B. as a stonecutter
    C. as the owner of the mill
    D. as Billy's angelic counterpart, the operator of a heavenly carousel
    E. as "Mr. God," sitting quietly in a New England parlor, with "Mrs. God" playing on the harmonium

3. *Allegro* (1947) is sometimes described as the first concept musical, telling the life story of Joseph Taylor, Jr., from birth to tough career choices in his mid-thirties. It used a constant Greek chorus, continuous action, and had no real sets, just props and furniture whisked on and off via treadmills. And, as one might have expected

with Agnes de Mille as director, it had four big ballets. Audiences and critics didn't take well to it, and due to its enormous operating costs, it lost money despite a decent run of 315 performances. Who was a "gofer" (general assistant) for the show, though he was only in his teens?

    A. Stephen Sondheim
    B. Fred Ebb
    C. Joe Layton
    D. Cy Coleman
    E. Michael Stewart

4. 1949's *South Pacific* returned the pair to the heights, capturing the Pulitzer for drama and running 1,925 performances. Based on James Michener's stories, it concerns the romance between a navy nurse, Nellie Forbush (Mary Martin), and a French plantation owner, Emile de Becque (opera star Ezio Pinza). The subplot involves the tragic love affair of a young officer (William Tabbert) for an island girl (Betta St. John). What does Lt. Cable try to give Bloody Mary (Juanita Hall) after he renounces Liat?

    A. a boar's tooth necklace
    B. his grandfather's watch
    C. DiMaggio's glove
    D. "fo' dolla'"
    E. a blueberry pie

5. Rodgers and Hammerstein's 1951 *The King and I* was written as a star vehicle for Gertrude Lawrence, who sadly died eighteen months into the run. The role of the King made a new star of Yul Brynner, who fortunately re-created the part in the movie version, winning the Best Actor Oscar. But due to Tony regulations about "above the title billing," he had to be content with the Featured Actor Tony. He played the King until his death in 1985, and will forever be linked to the role. Who among these other fine actors has *not* played the monarch of Siam in this classic musical?

    A. Farley Granger
    B. Darrin McGavin
    C. Rex Harrison
    D. Alfred Drake
    E. Lou Diamond Phillips

6. The duo followed *The King and I* with the backstage tale *Me and Juliet* (1953). George Abbott directed; Jo Mielziner's stage-within-a-stage was stunning; the cast was talented. But for whatever reason, it failed to catch on, though it did turn a profit. Who or what was "the Big Black Giant"?

    A. the sandbag jealous Bob drops at the end of act I
    B. the orchestra pit
    C. the nickname for Dario, the conductor
    D. the audience
    E. the eighty-five tons of scenery on trucks with synchronized motors

7. 1955's *Pipe Dream* was troubled all the way. Rodgers wrote a lush score, but had surgery and was absent during critical rehearsals. Hammerstein's libretto was pieced

together while John Steinbeck turned out chapters of a new novel (*Sweet Thursday*), using characters from *Cannery Row*. Somehow, the flavor of Steinbeck's people and what Hammerstein envisioned didn't mesh. Rodgers admitted the show was "not well produced" and opera star Helen Traubel got poor reviews. In the show, what was the name of "the Happiest House on the Block"?

    A. the Bear Flag Cafe
    B. Cannery Row
    C. Western Biological Laboratory
    D. "The Pipe"
    E. Sonny Boy's Pier Restaurant

8. *Flower Drum Song* (1958), while not regarded with the honor given to other Rodgers and Hammerstein works, nonetheless was a hit, running for 600 performances. It was based on C. Y. Lee's novel about generational and cultural clashes among Chinese immigrants in San Francisco. Who was the novice director?

9. *The Sound of Music* (1959) would be Rodgers and Hammerstein's last show; Hammerstein died of stomach cancer the following year. The story of the Von Trapp family singers starred Mary Martin and was a smash, while the 1965 movie with Julie Andrews was an even greater success. What was the last lyric Hammerstein wrote?

    A. "Do-Re-Mi"
    B. "Climb Ev'ry Mountain"
    C. "The Sound of Music"
    D. "Edelweiss"
    E. "The Lonely Goatherd"

10. The year 1996 saw *State Fair*, Rodgers and Hammerstein's 1945 movie musical (itself remade in 1962 with new songs by Rodgers) revised into a stage production. To eke out the score, cut songs from other shows by the duo were added to the two movie scores. What show was the original source for "When I Go Out Walking with My Baby" and "Boys and Girls Like You and Me"?

    A. *Allegro*
    B. *Carousel*
    C. *Me and Juliet*
    D. *Pipe Dream*
    E. *Oklahoma!*

Answers on page 214.

Jerry Bock and Sheldon Harnick

Jerry Bock and Sheldon Harnick comprised a formidable duo in the Golden Age of musicals, creating seven shows in all. These included smashes like *Fiddler on the Roof*, for years the longest-running show in history, and *She Loves Me*, a cult favorite with romance, comedy, and finely portrayed characters. Their skill was evident in every score. Harnick has listed his basic requirements for a good lyric: it should continue the plotline's flow, give insight into the character, heighten climatic moments, and embellish the period and the setting. Bock's music, ranging from rich and melodious ballads to pastiche to moving character pieces, perfectly complemented his partner's words.

1. One of Sheldon Harnick's early successes was "Boston Beguine," satirizing censorship in Beantown, written for the acclaimed revue *New Faces of 1952*. Who introduced it?
   A. June Carroll
   B. Paul Lynde
   C. Alice Ghostley
   D. Eartha Kitt
   E. Carol Lawrence

2. Jerry Bock's early work included music for a revue, *Catch a Star* (1955), with sketches by a comedy writer named Neil Simon. The following year, he provided the music and some lyrics for *Mr. Wonderful*, with help from Larry Holofcener and George Weiss. Jule Styne produced the show, which starred Sammy Davis, Jr., in a role fairly similar to his own nightclub act. Olga James played Sammy's love interest, but what actress had a supporting role?
   A. Chita Rivera
   B. Carol Haney
   C. Gwen Verdon
   D. Millicent Martin
   E. Edie Adams

3. Bock then wrote some songs for the *Ziegfeld Follies of 1956*, which closed in Boston. Not long after, Jack Cassidy introduced Bock to Harnick, and Broadway history was made. Their first joint effort, *The Body Beautiful* (1958), didn't last long, hampered by a formulaic plot and a cast of non-singers, but the pair attracted attention. Producers Hal Prince and Robert Griffith admired the score, and tapped them for their next show.
   What sport was featured in *The Body Beautiful*?
   A. lacrosse
   B. hockey
   C. body building
   D. surfing
   E. boxing

4. Only a handful of musicals ever won a Pulitzer Prize, but Bock and Harnick's *Fiorello!* (1959) did. The show, starring previously unknown Tom Bosley as Fiorello LaGuardia, had a book written by Jerome Weidman and George Abbott, and ran for 795 performances. Bock and Harnick's score ranged from ballads evoking the flavor of early-twentieth-century music to sharp, satirical masterpieces, deftly merging background details, plot points, and lots of humor.
   Which of the following is *true* about the first three songs Bock and Harnick wrote for *Fiorello!*?
   A. director Arthur Penn disliked them because they were too light in tone
   B. director George Abbott disliked them because they were too satirical
   C. they wrote them in Jerome Weidman's basement

D. they wrote them without knowing who the central character of the show would be

E. they wrote them in a single weekend

5. Despite assembling the same team as *Fiorello!* (Abbott, Weidman, Griffith, Prince), Bock and Harnick's next show, *Tenderloin* (1960) didn't last a year. The setting was once again a period piece, this time concerning a minister (Maurice Evans) trying to clean up vice in 1890s New York. Unfortunately, audiences seemed to find vice more interesting than virtue. Bock and Harnick's score still had some gems, including one song sung by the brash reporter Tommy (Ron Hussman), cheerfully describing tales of girls gone astray, who found happiness and rosy cheeks through immoral actions.

For one gal, the path to sin began when she was given which of the following?

A. artificial flowers

B. educated fleas

C. lobster

D. a kiss on the hand

E. rahadlakum

6. Bock and Harnick's next show was one of those musicals that wasn't a commercial success, but became a cult classic with a score deeply loved by many. *She Loves Me* (1963) was an intimate show based on the Miklos Laszlo play *Parfumerie* and its film version, *The Shop Around the Corner* by Ernst Lubitsch. Hal Prince had double duty as producer-director, and Joe Masteroff wrote a book that melded almost seamlessly with the score. In one of Broadway's greatest romances, Barbara Cook and Daniel Massey played Amalia and Georg, two clerks who feud at work while unaware they are lonely-hearts club pen pals.

Each of the characters in the 1930s Hungarian cosmetics shop has his or her own delightful story arc and number. The delivery boy, Arpad (Ralph Williams), earnestly wants to move up in his responsibilities, so he describes his extensive knowledge of the business to his boss. According to Arpad, what are the three elements of a fine perfume?

7. Bock and Harnick's next work would be their greatest hit: 1964's *Fiddler on the Roof*, which for years held the status of longest-running Broadway show at 3,242 performances. Prince produced, but Jerome Robbins handled direction and choreography in what would be his last book musical. Joe Stein adapted the stories of Sholom Aleichem's Jewish milkman Tevye (Zero Mostel), whose family faces the challenging social and political upheavals of early twentieth-century Russia.

When *Fiddler* was in tryouts, it was running far too long. Two fine songs were cut to speed things along, their material boiled down into several lines of dialogue. One song, "When Messiah Comes," was an irreverent piece that highlighted Zero Mostel's comic skills. What was the subject matter of the other song?

A. Motel's new sewing machine

B. a duet for the younger daughters

C. Perchik demonstrating the new dances in Kiev

D. Golde describing her hopes for her daughters' futures

E. the death of Tevye's horse

8. When shows on the road are ailing, sometimes additional librettists or songwriters are called in to help. Over the years, Harnick provided additional lyrics to two troubled shows, and he and Bock wrote songs for another pair. Which of the following shows did Harnick *not* work on?

   A. *Shangri-la*
   B. *A Family Affair*
   C. *Her First Roman*
   D. *Baker Street*
   E. *Portofino*

9. Bock and Harnick decided to try something different in 1966. They created a musical of three thematically similar one-acts, *The Apple Tree*. They wrote the libretto themselves, with some additional material by Jerome Coopersmith, adapting Mark Twain's *Extracts from Adam's Diary;* Frank Stockton's story, "The Lady or the Tiger?"; and Jules Feiffer's *Passionella,* an updating of the Cinderella story. The show, highlighted by Barbara Harris' Tony-winning turn, ran for 463 performances.

   The show's director had previously done a summer production featuring Feiffer material, starring Dorothy Loudon and using music by Stephen Sondheim, in 1962, but it never got to New York. He convinced Bock and Harnick to use *Passionella* as their third act; they had wanted to use Bruce Jay Friedman's *Show Biz Connections.* Who directed *The Apple Tree*?

   A. Joe Layton
   B. Robert Lewis
   C. Mike Nichols
   D. Gower Champion
   E. George Abbott

10. The final Bock and Harnick musical was 1970's *The Rothschilds.* Since then, Bock has worked on a murder-mystery musical and one based on the U.S. income tax code, both unproduced. Harnick teamed with Richard Rodgers for the Broadway flop *Rex,* with Michel Legrand on a stage version of his film *The Umbrellas of Cherbourg,* and with Joe Raposo on an adaptation of the film *It's a Wonderful Life.* Both *Umbrellas* and *Life* have had regional productions.

    But Bock and Harnick's final collaboration, while not a financial hit, has some of their deftest writing, covering the turbulent years around the turn of the nineteenth century. Because the show centered on a Jewish family with lots of offspring, many people dismissed it as another *Fiddler on the Roof,* which is absurd. *Fiddler* is set in a village and shows the passing of a traditional way of life and its effect on families. *The Rothschilds,* set throughout Europe, encompasses the Napoleonic Wars, the establishment of international financial markets, and the advent of increasingly democratic governments.

    Hal Linden won a Tony as Mayer Rothschild, the patriarch who sees his family move from the Jewish ghetto to become the bankers of Europe. The Best Featured Actor Tony also went to a member of the cast, who portrayed multiple roles as key figures in different governments. Who was it?

    A. Chris Sarandon
    B. Paul Hecht

C. Keene Curtis
D. William Daniels
E. Len Cariou

Answers on page 215.

Frank Loesser and Burton Lane

These Broadway greats never worked together, but I've combined them in one quiz since their output is small compared to other songwriters. And they're alliterative.

1. Frank Loesser had success in Hollywood (an Oscar for "Baby, It's Cold Outside") in addition to penning popular wartime songs. But Broadway fans honor him for the five shows he wrote before his untimely death at fifty-eight. His first hit was *Where's Charley?*, the 1948 musical version of the 1892 farce *Charley's Aunt*, which starred Ray Bolger. Bolger stopped the show every night with the audience-participation number "Once in Love with Amy." But the number didn't start as a smash. Shortly after opening, Bolger forgot the lyrics to the second verse. Bobby, a young boy whose dad was involved with the show, began calling out the words he'd learned when attending rehearsals. Bolger, somewhat irked, decided to ask the entire audience to join in a sing-along...and Broadway history was made. Bobby was the seven-year-old son of:

   A. producer Cy Feuer
   B. producer Ernest Martin
   C. composer Frank Loesser
   D. stage manager Robert E. Griffith
   E. librettist-director George Abbott

2. Loesser's *Guys and Dolls* (1950) may be the most perfectly constructed musical comedy of all time. Based on Damon Runyon's tales of gamblers and their girls, the show was recognized as an instant classic. Which of these locations is *not* mentioned when the boys are arranging the site of the "oldest established permanent floating crap game in New York"?

   A. Mindy's Restaurant
   B. the back of the police station
   C. the Biltmore Garage
   D. the gym of P.S. 84
   E. the stock room at McCloskey's

3. Loesser wrote the book himself for 1956's *The Most Happy Fella*, based on Sidney Howard's *They Knew What They Wanted*. He worked on this musical ("with lots of music") for five years, adding characters, using operatic and classical forms, and eventually created a heartwarming masterpiece. The title song begins with the postman calling out names of letter recipients, ending with the latest delivery in the mail-order romance of vineyard owner Tony Esposito. What was unusual about the names of the people who got mail?

4. 1960's *Greenwillow* was a disappointment, despite its rich score. Audiences never got behind the invented folktale about the family Briggs, whose eldest sons are doomed to follow the call to wander. Musical newcomer Anthony Perkins played Gideon, who thinks the curse is about to inflict him, causing his girlfriend (Ellen McCown) much heartache. Who played Gramma Briggs, the turnip-chewing matriarch, who lies about her former suitor's deathbed conversion in order to keep a much-needed cow?

    A. Isabella Hoopes
    B. Patricia Neway
    C. Kay Medford
    D. Hermione Gingold
    E. Pert Kelton

BROADWAY BONUS: What was the cow's name (her real name) in *Greenwillow* and what did she do during the Philly tryout?

5. A deliciously evil satire of corporate America, *How to Succeed in Business Without Really Trying* won a Pulitzer for Loesser and book writer Abe Burrows in 1961. Loesser didn't think much of his and called it his "Putziller." He was initially reluctant to take on the job, and did so out of loyalty to producers Cy Feuer and Ernest Martin, who had backed *Guys and Dolls*. That said, every number was perfectly complementary to the material; as Feuer put it, "Loesser was laying down a bunt for the sake of the show." And he could be endlessly creative, as in the orchestrations for "I Believe in You," which placed something unusual in the pit. What was it?

    A. slide whistles
    B. cowbells
    C. whoopee cushions
    D. telephones
    E. kazoos

6. Loesser was also a brilliant businessman. He established his own music company, Frank Music, to publish his own songs and develop other songwriters. Which of these songwriters was *not* part of the Frank Music catalog?

    A. Robert Wright and George Forrest
    B. Stephen Sondheim
    C. Richard Adler and Jerry Ross
    D. Mark Bucci
    E. Meredith Willson

7. Burton Lane's career spanned fifty years and included many collaborators. He contributed songs to over twenty-five films, and his Broadway productions, while far fewer in number, include the classic *Finian's Rainbow*. He first teamed with Yip Harburg for 1940's *Hold On to Your Hats*, notable as the last Broadway show for which early great?

    A. Al Jolson
    B. Eddie Foy

C. Eddie Cantor
D. Ed Wynn
E. George M. Cohan

8. Lane and Harburg's masterpiece was 1947's *Finian's Rainbow*, which ran for 725 performances. Lane used a variety of musical styles: blues, gospel, waltz, and sprightly, impish ditties for Og, the leprechaun. Half the score became standards, with the smash being "Old Devil Moon." Central to the plot was Finian's pot of gold, stolen from Og. Why did Finian bury the gold in Rainbow Valley?

9. Lane wrote the 1951 movie *Royal Wedding* with Alan Jay Lerner, and teamed with him again for 1965's *On a Clear Day You Can See Forever*. Lane's score was outstanding, but Lerner's book lacked focus. Barbara Harris played Daisy, John Cullum was the E.S.P. doctor who reveals her past life in Regency England. What was the name of Daisy's previous incarnation?
   A. Melisande
   B. Melissa
   C. Melinda
   D. Prudence
   E. Flora

10. Lane's last show was another effort with Lerner, 1979's *Carmelina*, the story of three American GIs all paying child support to the same Italian woman they met twenty years before in the war. It's a similar plot to the 1968 movie, *Buona Sera, Mrs. Campbell*, though Lerner always denied this. (For that matter, it's pretty much *Mamma Mia!*'s plot, too.) Star Cesare Siepi was so disgruntled after the seventeen-performance run, he refused to take part in the cast recording. Who took his place?
   A. Hershel Bernardi
   B. Michael King
   C. Topol
   D. Paul Lipson
   E. Paul Sorvino

Answers on page 215.

Lynn Ahrens and Stephen Flaherty

In the fifties and sixties, long-standing songwriting teams were a mainstay of Broadway: Rodgers and Hammerstein, Lerner and Loewe, Bock and Harnick, Kander and Ebb. These days, such dynamic duos are hard to find. Perhaps the most versatile of the modern-era pairs is Lynn Ahrens and Stephen Flaherty. They met at the BMI Workshop in 1982, and began working together not long after, collaborating on eight stage musicals and an award-winning animated film, as well as doing some work individually. Their efforts have not always met with commercial success, but true Broadway fans appreciate their intelligent scores, their daring variety of subject matter, and their theatricality.

1. Ahrens and Flaherty's first work was the musical farce *Lucky Stiff*, based on the novel *The Man Who Broke the Bank at Monte Carlo*. The show debuted in 1988 at Playwrights Horizons and won the Richard Rodgers Award. Farce is difficult, but Ahrens' libretto deftly handled the convoluted plot, in which Harry Witherspoon must fulfill the bizarre terms of his uncle's will to get his millions. Flaherty's score was lively and often hilarious. What is Harry Witherspoon's occupation?
   A. the office nerd
   B. a shoe salesman
   C. a dentist
   D. a mobster
   E. owner of the Universal Dog Home

2. Ahrens and Flaherty next adapted a Caribbean story by Rosa Guy, *My Love, My Love*, about a tragic romance between a peasant girl and the wealthy youth whom she saves after he suffers a car accident. *Once on This Island* blended elements of *The Little Mermaid*, *Romeo and Juliet*, and Caribbean folk legends into a swirling tropical celebration of story and dance. Like *Lucky Stiff*, it opened at Playwrights Horizon, but later transferred to Broadway, where it ran 469 performances and won eight Tony nominations. Its success was no doubt helped by the presence of LaChanze as the ill-fated lover, and Graciela Daniele's direction and choreography. The character of Papa Gé is critical to the action. Who is he?
   A. the young man's father
   B. the god of water
   C. Death
   D. the god of love
   E. the girl's father

3. The pair had less success with their next venture, 1992's *My Favorite Year*, an adaptation of the popular movie about a young man (Evan Pappas) who works for a comedy television show in the fifties, and how he handles an out-of-control movie actor (Tim Curry) who is that week's guest star. The show didn't fare well, despite some fine numbers (especially the scene-setting opening), but it did capture a Tony. Who won it?
   A. Tim Curry
   B. Ahrens and Flaherty (Best Original Score)
   C. Lainie Kazan
   D. Andrea Martin
   E. Patricia Zipprodt (Best Costume Design)

4. Lynn Ahrens teamed up with composer Alan Menken for a holiday show based on Charles Dickens' *A Christmas Carol* that became a New York fixture from 1994 to 2003, with many leading men tackling the role of Scrooge. It generated a popular song, "A Place Called Home," and was filmed for television with an all-star Broadway cast (Kelsey Grammer, Jason Alexander, Jane Krakowski, Ruthie Henshall, and more). Where did the stage show play?
   A. Madison Square Garden's downstairs theatre
   B. Radio City Music Hall

C. the Hippodrome
D. 30 Rock
E. Lincoln Center

5. Perhaps Ahrens and Flaherty's most highly acclaimed score was 1998's *Ragtime*. With a book by Terrence McNally based on E. L. Doctorow's kaleidoscopic novel of America at the dawn of the twentieth century, *Ragtime* told the intertwined tale of three families: white Protestant, black, and Jewish immigrant. Ahrens and Flaherty, McNally, Audra McDonald (Best Featured Actress), and William David Brohn (Best Orchestrations) all took home Tonys, but the lion's share that year went to *The Lion King*. *Ragtime*'s struggles didn't end there, for producer Livent went bankrupt while the show was on tour. Still, the epic saga and the dazzling score have remained in the consciousness of musical fans, and the show was revived in 2009.

   One of the treats of *Ragtime* is its melding of fictional and historical characters. Which of the following is *not* a real-life character in *Ragtime*?
   A. Emma Goldman
   B. Baron Ashkenazy
   C. Stanford White
   D. Matthew Henson
   E. Evelyn Nesbitt

6. Lynn Ahrens was no stranger to material for children, having written many of the songs for the long-running series of animated educational shorts known as *Schoolhouse Rock*, starting back in 1973 (Flaherty co-wrote one in 1995). The duo also had success with the children's animated feature, *Anastasia* (1997), with the voice talents of Liz Callaway, Angela Lansbury, Bernadette Peters, Hank Azaria, and Kelsey Grammer. So it wasn't surprising when they got the rights to the works of Theodor Geisel, better known as Dr. Seuss. In late 2000, *Seussical* debuted, combining plot elements and characters from *Horton Hears a Who*, *Horton Hatches the Egg*, *The Cat in the Hat*, and other Seuss works. *Seussical* didn't last long on Broadway, but the show was revised to tour, and the cut-down version has proved very popular with school and regional companies.

   The revised *Seussical* focuses more on the character of JoJo, a boy who dreams up the Seussian world and later plays the son of the mayor of Whoville. The tiny Whos are in danger because no one in the Jungle of Nool can hear them or believes they even exist, save Horton the Elephant. What word does JoJo shout that is finally heard?
   A. Seuss!
   B. Yopp!
   C. Solla Sollew!
   D. Oobleck!
   E. Think!

7. Ahrens and Flaherty and McNally reunited for the 2002 off-Broadway production of *A Man of No Importance*. The story concerns Alfie (Roger Rees), a bus driver in 1964 Dublin with a passion for theatre. Alfie is a closeted gay, trying to come to terms with who he is in a world where such attitudes were considered deviant. Alfie hopes

his community theatre group, the St. Imelda's Players, will stage a work by Oscar Wilde (Wilde's ghost is also a character in the musical). What play is it?

A. *A Woman of No Importance*
B. *An Ideal Husband*
C. *The Importance of Being Earnest*
D. *Lady Windermere's Fan*
E. *Salome*

8. Ahrens and Flaherty went even further back in time for 2005's off-Broadway production of *Dessa Rose*, starring LaChanze and Rachel York, with direction and choreography by Graciela Daniele. The tale is told as an oral history, with both women in their eighties at the start of the show, then transforming into their younger selves. Who are Dessa Rose and Ruth?

A. a runaway black slave and an abandoned white farmwife, ca. 1847
B. a sweatshop worker and the factory owner's wife, ca. 1918
C. two women camp followers during the Civil War
D. the Wicked Witch of the East and a promising writer in 1930s New York
E. barnstorming women pilots, ca. 1937

9. In 2006, Stephen Flaherty worked on a project in Chicago with writer/director Frank Galati, creating a chamber musical about the life of a noted American writer. The show, titled *Loving Repeating*, was a limited run, but fortunately has had a cast recording (thank you, Jay Records!). Flaherty experiments with a wide variety of musical styles, combining his melodies with a unique woman's voice. Who is the subject of this musical?

A. Emily Dickinson
B. Gertrude Stein
C. Erma Bombeck
D. Dorothy Parker
E. Edna St. Vincent Millay

10. Ahrens and Flaherty's *The Glorious Ones* (2007) was an off-Broadway show about a seventeenth-century troupe of commedia dell'arte players in Italy. The stellar cast of Marc Kudisch, Natalie Venetia Belcon, and Erin Davie was directed by Graciela Daniele, and the score was bawdy, broad, and dramatic (thanks again to Jay Records for preserving it). *The Glorious Ones* may not have found an audience, but several of the songs have been recorded or used in concert and cabaret acts. One of these is an outstanding "actor's anthem," which was the show's eleven o'clock number. What is the song?

A. "Madness to Act"
B. "Rise and Fall"
C. "The Comedy of Love"
D. "Opposite You"
E. "I Was Here"

Answers on page 216.

Leonard Bernstein and Marc Blitzstein

As these two talented composers were lifelong friends and their combined output on Broadway was relatively small, I've combined them in a single quiz.

1. By the early forties, Leonard Bernstein was already established as a wunderkind in classical music, having conducted the New York Philharmonic. In 1944, he wrote the music for a ballet, *Fancy Free*, choreographed by Jerome Robbins, which producer/designer Oliver Smith believed had Broadway potential. Robbins, Bernstein, and his pals, lyricists Betty Comden and Adolph Green (Bernstein had been part of their nightclub act, the Revuers)—under the guidance of veteran director George Abbott—expanded the ballet into the wartime hit *On the Town* (1944). The plot concerned the romantic adventures of three sailors on a day's leave in New York. Abbott had his favorite orchestrator, Don Walker, work on the comedy numbers, but whom did Bernstein pick to orchestrate the rest of the show, giving it a more symphonic sound?
   A. Robert Russell Bennett
   B. Hershy Kay
   C. Irwin Kostal
   D. Ralph Burns
   E. Philip Lang

2. In 1950, Bernstein was asked to provide incidental music for a play, but got carried away and wrote five songs and two choruses as well, despite the fact that the leads (Jean Arthur and Boris Karloff) were not singers by any stretch of the imagination. When the show went into production, Bernstein was in Europe and he named Marc Blitzstein as his "deputy" regarding any song changes. Blitzstein admitted he didn't do much, and was paid $200 out of Bernstein's royalties. What was the subject of the show? (Hint: Bernstein's buddies Comden and Green would later tackle the same subject.)

3. Bernstein had promised his mentor, Sergei Koussevitzy, that he would stick to serious composing and stay away from those show tunes. But when the producers of *Wonderful Town* (1953) needed new songwriters at very short notice, director George Abbott knew he needed people who could work fast, so he found Comden and Green. They contacted Bernstein. The composer responded to the challenge of writing a show in five weeks, and was thrilled by the possibilities for pastiches of thirties musical styles—swing, South American, Irish clogs. And there was the difficulty of writing for the lead's limited vocal abilities. Star Rosalind Russell had previously described her voice as "so bass, it's viol," and she couldn't handle one number, "The Story of My Life." She wanted a song that went "Da...da...da...da...da...da...joke." What song did Bernstein, Comden, and Green devise in its place?
   A. "Ohio"
   B. "Conga!"
   C. "One Hundred Easy Ways to Lose a Man"
   D. "Swing"
   E. "Conversation Piece"

4. *Candide* (1956) may have only lasted seventy-three performances, but Bernstein's magnificent score lives on forever in the hearts of Broadway buffs. The show had a hodgepodge of lyricists: John Latouche, Dorothy Parker, librettist Lillian Hellman, Richard Wilbur, and Bernstein himself, all taking their inspiration from Voltaire's classic novel. One of the songs for which Bernstein did the lyrics was the Old Lady's "I Am Easily Assimilated." In which language does the Old Lady *not* sing?

    A. Russian
    B. German
    C. Spanish
    D. Portuguese
    E. French

BROADWAY BONUS: Who gave Bernstein an uncredited hand with the lyrics for this song?

5. Bernstein, Arthur Laurents, and Jerome Robbins had been kicking around the notion of an updated *Romeo and Juliet* for years, possibly with the lovers coming from Jewish and Catholic families. Then, while lounging by the pool at the Beverly Hills Hotel, they noticed a headline about Latino gang wars in Los Angeles, and that headline led to *West Side Story* (1957). Bernstein was going to do the lyrics, but as he was working on *Candide* at the same time, Stephen Sondheim joined the creative team. (In a generous gesture, Bernstein even had his name removed as co-lyricist.)

    The dual evolution of the two shows made for some interesting connections. Two songs in *West Side Story* were set to discarded songs from *Candide*. One was "One Hand, One Heart." What was the other?

    A. "Maria"
    B. "Something's Coming"
    C. "Tonight"
    D. "A Boy Like That"
    E. "Gee, Officer Krupke"

6. *West Side Story*, while groundbreaking in many ways, didn't become accepted as a true classic until after the 1961 Academy Award–winning movie. Bernstein continued his work with the New York Philharmonic, wrote *Mass* to inaugurate the Kennedy Center in 1971, and supervised the 1974 revival of *Candide*. But he didn't write another original musical until 1976's *1600 Pennsylvania Avenue*. This show, written with veteran Alan Jay Lerner, examined a century of life at the White House, with the same man and woman (Ken Howard and Patricia Routledge) playing a succession of Presidents and First Ladies, and another couple, a pair of black servants (Gilbert Price and Emily Yancy) giving the perspective of the downstairs staff. The show was a disaster. Bernstein wanted to abandon it in Philadelphia, but Lerner pressed for a New York opening... and the show closed six performances after that.

    For all the muddle of the script, there was good music in *1600 Pennsylvania Avenue*, but Bernstein and Lerner refused to allow a cast album recording. In 2000, their respective estates relented, and a shortened (some eighty minutes) concert version was recorded. What is the new version called?

7. The connections between Leonard Bernstein and Marc Blitzstein go back to the late thirties, when Bernstein staged and played accompaniment at the Boston premiere of Blitzstein's *The Cradle Will Rock*. Which of the following is *not* true?
    A. Bernstein named his daughter Nina after the heroine in Blitzstein's *Reuben Reuben* and asked the composer to be her godfather
    B. Bernstein conducted the 1953 Brandeis University production of Blitzstein's adaptation of *The Threepenny Opera*, which would soon after become an off-Broadway hit
    C. Blitzstein left his unfinished opera about Sacco and Vanzetti to Bernstein in his will
    D. Blitzstein wrote the lyrics for an unfinished musical, *A Pray by Blecht*, based on Brecht's *The Exception and the Rule*, in 1968, with music by Bernstein, book by John Guare, and direction by Jerome Robbins
    E. Bernstein dedicated his 1955 opera, *Trouble in Tahiti*, to Blitzstein

8. Blitzstein was a few years older than Bernstein, and likewise was a musical prodigy. He soloed with the Philadelphia Philharmonic at sixteen, and later studied with Arnold Schönberg. He placed a few songs in the 1930 edition of the *Garrick Gaieties* and the 1935 revue *Parade*. His best-known work, *The Cradle Will Rock* (1937), concerned the anti-establishment tale of Larry Foreman (Howard da Silva), and his attempt to unionize Steeltown, U.S.A. The show was backed by the Federal Theatre, part of FDR's Works Project Administration (WPA). As the opening drew near, those in the Federal Theatre grew uneasy about the inflammatory nature of Blitzstein's material in an era of bloody strikes and labor uprisings, and padlocked the theatre rather than let the show open. Blitzstein, John Houseman, and most of the cast then guided their audience to a vacant theatre blocks away. Since the actors were forbidden to take the stage, they performed their roles from their seats, high-lighted by a single spotlight, while Blitzstein accompanied them on a hastily delivered piano. The most unusual opening night in history guaranteed the show musical immortality—probably far more than the material itself ever deserved.

    Cradle had its genesis in 1935, when Blitzstein performed a sketch and a song about a prostitute ("Nickel Under the Foot"). Someone told him he should expand that into a full theatrical piece. Who was it?
    A. Kurt Weill
    B. John Houseman
    C. Bertolt Brecht
    D. Orson Welles
    E. Burgess Meredith

9. Blitzstein worked again with Houseman and his Mercury Theatre, providing music for their *Julius Caesar* in 1937. During the war, he contributed to Kurt Weill's revue *Lunchtime Follies*. Lillian Hellman then co-produced a reading of a left-wing piece by Blitzstein that found no other backing, which led to his writing the incidental music for her 1946 play, *Another Part of the Forest*. They collaborated again in 1949

on *Regina*, a hard-to-categorize show. Some regard it a musical, some an opera, but whatever you call it, it wasn't a success, lasting only fifty-six performances. What Hellman work was its source?

    A. *Another Part of the Forest*, expanding on the earlier incidental music
    B. *The Children's Hour*
    C. *The Little Foxes*
    D. *The Watch on the Rhine*
    E. *Toys in the Attic*

10. Perhaps Blitzstein's finest score came in 1959's *Juno*, based on O'Casey's *Juno and the Paycock*, with libretto by Joseph Stein. The struggles of an Irish family during the turbulent and violent twenties were perhaps too grim for audiences, and it closed after sixteen performances. *Juno* starred Shirley Booth and Melvyn Douglas, and had dazzling choreography by Agnes de Mille, but the lack of a firm directorial hand hurt its chances. Tony Richardson initially had the helm, but his departure led to the hiring of Vincent Donehue ("an absolute boob," according to de Mille). Donehue was soon fired, and the inexperienced Jose Ferrer took over. The best thing about *Juno* was that Columbia Records decided to record this glorious flop of a show. Thank you, Goddard Lieberson of Columbia!

Tommy Rall played the son, Johnny, who is taken in by the British and violently interrogated. De Mille staged a twelve-minute dance in which Rall portrays Johnny's feelings after this treatment. The dance was based on Irish clog dancing and was known as:

    A. a "shoutin'"
    B. the "pains in me legs"
    C. the Banshee's reel
    D. a river dance
    E. a "haunt"

Answers on page 217.

Alan Jay Lerner and Frederick Loewe

Alan Jay Lerner wrote the books and lyrics for over a dozen stage musicals, including the classic *My Fair Lady*, for years the longest-running musical in history, and earned Oscars for his work in Hollywood on *An American in Paris* and *Gigi*. His best known collaborator was Frederick Loewe, although he worked with six other composers throughout his long career. His work was erudite and witty, and often laced with sophisticated humor.

1. Alan Jay Lerner's family owned the successful dress shops, the Lerner Stores, and he attended private academies before college. His father hoped he would go into the diplomatic service, but Lerner's passion was the theatre. He was working on radio scripts when he met Austrian composer Frederick Loewe, who was looking for a lyricist. Loewe had been a successful young pianist in Europe, but came to America in 1924 in his early twenties with his father, a noted operetta star. Accounts vary regarding the actual circumstances about the first meeting between Lerner and Loewe, but most agree on the place. Where did they meet?

A. Harvard, where Lerner wrote for the *Hasty Pudding* shows

B. Columbia University, where they both worked on the variety shows

C. at the radio station that broadcast *Your Hit Parade*, where Loewe was a musician and Lerner wrote the scripts

D. at the opening of Rodgers and Hammerstein's *Oklahoma!*

E. at the Lambs Club

2. As with many new teams, Lerner and Loewe struggled at first. What was the title of their first Broadway show, which lasted a mere two months on the street in 1943?

    A. *The Life of the Party*

    B. *The Patsy*

    C. *What's Up*

    D. *Great Lady*

    E. *Here's Love*

3. Lerner and Loewe's next show, *The Day Before Spring* (1945) also didn't run long, but attracted some notices comparing them to Rodgers and Hammerstein. The show used innovative ballets to reveal character, and the action revealed differing viewpoints of the same events. What was the plot?

    A. a married couple attends their college reunion, where the wife meets the man she nearly eloped with ten years ago

    B. an angel helps the Notre Dame football team defeat Army

    C. an account of the life of Polish leader Thaddeus Kosciuszko, who helped the Continental Army in the American Revolution

    D. an East Indian potentate crash-lands in a girls' school, where he gets quarantined

    E. a clerk is hit on the head and dreams he is Goya painting the nude Duchess of Alba

4. Success came to the duo with 1947's fantasy, *Brigadoon*, about the little Scottish town that appears in the mist for a single day every century, and the two Americans who stumble into it. Lerner divorced his first wife, Ruth Boyd, and married *Brigadoon*'s leading lady, Marion Bell, but the romantic turmoil didn't affect the quality of the show, which ran for 581 performances. Robert Lewis directed Lerner's libretto, and Agnes de Mille handled the lively choreography.

    Brigadoon's first major choral number features the villagers gathering in Mac-Connachy Square. What *can't* you buy there on market day?

    A. ale

    B. fish

    C. candy

    D. milk

    E. wool

5. Throughout their relationship, Lerner and Loewe did not always get along. Despite the success of *Brigadoon*, they went their separate ways in 1948, and Lerner teamed with another composer of Germanic ancestry, Kurt Weill, for the highly unusual *Love Life*. Like *Allegro* in the previous year, *Love Life* was an early concept show, focusing on the effects of societal change on the American family over a century. As with *Allegro*, it may have been too out of the ordinary for its time, lasting only 252 performances.

Who starred opposite Ray Middleton?
A. Irra Petina
B. Marion Bell
C. Patricia Morison
D. Mary McCarty
E. Nanette Fabray

6. Lerner reunited with Loewe for 1951's *Paint Your Wagon*. Set in California in 1853, it focused on a group of gold miners and the development of their community, as well as their need for more women. The shortage is solved by the arrival of the Fandango Girls, who got to do a lot of Agnes de Mille dances. Although it had some lovely songs, including "I Talk to the Trees" and "Wand'rin' Star," *Paint Your Wagon* closed in the red at 289 performances.

   In the show, who are Maria and Joe and Tess?

7. Lerner also worked on two movies in 1951, *Royal Wedding*, with Burton Lane as composer, and *An American in Paris*, which used Gershwin songs in a new script by Lerner, one which earned him an Oscar for Best Screenplay. In 1954, Lerner was toiling on a musical based on *Li'l Abner* when he saw that Gabriel Pascal had died. Pascal had held the rights to George Bernard Shaw's *Pygmalion*, and had approached many songwriters, including Lerner and Loewe, about adapting it. They had tried back in 1950 before abandoning it. Reading the obituary, Lerner's interest in *Pygmalion* revived, and he convinced Loewe to tackle it again, despite not knowing who might hold the rights after Pascal's death.

   The result, *My Fair Lady*, was one of the greatest musicals of the Golden Age, running an astonishing 2,717 performances. Rex Harrison played Henry Higgins, the misogynistic phonetics professor who transforms Eliza, a Cockney flower girl (Julie Andrews), into a lady by teaching her proper speech. Moss Hart directed Lerner's book, which incorporated vast chunks of Shaw, but brilliantly opened up action only alluded to in the original, especially for scenes involving Eliza's father (Stanley Holloway).

   My Fair Lady was a smash even during tryouts, but it was running long. They ultimately cut "Come to the Ball" and "Say a Prayer for Me Tonight" (later used in *Gigi*). There was one song that Loewe and Hart wanted cut, but Lerner defended it, and it remained in the final score. What was it?
   A. "On the Street Where You Live"
   B. "A Hymn to Him"
   C. "You Did It"
   D. "Without You"
   E. "I'm an Ordinary Man"

8. Lerner and Loewe followed that classic musical with one of the greatest film musicals, 1958's *Gigi*. But how to follow such successes? The duo settled on an unusual topic, the novel *The Once and Future King*, by T. H. White, about the life of King Arthur. Lerner's libretto settled on one aspect of the book, the love triangle between Arthur (Richard Burton), Guenevere (Julie Andrews), and Lancelot (Robert Goulet).

Camelot, as the show became known, had trouble from the start. Lerner's fourth wife left him during its development; he began using amphetamines; and he was hospitalized with bleeding ulcers. Moss Hart suffered a massive heart attack, leaving Lerner as director for a time. (Hart would die not long into *Camelot*'s run.)

The show was extremely expensive (jokingly called "Costalot") and even after many cuts, still ran long. A featured spot on *The Ed Sullivan Show* saved the day. Sullivan was honoring Lerner and Loewe on the fifth anniversary of *My Fair Lady*, and had cast members from *Camelot* perform some numbers, including Burton and Andrews. The following morning, there were long lines at the box office, and the show survived.

Camelot reunited almost the entire creative staff from *My Fair Lady*. Along with Lerner, Loewe, Hart, Andrews, and actor Robert Coote, all of the following except one worked on both shows. Who of these *My Fair Lady* veterans did not work on *Camelot*?

A. Hanya Holm, choreography
B. Robert Russell Bennett, orchestrations
C. Oliver Smith, set design
D. Cecil Beaton, costumes
E. Franz Allers, conductor

9. Loewe, who had suffered a heart attack in 1958, retired to Palm Springs after *Camelot*. He would work again with Lerner on the 1973 stage version of *Gigi*, and the 1974 film musical *The Little Prince*. Lerner would go on to write six more musicals with different composers, but would never come close to the success he had with Loewe.

He first worked, rather fitfully, given his addiction to pills and injections, with Richard Rodgers, on a musical about a girl with ESP who could talk to flowers. Rodgers needed a new lyricist after Hammerstein's death; who better than the man who wrote *My Fair Lady*? But Rodgers grew fed up with Lerner's dilatory ways, and the task of composing passed to Burton Lane, who was at least familiar with how Lerner worked. (Or didn't work, as the case might be.)

The show was 1965's *On a Clear Day You Can See Forever*, in which Barbara Harris played Daisy, the girl with ESP, and John Cullum played Mark, the psychiatrist investigating her abilities. Unfortunately, Lerner was deep in his drug addiction during the creation of the show, and the muddled book is proof. *On a Clear Day* lasted only 280 performances. The score still has much to offer, including one of Lerner's best "list songs." In "Come Back to Me," Mark suggests numerous ways for Daisy to return to him. Which is *not* one of them?

A. in a stagecoach
B. by airplane
C. by mail
D. on horse
E. swimming

10. Lerner would work with Lane once time, for the 1979 flop, *Carmelina*. His track record in his later years was not good: *Lolita, My Love* (music by John Barry) would close out of town in 1971; the enormous catastrophe that was *1600 Pennsylvania*

Avenue (music by Leonard Bernstein) tallied seven performances in 1976; and *Dance a Little Closer* (music by Charles Strouse) managed but a single night in 1983. Suffering poor health in the eighties, he turned down the offer to do the lyrics for *Les Misérables*. He did write some lyrics for Andrew Lloyd Webber's *The Phantom of the Opera*, ones not used in the final score, before dying of lung cancer in 1986.

The longest-running of Lerner's later shows was 1969's *Coco*, with music by Andre Previn, which ran for 329 performances, largely on audiences wanting to see Katharine Hepburn in her first Broadway musical. She played Coco Chanel in the later years of her life, something that annoyed the fashion designer, since Lerner had told her the plot would focus on her youth. She also had assumed it was Audrey, not Kate, Hepburn, in the lead role!

Who replaced Hepburn during the run, leading to the show's closing two months later?

   A. Jeanmaire
   B. Danielle Darrieux
   C. Lilo
   D. Rosalind Russell
   E. Maria Karnilova

Answers on page 217.

George and Ira Gershwin

Ira Gershwin and his younger brother George, sons of Russian immigrants, were living on the Lower East Side when their parents purchased a piano. As the eldest, Ira was supposed to get the lessons, but George sat down at the newly installed instrument and played several hit songs. He had visited a neighbor who owned a player-piano and committed the sequence of keys to his incredible memory. George got the lessons, and the rest is history.

In his teens, George was a "song plugger" for a Tin Pan Alley publisher before he began selling his own material and getting songs interpolated into some Broadway shows. Young producer Alex Aarons took a chance on him, and *La, La, Lucille* (1919) was his first complete score.

1. For five years (1920–1924), George had songs in *George White's Scandals*, including his early hits "I'll Build a Staircase to Paradise" and "Somebody Loves Me," with lyrics by Bud DeSylva and DeSylva and Ballard MacDonald. But it was his father who suggested the best lyricist for George's complicated rhythms: "Why not try your brother?" Ira's quick wit and verbal flair were indeed the perfect match. Why did Ira choose the pseudonym "Arthur Francis" for some of his early lyrics for George's songs? Hint: there's a family connection.

2. George and Ira's first big hit was 1924's *Lady, Be Good!*, with book by Guy Bolton and Fred Thompson and starring Fred and Adele Astaire. *Lady, Be Good!*, with its jazz-influenced score, would run for over three hundred performances, and is today seen as a landmark show for the era. Which song used a piece George had previously written that he called "Syncopated City"?

A. "Oh, Lady, Be Good"
B. "The Half of It, Dearie, Blues"
C. "Hang On to Me"
D. "Fascinating Rhythm"
E. "Little Jazz Bird"

3. *Tip-Toes* (1926) reunited the creative team from *Lady, Be Good!* with the same producers, Alex Aarons and Vinton Freedley—the second of the seven Gershwin shows they would produce. This was a zippy, often satirical piece about a flapper and her uncles, and Ira gave full rein to his love of the vernacular in lyrics. Whose comic style did he hope to emulate in some of his lyrics for *Tip-Toes*?
   A. Alexander Woolcott
   B. Lorenz Hart
   C. Irving Berlin
   D. W. S. Gilbert
   E. P. G. Wodehouse

4. The brothers followed up *Tip-Toes* with another success in *Oh, Kay!* (1926), starring Gertrude Lawrence and Victor Moore. Howard Deitz helped with some lyrics when Ira had an emergency appendectomy. The plot (book by Guy Bolton and P. G. Wodehouse) was classic twenties' fluff about rumrunners during Prohibition, but the score was studded with hits: "Clap Yo' Hands," "Do, Do, Do," "Maybe," and "Someone to Watch Over Me." What prop was Gertie Lawrence holding when she introduced "Someone to Watch Over Me"?
   A. a teddy bear
   B. a stuffed lamb
   C. a feather duster, since she was in disguise as a maid
   D. a long, long scarf
   E. a rag doll

5. *Funny Face* (1927) was another hit starring the Astaires and Victor Moore. Fred played the guardian of three girls, and the show incorporated many topical subjects, including aviation (Lindbergh had just flown the Atlantic) and flappers. The show had a rough tryout, with much of the score tossed along the way, but the songs that made the final cut ("The Babbitt and the Bromide," "My One and Only," and "'S Wonderful," to name a few) were tops. It was the inaugural show at the Alvin Theatre. Who was the theatre named after?

6. *Rosalie* (1928) ended up a success because of its star, Marilyn Miller, not the score. George and Ira were working on two other shows at the time, but when producer Flo Ziegfeld talked, people listened. The brothers contributed about half the songs, using a lot of trunk material, as did the songwriter(s) responsible for the other half (working on *three* other shows at the time!). Who was/were the other songwriter(s)?
   A. Rudolf Friml
   B. DeSylva, Brown, and Henderson
   C. Sigmund Romberg
   D. Rodgers and Hart
   E. Jerome Kern

7. *Girl Crazy* (1930) shows up on the radar of many Broadway buffs because it marked the sensational debut of Ethel Merman (though Ginger Rogers was the lead). The goofy story had a New York playboy heading to Arizona, leading to fun with cowpokes and chorines. The phenomenal score includes hits like "But Not for Me," "I Got Rhythm," "Sam and Delilah," "Could You Use Me?," and "Embraceable You." This jazzy songfest had a ton of heavy hitters playing in the pit. Who was *not* in the orchestra for *Girl Crazy*?
   A. Gene Krupa
   B. Jimmy Dorsey
   C. Benny Goodman
   D. Glenn Miller
   E. Bunny Berigan

❧ ❧

BROADWAY BONUS: Who helped design the choreography for Ginger Rogers in "Embraceable You"?

❧ ❧

8. The brothers worked on the satiric musical *Strike Up the Band* with librettist George Kaufman, but it closed during its tryout in 1927. They tried again three years later. Morrie Ryskind revised Kaufman's book, toning down some of the sharper satiric elements. Which of the following is *not* true about the 1930 version?
   A. it changed the product over which the U.S.A. and Switzerland are at odds from cheese to chocolate
   B. the war plot became a dream sequence
   C. nearly a dozen songs were cut
   D. it restored "The Man I Love," which had been cut
   E. it rewrote the comic role of "George Spelvin" to fit the burlesque style of Paul McCullough, who was playing a sidekick to his longtime partner, Bobby Clark

9. *Of Thee I Sing* (1931) ran for 441 performances and became the first musical to win the Pulitzer Prize, which was awarded to Ira for his lyrics and to Kaufman and Ryskind for their libretto, but not to George! (The Pulitzer committee has since then added George's name, but he didn't get any of the money.) This satire of politics introduced John Wintergreen, running for president on a ticket of love. He gets into trouble, however, when he prefers Mary Turner and her homemade muffins over the girl who won the contest, Diane Devereaux, to be his sweetheart. This turns into an international fracas when Diane's French ancestry is revealed, and the French ambassador files a protest. The honor guard accompanying the ambassador has a lovely bit of French nonsense penned by Ira to some trunk music George had left over from *Girl Crazy*. What typically "French" item listed below is *not* mentioned in Ira's lyrics?
   A. escargot
   B. crêpes-suzette
   C. Chevrolet coupé
   D. Lafayette
   E. Maurice Chevalier

10. The brothers followed this smash with two flops in 1933, *Pardon My English* and the ill-advised sequel to *Of Thee I Sing*, *Let 'Em Eat Cake*. Their next effort was the classic *Porgy and Bess*, written in collaboration with DuBose Heyward, who had written the novel (and with his wife, Dorothy, the later play) *Porgy*, about a poor black community on the South Carolina coast. *Porgy and Bess* debuted in 1935 and was met with mixed reactions. It did not run long, and George and Ira, like many of their Broadway brethren, headed to Hollywood. They wrote several film scores, including two (*Shall We Dance* and *A Damsel in Distress*) for their old pal Fred Astaire. But then George died in 1937 of a brain tumor, never seeing the success of the 1942 revival of *Porgy and Bess*. What a treasure the musical world lost! Thankfully, Ira would live for many more years, and write more brilliant, idiosyncratic lyrics for Jerome Kern, Kurt Weill, and Harold Arlen, among others.

Which of the following is *not* true about *Porgy and Bess*?

A. the score was valued at a mere $250 when George's estate was totaled in 1937

B. the Danish so admired it they staged despite Nazi opposition and used "It Ain't Necessarily So" to block German broadcasts

C. Oscar Hammerstein II and Jerome Kern considered doing a musical *Porgy* based on Heyward's play with Al Jolson playing the lead in blackface

D. the *New York Times* was so confused about whether it was an opera or a musical that they sent both their music critic and their theatre critic to the premiere

E. *Porgy and Bess* arose out of George's one-act black opera, *Blue Monday Blues*, which played for one night during the *George White's Scandals of 1922* before being cut.

Answers on page 218.

Charles Strouse and Lee Adams

1. Charles Strouse, working with Lee Adams and other lyricists, may not have had the success that Rodgers and Hammerstein did, but his few hits were socked right out of the park, and his flops generally have something interesting about them. He and Lee Adams worked on summer amateur productions before they cracked the big time in a big way with *Bye Bye Birdie* in 1960. Fellow novice Michael Stewart wrote the book, a cast of fresh faces starred, and Gower Champion was the innovative director-choreographer. Which 1950s pop idol were Strouse and Adams spoofing with the character Conrad Birdie?

2. Strouse and Adams' next offering, 1962's *All American*, didn't fare so well. Their score had promise, but the story of a European immigrant (Ray Bolger) using his engineering background to help his college's football team offered little to work with, and Joshua Logan's direction was subpar. Who wrote the libretto, and clearly learned plenty about what constitutes a flop musical?

A. Robert Lewis Taylor

B. Larry Gelbart

C. Samuel Taylor

    D. Jerome Weidman

    E. Mel Brooks

3. *Golden Boy* (1964) might have been Strouse and Adams' most dynamic score. This adaptation of Clifford Odets' play starred Sammy Davis, Jr., and ran 569 performances…and still wound up in the red. Whenever Sammy was out ill—which was frequently—box office plummeted. How did the show open?

    A. a brassy overture, followed by a Harlem neighborhood celebration

    B. no overture, but an ode to 1617 Broadway

    C. no overture, but six boxers working out in a gym, accompanied by lots of percussion

    D. Sammy played the overture on a solo trumpet

    E. no overture, but a bunch of guys on a train discussing fight cards

4. Strouse and Adams didn't do much better with *It's a Bird…It's a Plane…It's Superman* (1966), which ran a lackluster 129 performances, despite a delicious cast, a bouncy score, and clever direction from Hal Prince. The villain, Dr. Abner Sedgwick, has lost the Nobel Prize ten times. Which of these scientific studies was *not* mentioned in the professor's cry for "Revenge"?

    A. fission

    B. neutron systems

    C. kryptonite analysis

    D. light diffusion

    E. colloid chemistry

5. *Applause* (1970) brought Strouse and Adams (and star Lauren Bacall) back to blockbuster status. Comden and Green wrote the libretto, which was based on the film *All About Eve* and the short story "The Wisdom of Eve." Unfortunately, not everything went smoothly. During out-of-town tryouts, the actress playing Eve was replaced by Penny Fuller. Who previously held this key role?

    A. Diane McAfee

    B. Betty Buckley

    C. Dilys Watling

    D. Susan Browning

    E. Bernadette Peters

6. Strouse worked with Adams on 1972's *I and Albert* based on Queen Victoria and the love of her life, Prince Albert. It ran but a few short months in London. His next project would fare much better. Much, much better. *Annie*, the tale of the spunky little redheaded orphan, debuted in 1977 and joined the ranks of the longest-running musicals ever, winning seven Tonys. Martin Charnin provided the lyrics and directed as well. In the script, Daddy Warbucks offers a hefty reward on a popular radio show to help find Annie's parents. Who sponsors the radio program, "The Hour of Smiles," at the NBC Studios in Rockefeller Center?

    A. Warbucks Enterprises

    B. Ovaltine

    C. Beau Brummell Menswear

D. Pepsodent

E. Oxydent

7. Following *Annie*'s success, Strouse and Charnin tossed up a brick with *A Broadway Musical*. Strouse and new lyricist David Rogers also flopped with 1979's London production of *Flowers for Algernon*, based on Daniel Keyes' classic science-fiction story. This piece had previously been adapted into a hit TV play and film (*Charly*), but somehow didn't work as a musical. The transfer to Broadway, retitled *Charlie and Algernon*, lasted seventeen performances. Michael Crawford in London and P. J. Benjamin in New York as Charlie were upstaged by their titular counterpart, Algernon. This performer was highly praised in reviews for his dancing skills, but critics speculated he would be denied Tony consideration because of discrimination. Why?

8. Strouse worked with Alan Jay Lerner on what proved to be the lyricist/librettist's final show, 1983's *Dance a Little Closer*, an update of Robert Sherwood's Pulitzer winner, *Idiot's Delight*. For all that, it lasted one night, but the score has some worthwhile numbers, including the title tune. The melody for this was recycled from which earlier Strouse show?

   A. the London production of *Golden Boy*

   B. *The Nightingale*, a children's opera performed in England

   C. *Bojangles*, an unproduced show about Bill Robinson

   D. *Mayor*, an off-Broadway show about Ed Koch

   E. *Bring Back Birdie*

9. Like *Dance a Little Closer*, *Rags* (1986, lyrics by Stephen Schwartz) flopped, but does offer listeners a few musical gems among the dross. While *Ragtime* (Ahrens/Flaherty), which similarly examined the immigrant experience in the early twentieth century, included numerous real-life figures who played off the fictional protagonists, *Rags* featured only two historical characters: Tammany politician "Big Tim" Sullivan and:

   A. Andrew Carnegie

   B. Sophie Tucker

   C. Fanny Brice

   D. Jacob Adler

   E. Fiorello La Guardia

10. Strouse's latest musical debuted in Los Angeles in 2009, with plans to move to Broadway in 2010. It boasts a book by Bob Martin and lyrics by Susan Birkenhead, and is very loosely based on a movie from the late sixties for which Strouse had done the music. What was the source for this new show?

    A. *The Night They Raided Minsky's*

    B. *Rosemary's Baby*

    C. *The Lion in Winter*

    D. *Planet of the Apes*

    E. *Bonnie and Clyde*

Answers on page 219.

Harvey Schmidt and Tom Jones

Harvey Schmidt and Tom Jones met at the University of Texas, Austin, and began collaborating on school productions, some of which were so popular, seats were sold at the windows. They would continue working together for over fifty years. This is one of the more challenging quizzes, since some of the questions are based on anecdotes or obscure shows.

1. Schmidt and Jones' first major collaboration after each had finished military service proved to be their most famous work. *The Fantasticks* opened at the Sullivan Street Theatre in 1960 and ran for forty-two years, the longest-running musical of all time. How did it last so long? Maybe because the material itself—a boy, a girl, two fathers, a wall—is so blessedly simple it can't ever become dated. Maybe because Schmidt and Jones and director Word Baker blended together many different theatrical elements, from commedia to vaudeville to Shakespearean, in the staging. And maybe because it's just about as perfect as a show can be.
   How many performances did *The Fantasticks* run at the Sullivan?
   A. 5,683
   B. 7,485
   C. 17,162
   D. 37,428
   E. 525,600

2. Tom Jones was in the original cast of *The Fantasticks*, performing under a pseudonym. What was it?
   A. Jay Hampton
   B. Ed Rostand
   C. Thomas Bruce
   D. George Spelvin
   E. Walter Plinge

3. During its run of forty-two years, many actors had the chance to perform in *The Fantasticks* at the Sullivan. Who among the following was *not* in it?
   A. Jerry Orbach
   B. Kristin Chenoweth
   C. Bert Convy
   D. F. Murray Abraham
   E. Joel Grey

4. In 1963, Schmidt and Jones teamed up with N. Richard Nash for an adaptation of his play *The Rainmaker*, the story of a spinster in a drought-stricken Texas town and the con man who claims he can bring rain. *110 in the Shade* boasted a lovely score—in fact, Schmidt and Jones wrote 114 songs before settling on the final numbers. The outstanding 2007 revival, featuring Audra McDonald and John Cullum, restored one of those cut songs. What was it?
   A. "110 in the Shade"
   B. "Evenin' Star"

C. "Sweetriver"
D. "Too Many People Alone"
E. "Inside My Head"

5. Schmidt and Jones had another huge hit in *I Do! I Do!* (1966), directed by Gower Champion and starring Mary Martin and Robert Preston. It tells the story of a couple through fifty years of married life. Jones wrote the libretto, which was based on Jan de Hartig's play *The Fourposter*. At the show's end, Agnes and Michael move out of their large house. They leave a gift for the newlywed couple who will be the new owners: a bottle of champagne and a pillow inscribed:
   A. "Home Sweet Home"
   B. "I Love My Wife"
   C. "A Penny Saved"
   D. "Love Conquers All"
   E. "God Is Love"

6. Schmidt and Jones created a heavily allegorical show in 1969's *Celebration*, which closed after fourteen weeks. There were only four principals. Which of the following was *not* a character in *Celebration*?
   A. Potemkin
   B. Orphan
   C. James J. Ratfink
   D. Angel
   E. Edgar Allen Rich

7. Schmidt and Jones have spent over twenty years tinkering with a musical based on the life of French author Colette, with versions appearing in 1970, 1982, 1983, and 1991, and a studio cast recording in 1994. Who among the following actresses did *not* play Colette?
   A. Dorothy Loudon
   B. Zoe Caldwell
   C. Jana Robbins
   D. Betsy Joslyn
   E. Diana Rigg

8. Schmidt and Jones' musical version of *Our Town*, *Grover's Corners*, was originally slated for Broadway in 1985, then was shelved and rescheduled for a national tour in late 1989. Who was going to play the Stage Manager on the tour, but had to withdraw?
   A. Tom Jones
   B. John McMartin
   C. Mary Martin
   D. Paul Newman
   E. Len Cariou

9. Schmidt and Jones wrote a chamber piece, *Mirette*, that was first performed in 1996 and has had several mountings since then. Based on an award-winning children's book, the show concerns:

A. a little girl in Paris who has her appendix out

B. two kids and what they do on a snowy day

C. a little girl who lives at the Palace Hotel

D. a witch with a magic pasta pot

E. a little girl who befriends a tightrope walker who has lost his nerve

10. Schmidt and Jones actually began work on *Roadside* before they created *The Fantasticks*, but they couldn't get the rights to the play they wanted to adapt, so the project faltered after they had written six songs. The show, which tells about a traveling theatrical family in Texas around 1900, finally made it to off-Broadway in 2001. What did it have in common with *Oklahoma!*?

A. a box social

B. a traveling salesman

C. a dream ballet

D. both are based on plays by Lynn Riggs

E. the theme of statehood

Answers on page 220.

John Kander and Fred Ebb

1. John Kander and Fred Ebb wrote the scores to over a dozen Broadway shows, some of them true classics. *Flora, the Red Menace* (1965) was their first show together, featuring a fabulous newcomer named Liza Minnelli. Set in the 1930s, it told of unemployed Flora, who joins the Communists at the urging of her geeky boyfriend. Ageless George Abbott directed his 105th show (though producer Hal Prince always wished *he* had). According to Flora, how does happiness come in?

2. *Cabaret* (1966) marked Kander and Ebb's first hit. Hal Prince directed—the first of his pioneering musicals—and Joe Masteroff wrote the book, based on Isherwood's *I Am a Camera*. *Cabaret* is such a strong show, it has seen success while being re-imagined by drastically different directors, in Fosse's 1972 film and Mendes' 1998 revival. How did the idea for "If You Could See Her" originate in the original production?

A. from a revue Prince saw in Russia

B. Lotte Lenya recalled going to the Berlin Zoo with Kurt Weill

C. Joel Grey had a gorilla mask at rehearsals

D. it came to Fred Ebb in a dream

E. Joe Masteroff suggested it

3. Fresh off their success with *Cabaret*, the duo wrote *The Happy Time* (1968) for David Merrick, with Gower Champion directing. While the creative parties meshed well for *Cabaret*, that wasn't the case with *The Happy Time*. The show didn't do well, but who got great notices playing the lively grandfather?

A. Howard da Silva

B. David Wayne

C. David Burns

D. Charles Ruggles

E. Rex Everhart

4. Working again with Prince, Kander and Ebb fared better with 1968's *Zorba*, based on Kazantzakis' novel and starring Hershel Bernardi as the irrepressible Greek. The pair read the novel at Prince's urging, but were initially reluctant to take it on. Then Prince described his concept for the opening and won them over. Where does *Zorba* open . . . and why is this unusual?

5. The year 1975 brought us *Chicago*, for which Ebb wrote the libretto with director-choreographer Bob Fosse. This was billed as "a musical vaudeville" about those "scintillating sinners," Roxie (Gwen Verdon) and Velma (Chita Rivera), and their slick lawyer, Billy Flynn (Jerry Orbach). Roxie, while on the stand, uses all the tricks Velma planned to use at her trial. What was she wearing?
  A. a lavaliere down to there
  B. her granny's shawl
  C. a Victorian cameo pin
  D. an Alice Blue Gown
  E. silver shoes with rhinestone buckles

6. 1977's *The Act* saw the duo writing for their favorite performer, Liza Minnelli, but on a show plagued with out-of-town troubles, not the least of which was director Martin Scorsese's lack of familiarity with stage productions. Gower Champion managed to salvage the show in three weeks. Liza played Michelle Craig, a washed-up movie star now performing in Vegas. The frisky number on adultery, "Arthur in the Afternoon" was originally written for *A Family Affair* (1962—Kander and James Goldman), but the subject wasn't Arthur. It was:
  A. Sally
  B. Tilly
  C. Mamie
  D. Selma
  E. Jenny

7. The duo wrote *Woman of the Year* for Lauren Bacall in 1981. Based on the Hepburn-Tracy film, it turned the political reporter into a TV interviewer and the sportswriter into a cartoonist (Harry Guardino). Bacall was game for anything, including being tossed around the stage in "One of the Boys" and obviously relishing the huge laughs Marilyn Cooper generated in "The Grass Is Always Greener." Who provided the voice of "Katz," the character in Guardino's comic strip?
  A. John Kander
  B. Tommy Tune
  C. James Coco
  D. Fred Ebb
  E. Robert Moore

8. *Kiss of the Spider Woman* in 1993 had Kander and Ebb writing songs for Terrence McNally's libretto, based on Puig's novel set in a Latin American prison. Prince directed, and the show took several years to go from workshop to Broadway. Brent Carver played gay prisoner Molina, who escapes from the horrors around him by recollecting the spectacular movies of his favorite actress, Aurora, played by the ageless Chita Rivera. What did Molina insist on putting in a mannequin's purse, even though no one could see it?

A. a Balanciaga scarf
B. a bottle of perfume by Lanvin
C. a silver compact
D. a chinchilla muff
E. a bottle of lilac water

9. Kander and Ebb worked with Scott Ellis, David Thompson, and Susan Stroman on 1997's *Steel Pier*, set in a 1930s dance marathon. The show used an amazing array of period dance styles and had a fine cast (Gregory Harrison, Karen Ziemba, Daniel McDonald, Debra Monk), but audiences had trouble accepting that the hero was a ghost. (I liked it, but I have no problems with singing, dancing ghosts.) What future Tony winner had a small, but choice, role?
   A. Idina Menzel
   B. Kristin Chenoweth
   C. Sara Ramirez
   D. Harriet Harris
   E. Jane Krakowski

10. *Curtains* in 2007 got to Broadway a year after Fred Ebb's death. The show, which lovingly combines a spoof of 1950s musicals with a backstage murder and two romances, was one the pair had worked on for years. Peter Stone, who died in 2003, wrote the original libretto. Who helped Kander revise the book and complete the lyrics?
   A. Terrence McNally
   B. Douglas Wright
   C. Thomas Meehan
   D. John Guare
   E. Rupert Holmes

❧ ❧

BROADWAY BONUS: What was the original title of *Curtains*?

❧ ❧

Answers on page 220.

Betty Comden and Adolph Green

1. Betty Comden and Adolph Green comprised one of the most talented and productive writing teams in Broadway history, penning lyrics and libretti for shows in five decades, not to mention some of the finest movie musicals ever made. In the 1930s, they formed a successful nightclub act, the Revuers, with their friend Judy Holliday. In 1944, they hit the big time with the wartime tale of sailors on leave in *On the Town*, with music by their pal, Lenny Bernstein. They performed in the piece as well. What were their roles?

2. *Two on the Aisle* was a 1951 revue that saw Comden and Green collaborating with Jule Styne. Bert Lahr and Dolores Gray, though feuding offstage, put the laughs over while onstage. One of the best numbers was the murderous lickety-split "If You

Hadn't (But You Did)." The jealous singer accuses her Joe of flings with all these dames but one. Who?

    A. Gwen

    B. Sue

    C. Kate

    D. Ivy

    E. Geraldine

3. Comden and Green and Bernstein produced the charming score for *Wonderful Town* (1952) in just over a month. The tale of two sisters hoping for careers in the Big Apple in the 1930's, it was based on Ruth McKerney's stories in *The New Yorker*, collected as *My Sister Eileen*. The original songwriters had been fired, and producer Robert Fryer needed a score quickly or he'd lose his star, Rosalind Russell. The trio came through. During "A Conversation Piece," Ruth desperately tries to start a nice, friendly chat by mentioning a classic novel she'd been reading. What was it?

    A. *Of Mice and Men*

    B. *Ivanhoe*

    C. *Wuthering Heights*

    D. *Pride and Prejudice*

    E. *Moby-Dick*

4. There had been stage versions of *Peter Pan* long before the 1954 version starring Mary Martin. This production began on the West Coast with Edwin Lester's Civic Light Opera and featured a score by Moose Charlap and Carolyn Leigh. Director-choreographer Jerome Robbins brought in his old pals, Comden and Green, to revise J. M. Barrie's original 1904 libretto and to add six more songs (music by Styne). The show was filmed for television and remained popular for decades. Martin, her costar Cyril Ritchard, and stage technician Richard Rodda picked up Tonys. Martin also won a Donaldson. How did Ritchard fare at the Donaldsons?

5. Comden and Green teamed with fellow Revuer Judy Holliday and old comrades Jerome Robbins and Jule Styne for 1956's *Bells Are Ringing*, the saga of the answering-service operator who meddles in the affairs of her clients—and is secretly in love with one. Which song did Comden and Green add after the show had been running a year? Hint: this song—and another new tune—wound up in the movie version.

    A. "Independent"

    B. "Is It a Crime?"

    C. "(It's) Better than a Dream"

    D. "Do It Yourself"

    E. "Long Before I Knew You"

6. *Do Re Mi* (1960) saw Comden and Green and Styne spoofing the music industry with star comics Phil Silvers and Nancy Walker (who had been in *On the Town*). It ran more than a year, but still ended up in the red. Who are the three retired gangsters whose help Herbie (Silvers) seeks?

    A. Paul Revere, Epitaph, and Valentine

    B. Tom, Dick, and Harry

    C. Groucho, Harpo, and Chico

D. Fatso, Stein, and Brains

E. Benny, Rusty, and Big Jule

7. The same trio worked on 1961's *Subways Are for Sleeping*, today best remembered for producer David Merrick's publicity stunt in which he found seven men whose names matched those of the critics, and got them to write rave reviews. The story of oddball New Yorkers wasn't a big hit, despite an attractive score and the equally attractive presence of Phyllis Newman (Mrs. Adolph Green) in a towel. Newman brought the house down with "I Was a Shoo-In," in which her character, Martha, describes the one-woman Civil War saga she used to impress beauty contest judges. How did the Southern belle "Emmelina Sue" distract "Cousin Willie" so her Yankee lover could escape?

   A. she gave him mint juleps

   B. she baked him homemade corn muffins

   C. she danced a polka

   D. she took him for a walk through the bayou

   E. she served him Southern Comfort

8. Following the disappointment of *Fade Out, Fade In*, Comden, Green, and Styne reunited for *Hallelujah, Baby!* in 1967. It got mixed reviews, but did well at the Tonys. The show told the story of Georgina, from her days working in a kitchen to stardom, and spanned sixty years. Leslie Uggams (in a role written for Lena Horne) managed to shine despite Arthur Laurents' problematic book. What did *Hallelujah, Baby!* have in common with 1948's *Love Life* by Lerner and Weill?

9. Comden and Green wrote the book for Strouse and Adams' score for *Applause* (1970), the musical version of *All About Eve*, starring Lauren Bacall. Who replaced Bacall in the run and what was her connection to this story?

10. Comden and Green returned to double duty (book and lyrics) for 1978's *On the Twentieth Century*, with Cy Coleman's score and Hal Prince's brilliant direction. On the liner between Chicago and New York City, desperate producer Oscar Jaffe (John Cullum) tries to lure Lily Garland (Madeline Kahn) back to Broadway, even faking his own death-bed scene to get her to sign the contract. How does Lily sign the contract?

   A. "Repent, for the time is at hand"

   B. Mildred Plotka

   C. Babette Veronique

   D. Toots Galore

   E. Peter Rabbit

Answers on page 221.

Richard Rodgers and Lorenz Hart

1. In 1919, sixteen-year-old Richard Rodgers met twenty-three-year-old Lorenz Hart, discovered a shared love of Kern's Princess Theatre shows, and began a partnership that would last nearly a quarter century. Their first hit song was "Manhattan" (*Garrick*

Gaieties of 1925), which paved the way for their first successful book show, *Dearest Enemy*. Based on a legend about an American woman who patriotically distracted some British officers during the Revolution, this snappy comedy ran for 286 performances in 1925. What historical figure appeared at the end?

  A. George Washington
  B. Paul Revere
  C. Peter Stuyvesant
  D. John Adams
  E. Theodore Roosevelt

❦ ❦

BROADWAY BONUS: How did star Helen Ford make her entrance in *Dearest Enemy*?

❦ ❦

2. Here's all the duo did in 1926: *The Girl Friend* (a silly show about bicycle races), another *Garrick Gaieties* ("Mountain Greenery"), a London hit called *Lido Lady*, and at year's end, *Peggy-Ann* and *Betsy*, which opened a day apart. *Betsy* flopped, though producer Flo Ziegfeld hired Irving Berlin to add a song...a little tune called "Blue Skies." *Peggy-Ann*, however, was a hit. It billed itself as "the utterly different musical comedy," and lived up to that. All of the following facts about *Peggy-Ann* are true *except:*

  A. it was plotless, describing a poor girl's spectacular and bizarre dreams
  B. it was full of Freudian overtones
  C. it began with no music at all
  D. it included a talking fish
  E. it had an elaborate "Hollywood Dream" sequence that was cut

3. *A Connecticut Yankee* proved a hit for the duo in 1927. They revised it in 1943, just prior to Hart's death from pneumonia. The revival included six new numbers and increased the focus on Morgan le Fay (Vivienne Segal), who got to sing some of Larry Hart's wickedest lyrics in "To Keep My Love Alive." Morgan doesn't divorce her unwanted hubbies; she uses other methods to get rid of them. Which method was *not* on her list?

  A. blunt object (a harp)
  B. stabbing
  C. a shove off a balcony
  D. bow and arrow
  E. arsenic

4. Rodgers and Hart finished the twenties and headed into the Depression with a series of flops and an unhappy stay in Hollywood. (They were still turning out great songs, though.) Back on Broadway, *Jumbo* (1935) lost money, too, because of the production costs involved in putting on the gargantuan musical circus in the Hippodrome. Who played Jumbo?

  A. Jimmy Durante
  B. Billy Rose
  C. John Hay "Jock" Whitney
  D. Poodles Hannaford
  E. Big Rosie

5. The pair next wrote the score and the book (with George Abbott) for the smash success *On Your Toes* (1936), the ballet-jazz musical. This show featured one of Broadway's most famous ballets, "Slaughter on Tenth Avenue," choreographed by George Balanchine. What nursery rhyme theme did Rodgers use to underscore the entrance of the cops?
    A. "The Cat and the Fiddle"
    B. "Goosey Goosey Gander"
    C. "Three Blind Mice"
    D. "Hickory Dickory Dock"
    E. "Three Little Kittens"

6. You could find all of the following at *Babes in Arms* (1937) *except:*
    A. someone with an extremely limited vocal range
    B. slightly smelly performing seals
    C. a character named for a holiday
    D. a banquet of sandwiches and beans
    E. a gal who prefers the bleacher seats at ball games

7. *I'd Rather Be Right* in 1937 had Rodgers and Hart writing a political satire for George M. Cohan's return to the stage. Cohan hated the pair, and FDR, too, but that didn't stop him from taking on the role of a sitting president and singing a score other than his own. He did occasionally alter Hart's lyrics, however. Who wrote the book spoofing New Deal agencies, FDR's attempt to pack the Supreme Court, and balancing the budget?
    A. George Abbott
    B. Kaufman and Hart (Moss, not Lorenz)
    C. Hecht and MacArthur
    D. Herbert Fields
    E. Guy Bolton

8. Rodgers and Hart created one of their finest scores for *The Boys from Syracuse*, the musical version of Shakespeare's *The Comedy of Errors*. What gave Lorenz Hart the idea for the show?

9. What was noteworthy about the casting of one of the roles in Rodgers and Hart's 1941 masterpiece, *Pal Joey*, given the subject matter of the song "Zip"?

10. *By Jupiter* in 1942 was set in ancient Greece, pitting the boys (Hercules and Theseus) against the girls (Queen Hippolyta and her Amazons). The show was a success and would have run longer than its 427 performances but star Ray Bolger left because:
    A. he went to entertain the troops overseas
    B. he was drafted
    C. he demanded a raise and didn't get it
    D. he was injured dancing
    E. he was cast in the movie version of *The Wizard of Oz*

Answers on page 221.

Act One: Scene Two

Jerry Herman

1. Jerry Herman's songs first attracted attention in two revues, *Nightcap* (a late show in a supper club) and *Parade* (1960, off-Broadway). The material was comic and fresh, ably put over by performers who would also make names for themselves. Who sang in both shows and remained a lifelong friend of Herman's?
   A. Kenneth Nelson
   B. Dody Goodman
   C. Estelle Parsons
   D. Charles Nelson Reilly
   E. Phyllis Newman

2. Herman teamed up with librettist Don Appell for his first Broadway show, 1961's *Milk and Honey*. They traveled to Israel for ideas, and were well treated by the government, though they found more interesting source material when they sneaked away from the sanitized tours and investigated on their own. Molly Picon, star of Yiddish theatre, helped turn *Milk and Honey* into a 543-performance hit. Clara (Picon) is the leader of a group of Jewish widows touring Israel looking for new husbands. She finds one. What's his name?
   A. Sol Horowitz
   B. S. I. Jacobowsky
   C. Phil Arkin
   D. Hymie Weiss
   E. Ephraim Levi

3. Herman's next show was one of the biggest smashes in musical history: 1964's *Hello, Dolly!*, which ran for 2,844 performances. *Dolly!*'s book was by Michael Stewart, David Merrick produced, and Gower Champion handled direction and choreography. Carol Channing, who already had the role of a lifetime in Lorelei Lee, now found herself another.

   A true Broadway buff knows the famous anecdotes associated with *Hello, Dolly!*: how Ethel Merman rejected the role, but wound up the last original Dolly; how Herman convinced Merrick he could write the score by creating four songs in three days; the tryout hell when Merrick brought in Bob Merrill (who worked on two songs) and Strouse and Adams (who wrote an unused song, but got rewarded with a title credit on "Before the Parade Passes By"), and how Herman triumphantly came up with his own "Parade," waking Channing and Champion in the middle of the night to play it; and how it won a record ten Tony Awards. But do you know which song was cut *after* the New York opening?
   A. the overture
   B. "Love, Look in My Window"
   C. "World, Take Me Back"

D. "You're a Damned Exasperating Woman"

E. "Come and Be My Butterfly"

4. Herman followed that big-lady hit with another, 1966's *Mame* (1,508 performances). Angela Lansbury starred, winning the first of her Tonys; Jerome Lawrence and Robert E. Lee wrote the libretto from their play, *Auntie Mame*; and Gene Saks directed. Given that Herman is a teetotaler, it's impressive how many alcohol-related lyrics he created for bohemian Mame. You can find all of the following beverages *except* one in the songs or the libretto of *Mame*. What is it?

A. mint julep

B. Scotch

C. martini

D. pousse café

E. a recent vintage (with fresh bubbles)

5. While *Hello, Dolly!* and *Mame* ran for years, 1969's *Dear World* managed just a couple of months. The initial concept had promise—Jean Giraudoux's *The Madwoman of Chaillot*—and the amazing Angela Lansbury in the lead, but the show was troubled from the start. The director, choreographer, a principal cast member, and the dance music director were all replaced in tryouts, and the show was endlessly doctored. Producer Alexander Cohen booked it into a huge theatre when an intimate setting would have better served. Nor did audiences enjoy seeing the woman who had been glamorous Mame Dennis covered in eye shadow and dressed in rags.

What is the Countess Aurelia, the Madwoman, looking for?

A. a nine-foot-long feather boa

B. an imaginary dog called Dickie

C. radioactive water

D. a stone gargoyle that opens a trap door

E. pearls

6. *Mack and Mabel* (1974) reunited Herman with Champion and Stewart from *Hello, Dolly!* to tell the tale of silent movie maker Mack Sennett and his star Mabel Normand. While many argue this is Herman's best score, the show that did well in West Coast tryouts failed to catch on in New York. Champion wanted to keep things dark and serious (his "Chekhov period," as Herman put it); changes on the road hurt rather than helped; David Merrick didn't support the show; and though the stars, Robert Preston and Bernadette Peters, were fabulously talented, the age difference bothered audiences. *Mack and Mabel* has been revised in a hit British production, proving there's life in an old score yet.

One of the changes that hurt was Champion's altering the Keystone Kops number. The raucous "Hit 'Em in the Head" was replaced with "Every Time a Cop Falls Down (My Heart Leaps Up)" and the choreography became more of a soft-shoe. Why did Champion want the number changed?

❧ ❧

BROADWAY BONUS: There was an even earlier version of the Kops number, used in the San Diego tryout. What was it called?

❧ ❧

---

7. After *Mack and Mabel*'s dismal showing, Herman spent the rest of the decade working in interior design, buying and renovating houses. But Michael Stewart got him back on Broadway with material that made Herman hesitate from the start: *The Grand Tour* (1979), a tale of a Jewish refugee and an aristocratic, anti-Semitic Polish officer making their way through Nazi-occupied France to England. Herman was glad of the opportunity to work with star Joel Grey, but was far from comfortable with the subject matter. Gerald Freeman directed, but who came in and doctored the show in San Francisco?

   A. Gower Champion
   B. Gene Saks
   C. George Abbott
   D. Peter Stone
   E. Tommy Tune

8. Speaking of doctoring, producer Alexander Cohen asked Herman to see *A Day in Hollywood/A Night in the Ukraine* (1980) while in previews. Herman suggested an establishing number in the opening and something stronger for Priscilla Lopez. Cohen asked Herman if he'd do the work, but remembering his own unhappiness at Merrick's use of interpolators in *Dolly!*, refused unless songwriters Dick Vosbugh and Frank Lazarus consented. They did, and Herman wrote three numbers: the establishing song, "Just Go to the Movies," the serious number for Lopez ("Best in the World"), and a funny take on a famous movie couple. What duo did Herman parody in the third song?

   A. Clark Gable and Claudette Colbert
   B. Nelson Eddy and Jeanette MacDonald
   C. Fay Wray and King Kong
   D. Mary Pickford and Douglas Fairbanks
   E. Mickey Rooney and Judy Garland

9. Herman saw the film *La Cage aux Folles* in 1978 and immediately wanted to turn it into a musical, but Alan Carr held the rights and Maury Yeston was working on the score. When that was shelved in favor of *Nine*, Herman got his chance. Working with director Arthur Laurents and librettist Harvey Fierstein, Herman helped create the first musical with gay leads. *La Cage* opened in 1983 and ran for 1,761 performances. When did Albin (George Hearn) and Georges (Gene Barry) take their memorable walk on that sandy beach?

   A. September
   B. October
   C. June
   D. May
   E. August

10. *Jerry's Girls* began as an off-off-Broadway revue in 1981, with Herman himself in the cast. It toured in 1984 and moved to Broadway in 1985 for 139 showings. It would have run longer, but one of the stars broke her leg in a car accident. Which one of these actresses was in both the 1984 tour and the Broadway production?

    A. Chita Rivera
    B. Dorothy Loudon

C. Carol Channing
D. Andrea McArdle
E. Leslie Uggams

Answers on page 222.

Kurt Weill

1. Kurt Weill had a celebrated career in Germany, highlighted by his collaboration with Bertolt Brecht (*The Threepenny Opera, Happy End, The Rise and Fall of the City of Mahagonny*) until he was forced to flee the Nazis. His Broadway output before his untimely death at fifty was not always commercial, but, oh, that music! His first piece written for Broadway was the 1936 antiwar satire/fantasy *Johnny Johnson*, produced by the Group Theatre. Which of the following is *not* true about *Johnny Johnson*?

    A. a row of cannons sings a lullaby to soldiers
    B. Weill felt the best song, "Farewell, Good-bye," was cut
    C. Johnny tries to pacify the Allied High Command using laughing gas
    D. Elia Kazan directed
    E. "Oh, the Rio Grande" featured a banjo accompaniment in Weill's orchestrations

2. Audiences might not have cared for *Johnny Johnson*, but playwright Maxwell Anderson did, and teamed with Weill on *Knickerbocker Holiday*, re-imagining Washington Irving's Peter Stuyvesant as a kind of seventeenth-century FDR. The show originated one of Weill's biggest hits in "September Song." Who initially suggested using Irving's work and was cast as the lead, Bram Broeck, only to abandon the role when he saw Stuyvesant's part taking over the show? Hint: this versatile actor-director-producer didn't do many musicals, but had the lead in a 1950 flop that lasted three nights.

    A. Frank Morgan
    B. William Gaxton
    C. Howard da Silva
    D. Eddie Albert
    E. Burgess Meredith

3. In 1941, Weill and librettist-director Moss Hart got Ira Gershwin to return to lyric writing (he had been semi-retired since George's death) for *Lady in the Dark*, a highly unusual hit about a troubled executive (Gertrude Lawrence) seeking psycho-analysis. The musical sequences took place in the dreams revealed on the shrink's couch. In one, Liza's former high-school classmates look back on their school days. What did they say they read in class?

    A. *Romeo and Juliet*
    B. *The Divine Comedy*
    C. *Les Misérables*
    D. Arthurian romances
    E. "Kubla Khan"

4. *One Touch of Venus* (1943, book by S. J. Perelman; lyrics by Ogden Nash) was Weill's longest-running hit. It starred Mary Martin as a statue of Venus that comes to life when barber Rodney Hatch places a ring on the statue's hand. Venus temporarily disposes of Rodney's obnoxious fiancée, Gloria, by magically sending her to:
  A. the North Pole
  B. Ozone Heights
  C. New Jersey
  D. Anatolia
  E. Mount Olympus

5. Weill paired with Gershwin again on 1945's *Firebrand of Florence*, which starred Weill's wife, Lotte Lenya, but the songwriters' intentions didn't mesh with the director and librettist's and it flopped. What was it called during its Boston tryout?
  A. *Much Ado About Love*
  B. *It Happened in Florence*
  C. *Make Way for Love*
  D. *Life, Love and Laughter*
  E. *The Dagger and the Rose*

6. Weill stretched himself further with 1947's *Street Scene*, a biting American opera with lyrics by Langston Hughes and book by Elmer Rice, both newcomers to Broadway. It earned Weill a Tony for his score and has been a favorite of opera companies since then. What does Harry Easter tell Rose is "just a few blocks over"?
  A. a primrose path
  B. lilac bushes
  C. Julia Riehman High School
  D. Broadway
  E. a castle in Spain

7. The ever-versatile Weill tackled one of Broadway's first concept shows with lyricist-librettist Alan Jay Lerner in *Love Life* (1948), telling the tale of the marriage of Sam and Susan Cooper from 1790 to 1948. Sam and Susan don't age. Instead, we see how the changes in society (industrialism, the women's rights movement, mass communication) affect marriage, all in the form of a vaudeville. It opened with a magic act and ended with a minstrel show. Who choreographed the famous dream ballet "Punch and Judy Get a Divorce"?
  A. Agnes de Mille
  B. Michael Kidd
  C. George Balanchine
  D. Jack Cole
  E. Hanya Holm

8. Weill reunited with Maxwell Anderson for 1949's "musical tragedy" *Lost in the Stars*, based on Alan Paton's novel *Cry, the Beloved Country*. Where does the Reverend Stephen Kumalo live?
  A. Kenya
  B. New Zealand
  C. Georgia

D. Tanzania

E. South Africa

9. Weill and Brecht's *The Threepenny Opera* had had a disastrously short run on Broadway (twelve performances) in 1933. Marc Blitzstein's 1952 adaptation (with Lenya re-creating her role as Jenny) would run for 2,611 performances off-Broadway. Before his death in 1950, Weill had tried for years to get several Americans interested in translating *Threepenny*. Who was *not* among the people he courted?

   A. Maxwell Anderson

   B. Ben Hecht

   C. Charles MacArthur

   D. Ann Ronell

   E. Howard Dietz

10. Broadway got to hear Weill again in the brief run of Hal Prince and Alfred Uhry's *LoveMusik* (2007), which told the story of the composer's (Michael Cerveris) relationship with Lotte Lenya (Donna Murphy). Much of the material was adapted from letters Weill and Lenya wrote to each other. What song does Lenya sing when she auditions for Brecht (David Pittu)?

   A. "Alabama Song"

   B. "Moritat"

   C. "Song of the Rhineland"

   D. "Berlin im Licht"

   E. "Pirate Jenny"

Answers on page 223.

Cole Porter

Unlike many of his contemporaries, who came from poor or modest Jewish immigrant families, Cole Porter was born into a wealthy, Midwestern Protestant clan. He attended Yale, where his football songs are still sung, and his first Broadway offering, *See America First* (1916), was a two-week flop. He went to France, and through the twenties placed songs in shows in London and Paris, as well as a few Broadway revues. *La revue des Ambassadeurs* (1927) was a hit, which led to *Paris* (1928), starring Irene Bordoni and the source of two standards, "Let's Misbehave" and "Let's Do It." *Wake Up and Dream* did well in London in 1929, but not so on a Broadway reeling from the stock market crash.

1. Porter teamed up with librettist Herbert Fields in 1929 for *Fifty Million Frenchmen*, the first of seven shows they would do. The plot was standard for the times: the young rich guy must do something on a bet (here, pose as a tour guide) to win his gal. The score, however, was full of great songs, including "You Do Something to Me," "Find Me a Primitive Man," "You Don't Know Paree," and "You've Got That Thing." The production got mixed reviews, but one prominent name actually took out a paid ad saying it was the best show in years and worth the price of admission just to hear the lyrics. Who was this early avid supporter of Porter?

A. Noel Coward
B. Vincent Youmans
C. Irving Berlin
D. Jerome Kern
E. Lorenz Hart

2. Porter and Fields' next show, *The New Yorkers* (1930), had a short run, but gave the public "Love for Sale," a song frequently censored for its subject matter. *The Gay Divorce* in 1932, with book by Dwight Taylor, did far better at 248 performances. The show starred Fred Astaire, Claire Luce, and Luella Gear. Astaire would later star in the movie version (*The Gay Divorceé*), which cut nearly all of Porter's great score. Porter often accommodated singers, tailoring songs to fit their needs, but when Astaire wanted one song from *The Gay Divorce* cut because he found it difficult to sing, Porter flatly refused. What was the song? Hint: it was one of the few that made it into the movie score.
   A. "After You, Who?
   B. "I've Got You on My Mind"
   C. "Night and Day"
   D. "You're in Love"
   E. "The Physician"

3. Porter's next show was London's *Nymph Errant* (1933), starring Gertrude Lawrence. He came back to Broadway in 1934 with the second-longest-running book show for the decade in *Anything Goes* (420 performances). Vinton Freedley produced the show, which starred William Gaxton, Victor Moore, and Ethel Merman, in the first of her many Porter shows. Guy Bolton and P. G. Wodehouse wrote the initial treatment, which was set on an ocean liner. There is a persistent legend that the script was rewritten by Russel Crouse and Howard Lindsay (the director) because of similarities to the recent fatal shipwreck of the *Morro Castle*. In fact, there was a bomb scare, but no shipwreck in the first version. Freedley simply didn't like it, but since Bolton was recovering from surgery and Wodehouse was in England with a play and a new novel, he called on Crouse and Lindsay to rewrite.

   Anything Goes boasted hit after hit, but perhaps the quintessential Porter "list song" was "You're the Top." You can find literary allusions to all of the following in its lyrics *except*:
   A. John Donne
   B. Eugene O'Neill
   C. John Keats
   D. William Shakespeare
   E. George Jean Nathan

❦ ❦

BROADWAY BONUS: What real-life incident caused Porter to change an early lyric for "I Get a Kick Out of You"?

❦ ❦

4. With *Anything Goes* playing to full houses, Porter, Moss Hart and Monty Woolley went on an around-the-world cruise. While traveling, they created 1935's *Jubilee*.

The show didn't run long and two of its songs ("Begin the Beguine" and "Just One of Those Things") didn't become hits until much later. The plot concerned the comic adventures of a royal family pretending to be commoners. The King, the Queen, and the Princess all fall for characters who are thinly disguised versions of *three* of the following thirties celebrities. Remember, pick three answers!

    A. Noel Coward

    B. Elsa Maxwell

    C. Aimee Semple McPherson

    D. Johnny Weismuller

    E. Alexander Woollcott

5. Many of the people responsible for *Anything Goes*—Freedley, Crouse, Lindsay, Merman, and Gaxton—joined Porter for 1936's *Red, Hot and Blue*, though Gaxton would quit and be replaced by Bob Hope. Jimmy Durante came on for the comic role. The run wasn't long, but "De-Lovely," "Ridin' High," and "Down in the Depths" became hits. After the film *Rosalie*, Porter was working on 1938's *You Never Know* when he suffered a devastating riding accident that crushed both legs and left him in lifelong pain. *You Never Know* managed a few months, but Porter was back on top with Sam and Bella Spewack's *Leave It to Me* (1938, 291 performances), the start of a long run of hits. *Du Barry Was a Lady* in 1939 chalked up 408 performances with Ethel Merman and Bert Lahr in the leads. Who had the second female role?

    A. Betty Hutton

    B. Mary Martin

    C. Betty Grable

    D. Eve Arden

    E. Betty Garrett

6. Merman returned in Porter's next smash, 1940's *Panama Hattie* (501 performances), which was followed by *Let's Face It* (1941, 547 performances with Danny Kaye); Merman again in *Something for the Boys* (1943, 422 performances); and 1944's *Mexican Hayride* (481 showings, starring comic Bobby Clark). For one of these shows, Porter wrote a song on a $25 bet with his pal Monty Woolley that he couldn't turn a commonplace saying into a song. Porter did, and got a hit ballad out of it, along with the money. What was the phrase and what was the show?

7. The string of successes ended with two disasters, *Seven Lively Arts* (1944) and the bloated Orson Welles production of *Around the World in Eighty Days* (1946). Word on the street was that Porter was washed up and unable to write for the more-integrated shows of the post-*Oklahoma!* era. He proved them wrong with 1948's *Kiss Me, Kate*, his longest-running show at 1,077 performances. The production starred Alfred Drake, Patricia Morison, Lisa Kirk, and Harold Lang, but the show-stopping number went to the two gangsters, Harry Clark and Jack Diamond. The thugs find their exposure to *The Taming of the Shrew*, the show-within-the-show, has taught them how to use Shakespeare to win over the ladies. In addition to citing the poem "Venus and Adonis" in their smash number, "Brush Up Your Shakespeare," the gangsters make reference to fourteen plays by the Bard. How many can you name?

8. Porter followed up his biggest success with one of his loveliest scores in *Out of This World* (1950), based on the Amphitryon legend. Unfortunately, this tale of Olympian gods and goddesses flopped after a few months. The book by Dwight Taylor and Reginald Lawrence was chaotic and on the vulgar side. One of the best things about the show was the return to Broadway after twenty-three years of Charlotte Greenwood in the role of Juno. In which number did she bring down the house with her signature high kicks?
    A. "From This Moment On"
    B. "Cherry Pies Ought to Be You"
    C. "I Got Beauty"
    D. "Nobody's Chasing Me"
    E. "I Sleep Easier Now"

9. *Can-Can* in 1953 helped Porter get through depression after the death of his mother. With a book by Abe Burrows and lively choreography by Genevieve Pitot, *Can-Can* lasted nearly nine hundred performances. The thin plot concerned the unlikely love affair between the woman who runs a nightclub where the indecent dance, the can-can, is performed, and the official determined to shut her down. Still, Porter's Francophile leanings gave true Gallic character to the score. Name the two song titles derived from French phrases.

10. Porter's final Broadway show was *Silk Stockings* (1955), a 478-performance hit. The show endured tryout hell, with producers Feuer and Martin getting rid of the original librettists (George S. Kaufman and his wife, Leueen MacGrath), director Kaufman, the second female lead, and twelve Porter songs. The show was based on the film *Ninotchka*, about a stern female Soviet official (Hildegarde Neff) who comes to Paris to investigate some of her colleagues with capitalistic leanings. Naturally, she falls for Steven, an American (Don Ameche). But before Steven wins her over, she discusses male and female relationships in a very scientific way, using some of Porter's especially clever lyrics. Which scientist does Ninotchka cite as most learned in sexual relations?
    A. Babinsky
    B. Markovitch
    C. Napoleon
    D. Ivanov
    E. Kamichev

Answers on page 224.

Stephen Sondheim

Beyond a doubt, Stephen Sondheim is one of the seminal figures in the history of Broadway, taking the musical where it had never been before. Each of his shows has its own unique character, as fits such diverse subject matter as adaptations of ancient comedy, the opening of Japan in 1853, a pointillist painting, or a vengeful Victorian barber. The one constant is that each of his works is relentlessly well crafted.

In his youth, Sondheim became friends with James Hammerstein, son of Oscar, and the Hammersteins became his surrogate family. As his interest in theatre grew, Oscar acted as his mentor, patiently reviewing his early efforts. Sondheim worked as a gofer on Hammerstein's *Allegro* and after college, wrote scripts for the television series *Topper*. In 1955, he composed the score for his first musical, *Saturday Night*, which folded before opening when producer Lemuel Ayers died. Despite being a newcomer to Broadway, he then wrote the lyrics to two classic shows, *West Side Story* (1957) and *Gypsy* (1959).

1. It wasn't until 1962 that Broadway finally heard Sondheim's music, in *A Funny Thing Happened on the Way to the Forum*, which ran for 964 performances. With a jam-packed libretto by Burt Shevelove and Larry Gelbart after the Roman comedies of Plautus, this show was a vaudevillian-style farce with Zero Mostel romping as Pseudolus the slave. *Forum* took years to reach Broadway, shuffling through several producers and directors. George Abbott had the final directing credit, though Jerome Robbins did some critical doctoring during out-of-town tryouts. Robbins' most valuable suggestion was to replace the opening number with something more in keeping with the frenetic, hilarious tone of the show. Sondheim's solution was "Comedy Tonight," which let the audience know exactly what they were going to get.

   What song did "Comedy Tonight" replace?

   A. "Invocation"

   B. "Once Upon a Time"

   C. "The Echo Song"

   D. "Love Is in the Air"

   E. "I Do Like You"

   Although *Forum* did well at the Tonys, Sondheim's delightful score wasn't even nominated. His next work, *Anyone Can Whistle* (1964), was daring and innovative—the story of a corrupt town, a "miracle," and speculation on sanity—and it lasted nine performances. *Do I Hear a Waltz?* in 1965 saw Sondheim providing the lyrics to Richard Rodgers' music and Arthur Laurents' book. This was apparently an unpleasant time for most of the participants, though some of the songs are lovely.

2. In 1970, he teamed with longtime friend Harold Prince for the first of five landmark musicals that would forever change the face of the field. Based on a series of one-acts George Furth had written about marriage, *Company* described the relationships between a single man, Robert, his five pairs of married friends, and his three girlfriends. The creators presented the show in nonlinear format: a series of fragmented, but related, scenes. Sondheim's score probed the depths of Robert's psyche at the same time it reflected the brassy, driven pulse of contemporary Manhattan and the complicated relations of his friends. Prince brilliantly directed the show, and Michael Bennett provided an astonishing amount of choreography for a cast that included no true dancers save Donna McKechnie.

   Boris Aronson's glass and chrome set, depicting the couples' apartments as abstract cubes, was critical to both the staging and the score. Sondheim has said he couldn't write the opening number without seeing it.

   What in particular did the set have to do with the fifteen-second sustained note on the word "love" and on Bennett's choreography in that opener?

Company swept the Tonys and ran for 706 performances, leading to the team's next project, *Follies* (1971). This show was originally conceived by Sondheim and librettist James Goldman as a murder mystery about former chorus girls, but when Hal Prince got involved, it became more surreal—a magnificent statement about the past, aging, memory, and decisions, using show business as a metaphor for life. The setting remained that of a reunion of showgirls from the "Weismann Follies," and in keeping with that notion, Sondheim crafted a score full of effective pastiches of the styles of older songwriters. Match each *Follies* song with its source of inspiration.

3. "One More Kiss"

A. Irving Berlin

4. "The Story of Lucy and Jessie"

B. Jerome Kern

5. "Losing My Mind"

C. Rudolph Friml/Sigmund Romberg

6. "Beautiful Girls"

D. DeSylva, Brown, and Henderson

7. "Broadway Baby"

E. George Gershwin

8. "You're Gonna Love Tomorrow"/ "Love Will See Us Through"

F. Cole Porter

9. Though recognized today as a masterpiece, *Follies*, which lasted 522 performances, could not overcome its incredible expenses, and was beaten at the Tonys by the far less rueful *Two Gentlemen of Verona*. Fortunately for Sondheim and Prince's fortunes, 1973's *A Little Night Music* was a commercial as well as a critical success, running 601 performances and garnering six Tony Awards. Hugh Wheeler wrote the book, adapting Ingmar Bergman's film *Smiles of a Summer Night*. The plot concerned the romantic entanglements of a middle-aged actress; her lawyer-lover of many years ago; her current lover, a jealous, egotistical count; the count's wife; the lawyer's son; and the lawyer's still virginal (and much younger) new wife. Glynis Johns and Len Cariou headed the cast as actress Desirée and lawyer Fredrik.

Surveying their foolish escapades is Desiree's aged mother, Madame Armfeldt (Hermione Gingold, in a role she wanted so desperately she auditioned, even though she hadn't auditioned in decades). Sondheim wrote some of his wittiest lyrics for Madame Armfeldt's solo, "Liaisons," in which she describes how sexual relations have changed. Which of the following did she *not* acquire through her liaisons over the years?

A. the deed to a duchy
B. pearls
C. pendants of fire-opals
D. a painting by Titian
E. a chateau

10. Sondheim reunited with Burt Shevelove on another classical project in 1974, a musical treatment of Aristophanes' *The Frogs*. In the original ancient Greek comedy, the god of drama, Dionysus, goes to Hades to bring back the avant-garde Euripides to improve the state of theatre. He ends up choosing the more traditional Aeschylus after the shades of the deceased playwrights have a competition. Shevelove updated the material to feature George Bernard Shaw and Shakespeare, and Sondheim provided a lively score for the brief piece that was performed in the Yale University swimming pool (to mimic the River Styx). Thirty years later, Nathan Lane expanded the work and starred in it on Broadway.

In the original production, Broadway veteran Larry Blyden played Dionysus, while Yale drama students comprised much of the cast, often splashing in the pool as the frogs. There was a lot of future talent in that pool. Who was *not* among the cast of the Yale production of *The Frogs*?

    A. Patti LuPone
    B. Sigourney Weaver
    C. Christopher Durang
    D. Meryl Streep
    E. Robert Picardo

11. Sondheim's next musical, *Pacific Overtures*, was far removed from classical comedy. Playwright John Weidman had written a play about Commodore Matthew Perry, whose expedition in 1853 opened Japan to Western trade and influences, ushering in a chaotic era of political and social change. Unconventional material for a play, but even more unlikely for a musical—but not for Sondheim and Prince. Weidman adapted his play into a series of linked sketches reflecting the effects of the West on isolated Japan, and Sondheim devised a score that evoked the tones of Asian music without being completely alien to the ears of a Broadway audience. Prince staged the work in bold, Kabuki fashion, utilizing the *hanamichi* (runway) and having men play all the women's roles until the final, contemporary scene. Boris Aronson designed the sets, his last masterful work.

But perhaps it was too much to expect theatre parties and tired businessmen to go for a musical in which the protagonists are really Japanese and Western cultures. *Pacific Overtures*, while brilliant, struck too many as a cold show. Those of us who are fans, however, will never forget this show, especially the depiction of Commodore Perry as:

    A. a black dragon
    B. a puppet
    C. a Kabuki lion
    D. a *kurombo*, all clad in black
    E. a samurai

Sondheim and Prince's next collaboration, *Sweeney Todd: The Demon Barber of Fleet Street* (1979) is regarded by many as one of the era's masterpieces. The tale of a murderous Victorian barber and his accomplice, the baker who disposes of the corpses, thrilled audiences for 558 performances, and swept the Tonys, including awards for Sondheim, Prince, and leads Len Cariou and Angela Lansbury.

Since *Sweeney* is so important, it gets a mini-quiz of its own.

12. Mrs. Lovett tells the Beadle Sweeney is a newcomer to London from which city?

13. The story of *Sweeney Todd* goes back to the "penny dreadfuls" of the 1840s. How did Sondheim get the idea for turning it into a musical?

14. One song was cut. What was it and why did it get the ax?

15. If you were a Victorian wigmaker, you'd know the difference between ash and flaxen locks.

16. Why didn't *Sweeney Todd* play out-of-town previews?

17. How many bells are in the Tower of Bray?

18. Who took over the lead roles from Len Cariou and Angela Lansbury?

19. What musical clue to the plot is hidden in "Poor Thing"?

20. Why didn't Len Cariou sing a line in "My Friends" as Sondheim originally wrote it?

21. Why did the cast members object to Pirelli's wagon?

22. Hal Prince's wife had been after him to do a show using teenagers and young people, and he thought he found a good subject in a 1930s comedy about three friends. *Merrily We Roll Along* in 1981 updated the story (book by George Furth), but kept the device of having the plot run backward in time, from 1980 to 1955. Sondheim created one of his finest scores, blending motifs and themes, and illustrating the growing fractures in the trio's friendship.

Yet *Merrily* did not find an audience and lasted just two weeks. Its failure brought an end—at least for many years—to the Sondheim-Prince collaborations.

Which 1930s playwright/s wrote the original play *Merrily We Roll Along*?

    A. Robert Sherwood
    B. George Kaufman and Moss Hart
    C. Philip Barry
    D. Julian Thompson
    E. Ben Hecht and Charles MacArthur

23. In the eighties, Sondheim found a new collaborator, writer-director James Lapine. Lapine was much younger, with a background in poetry and photography. While discussing possible projects, they mused over the many figures depicted in Georges Seurat's *A Sunday Afternoon on the Island of la Grande Jatte*. That became the basis for 1984's *Sunday in the Park with George*, which starred Mandy Patinkin as the painter and Bernadette Peters as his mistress and model. *Sunday* ran for 604 performances, but while it did not win the Tony, it became the sixth musical in history to receive the Pulitzer Prize for drama.

While researching Seurat, Sondheim realized that pointillism had interesting parallels in music and reflected that in the score. Seurat's love of color also comes through in the lyrics, many of which describe the painter at work. Which color is mentioned most often?

    A. purple
    B. yellow
    C. green
    D. red
    E. blue

24. Sondheim and Lapine's second work together was 1987's *Into the Woods*, which looks at fairy tales beyond their simplistic happy endings and into their examples of social irresponsibility. All of the fairy tale characters in the show want something and selfishly go to extremes to get their desires. Their actions, as seen in the darker second act, have an effect on their community and they can survive only by pulling together. *Into the Woods* was a hit, running 764 performances, and Lapine would revive the show (with some changes) in 2002.

Bernadette Peters, on her way to becoming a key Sondheim interpreter, played the Witch opposite Chip Zien and Joanna Gleason as a childless baker and his wife. This couple was invented by Lapine and Sondheim, but the other characters derive from classic children's stories. Which classic character/s was/were cut early in development?

- **A.** Hansel and Gretel
- **B.** Rumpelstiltskin
- **C.** the Frog King
- **D.** Puss in Boots
- **E.** the twelve dancing princesses

25. Sondheim reunited with librettist John Weidman, who had written the book for *Pacific Overtures*, for another historically based musical, 1991's *Assassins*. Sondheim's most controversial work, *Assassins* focuses on nine successful and unsuccessful presidential assassins and their place in American society and culture. The versatile score ranged from Sousa marches to folk numbers to seventies pop, and Weidman's book took the figures out of their historical context, having them mingle in a *Twilight Zone*–style bar, talking with each other despite having existed in different eras.

The show was staged by director Jerry Zaks in revue form, and played off-Broadway in a limited run. When the show finally appeared on Broadway in 2004, it won the Tony as Best Revival, although it technically wasn't one. It has become one of Sondheim's most produced shows in regional and college theatres.

Which historical figure appears in both *Assassins* and *Ragtime*? Hint: this character doesn't get to sing in *Assassins*.

26. 1n 1994, Sondheim and Lapine created *Passion*, a chamber musical inspired by an Italian film that was itself based on a nineteenth-century novel. The tale centers on a trio: handsome soldier Giorgio (Jere Shea), his married mistress Clara (Marin Mazzie), and Fosca (Tony winner Donna Murphy), the ill and neurotic cousin of the commander of Giorgio's regiment, who develops an obsession for the young soldier. Sondheim has described his work in general as "unexpected," a word that certainly applies to *Passion*. Love triangles are a staple of theatre, but this was a very different triangle, and audiences did not always warm to it, even though Sondheim provided another brilliant, heartbreaking score.

During the action, Giorgio's commander reveals that Fosca had been married before, to a man who was a fraud and a bigamist. Where did "Count" Ludovic's wife and child live?

- **A.** Croatia
- **B.** Austria
- **C.** Dalmatia
- **D.** Milan
- **E.** Boca Raton

27. The latest Sondheim book show was one that appeared off-Broadway in 2008. It starred Michael Cerveris and Alexander Gemignani as real-life brothers Addison and Wilson Mizner, and chronicled the years from the Alaskan gold rush through the thirties. The musical had a long and complicated history: Sondheim had been interested in the Mizners for years, and the much revised material (libretto by John Weidman) saw directors Sam Mendes and Hal Prince each take a shot before John Doyle (who had recently staged acclaimed Broadway revivals of *Sweeney Todd* and *Company*) mounted the Public Theatre production.

The show's title changed repeatedly, too. Which of the following was *not* a title for Sondheim's musical about the Mizners?

A. *Road Show*
B. *Wise Guys*
C. *Bounce*
D. *Gold!*
E. *Sentimental Guy*

Answers on page 225.

Irving Berlin

When Jerome Kern was asked to define Irving Berlin's place in American music, he snapped, "Irving Berlin has no place in American music. Irving Berlin *is* American music." The diminutive Russian immigrant, the son of a cantor, spent his whole life making music. As a youth, he was a singing waiter, and published his first song in 1907 at the age of nineteen. He next worked as a Tin Pan Alley songwriter, eventually becoming a major music publisher himself.

He began placing songs in Broadway shows in his twenties, his first big hit being "Alexander's Ragtime Band" in 1911. His first full score was 1914's *Watch Your Step*, featuring Vernon and Irene Castle and their "Syncopated Walk."

1. Over two-thirds of Berlin's shows were revues, so while many of his songs became standards, the shows in which they first appeared are rarely revived. One of these, *Yip Yip Yaphank*, had a rather unusual history. After war had been declared, Berlin was a recruit at Camp Upton. The camp commander hoped to raise money for a new building, and Berlin had the notion of creating a revue about army life, which would be performed entirely by soldiers. Harry Ruby helped fashion the final sketches, which were full of humor and satire, including soldiers dressed as chorus girls. The show raised over eighty thousand dollars, but oddly enough, the proposed building was never built. Sgt. Berlin himself performed the number that became best known. What was it?

✻ ✻

BROADWAY BONUS: Berlin cut a number from *Yip Yip Yaphank* that he felt was too solemn for the comic revue. It gained fame years later. What was it?

✻ ✻

2. Berlin wrote for the *Ziegfeld Follies* in 1910, 1911, 1912, 1916, 1918, 1919, 1920, and 1927. Many regard the 1919 edition as the best in the series, and Berlin wrote most of the score, many of which became hits. Which of these songs from the 1919 *Follies* was *not* by Irving Berlin?

   A. "How Ya Gonna Keep 'Em Down on the Farm (After They've Seen Paree)?"
   B. "A Pretty Girl Is Like a Melody"
   C. "You Cannot Make Your Shimmy Shake on Tea"
   D. "Mandy"
   E. "I Love a Minstrel Show"

3. Sam Harris and Berlin decided they wanted to build a theatre of their own and produce their own revues, less extravagant than Ziegfeld's, but with plenty of good music and classic comedy by George Kaufman and Robert Benchley, among others. The theatre was the Music Box, and the shows were the *Music Box Revues*, which ran annually from 1921 to 1924. When the series ended, Berlin kept the theatre, though Harris began selling his shares to the Shuberts.

    Berlin then wrote the score for the Marx Brothers' *The Cocoanuts* (1925), and added a little number called "Blue Skies" to Rodgers and Hart's *Betsy* (1926), a song which would soon appear in the first film musical, *The Jazz Singer*.

    When the Depression hit, Berlin, Moss Hart, Kaufman, and Harris put together a screwball show to lift New Yorkers' spirits. *Face the Music* (1932) was a silly tale involving corrupt Broadway producers (nah, that idea would never work!), but it was loaded with hits, including the pick-me-up numbers "Let's Have Another Cup o' Coffee" and "I Say It's Spinach and the Hell with It." What was the inspiration for "I Say It's Spinach"?

   A. FDR said he didn't like that vegetable
   B. an overheard conversation in an Automat
   C. Berlin's daughter wouldn't eat her veggies
   D. Berlin himself hated spinach
   E. it's the caption of a *New Yorker* cartoon

4. *As Thousands Cheer* in 1933 was a smash revue that ran for 400 performances—a monster show for the era. Moss Hart wrote the sketches; the star-powered cast included Ethel Waters, Marilyn Miller, Clifton Webb, and Helen Broderick. Miller and Webb complained to Berlin, refusing to take their bows with Waters, who was black. Berlin said that was fine—he'd cut *all* curtain calls. They changed their minds.

    The show's theme was that of a newspaper, with different numbers representing different sections. "Easter Parade," for example, reproduced the rotogravure section, and the show ended with a news feature on a Supreme Court decision declaring the use of reprises to end a musical as unconstitutional. What part of a newspaper was *not* represented in *As Thousands Cheer*?

   A. the classified ads
   B. the weather report
   C. the comics
   D. a news account of the lynching of a Negro man
   E. the Miss Lonely Hearts column

5. Following *As Thousands Cheer*, Berlin spent some years in Hollywood, giving us classic scores like *Top Hat* and *Holiday Inn*. He had a Broadway hit with 1940's

Louisiana Purchase, which parodied Governor Huey Long. And when the United States entered the war, he put together another military revue, *This Is the Army*, benefiting the Army Emergency Relief Fund. He worked again at Camp Upton, using an all-soldier cast, and insisted that the cast include blacks, although the army was still segregated. The show was a hit on Broadway, toured the nation, and was filmed. When the Roosevelts attended, a number with a soldier on K.P. duty had to be altered: security did not want a man with a meat cleaver standing fifteen feet from FDR!

The tour continued to American bases in England where it was so popular, General Eisenhower requested that the company perform closer to the front. *This Is the Army* was staged for thousands of soldiers in Italy, Egypt, New Guinea, the Philippines, Okinawa, and Iwo Jima, ending in Hawaii. Berlin accompanied the unit throughout the tour, enduring shelling, a typhoon, vaccinations against tropical diseases, and the eruption of Mount Vesuvius. The stage version raised over two million dollars for the Fund; the movie earned over ten million.

True or false: Sgt. Berlin reprised his number from *Yip Yip Yaphank* in *This Is the Army*.

6. After the war's end came Berlin's biggest hit—for a show he wasn't supposed to write. Jerome Kern, contracted for the score of *Annie Get Your Gun*, suffered a fatal stroke. Producers Rodgers and Hammerstein asked Berlin if he'd take the job. He wasn't sure if he could handle "the hillbilly sound," but using the libretto by Dorothy and Herbert Fields for inspiration, he knocked out ten songs in eight days. Legend has it he wrote "Anything You Can Do" in a taxicab. The 1946 show, starring the amazing Ethel Merman as sharpshooter Annie Oakley, ran for 1,147 performances. Because of its combination of strong book and many classic songs, it is probably Berlin's best-known work.

Ray Middleton played Frank Butler, Annie's rival sharpshooter and love interest. Frank declares he's "A Bad, Bad Man" whose exploits have made it impossible for him to return to parts of the country. Which of these locales is *not* on his list?
   A. Texas
   B. Wyoming
   C. Arkansas
   D. Omaha
   E. Tennessee

7. *Miss Liberty* (1949), with book by Robert Sherwood, direction by Moss Hart, and choreography by Jerome Robbins, was a failure at 308 performances. The plot concerned two rival newspapers in the 1880s and the creation of the Statue of Liberty. Berlin got a standard out of "Let's Take an Old-Fashioned Walk," which was recorded by Sinatra, Como, Martin, and other crooners. But late forties audiences found the musical unappealing.

Berlin nearly always wrote his own lyrics, but he had a co-lyricist for the final number. Who was it?
   A. Robert Sherwood
   B. Cole Porter
   C. Emma Lazarus

D. Moss Hart

E. Joseph Pulitzer

8. Berlin was soon back on top with *Call Me Madam* (1950), starring Ethel Merman as a thinly disguised version of Perle Mesta, society hostess turned into a U.S. ambassador. *Madam*, with book by Russel Crouse and Howard Lindsay, direction by George Abbott, and choreography by Jerome Robbins, ran for 644 performances. Several songs became hits, including "They Like Ike," which was revised into a campaign song for Eisenhower; "It's a Lovely Day Today"; and "You're Just in Love," a eleven o'clock quodlibet for Merman and Russell Nype that brought the house down every night (reportedly seven encores in Boston).

    The Merm was, of course, one of a kind, but who was her standby and later played "The Hostess with the Mostes'" on tour?

A. Reta Shaw

B. Vivian Blaine

C. Helen Gallagher

D. Elaine Stritch

E. Nanette Fabray

9. Berlin's last original Broadway musical was *Mr. President* (1962), which steamed into town with a two-million-dollar advance and promptly steamed out as soon as the advance vanished. Cold War tensions didn't help audiences warm to the muddled tale of a family in the White House, despite the charming presence of Nanette Fabray and Anita Gillette. Berlin, after more than a half century of writing show tunes, realized that the contemporary music scene was changing, and acknowledged that in one number. Well, he tried. While some of the older characters longed to waltz again, the younger set clearly prefer which of these dances?

A. the "Beltway Bossa Nova"

B. the "Washington Square Dance"

C. the "Congressional Boogaloo"

D. the "Washington Twist"

E. the "Mashed Potato"

10. Berlin had one more song hit up his sleeve. It came in the 1966 revival of *Annie Get Your Gun*, which starred Ethel Merman, twenty years after she first plugged bull's-eyes. Despite being long in the tooth, she was still the Merm, and the show was a smash all over again. Berlin wrote a new comedy duet for Merman and Bruce Yarnell in the contrapuntal style of *Call Me Madam*'s "You're Just in Love." It got so many encores on opening night that some critics had to leave before the finale to file their reviews on time. What was the song?

Answers on page 226.

Cy Coleman

1. Cy Coleman, one of Broadway's premiere composers, wrote the scores for ten different shows, working with several different lyricists. He began as a child prodigy, then

performed as a jazz pianist in nightclubs. His first show was *Wildcat* in 1960 (lyrics by Carolyn Leigh). The big draw was the star/producer, Lucille Ball, who played Wildcat Jackson, a fast-talkin' gal who gains both a husband and a gusher in this tale of the oil boom of 1912. But she left when the rigors of stage performances wore on her, pleading illness and exhaustion, and *Wildcat* promptly folded. Who wrote the libretto?

   A. Jerome Weidman

   B. N. Richard Nash

   C. Richard Morris

   D. Abe Burrows

   E. Michael Stewart

2. You'd think with the talent involved—a Neil Simon libretto based on a Patrick Dennis novel, Cy Feuer and Bob Fosse's direction, Fosse dances, Coleman and Leigh's songs, and Sid Caesar in the lead—*Little Me* would have been a smash. Yet it never took off, despite a fine score. Caesar played seven roles himself, while the lead female role of Belle Poitrine (neé Schlumpfort) was portrayed by two actresses, one older, one younger. Who were they?

3. *Sweet Charity* (1966) was one of Coleman's biggest hits. He teamed with the ageless Dorothy Fields for lyrics. Fosse directed his brilliant wife, Gwen Verdon, as the irrepressible Charity Hope Valentine, the dance hall gal with the ever hopeful attitude. What name is tattooed on Charity's arm?

   A. Bobby

   B. Oscar

   C. George

   D. Billy

   E. Charlie

4. Coleman rejoined Fields (her last show after a half century in the biz) for the 1973 Michael Bennett production, *Seesaw*. The show, featuring a romance between a Midwestern lawyer and a nutty New York dancer, wasn't a success, but it did create a hit song. "It's Not Where You Start" was originally written five years before for an unproduced musical about which First Lady?

   A. Eleanor Roosevelt

   B. Dolly Madison

   C. Rachel Jackson

   D. Abigail Adams

   E. Edith Wilson

5. After Fields' death, Coleman worked with Michael Stewart on the sexy, swinging *I Love My Wife* (1977). While dwarfed by the season's smash about that orphan kid, it proved a hit. True or false: it was based on the film *Bob and Carol and Ted and Alice*.

6. Coleman, ever versatile, produced a delightful operetta-style score for the over-the-top antics of scheming producer Oscar Jaffe and his protégé-turned-star Lily Garland in *On the Twentieth Century* (1978). Comden and Green wrote the book and lyrics, while Hal Prince kept the frenetic pace going. Imogene Coca captivated

audiences as the religious nut, Mrs. Primrose, but she wasn't the first choice. Which of the following actresses turned down the part, claiming the lyrics to "Repent" were too dirty?

   A. Ethel Merman

   B. Lillian Roth

   C. Ethel Shutta

   D. Mildred Natwick

   E. Gretchen Wyler

7. Coleman had Stewart as lyricist again for the cleverly staged circus bio-musical *Barnum* (1980). Which of the following circus acts was *not* re-created in *Barnum*?

   A. Jumbo the elephant

   B. the oldest woman in the world

   C. General Tom Thumb

   D. Sophie the seal

   E. Jenny Lind, the Swedish nightingale

8. My personal favorite among Coleman's shows is 1989's *City of Angels* (David Zippel, lyrics; sidesplitting libretto, Larry Gelbart), about the creation of a detective movie in the 1940s. Coleman's jazzy score perfectly complemented Gelbart's plot and director Michael Blakemore added the crowning touch by dividing the set into black-and-white for the movie screenplay scenes and color for the "real life" scenes. Identify the earlier title (or titles) of Gelbart's libretto.

   A. *Double Talk*

   B. *Death Is for Suckers*

   C. *Double Exposure*

   D. A and B

   E. B and C

9. Coleman reunited with Comden and Green for 1991's Tony-winning *The Will Rogers Follies*. Directed by Tommy Tune and with a book by Peter Stone, it presented the comedian's life as a kind of Ziegfeld revue. Whose tape-recorded voice portrayed Flo Ziegfeld?

   A. Gregory Peck

   B. Donald Trump

   C. Burt Lancaster

   D. John Houseman

   E. Robert Mitchum

10. Coleman's final score was for 1997's *The Life*, a saga of prostitutes and pimps on 42nd Street. Ira Gassman did the lyrics and collaborated on the book with Coleman and David Newman. This show took years to get from workshop to the Great White Way, including time spent producing an all-star concept album. Despite some good songs, it flopped. How many years did it take from workshop to Broadway? Hint: it equals how many millions *The Life* lost.

   A. 4

   B. 5

   C. 6

D. 7

E. 8

Answers on page 227.

Andrew Lloyd Webber

1. Andrew Lloyd Webber and his friend Tim Rice began working together as teens in the mid-sixties. In 1968, they created a cantata for a children's school concert based on the Biblical story of Joseph, which attracted a good notice from music critic Derek Jewell, whose son attended the school. Lloyd Webber and Rice continued to expand and revise the piece, which gained popularity through many regional performances, including the Edinburgh Festival. It made it to the West End in 1973 and off-Broadway three years later. The work was *Joseph and the Amazing Technicolor Dreamcoat* and it established the pair in the world of musical theatre.

What color is *not* mentioned in Joseph's coat?

A. lilac

B. turquoise

C. russet

D. mauve

E. azure

2. As possibilities for their next project, the duo next compiled a list of historical figures who died young, but had an impact on the world. They tinkered with *Come Back, Richard, Your Country Needs You*, based on the life of medieval king Richard the Lionhearted and his troubadour, Blondel, before shelving it. (Rice would revise this material as *Blondel* in 1983 with music by Stephen Oliver.) They settled on *Jesus Christ Superstar*, but unlike *Joseph*, this would not be a kids' show. They created a concept album in 1970, and its success led to a Broadway opening. Tom O'Horgan, who had done another rock musical, *Hair*, directed, filling the show with spectacle and special effects. Ben Vereen got raves as Judas, and the show ran for 721 performances. Not bad, but the London production, directed by Jim Sharman as more in keeping with the creators' intentions, ran for eight years.

On that fateful concept album, the part of Jesus was sung by the lead singer of which rock group?

A. The Who

B. Emerson, Lake and Palmer

C. the Moody Blues

D. Deep Purple

E. Jethro Tull

3. Lloyd Webber next wanted to adapt P. G. Wodehouse's stories about the incomparable manservant, Jeeves, but Rice abandoned it. Alan Ayckbourn handled the book and lyrics for Lloyd Webber's *Jeeves* in 1975, but it flopped miserably. (They revised it again in the 1990s, and it limped along on Broadway in 2001 for several months.) Rice then heard a radio play about Eva Peron and had the notion of telling her story, using the figure of an Everyman, "Che," as a commentator. The concept album of *Evita* was a smash. Hal Prince came across the Atlantic to direct the stage version with Elaine Paige and would also handle the hit Broadway production in 1979 (567 performances). *Evita* would sweep the Tonys, winning seven, including awards for Patti LuPone, Mandy Patinkin, Prince, and Lloyd Webber and Rice's book and score.

Where does Eva go on her Rainbow tour?

4. *Song and Dance* (1982, London) began as a one-act, *Tell Me on a Sunday* (1979), about a British girl, Emma, in the States. Don Black wrote the lyrics for the piece, which was then paired with a 1978 work, *Variations*, the "dance" half of *Song and Dance*. Richard Maltby, Jr., directed the Broadway production, which opened in 1985 (474 performances) and earned Bernadette Peters a Tony. Who played Emma at the end of the Broadway run?
   A. Melissa Manchester
   B. Betty Buckley
   C. Marti Webb
   D. Loni Ackerman
   E. Elaine Paige

5. Lloyd Webber had had the idea for a show based on T. S. Eliot's poems about cats for years, but nobody thought it would work until British producer Cameron Mackintosh suggested that Trevor Nunn of the Royal Shakespeare Company get involved. Nunn looked at Eliot's papers with his widow's permission, and concocted the notion of a Heaviside Layer, to which good cats may ascend after their nine lives. The result was *Cats*, one of the longest-running shows in history (London, 8,950 performances; Broadway, 7,485 performances). When creating the show, Lloyd Webber and Nunn realized they needed a big number for Grizabella, though there wasn't anything appropriate in Eliot's cat poems. Using parts of another Eliot poem, "Rhapsody on a Windy Night," who helped write the lyrics to "Memory"?
   A. Don Black
   B. Tim Rice
   C. Richard Stilgoe
   D. Trevor Nunn
   E. Charles Hart

6. As a longtime rail buff, Lloyd Webber had enjoyed the British children's books by the Rev. Ardry about Thomas the Tank Engine. He worked up some sketches of a train adventure for his kids in 1982, but seeing an old steam railroad in Connecticut gave him the notion of a train Cinderella story. Richard Stilgoe wrote the lyrics for *Starlight Express*; Lloyd Webber composed pastiches of American musical styles, from country to gospel; and Trevor Nunn returned to direct. The show opened in London in 1984 and ran for an amazing eighteen years, as audiences marveled at actors on wheels whizzing around John Napier's set of tracks and bridges running out into the house. The Broadway production in 1987 managed 761 performances, but lost money; for whatever reason, the trains didn't catch on with American audiences.

Which of the following was not a name for a train in *Starlight Express*?

A. Diesel
B. Rusty
C. Electra
D. Greaseball
E. Red Caboose

7. Lloyd Webber next wanted to do "a romantic musical." Fortunately, so did Hal Prince after a few gritty, serious flops. They created what is now the longest-running musical in Broadway history, *The Phantom of the Opera* (1988). Richard Stilgoe, and then Charles Hart, came in to work on the lyrics; Michael Crawford and Sarah Brightman (then Mrs. Lloyd Webber) starred; and the show shattered records on both sides of the Atlantic. Which of the following is *not* true about *The Phantom of the Opera*?

   A. the Phantom's name is Erik
   B. the chandelier weighs 3/4 of a ton and has 6,000 beads
   C. Lloyd Webber asked Lionel Bart to do the lyrics, but he was too ill
   D. five men who played Raoul on Broadway would go on to play the title role
   E. over 80 million people have seen it

8. *Aspects of Love* had a lengthy history before reaching Broadway in 1990. Lloyd Webber had long been intrigued with David Garnett's book, and, with Tim Rice, first tinkered with it in 1980. Rice moved on to *Chess*, and Lloyd Webber created a cabaret version with Trevor Nunn in 1983, but then used some of that music for *Phantom*. For the final version of *Aspects*, he used some material he had written with Rice for the short piece called *Cricket* (1986), written for the Queen. Don Black and Charles Hart wrote the lyrics for *Aspects*, a chamber piece of shifting, kaleidoscopic love relationships. As with some of Lloyd Webber's other works, it did better in the West End (1,325 performances) than New York (337).

   Which British actor was originally going to play Uncle George, but withdrew shortly before the London opening, believing his singing wasn't strong enough?

   A. Sean Connery
   B. Roger Moore
   C. Sylvester McCoy
   D. Patrick McNee
   E. David McCallum

9. Lloyd Webber had hoped to do a musical version of the classic film *Sunset Boulevard* since the 1970s. He worked with screenwriter Christopher Hampton and lyricist Don Black to create a work that wasn't through-sung as many of his musicals were, but was heavily underscored. Patti LuPone opened as Norma Desmond in London in 1993, Glenn Close on Broadway the following year. (See the Patti LuPone quiz for further details.) The musical was a fairly faithful adaptation of the film, with a jazzy beat for the industry insiders and appropriate star-power numbers for Norma.

   What's the title of the script Joe and Betty write?

   A. "Blind Windows"
   B. "Girl Meets Boy"
   C. "Salome"
   D. "Mad About the Boy"
   E. "Bases Loaded"

10. Following *Sunset Boulevard*, Lloyd Webber presented his revised *By Jeeves* in London (1996) and New York (2001). Two other shows failed to reach Broadway. *Whistle Down the Wind*, based on the film in which poor rural children mistake a runaway convict for Jesus, had a West End run from 1998 to 2001, but folded in Washington. *The Beautiful Game*, which centered on soccer fans in 1960s Northern Ireland, ran in London in 2000. He produced *Bombay Dreams* in 2004, with music by A. R. Rahman and lyrics by Don Black. Lloyd Webber returned to composing with lyricist David Zippel and old comrades Trevor Nunn and Michael Crawford for *The Woman in White*, based on the Wilkie Collins novel. This spooky tale starred Maria Friedman, who came over for the brief Broadway run in 2005 despite a recent diagnosis of breast cancer. Michael Ball replaced Crawford as the fiendish Count Fosco.

The Woman in White was:
- **A.** a ghost
- **B.** a Victorian governess
- **C.** a mysterious bride
- **D.** a girl trapped in an asylum against her will
- **E.** Count Fosco's pet mouse

Answers on page 227.

William Finn

William Finn is one of the most talented and innovative songwriters working in theatre today. His songs are always highly crafted, and his lyrics are insightful and enlightening. In addition to composing, he teaches at NYU's graduate school, helping future musical theatre innovators.

1. William Finn's first produced musical was *In Trousers* (1979, off-Broadway), the first of three short musicals dealing with a Jewish man, Marvin, who leaves his wife and son for his lover, Whizzer. Finn wrote the book, music, and lyrics for *In Trousers*, and directed the original production. He revised it in 1981, adding and deleting songs and giving Marvin's wife a name (Trina), and again in 1985, when it played at the off-Broadway Promenade Theatre. Who played Marvin in the 1979 and 1985 productions, and what roles did these actors play in the other parts of the Marvin trilogy?

2. Marvin's story continues in 1981's *March of the Falsettos*, directed by James Lapine. Marvin attempts to balance his life between his lover and his ex-wife and son, while his psychiatrist, Mendel, marries his ex-wife. His son, Jason (who may be the most intelligent character in the trilogy), comes to grips not only with his father's sexuality, but his own individualism.

Finn added a song to the Los Angeles production of *March of the Falsettos* that was originally written for 1981 version of *In Trousers*. What was it?
- **A.** "The Thrill of First Love"
- **B.** "My Father's a Homo"
- **C.** "I'm Breaking Down"
- **D.** "The Games I Play"
- **E.** "Making a Home"

3. In 1983, Finn wrote the score for a musical set in a New York soup kitchen during the Depression, *America Kicks Up Its Heels*, which lasted only a handful of performances. In 1987, he penned the lyrics to Astor Piazolla's music for the off-Broadway show *Tango Apasionado*, which was later remounted and briefly ran on Broadway as *Dangerous Games*. Librettists Graciela Daniele (who also choreographed and directed) and Jim Lewis dedicated the show to the *desparecidos*, those who vanished following arrests by Argentina's military dictators. What Greek legend acts as an analogy to the plight of the "disappeared ones"?

    A. Antigone
    B. Prometheus
    C. Demeter and Persephone
    D. Orpheus and Eurydice
    E. Pygmalion and Galatea

4. Finn revised *America Kicks Up Its Heels* as 1989's *Romance in Hard Times* for the Public Theatre, but it too flopped. He had far better luck with *Falsettoland* (off-Broadway, 1990). The third installment of the Marvin trilogy, it addressed the devastating impact of AIDS on Marvin's extended family. In 1992, Finn and Lapine combined *March of the Falsettos* and *Falsettoland* into *Falsettos*, which ran on Broadway for 487 performances and won Tonys for Best Book and Best Score. Stephen Bogardus, Michael Rupert, Chip Zien, and Heather MacRae from the off-Broadway productions reprised their roles.

In *Falsettoland*, who (or what) does everyone hate?

    A. his psychiatrist
    B. his parents
    C. the umpire
    D. bar mitzvahs
    E. racquetball

5. In the early 1990s, Finn began writing lyrics to Jerry Bock's music for a project that never came to fruition. Finn abandoned it first, then Bock did too, after trying his hand at lyric writing. What was the plot based on?

    A. the works of Jorge Luis Borges
    B. the movie *Groundhog Day*
    C. Tevye's family after they came to America
    D. Noel Coward's *Hay Fever*
    E. the U.S. income tax code

6. In 1998, Finn and several other playwrights (he's multitalented), including John Guare, Tony Kushner, and Wendy Wasserstein, wrote one-act plays inspired by Shakespearean sonnets for the Acting Company. Finn's work, titled *Painting*, was based on Sonnet 102. What celebrated composer contributed incidental music in this production?

    A. Jason Robert Brown
    B. Jeanine Tesori
    C. Andrew Lippa
    D. Adam Guettel
    E. Michael John LaChiusa

7. Following his own serious battle with a misdiagnosed brain tumor, Finn collaborated with librettist-director James Lapine on the off-Broadway show *A New Brain* (1998). The plot centered on a songwriter, Gordon Schwinn (Malcolm Gets), who is hospitalized with a brain disorder and fears death in large part because of all the songs he hasn't yet had the chance to write. Kristin Chenoweth was in the ensemble, and also played the Mean Nurse and a waitress serving which of the following dishes?

   A. calamari

   B. f***ing rolls

   C. fettucini Alfredo Drake

   D. egg rolls

   E. a plate of sardines

8. Finn's next hit was 2005's *The 25th Annual Putnam County Spelling Bee*, a show about competitors in a middle-school spelling contest. The score is delightfully quirky and sometimes quite moving; Finn's personal favorite is the heartbreaking "I Love You Song." Part of the show's charm came from the use of four audience members as fellow participants, which harkens back to its roots in improvisational theatre. *Spelling Bee* began as *C-R-E-P-U-S-C-U-L-E*, an improv piece at Rebecca Feldman's The Farm. A friend of Finn's saw the potential for a musical, and sent him a videotape. One of Finn's former NYU students, Rachel Sheikin, wrote the libretto, winning the Tony for Best Book. (Dan Fogler, who originated the role of William Barfée in *C-R-E-P-U-S-C-U-L-E*, won the Tony for Best Featured Actor.)

   Spelling Bee was a 2004 workshop that turned into an off-Broadway success, moving to Broadway's Circle in the Square Theatre in 2005 for a 1,136-performance run.

   Who was Finn's friend whose insight helped bring about one of the most unusual musicals of the decade?

   A. Graciela Daniele

   B. Alison Fraser

   C. James Lapine

   D. Carolee Carmello

   E. Wendy Wasserstein

❧ ❧

BROADWAY BONUS: What is the mascot of the Putnam Valley Middle School? And when Julie Andrews joined the spellers one night, what word did she misspell?

❧ ❧

9. Finn's songs have been performed in three different revues, all of which have been released as albums. Two of them, *Infinite Joy* (2000) and *Make Me a Song* (2007) consisted largely of material included in or cut from Finn's musicals, both produced and unproduced. The third, *Elegies: A Song Cycle* (2003) collected songs written to commemorate the passing of friends and family, including his mother, and several gay friends who died of AIDS. But while the songs tug at one's heart, the overall effect is a celebration of life.

   What noted theatrical figure was among those Finn commemorated in *Elegies*?

A. Joseph Papp
B. Boris Aronson
C. Vincent Sardi, Jr.
D. Jule Styne
E. Imogene Coca

10. Dedicated Finn fans know he has been working for many years on a musical adaptation of a classic American comedy. It sadly seems the show will be relegated to the Land of Lost Musicals, but at least we can hear some of the songs in various Finn collections. What was the basis for the proposed musical?
    A. Kaufman and Hart's *You Can't Take It with You*
    B. Wilder's *The Skin of Our Teeth*
    C. Barry's *The Philadelphia Story*
    D. Kaufman and Hart's *Beggar on Horseback*
    E. Kaufman and Ferber's *The Royal Family*

Answers on page 228.

Jerome Kern

1. Jerome Kern was one of the early giants of American musical theatre, and he helped create this unique art form. He spent many of his formative years writing interpolations for shows both in London's West End and on Broadway. Who produced most of these early twentieth-century shows containing early Kern tunes (and who hired him in England, mistakenly believing he was a Brit)?
    A. Florence Ziegfeld
    B. David Belasco
    C. Charles Dillingham
    D. Charles Frohman
    E. Jay Shubert

❧ ❧

BROADWAY BONUS: How did this producer die, and how did this relate to Kern?

❧ ❧

2. One of Kern's early commercial hits was an interpolation, "They Didn't Believe Me," which appeared in:
    A. *The Earl and the Girl*
    B. *The Girl from Utah*
    C. *The Girl and the Wizard*
    D. *The Girls of Gottenberg*
    E. *The "Mind-the-Paint" Girl*

3. In 1915, agent Bessie Marbury developed a plan to save Ray Comstock's tiny (299 seats) Princess Theatre. They would limit productions to a modest budget, a two-set maximum, a small cast and orchestra, and use contemporary settings to avoid the costs of exotically costumed operettas. These intentions fit well with Kern, who had

been working toward more integrated musicals. Collaborating with librettist Guy Bolton and lyricist P. G. Wodehouse, he forever changed musical theatre, creating a series of intimate, energetic shows with characters and songs that fit naturally into the action. They proved quite popular, and greatly influenced the next generation of Broadway songwriters, including George Gershwin and Rodgers and Hart. Which of the following was a "Princess show" that opened at the much larger Longacre Theatre?

A. *Oh, Boy!*

B. *Oh, Lady! Lady!*

C. *Leave It to Jane*

D. *Very Good Eddie*

E. *Nobody Home*

4. Flo Ziegfeld, master of the revue, wanted to get in on the growing popularity of the musical comedy. He assembled a dream team that, through much turmoil, created the 1920 blockbuster *Sally*. With Kern's score, Bolton's book, Joseph Urban's sets, and the fabulous Marilyn Miller as the poor dishwasher who eventually weds the rich gent, it ran for 570 performances. The score included several numbers originally written for other shows, a common occurrence in the era. Two of the biggest hits, "Look for the Silver Lining" and "Whip-poor-will," came from *Zip! Goes a Million*, a Princess show that closed in tryouts in 1919. Who was the lyricist?

A. Clifford Grey

B. Anne Caldwell

C. Herbert Reynolds

D. Bud (B.G.) DeSylva

E. Howard Dietz

5. Kern teamed up for the first time with lyricists/librettists Otto Harbach and Oscar Hammerstein II in 1925's smash *Sunny*, again starring Marilyn Miller (but lavishly produced by Ziegfeld's rival Charles Dillingham). It was a whimsical spectacle, with scenes set in a circus, on an ocean liner, and during a fox hunt, all the while keeping room for Miller's tap-dance specialty, Ukelele Ike's specialty (performed at precisely 10:00 p.m.), and live circus animals. What was the hit song from *Sunny*?

A. "Whose Baby Are You?"

B. "Babes in the Woods"

C. "Make Believe"

D. "Till the Clouds Roll By"

E. "Who?"

6. Kern had read Edna Ferber's sprawling novel *Show Boat* and saw the possibilities in it. At a Broadway opening, he approached a man whom he knew was a friend of the author and asked if he could arrange a meeting. The man turned to the woman next to him and said, "Ferber, this is Jerome Kern. Kern, this is Ferber." Who was the man?

7. Having gotten the rights from Ferber, Kern paired once again with Oscar Hammerstein to create *Show Boat* (1927), one of the masterpieces of musical theatre. It broke ground as no show had done before, with its integrated cast, a saga that spanned

more than forty years, its controversial and dramatic storyline, and its use of music as subtext. Kern took a year to complete the score, and Flo Ziegfeld backed the show, providing Joseph Urban sets and a cast of nearly one hundred. Who was *not* a member of that opening-night cast?

    A. Howard Marsh

    B. Norma Terris

    C. Helen Morgan

    D. Paul Robeson

    E. Charles Winninger

8. What gave Kern the inspiration for the melody of "I've Told Ev'ry Little Star," the hit from 1932's *Music in the Air*?

    A. a green finch

    B. a Nantucket songbird

    C. Dorothy Hammerstein's canary

    D. a rippling brook

    E. a Bavarian linnet

9. Kern and Otto Harbach paired for the 1933 hit *Roberta*, a show that got its success from its incredible score, since the plot involving a Russian princess, a Parisian dress shop, and an American football player was fairly trite. Which of these hits was *not* included in *Roberta*'s Broadway score?

    A. "Lovely to Look At"

    B. "Smoke Gets in Your Eyes"

    C. "The Touch of Your Hand"

    D. "You're Devastating"

    E. "Yesterdays"

10. Kern had agreed to work on a new show with lyrics to be written by Dorothy Fields (with whom he had worked in Hollywood) when he died following a stroke in 1945. The show was produced the following year with a different composer/lyricist. Who was it and what was the show?

Answers on page 229.

Jule Styne

Jule Styne was one of the greats of Broadway. Born in 1905, he began as a child prodigy, but ended up preferring popular music to classical, especially after suffering an injury to his fingers. He formed his own dance band, was a player in burlesque pits, then headed to Hollywood. Styne worked as a vocal coach at first, then began composing for films in the late thirties and forties, ending up with ten Oscar nominations and one win ("Three Coins in the Fountain"). When he came to Broadway, he wrote the scores for a couple dozen shows, ranging from smash hits like *Funny Girl* to disasters that closed on the road like *Prettybelle*. He also occasionally directed and was a notable producer; his revival of *Pal Joey* in 1952 made many people realize the importance of that show.

1. Jule Styne, like Cy Coleman, worked with many different lyricists over his long career, teaming most often with Sammy Cahn, Betty Comden, and Adolph Green. Who among the following did *not* pen lyrics to a Styne tune?
   A. Don Black
   B. Yip Harburg
   C. Dorothy Fields
   D. Herb Gardner
   E. Stephen Sondheim

2. While Styne and Sammy Cahn had had good fortune in Hollywood, their first musical, *Glad to See You!*, closed in Philadelphia in 1944. Undaunted, they tried again in 1947 with *High Button Shoes*, a smash comedy that ran for 727 performances. The story was set in 1913 New Jersey, where con man Harrison Floy (Phil Silvers) tries to fleece the Longstreet family. George Abbott directed the romp, and, with Silvers, heavily revised Stephen Longstreet's original libretto. Jerome Robbins' choreography, including the landmark "Mack Sennett Ballet," helped win over audiences, and a couple of Styne's songs ("Papa, Won't You Dance with Me?" and "I Still Get Jealous") became hits.

   Silvers was the standout character, but he was backed by forty-seven-year-old Jack McCauley as Papa Longstreet, and a twenty-five-year-old actress as Mama (with a thirteen-year-old stage son!). Who was the young, talented lady playing a character beyond her years?
   A. Yvonne de Carlo
   B. Vivian Blaine
   C. Nanette Fabray
   D. Judy Holliday
   E. Beatrice Arthur

3. Styne followed *High Button Shoes* with an even bigger hit, 1949's *Gentlemen Prefer Blondes*. Leo Robin penned the lyrics for Styne's lively score, and Anita Loos wrote the book based on her own novel. The show starred Carol Channing and Yvonne Adair as gold diggers Lorelei Lee and Dorothy Shaw, out looking for sugar daddies in the Roaring Twenties. Wealthy Henry Spofford (Eric Brotherson) romances Dorothy, but she isn't sure she'd fit in the locale he suggests as their possible future home. Where was it?
   A. Greenwich Village
   B. Chelsea
   C. Little Rock
   D. the Left Bank of the Seine
   E. Rittenhouse Square

4. Throughout the fifties, Styne became a double threat on Broadway. He produced *Make a Wish* (1951), *Pal Joey* (1952), and *Mr. Wonderful* (1956). As composer, he teamed for the first time with lyricists Betty Comden and Adolph Green for the 1951 revue *Two on the Aisle*, worked with Bob Hilliard on the flop *Hazel Flagg* (1953), then joined Comden and Green again at Jerome Robbins' request in 1954 to add songs to *Peter Pan*.

Styne, Comden, and Green's next offering would be one of their most successful shows. *Bells Are Ringing* in 1956, starring the wonderful comic talents of Judy Holliday, would stay on the boards for 924 performances. The show concerned the adventures of a young lady who works at a telephone answering service and meddles in the lives of her clients. She has fallen for one, a young playwright named Jeff (Sydney Chaplin). Jeff, who has never seen her, calls her one of the following names. What is it?

A. Granny

B. Ella

C. Melisande

D. Mom

E. Susanswerphone

5. The trio reunited in 1958 to provide nine songs for *Say, Darling*, a play by Abe Burrows and Richard and Marian Bissell. Richard Bissell had written the novel *7 1/2 Cents*, which he co-adapted into the musical *The Pajama Game*. He turned that experience into another novel, *Say, Darling*, which then became the 1958 play. Styne's songs were all intended as material for the show within the show, so *Say, Darling*, despite its fine pedigree, isn't a true musical. Robert Morse attracted the best notices, playing a character inspired by someone from *The Pajama Game*. Who was it?

A. Hal Prince

B. Bob Fosse

C. John Raitt

D. David Merrick

E. Agnes de Mille

6. The year 1959 saw Styne working with librettist Arthur Laurents, lyricist Stephen Sondheim, and director Jerome Robbins for one of the greatest musicals of all time, *Gypsy*, starring the one and only Ethel Merman. The show was based on the memoirs of stripper Gypsy Rose Lee, and Styne's years of playing in burlesque pits gave him the unique background to write the score. That said, he reworked one of the songs, "You'll Never Get Away from Me," from an earlier tune. Where did that melody first appear?

A. *The Little Colonel* (a Shirley Temple film)

B. *Three Coins in the Fountain* (film)

C. *Ice Capades of 1943*

D. *Michael Todd's Peep Show*

E. *Ruggles of Red Gap* (a TV musical)

7. Styne returned to Comden and Green for 1960's *Do Re Mi* and 1961's *Subways Are for Sleeping*, but it was with Bob Merrill that he had his longest-running show, *Funny Girl* (1964, 1,348 performances). They had previously worked on an animated television special, *Mr. Magoo's Christmas Carol*, and eagerly tackled the subject of the musical version of Fanny Brice's life, with libretto by Isobel Lennart. The star of the show was Barbra Streisand, in what would be her breakout role.

Yet all was not well in *Funny Girl*'s tryouts. One number was playing so poorly that director Garson Kanin wanted it cut. Which number was it?

A. "Don't Rain on My Parade"

B. "The Music That Makes Me Dance"

C. "I'm the Greatest Star"

D. "People"

E. "Cornet Man"

8. While *Funny Girl* ran and ran, Styne's next offering quickly vanished. *Fade Out—Fade In* (1964), a satire of Hollywood in the thirties written with Comden and Green, faded out after 199 performances. The show's fortunes were hurt when star Carol Burnett suffered an auto accident. She returned after an absence, but left again to work on a television program, leading to a lawsuit from the producers. Styne penned some nice tunes, but Comden and Green had better success spoofing Hollywood studios in *Singin' in the Rain*.

In *Fade Out—Fade In*, who or what was "Smaxie?"

A. Carol Burnett's pet dachshund

B. the name of a trained seal who was the logo for the studio

C. Tina Louise's sultry character

D. the title of the movie Burnett promotes on a sandwich board

E. the name of the diner where Burnett is discovered by studio boss Jack Cassidy

9. Styne's next show, while not as long running as *Gypsy* or *Funny Girl*, was the production that finally won Tonys for Best Musical and Best Composer. What was it?

10. Nearly all of the last ten shows on which Styne worked flopped, with runs in either single or double digits. *Prettybelle* (1971), with Angela Lansbury, closed in Boston. *Pieces of Eight* (1985) closed in Canada. *Lorelei* (1972), a reworking of *Gentlemen Prefer Blondes*, managed 320 performances in 1974 on the familiarity of the material and the presence of Carol Channing.

Sugar (1972), with lyrics by Bob Merrill and book by Peter Stone, was Styne's last hit. This David Merrick–produced show was an adaptation of the film comedy *Some Like It Hot*, with Robert Morse and Tony Roberts as the guys in drag on the run from the mob. Gower Champion directed, and with the help of associate choreographer Bert Michaels, devised an idea for a number that was highly dependent on rhythm. Styne remained unconvinced it could work until they demonstrated, using the drummer to produce the needed beats. The number, highlighting machine-gun taps, became a standout in the show. What was it?

A. "The Beauty That Drives Men Mad"

B. "We Could Be Close"

C. "Tear the Town Apart"

D. "Hey, Why Not?"

E. "Doing It for Sugar"

Answers on page 230.

Noel Coward

Noel Coward was one of the treasures of the British stage, but also attained great popularity in America. Born in 1899, he went onstage as a child performer, where he would meet his lifelong friend, Gertrude Lawrence. Coward was a quadruple threat: he could act, write, compose songs, and direct. As is the case for many composers who worked in the first half of the twentieth century, many of Coward's shows can't be revived today, either because of topicality or because musical conventions have changed too much. But a great number of Coward songs have stood the test of time on their own, as have many of his plays. He was a unique voice in the history of musical theatre, and truly deserved the title "the Master."

1. Late in World War I, Coward was drafted, but a concussion in training meant he never saw combat. He had already begun writing plays, and would have his first produced when he was just twenty. He then provided most of the songs and sketches for a 1923 revue, *London Calling!*, and ended up with the leading male role. One number, "Parisian Pierrot," became such a hit that Cecil Beaton later called it "the signature tune of the twenties," and it was lovingly spoofed in *The Boy Friend*.

   Who helped Coward with some of the dance numbers for *London Calling!*? Hint: this person also attended classes with Coward at the Guildhall School of Music, and his/her sibling married into the British aristocracy.
   A. Fred Astaire
   B. Ivor Novello
   C. Gertrude Lawrence
   D. Jack Hubert
   E. Beatrice Lillie

2. Coward's next play, *The Vortex* (1924), was a smash, but while he was performing in that show, he also worked on another revue and the play *Fallen Angels*. He came with *The Vortex* to Broadway, then returned to England, turning out more hit shows (*Hay Fever, Easy Virtue*) and the revue *This Year of Grace* (1928). This show starred Maisie Gay, Jessie Matthews, and Sonnie Hale, running nearly a year. Bea Lillie and Coward led the Broadway cast, which might have run longer, but Coward had a penchant for growing bored with a role after three months or so. The score provided Coward with many popular hits. Which of these standards was *not* from *This Year of Grace*?
   A. "The Lorelei"
   B. "World Weary"
   C. "Don't Let's Be Beastly to the Germans"
   D. "A Room with a View"
   E. "Dance, Little Lady"

3. Coward's 1929 operetta *Bitter Sweet* never won the critics, but still was a success everywhere except Broadway, where it opened not long after the stock market crash. It ran 769 performances in London, was filmed twice, and was a hit in Paris, too. The original production starred Peggy Wood and George Mextaxa, and supplied the standards "I'll See You Again" (the show's enduring theme) and "If Love Were All."

   In the plot, the young singer Sarah/Sari leaves her fiancé to wed her beloved Carl, who is
   A. a chemist (pharmacist)
   B. an army officer
   C. a butcher

D. a starving artist

E. a music teacher

4. The comedy *Private Lives* (1930) was another great success, and Coward and Gertie Lawrence performed in it on both sides of the Atlantic. Coward's 1931 production wasn't exactly a musical, but it was more than a mere play with music. This spectacle included a gigantic cast (400 extras alone), requiring 3,700 costumes. It boasted a show-within-the-show, which used a number of original Coward songs, as well as many period pieces, as the action encompassed 1899 to 1930. The historical events covered included the Boer War, Victoria's Jubilee, the sinking of the *Titanic*, and World War I. It may have helped inspire the television series *Upstairs, Downstairs*. What was it?

A. *Sigh No More*

B. *Hands Across the Sea*

C. *Operette*

D. *Cavalcade*

E. *Ace of Clubs*

5. Coward's 1932 play, *Design for Living*, opened in New York, starring Coward and the Lunts. Coward had favored a Broadway opening to avoid the British censor, which he feared would reject the play's sexual themes. It was a success, but he would not fare well with his next musical revue, *Words and Music* (1932). The revue flopped, though two Coward perennials debuted in it: "Mad Dogs and Englishmen" and "Mad About the Boy." In the latter, women from different walks of life describe their adoration of a fictional movie star. Which real-life actor is *not* mentioned?

A. Rudolph Valentino

B. John Barrymore

C. Gary Cooper

D. Ronald Colman

E. Douglas Fairbanks

6. *Conversation Piece* (1934) was an operetta set in Regency England about a poor and exiled French duke, hoping to make a good marriage for his ward. "I'll Follow My Secret Heart" became the theme of the show, since the girl falls for her guardian. Coward said the show was "conceived, written, and composed" with one actress in mind. The show might have run longer, but the actress had to leave for another commitment. Who was she?

A. Fifi d'Orsay

B. Yvonne Printemps

C. Simone Simon

D. Beatrice Lillie

E. Lucienne Boyer

7. In 1936, Coward wrote a series of ten short plays, which he combined into two evenings of performances called *Tonight at 8:30*. He then wrote another operetta (*Operette*) that flopped, since 1938 audiences preferred musical comedies like *Me and My Girl*. He next revised his revue *Words and Music* for Broadway in 1939 (now called *Set to Music*) and inserted a song from *Operette*, "The Stately Homes of

England," which became quite popular. In this satire, Charles I and which other monarch reportedly used the lavatory?

A. George IV
B. Richard III
C. Aethelred the Unready
D. Henry IV (part one)
E. Edward the Confessor

8. In the years leading up to the war, Coward traveled, wrote plays, then began working secretly for the British Bureau of Propaganda in Paris and later for British Intelligence, helping to sway American opinion toward Britain. He toured for the troops, wrote and performed in the patriotic film *In Which We Serve*, and also wrote *Blithe Spirit* during a six-day holiday in Wales in 1941. It would become his longest-running show, lasting four and a half years in London. Years later, Coward would direct the Broadway musical version, *High Spirits*, for which he did not do the score. (He tried once, but remarked, "I never could get it out of [the characters'] living room!")

The postwar years seemed to find Coward out of fashion. His plays did decent business, but his musicals largely failed. His period operetta with the miscast Mary Martin, *Pacific 1860*, lasted four months on the strength of their names in late 1946. *After the Ball*, a 1954 adaptation of *Lady Windermere's Fan*, also flopped.

He turned down Richard Rodgers' offer to play the king in *The King and I*, but did accept an offer to do a cabaret production (*Relative Values*) in 1951. Coward suddenly found himself in demand as a cabaret performer, and played to sold-out houses at the Desert Inn in Las Vegas in 1955, all of his profits going to cover his tax debt in England.

Part of his cabaret act included a Cole Porter song, which he had first used during his war tours, tailoring the lyrics to his audience. Porter and Coward were good friends, and Porter had given his permission for the alterations. The version Coward used in Las Vegas stopped the show. Which song was it?

A. "What Am I to Do?"
B. "Well, Did You Evah?"
C. "It's De-Lovely"
D. "Night and Day"
E. "Let's Do It"

9. Coward returned to Broadway with 1961's *Sail Away*, starring Elaine Stritch, whose work he had admired in the flop *Goldilocks*. Coward wrote the book and score, and directed as well, and the show lasted 167 performances. The plot was drastically rewritten while on tryout, focusing more on Stritch, the hostess on a cruise ship, and cutting other characters, songs, and story lines. Stritch got great notices, to say nothing of the best song, "Why Do the Wrong People Travel?" When those wrong people go to Greece, what do they drink?

A. dry martinis
B. Coca-Cola
C. ouzo
D. rum punch
E. Canada Dry

BROADWAY BONUS: Where did producer Morton Gottlieb get an extra $100,000 to cover costs in *Sail Away*? Hint: it has to do with ships.

10. Coward didn't write the book for his last original musical, *The Girl Who Came to Supper* (1963); Harry Kurnitz adapted the Terence Rattigan play *The Sleeping Prince*. The story concerned a Balkan prince at the 1911 coronation of George V who falls for an American chorus girl. It only lasted a few months, with critics calling it old-fashioned. Tessie O'Shea, in a supporting role that let her do some hilarious music hall numbers, nabbed a Tony Award.

Part of the show's trouble was its leading man, who came across as unappealing, though he initially seemed well cast. Who was it?

A. Rex Harrison
B. Christopher Plummer
C. Jose Ferrer
D. Noel Coward
E. Michael Redgrave

Answers on page 230.

Stephen Schwartz

1. Songwriter Stephen Schwartz has written some of Broadway's most popular shows. Like many of us, he fell in love with musicals when just a kid. As a nine-year-old, he attended *Shinbone Alley*, which his neighbor, George Kleinsinger, had helped write, and wound up hooked for life. He attended Carnegie Tech, where he worked on an early version of *Pippin*. His first big success was *Godspell*, a kind of sixties love-in retelling of the last days of Jesus, which had begun as a college project of director John Michael Tebelak. *Godspell* debuted off-Broadway in 1971 and played for 2,124 performances before transferring to the Great White Way for another 527 showings. In the "Prologue," Schwartz introduces the audience to the philosophical concepts of Western civilization's greatest thinkers, and how these men viewed God and society. Who is *not* among them?

A. Jean-Paul Sartre
B. Socrates
C. Frederick Nietzsche
D. Martin Luther
E. Karl Marx

2. After contributing some lyrics to Leonard Bernstein's *Mass*, Schwartz returned to his musical about the medieval emperor Charlemagne's son. Actually, anyone looking for historical accuracy in *Pippin* will flunk an exam in European history. Yes, *Pippin* concerns the generation gap, and attitudes toward war, love, and life, but while the setting is the kingdom of the Franks in the ninth century, the mindset is firmly entrenched in late-twentieth-century America. There was conflict in the production, as well as the script; director Bob Fosse drastically reworked the material (Schwartz later staged his version in some overseas productions).

The character Pippin decides he's "extraordinary," so he need not fret over commonplace things. Which of the following aggravations is on Pippin's list of things to ignore?

A. paying taxes
B. meeting the diplomat from the Byzantine Empire
C. ale that's gone sour
D. cleaning the chicken coop
E. a leaky moat

3. With *The Magic Show* (1974), Schwartz had three shows on Broadway at the same time. *The Magic Show* ran for 1,920 performances, largely on the incredible popularity of magician Doug Henning. To help promote the show, Henning sawed someone in half on a morning talk show. Who was it?

A. J. Fred Muggs
B. Connie Chung
C. Liza Minnelli
D. Barbara Walters
E. Dinah Shore

4. Many regard *The Baker's Wife* (1976) as Schwartz' best score, though the story, adapted by Joseph Stein from a movie by Marcel Pagnol, was perhaps too slight to support a full musical treatment. It endured tryout hell before folding in Washington, D.C., fortunately leaving behind a cast album. What was the name of the baker's cat, whose amorous prowling plays a role in the story?

A. Asparagus
B. Meowrice
C. Pompom
D. Fluffy
E. Minou

5. In 1978, Schwartz conceived a show based on Studs Turkel's oral history *Working*, in which people of many backgrounds discussed their jobs. Schwartz directed the revue, and a host of songwriters (James Taylor, Mary Rodgers, Nicki Grant, Craig Carnelia, Graciela Daniele, Matt Landers, and Susan Birkenhead) added material to Schwartz'. Though it had a short run, *Working* has proved popular with amateur and regional companies. For the opening number, Schwartz adapted a poem by a noted American writer. Who was it?

A. Abraham Lincoln
B. Langston Hughes
C. Walt Whitman
D. Ogden Nash
E. Groucho Marx

6. Schwartz directed the 1984 workshop of *Rags*, for which he wrote the lyrics to Charles Strouse's music. It lasted but four performances on Broadway in 1986, despite a lush score and a fine cast portraying turn-of-the-century immigrants in America. What did the cast do in an effort to stop the closing?

A. they picketed the *New York Times* for its bad review
B. they staged a sit-in
C. they dismantled the skeletal sets and played on a bare stage
D. they asked Teresa Stratas' friends in the opera community for help
E. they marched down Broadway to Duffy Square in protest

7. Schwartz returned to the source of his first success, the Bible, for his next big show, 1991's *Children of Eden*. (As Charles Vance has remarked, "Good book—and no royalties!") This was staged in London by John Caird, who also wrote the libretto and had co-directed *Les Misérables*. The talent involved was impressive, but the show wasn't. Nor did it succeed in a 1997 mounting at the Papermill Playhouse. Act I tells of Adam, Eve, Cain, and Abel; act II, the tale of Noah and the flood. What was God's name in the show?
   A. Father
   B. the Starkeeper
   C. the Dude
   D. Mr. God
   E. the Storyteller

8. Schwartz spent much of the 1990s writing for animated films and winning Oscars, including penning lyrics to two scores by which fellow theatre veteran?
   A. Charles Strouse
   B. Henry Krieger
   C. Alan Menken
   D. William Finn
   E. Marvin Hamlisch

9. *Wicked* (2003) gave Schwartz another monster hit. Winnie Holzman's adaptation of Gregory Maguire's novel about the witches of Oz, combined with Schwartz' lively score, colorful staging, and the one-two punch of Idina Menzel and Kristin Chenoweth, has been a crowd-pleaser since opening night. Oz is a magical world where animals can talk. What is Dr. Dillamond?
   A. a monkey
   B. a goat
   C. a highly magnified Wogglebug
   D. a pushmi-pullyu
   E. an elephant

10. Schwartz' next big project is an opera, *A Séance on a Wet Afternoon*, which debuted in Santa Barbara in late 2009. But he has written a smaller piece, a children's show, *Captain Louie*, with book by Anthony Stein, which is available in both a fifty-minute and a thirty-minute version suitable for schools. *Captain Louie* had a brief run off-Broadway in 2005 and toured the nation for the next two years. The plot concerns a young boy who moves to a new home and retreats into his imagination, where he is a pilot flying over his old neighborhood. It's based on a charming book, *The Trip*, by a noted children's author. Who is it?
   A. Maurice Sendak
   B. Bernadette Peters

C. Ezra Jack Keats

D. John Lithgow

E. Julie Andrews

Answers on page 231.

Harold Arlen

1. Harold Arlen was a skilled jazz musician who wrote for the Cotton Club, as well as composing many outstanding Broadway and Hollywood musicals, most notably the classic film version of *The Wizard of Oz*. His first hit, written at the urging of Harry Warren, helped land him a spot as a composer at Remick's. What was it?

   A. "Sweet and Hot"

   B. "Get Happy"

   C. "Linda"

   D. "I Gotta Right to Sing the Blues"

   E. "Between the Devil and the Deep Blue Sea"

2. Arlen played in the pit orchestra in a 1928 revue before his own songs made it to the Great White Way. What was the show?

   A. *George White's Scandals*

   B. *Greenwich Village Follies*

   C. *Earl Carroll Vanities*

   D. *Grand Street Follies*

   E. *Americana*

3. Arlen worked with many lyricists over the years. Who was *not* a lyricist for his music?

   A. Truman Capote

   B. E. Y. "Yip" Harburg

   C. Johnny Mercer

   D. Ira Gershwin

   E. Oscar Hammerstein II

4. Which of these stars was *not* in the cast of the 1934 Arlen revue, *Life Begins at 8:40*?

   A. Luella Gear

   B. Bert Lahr

   C. Ethel Waters

   D. Ray Bolger

   E. Frances Williams

5. In Arlen's 1937 satirical antiwar musical, *Hooray for What!*, what is the name of the scientist who invents a poison gas so deadly that world leaders send spies to steal the secret formula?

   A. Frankenstein

   B. Smiley

   C. Chuckles

D. Parker

E. Sedgwick

6. What number does Arlen himself perform (he was a fine singer!) on the cast album of *Bloomer Girl* (1944)?

7. What noted actress was supposed to play the lead in *St. Louis Woman* (1946), but pulled out after the NAACP blasted the show for "offering roles (i.e., gamblers and murderers) that detract from the dignity of our race"?

8. Which of the following floral-inspired names is *not* found among Madame Fleur's girls in 1954's *House of Flowers*?

A. Pansy

B. Gladiola

C. Violet

D. Tulip

E. Rose

9. *Jamaica* (1957) was a hit largely due to its star, Lena Horne, since it had a flimsy book that was originally written for Harry Belefonte and hastily revised. Arlen's calypso numbers were pleasant, if not his best work. The choreography wowed audiences, however. Who was responsible?

A. Jack Cole

B. Bob Fosse

C. Michael Kidd

D. Agnes de Mille

E. Jerome Robbins

10. *Saratoga* in 1959 proved to be Arlen's last score, a project so troubled he claimed illness and abandoned it, leaving Johnny Mercer to pen the remaining numbers. It should have worked: a plot based on a Ferber novel; director-librettist Morton da Costa, fresh from *The Music Man*; Carol Lawrence and Howard Keel starring; and Cecil Beaton costumes to stun the eye. And the score does have its charms. Which of the following numbers did Mercer compose the music for?

A. "Dog Eat Dog"

B. "Goose Never Be a Peacock"

C. "(Love Is) A Game of Poker"

D. "Love Hold Lightly"

E. "Gettin' a Man"

Answers on page 232.

Act One: Scene Three

Go into Your Dance
Choreographers

From the time those stranded French ballerinas teamed up with a Gothic melodramatic spectacle to create *The Black Crook* in 1866, dance has been an important part of the American musical. I've listed twenty-six of Broadway's finest choreographers. It's your job to match them with their dances in the opposite column. In some cases, the dances are from shows that have received revivals, which may or may not have used different choreography. I have listed either (o) for the original production or (r) for the revival.

1.	Rob Ashford	**A.**	"Laurey Makes Up Her Mind" (o)
2.	George Balanchine	**B.**	"Gentleman Jimmy"
3.	Michael Bennett	**C.**	"Marian the Librarian" (o)
4.	Patricia Birch	**D.**	"We Dance"
5.	Gower Champion	**E.**	"Too Darn Hot" (o)
6.	Wayne Cilento	**F.**	"Garden of Eden Ballet" (o)
7.	Jack Cole	**G.**	"We'll Take a Glass Together"
8.	Graciela Daniele	**H.**	"Forget About the Boy"
9.	Agnes de Mille	**I.**	"The Tree of Life Ballet"
10.	Ron Field	**J.**	"But Alive"
11.	Bob Fosse	**K.**	"Love Makes the World Go"
12.	Peter Gennaro	**L.**	"Let It Go"
13.	Hanya Holm	**M.**	"Magic to Do"
14.	Bill T. Jones	**N.**	"Conga!" (r)
15.	Michael Kidd	**O.**	"Who's That Woman?" (o)
16.	Joe Layton	**P.**	"The Bitch of Living"
17.	Gillian Lynne	**Q.**	"The Waiters' Gallop" (o)
18.	Kathleen Marshall	**R.**	"Slaughter on 10th Avenue"
19.	Jerry Mitchell	**S.**	"Fisch Schlapping Dance"
20.	Casey Nicholaw	**T.**	"The Jellicle Ball"
21.	Jerome Robbins	**U.**	"The Cookie Chase"
22.	Herb Ross	**V.**	"Mack Sennett Ballet"
23.	Susan Strohman	**W.**	"Not Since Nineveh"
24.	Lee (Becker) Theodore	**X.**	"We Go Together" (o)
25.	Tommy Tune	**Y.**	"Along Came Bialy"
26.	Onna White	**Z.**	"One Short Day"

BROADWAY BONUS: Hanya Holm staged an elaborate ballet for *Camelot* that had to be cut because the show was running hours too long and going far over budget. What was it about?

Answers on page 232.

Backstage Babble

Stagecrew

Of course, it's impossible to put on a show without a hardworking crew. I've listed a few crew members according to their particular skill. Your task is to come up with the character's name and the show in which each appears or is mentioned. Hint: most of these characters are known only by their first names and two share a name.

1. works the spotlight for the out-of-town musical *Robbin' Hood* _____

2. a jealous electrician _____

3. Margo Channing's hairdresser_____

4. chief of the stage flies, Paris Opera House_____

5. Roger de Bris' lighting designer _____

6. the bald doorman at the Weismann Theatre, c. 1941 _____

7. on the spotlight, Paramount Pictures (a Cecil B. DeMille Production)

_____

8. Lilli Vanessi's dresser/maid _____

9. Zach's assistant choreographer_____

Answers on page 233.

Ensemble Number

Supporting characters

It's easy to name the leads in a musical: Fred and Lily, Eva and Che, Stine and Stone, Giorgio and Fosca, Babe and Sid. But the leads aren't the whole story. Can you supply the names of these supporting characters?

1. The Kit Kat Klub girls and boys

2. The six other orphans at Miss Hannigan's

3. The three knights who want to escort Guenevere (extra credit for knowing which one gets resurrected by Lancelot)

4. Tevye's five daughters

5. The five other murderesses under Mama Morton's care

6. The three other acts competing with the Dreamettes at the Apollo

7. The three girls that hang out on Skid Row near Mushnik's (and just happen to sing terrific harmony)

8. Meyer Rothschild's five sons (extra credit for knowing where each goes)
9. Oscar Jaffe's assistants
10. The Pink Ladies and the Burger Palace Boys
11. The girls at Madame DuBonnet's Finishing School
12. The eight kids who are Corny Collins' Council Members (besides Link and Amber)
13. Charlie Anderson's six sons

〜〜〜〜〜〜〜〜〜〜〜〜〜〜〜〜〜〜〜〜〜〜〜〜〜〜〜〜〜〜〜〜〜〜〜

BROADWAY BONUS: Who are Wiggins, Duckbellows, Nipper, Perkins, and Macipper?

〜〜〜〜〜〜〜〜〜〜〜〜〜〜〜〜〜〜〜〜〜〜〜〜〜〜〜〜〜〜〜〜〜〜〜

Answers on page 233.

Ethel Merman

Ethel Merman was a one-of-a-kind Broadway original. From her startling debut in the Gershwins' *Girl Crazy* in 1930 to her appearance as the final Dolly in the original run of *Hello, Dolly!* in 1970, she was a monumental presence on the Great White Way. In her early days, she established a different kind of leading lady from the sweet Marilyn Miller types: bold, brassy, earthy, and perfect for musical comedy. She starred in Irving Berlin's two best book shows, *Annie Get Your Gun* and *Call Me Madam*, and originated perhaps the best female role in all musical history, that of Rose in *Gypsy*. Other Roses have followed; all are compared to Merman's. She could be abrasive and obscene, but she was a perfectionist in her work. She could tell if a single orchestra member was off-key, if a wrong gel was in a balcony light, and had no qualms about interrupting a performance to toss a drunk or tell stagehands listening to a ball game "to shut the bleep up." She had no formal musical training, hardly ever missed a performance, and never played in the chorus. With one exception, all her shows were hits. And then there was the voice that could be heard in the ticket lobby! No, Broadway will never see the likes of Ethel Merman again.

1. Ethel Zimmermann was a stenographer from Queens who did some singing on the side. Producer Vinton Freedley heard her at the Brooklyn Paramount and signed her for his new Gershwin show, *Girl Crazy*, starring Ginger Rogers and Willie Howard. The goofy story had a New York playboy sent to Arizona by his father, where the fellow falls for a Western gal. Merman (having dropped the Zim-) played a supporting character with little to do in the first act, but everyone realized a star had been born by the final curtain. Merman belted the daylights out of "Sam and Delilah" and "Boy! What Love Has Done to Me," but the smash was "I Got Rhythm."

   How long did Merman hold the "I" in "I Got Rhythm" while the orchestra continued playing the melodic line?
   A. ten bars
   B. twelve bars
   C. fourteen bars
   D. sixteen bars
   E. eighteen bars

2. While researching this quiz, I kept running into great Merman quotes. One of the following famous quotes is incorrectly attributed. Which?
   A. "You break all the rules of nature. Where do you breathe from?" —Grace Moore ("Necessity," answered Ethel.)
   B. (Kissing Ethel was) "somewhere between kissing your uncle and a Sherman tank." —Bert Lahr
   C. "Don't you go near (music teachers). They'll only get you self-conscious about your breathing and accent." —George Gershwin
   D. "Her voice is like another instrument in the orchestra." —Cole Porter
   E. "What will you do about your *hair*, Miss Merman?" —costume designer Mainbocher ("Wash it," said Ethel.)

3. Following *Girl Crazy*, Merman was in the highly acclaimed *George White's Scandals of 1931* and 1932's *Take a Chance*, where she had the hit "Eadie Was a Lady." Those shows led to her first of five shows with Cole Porter, *Anything Goes* (1934). Merman played Reno Sweeney, a sassy cross between Texas Guinan and Aimee Semple McPherson. She didn't get the leading man, William Gaxton, but she did get four out of five major songs. Which song wasn't introduced by Merman?
   A. "Blow, Gabriel, Blow"
   B. "I Get a Kick Out of You"
   C. "All Through the Night"
   D. "You're the Top"
   E. "Anything Goes"

4. Many of the same people responsible for *Anything Goes* reunited for 1936's *Red, Hot and Blue*. Producer Vinton Freedley had hoped to resign William Gaxton and comic Victor Moore, but Gaxton learned that while Freedley had promised him the largest role, he had promised Merman the same thing. So Gaxton walked, taking Victor Moore with him. Freedley didn't do badly in replacing them: Bob Hope (in his final Broadway role) and Jimmy Durante. Merman played "Nails" O'Reilly Duquesne, so smitten with Hope's character, she'd do anything for him, including finding his long-lost childhood girlfriend, known for a waffle-iron scar on her behind. Durante played the convict who's happier in prison than out of it. There was a dispute over the advertising: both Merman and Durante wanted top billing. Someone had the bright idea of putting their names in a crisscross, and alternating left and right each week. Who kept the peace between the two stars?
   A. Bob Hope
   B. Cole Porter
   C. Alex Aarons
   D. Howard Lindsay
   E. Monty Woolley

5. Merman's next Porter show, *Du Barry Was a Lady* (1939), ran for 408 performances, an amazing run in the Depression. Merman played a nightclub singer and Bert Lahr was the washroom attendant with a crush on her. He accidentally drinks a Mickey Finn and dreams he is King Louis XV and she is Madame du Barry. Betty Grable, the ingénue, had a great song in the second act while the show was in Boston, but Merman was singing it in New York. What was it?

A. "Katie Went to Haiti"
B. "When Love Beckoned"
C. "Give Him the Oo-La-La"
D. "Friendship"
E. "But in the Morning, No"

6. Merman's longest-running Porter show (501 performances) was *Panama Hattie* (1940). Bud DeSylva and Herbert Fields concocted a libretto about a nightclub owner in the Canal Zone who falls for a naval officer from an upper-class Philadelphia family (no, it's not Lt. Cable). Hattie must also win over the widowed officer's eight-year-old daughter, which she does in "Let's Be Buddies." Despite the dopey plot, the show gave us one of Porter's (and the Merm's!) best torch songs, "Make It Another Old-Fashioned, Please."

   Long before Annie and Sandy romped through New York or Elle and Bruiser tackled Harvard, Hattie had a poodle in Panama. The pooch was named for a heavily advertised product. What was its name?

   A. Serutan
   B. Pepsodent
   C. Bromo-seltzer
   D. Philip Morris
   E. Ovaltine

7. Merman's last show with Porter was 1942's *Something for the Boys*, which ran for 422 performances on a plot that featured Merman's character getting radio signals through her fillings and running a Texas ranch-style hotel for military wives that is mistaken for a bordello. She then was offered the lead in *Sadie Thompson* (1944), but quarreled with Howard Dietz over the lyrics, especially one that mentioned a French brand of lipstick (Mal Maison) unfamiliar to Merman. Merman left, June Havoc replaced her, and *Sadie* flopped.

   Merman's next show would be her most successful: 1946's *Annie Get Your Gun*, with songs by Irving Berlin and book by Dorothy and Herbert Fields. *Annie*, based loosely on the life of sharpshooter Annie Oakley, ran for 1,147 performances. Merman took shooting lessons and learned how to ride a motorcycle for the role, which was somewhat out of the ordinary for her. Annie could trade quips, in a countrified way, but she also had a more wistful and tender side than most characters Merman played.

   Annie's decision to throw the shooting match at the show's end may seem sub-missive and foolish given current attitudes about relationships, but audiences in 1946 (and 1966, when Merman played the revival) thought it was sweet. Who advises Annie to lose the match, and thus win Frank's heart?

   A. Buffalo Bill
   B. Pawnee Bill
   C. Dolly Tate
   D. Tommy Keeler
   E. Chief Sitting Bull

8. Merman and Berlin reunited for 1950's *Call Me Madam*, inspired by socialite-turned-ambassador Perle Mesta. Howard Lindsay and Russel Crouse wrote the

book, Jerome Robbins did the choreography, and Merman worked for the first time with director George Abbott. The role of Mrs. Sally Adams won Merman her only Tony as Best Actress; she would later receive a special Tony honoring her career. There were two cast albums made of *Call Me Madam*. Although RCA had invested in the show, Decca would not release Merman from her contract to record the album, so RCA used the original cast with Dinah Shore. Decca made its own version with Merman and Dick Haymes replacing Russell Nype.

The real Perle Mesta was the widow of a wealthy steel manufacturer, but her family was already rich. Berlin incorporated that background into a song for his character. Where did Mrs. Sally Adams' family fortune come from?

A. cheese manufacturing
B. they began with a still brewing moonshine, but later made vodka
C. Oklahoma oil fields
D. rubies and diamonds
E. Hollywood films

9. Though it ran for a year, *Happy Hunting* (1956) ended up in the red, Merman's sole flop. The usually reliable Lindsay and Crouse turned out a poor libretto, and the composers (Harold Karr and Matt Dubey) were novices. When Karr criticized Merman's singing, she told director Abe Burrows that she never wanted to talk with the songwriter again. But the killer feud was between Merman and her costar, Fernando Lamas, which was clearly visible onstage.

What was the inspiration for this mess?

A. Molnár's *The Good Fairy*
B. the wedding of Grace Kelly and Prince Rainier
C. Theodore Dreiser's "St. Columba and the River"
D. Arthur Kober's *Having Wonderful Time*
E. the romance of Wallis Simpson and King Edward VIII

10. Merman's last original role on Broadway would be her greatest: Rose, the stage mother determined to turn her kids into show business stars, in *Gypsy* (1959). Merman, who was not known for nuanced performances, stunned the audiences, especially with "Rose's Turn," in which the character has a breakdown.

Arthur Laurents (libretto) and Jerome Robbins (director/choreographer) wanted Stephen Sondheim, with whom they had worked on *West Side Story* to do the score, but after her experience in *Happy Hunting*, Merman wanted a more experienced composer. Jule Styne got the nod, but Sondheim initially didn't want to write just the lyrics, as he had in *West Side Story*. Who convinced Sondheim to take the job, and what did it have to do with Ethel Merman?

❀ ❀

BROADWAY BONUS: *Jenny Get Your Gun* was the original title of which Merman show?

❀ ❀

Answers on page 234.

David Merrick

David Merrick, sometimes called "the Abominable Showman," was a producer whose output and successes on Broadway surpassed all others, including the Shuberts and Ziegfeld. He cultivated his reputation as the most disagreeable man on the Street; fostered feuds among the creative staffs of his musicals to see what he could get out of them; wielded contracts as though they were lethal weapons; and concocted the most innovative publicity campaigns ever seen. This quiz is largely based on Merrick anecdotes, of which there are many, and is one of the more difficult ones. On the other hand, Merrick's deeds were fairly infamous, so I'm guessing many readers will know these stories.

1. David Merrick's birth name was Margulois. By the time he arrived in New York to take on show business, he had legally changed it. Why did he pick "Merrick?"
   A. it was his mother's maiden name
   B. it was the last name of his uncle
   C. it rhymed with derrick, so it sounded tough
   D. it rhymed with Garrick, the famous actor
   E. it sounded like "more rich," which he wanted to become

2. Through dogged persistence, Merrick got the rights to the famous trilogy *Marius*, *Caesar*, and *Fanny* by Marcel Pagnol and had S. N. Behrman and Joshua Logan condense them into a musical with a score by Harold Rome. *Fanny* (1954) was a success, not least because of Merrick's crazy publicity schemes. He did all of the following to promote the show *except*:
   A. placed stickers in men's rooms all over New York reading "Have you seen *Fanny*?"
   B. had hotel bellhops and operators page "Mademoiselle Fanny"
   C. had "Fanny" written in skywriting at Princess Grace's wedding
   D. tried to get the U.S. Weather Service to change the name of the next hurricane due to start with the letter *F* from Flora to Fanny
   E. set up an illegal papier-mâché statue of belly dancer Nejla Ates in Central Park, then made sure the reporters knew about it so they'd be there when the authorities removed it

3. *Destry Rides Again* (1959), with another fine score by Rome, was overshadowed by Merrick's production of *Gypsy*, which opened a month later. What happened during the production of *Destry* that led Merrick to chortle, "I couldn't buy publicity like this for five thousand dollars a week!"
   A. Andy Griffith developed a "bad boy" reputation
   B. a dangerous confrontation between the "whip dancers" during rehearsals
   C. a name-calling, slapping, slugging fight between star Dolores Gray and director Michael Kidd
   D. a quarrel between Rome and Leonard Gershe over the book
   E. the over-amplified mikes at the Imperial picked up sounds of actors going to the bathroom

4. Merrick next bought the rights to a little show about a Parisian hooker with a heart of gold called *Irma la Douce*. It had run for four years in Paris and was a hit in London before coming to New York (1960), where it ran for 527 performances and lead Elizabeth Seal won the Tony. True or false: to promote *Irma*, Merrick had men walking through Manhattan, wearing French berets and sandwich boards emblazoned with the show's logo and carrying rubber chickens, since in Parisian slang a *poule* (chicken) was a whore.

5. Merrick had plotted for years to run The Ad, possibly the greatest publicity stunt in Broadway history, in which he found seven men whose names were identical to those of the top critics. He wined and dined them, then took them to his 1961 show, *Subways Are for Sleeping*, and got rave comments from the bogus critics. When he submitted the quote ad, most newspapers recognized it as fraudulent and pulled it, but the *Post* didn't notice in time. The subsequent publicity about the publicity was exactly what Merrick wanted. Why did Merrick have to wait years to play his trick?

6. In 1963, there was a celebration in New York for Gordon Cooper, who had just returned from orbiting earth, and two other Mercury 7 astronauts. After the ticker-tape parade, they were invited to a Broadway show, and Merrick naturally arranged it that they saw one of his. Which one?
  A. *Stop the World, I Want to Get Off*
  B. *Oliver!*
  C. *110 in the Shade*
  D. *Carnival*
  E. *I Can Get It for You Wholesale*

7. Lionel Bart's *Oliver!* was a success in London, and Merrick grabbed the Broadway rights. What did Merrrick *not* do concerning *Oliver!* (1963)?
  A. posed as a "guest critic" on a New York radio station and called it the greatest show in history
  B. made Fagin less Jewish to avoid offending New York crowds
  C. sent the show on a lengthy and highly profitable tour before opening on Broadway in 1963
  D. drastically cut the number of orphans/pickpockets to save money
  E. spent $10,000 to lower the orchestra pit to get a more intimate sound, since the union contract required him to hire a larger number of musicians than in London

8. Merrick's biggest hit of the decade was 1964's *Hello, Dolly!* He had earlier produced Thorton Wilder's play *The Matchmaker* and knew it would make a good musical. He wanted to reunite his team from *Carnival*, director Gower Champion and song-writer Bob Merrill, but Merrill flatly refused to work with Champion again. So Merrick talked to a young composer named Jerry Herman, who was aching to do the show. Merrick wasn't so sure; the only work of Herman's he'd seen was *Milk and Honey*, set in Israel. Herman pleaded for a weekend to convince Merrick. He created four songs, impressing the producer with both the material and his speed. Three of those songs remained in the score. Which song of those listed below was *not* among that first weekend's work?

A. "Dancing"
B. "I Put My Hand In"
C. "Before the Parade Passes By"
D. "Put On Your Sunday Clothes"
(this question has only four options, so no **E**)

9. If Merrick's greatest hit was *Dolly!*, his greatest disaster was *Breakfast at Tiffany's* (1966), with Mary Tyler Moore and Richard Chamberlain starring in an adaptation of the famous film, itself based on a Truman Capote novella. Bob Merrill wrote the score, and after numerous personnel changes, Abe Burrows took over as librettist-director. But following a disaster in Philadelphia, Merrick jettisoned all of Burrows' book. Burrows would soon withdraw as director, replaced by Joseph Anthony. Whom did Merrick hire to pen the libretto *Tiffany's* used in its last gasp before Merrick pulled the plug in a spectacular closing announcement?
   A. Tennessee Williams
   B. Neil Simon
   C. Terrance Rattigan
   D. Edward Albee
   E. George Axelrod

10. One of the most famous stories about Merrick was how he kept the news of Gower Champion's death a secret until the opening-night curtain calls of *42nd Street* (1980). Was it meant as a public tribute? A genuine desire to get the best possible performance on opening night from the unknowing actors? A shameless bid for publicity? Whatever the reasons, Merrick admitted years later that while he knew some might have seen it as tasteless, he couldn't resist the opportunity.

    Some years into in *42nd Street*'s long run, Merrick had posters printed with his own image announcing, "David Merrick is holding the curtain for you!" and listing later start times for the show (at 2:15 p.m. and 8:15 p.m.). What was behind this move?

Answers on page 235.

Carol Channing and Jerry Orbach

If Broadway had a true Hall of Fame like baseball's Cooperstown instead of making do with the wall on the Gershwin Theatre, Carol Channing and Jerry Orbach would each have a wing of their own. Both had long, successful careers and helped create some of the most legendary characters in musical theatre.

1. Carol Channing had understudied Eve Arden in *Let's Face It*, but made her debut to rave notices in 1948's *Lend an Ear*. The hit of this highly popular revue by Charles Gaynor was "The Gladiola Girl." In this number, Channing and her able partners, William Eythe, Yvonne Adair, and Gene Nelson spoofed:
   A. opera
   B. celebrities and gossip columnists
   C. psychoanalysis

D. silent movie heroines

E. 1920s musical comedies

2. Channing's comic skills in *Lend an Ear* led to Jule Styne and Anita Loos' pushing for her to be cast as Lorelei Lee in *Gentlemen Prefer Blondes* (1949). This smash about flappers and their sugar daddies ran for 740 performances. What did Channing report was the costume designer's inspiration for "Diamonds Are a Girl's Best Friend"?

    A. the iceberg that sank the *Titanic*

    B. the Palace of Versailles

    C. an avalanche in the Rockies

    D. Tallulah Bankhead going down the Nile as Cleopatra

    E. the Pope on the balcony at the Vatican

3. Channing next replaced Rosalind Russell in *Wonderful Town*, then got the lead in *The Vamp*, a 1955 flop about silent movies (music by James Muncy, lyrics by John Latouche). Channing played Flora, a country girl catapulted into movie stardom. What is the name of Flora's silent movie role?

    A. Hedda

    B. Portia

    C. Betty Boop

    D. Delilah

    E. Helen of Troy

4. Channing then found the role of a lifetime as Dolly Gallagher Levi in 1964's *Hello, Dolly!*, though it took some work to convince director Gower Champion and producer David Merrick that she was right for the part. (Ethel Merman, who had been first offered the role, turned it down.) Channing has remarked that she "could play Dolly every day." What was she doing in Jerry Herman's hotel room, wearing a bathrobe, in the middle of the night when *Dolly!* was in tryouts in Detroit?

    A. the tub in her room backed up

    B. trying to thwart David Merrick's latest schemes

    C. rehearsing Champion's choreography

    D. listening to the composer play "Before the Parade Passes By," which he'd just written

    E. talking with Louis Armstrong on the West Coast

5. Channing reprised the role of Lorelei Lee in 1974's *Lorelei*, a kind of "revisal" of *Gentlemen Prefer Blondes*, the now older and widowed gold digger looking back on her life. Styne returned to write the new music, with Comden and Green penning new lyrics. *Lorelei* toured on an extended tryout for nearly a year, got decent reviews (Channing especially), but still wound up in the red. The order of the older songs was shuffled and some were given to different characters than in the original. By the time it got to Broadway, eleven of the original nineteen numbers survived, with four new songs added. Which of the following original *Gentlemen Prefer Blondes* numbers remained in the Broadway version of *Lorelei*?

    A. "Bye, Bye Baby"

    B. "House on Rittenhouse Square"

C. "You Say You Care"

D. "Gentlemen Prefer Blondes"

E. "Sunshine"

6. While Carol Channing was heading for the heights, a young performer named Jerry Orbach was getting started. At the age of twenty, he performed in the famous off-Broadway Marc Blitzstein adaptation of Brecht and Weill's *The Threepenny Opera* (1954), eventually moving up as a replacement for Macheath. Not long after, he would create the role of the Narrator (later called El Gallo) in the longest-running musical of all time, *The Fantasticks* (1960). The Narrator/El Gallo sets the tone for the romantic fantasy and comments on the action to the audience. Orbach got to introduce the show's biggest hit, "Try to Remember." When Orbach first played the role, there were nine characters in the show. In 1961, one part was cut. What was it?

7. Orbach's Broadway debut was the lead in the 1961 David Merrick production of *Carnival* (songs by Bob Merrill, book by Michael Stewart). Gower Champion's creative direction set the scene early in this show: with the curtain already up, the carnival troupe came on, the roustabouts set up the tent, the performers practiced their turns. Orbach's character was the bitter, crippled puppet master Paul, who falls for the young and innocent Lili (Anna Maria Alberghetti). Lili relates better to Paul's puppets than to the man himself, not realizing till the end that the puppets and Paul are one and the same. Which of the following is *not* one of Paul's puppets?

A. Horr'ble Henry

B. Marguerite

C. Renardo

D. Jacquot

E. Carrot Top

8. Following his success in *Carnival*, Orbach earned a Tony nomination for Featured Actor as Sky Masterson in the 1965 revival of *Guys and Dolls*. Ethel Merman then helped get him cast as Charlie in the 1966 revival of *Annie Get Your Gun*. In 1968, he originated another lead role in a Merrick show: Chuck Baxter in Burt Bacharach and Hal David's *Promises, Promises*, with book by Neil Simon, adapting the film *The Apartment*. It was Orbach's first over-the-title billing and earned him a Tony. *Promises* was innovative in its use of pop music; orchestrator Jonathan Tunick even placed vocalists in the pit to create backing vocals. Michael Bennett handled the choreography. Against the objections of others on the creative team, he vetoed including a full-blown chorus number for the song "She Likes Basketball." Instead, he staged it for Orbach alone. What prop did Orbach use in place of a basketball?

9. Orbach originated another classic role in 1975's *Chicago*, shyster Billy Flynn. He put his indelible mark on great numbers like "All I Care About," "They Both Reached for the Gun," and "Razzle Dazzle." *Chicago* was nominated for eleven Tonys, including one for Orbach, but lost all of them to *A Chorus Line*. Orbach ended up playing a crucial role in the way one number was staged. Bob Fosse's original staging for "Razzle Dazzle" featured numerous couples having simulated sex on a staircase. The blatant vulgarity of the number upset everyone, but the director refused to abandon

his pornographic vision until Orbach talked to him. How did Orbach convince Fosse to change the number?

    A. by pointing out they'd lose the matinee crowd

    B. by suggesting the increasing ill feelings might trigger another heart attack in Fosse

    C. by casually mentioning that Kander and Ebb were on the verge of walking out

    D. by describing the number in terms of the Brechtian Alienation Effect and musing that the sex on the stairs perhaps detracted from the (presumed) desired alienation of the audience at the end

    E. by getting Fosse's pals Herb Gardner and Paddy Chayefsky to talk to him

10. Orbach's final original Broadway role was that of Julian Marsh, the director in *42nd Street* (1980). This show was based on the film, with additional songs from other films by Harry Warren and Al Dubin to fill out the score. Gower Champion directed, though fatally ill, and the show ended up a huge success, running 3,486 performances. Orbach's confrontation with Wanda Richart, playing young actress Peggy Sawyer, sets up the show-stopping production number, "Lullaby of Broadway." What does he tell her are the most glorious words in the English language?

Answers on page 236.

Bob Fosse and Gwen Verdon

I've paired these two since their lives and careers were so closely connected that it only seemed fitting. It's one of the more difficult quizzes, so be warned!

1. Bob Fosse began dancing professionally as a child, tap-danced in strip joints, and played stock and regional theatre before gaining fame with his first wife, Mary-Ann Niles. They performed on Broadway in the revue *Dance Me a Song* (1950) and on television. Fosse played the lead in a summer production of *Pal Joey*, attracting Jule Styne's attention, but when Styne revived the show on Broadway, he cast Harold Lang. Fosse worked briefly in Hollywood with MGM, divorced Niles, and married Joan McCracken, then returned to the stage. On McCracken's recommendation, George Abbott hired him to do the choreography on *The Pajama Game*. Producer Hal Prince, nervous over Fosse's inexperience, asked Jerome Robbins to assist. Which Fosse number did Abbott want removed, but Robbins talked him into keeping it?

    A. "Steam Heat"

    B. "Hernando's Hideaway"

    C. "Once a Year Day"

    D. "Racing with the Clock"

    E. "I'm Not At All in Love"

2. Gwen Verdon, who would marry Fosse and be the principal interpreter of his choreography, was born to dance. Her mom had been a dancer, and she was part of a professional ballroom team while still a youth. She married in her teens, had a son, then returned to dance in her twenties with the Jack Cole Dancers, debuting on

Broadway in 1950's *Alive and Kicking*. She assisted Cole on the film version of *Gentlemen Prefer Blondes* before being cast by Cy Feuer in 1953's *Can-Can*. She literally stopped the show twice with her phenomenal dancing. Which number created such a tumult that Feuer had to drag her in her robe from her dressing room to acknowledge the cheers (which not doubt rang louder, given her half-dressed state)?

    A. "The Garden of Eden Ballet"
    B. "Maidens Typical of France"
    C. "Can-Can"
    D. "Apache Dance"
    E. "Quadrille Dance"

3. The team behind *The Pajama Game* (Abbott, Prince, Griffith, Adler, Ross) reunited for *Damn Yankees* (1955) and knew they wanted a dancer for the Devil's temptress, Lola. They signed Verdon, fresh off the smash *Can-Can*, and she and choreographer Fosse soon discovered a bond. They worked for hours on "Whatever Lola Wants" and "Who's Got the Pain?" and began an affair, which eventually led to Fosse's divorcing McCracken.

    Damn Yankees underwent many changes in its tryout. Which of the following is *not* true about the tryout version?

    A. Applegate and the Gossips sang a song called "Not Meg"
    B. the ending of the ball game had the umpire ruling Old Joe safe at home, not making a fantastic catch in the outfield
    C. the orchestrations on "Two Lost Souls" had a rock rhythm
    D. Lola remained a crone
    E. act I ended with a baseball ballet, including a bird (as a Baltimore Oriole) and a gorilla (a damn Yankee, of course)

4. Fosse helped Robbins with the "Mu-Cha-Cha" number in *Bells Are Ringing*, then worked on the films of *The Pajama Game* and *Damn Yankees*. He appeared opposite Verdon in the latter in "Who's Got the Pain?" The pair teamed up again with Abbott, Prince, and Griffith, but things would not go so smoothly with *New Girl in Town* (1957). An enormous conflict arose over one number, leading to a permanent split. Abbott, Prince, and Griffith would go on to *Fiorello!*, while Fosse and Verdon would tackle *Redhead*. What was the disputed number?

5. *Redhead* in 1959 (music by Albert Hague, lyrics by Dorothy Fields, book by Dorothy and Herbert Fields, with rewrites by Sidney Sheldon and David Shaw) starred Verdon as Essie, who works for her aunts in a London wax museum. Fosse had hoped to play the redheaded murderer (the title does not refer to Verdon's hair, but to a Victorian-era serial killer), but realized he couldn't both direct and perform. Which number did Verdon perform in male drag and derby hat, as seen in the show's logo?

    A. "Pick Pocket Tango"
    B. "Uncle Sam Rag"
    C. "Essie's Vision"
    D. "'Erbie Fitch's Twitch"
    E. "We Loves Ya, Jimey"

6. Verdon and Fosse secretly wed in 1960 when *Redhead* toured in Chicago, Fosse's hometown. For his next project, Fosse and producer Robert Whitehead worked on adapting the Preston Sturgis movie *Hail, the Conquering Hero*. Moose Charnap and Norman Gimbel wrote the songs while Larry Gelbart handled the book. Verdon worked as Fosse's uncredited assistant. *The Conquering Hero* ran into serious trouble on the road, leading to Whitehead firing Fosse from a show he initiated. Fosse said the production could keep the two major ballets he had choreographed, provided they remained intact. When they were altered for the show's very brief run (eight performances, 1961), he sued for damages and won. How much was he awarded?

   A. 7 1/2 cents
   B. tuppence
   C. six cents
   D. eight cents, one for each performance
   E. five hundred thousand dollars

❧ ❧

BROADWAY BONUS: What was Larry Gelbart's famous comment while on tryout with *The Conquering Hero*?

❧ ❧

7. Fosse came in at the last minute to help with choreography on 1962's hit *How to Succeed in Business Without Really Trying*. One number, which originally had a waltz tempo, was cut in Philly since Rudy Vallee was having trouble singing it. Fosse rescued it by changing the tempo and rehearsing new choreography with Verdon's assistance, all behind composer Frank Loesser's back. Instead of being angry at the change in his rhythm, Loesser was thrilled by the dance. What was the number?

   A. "Coffee Break"
   B. "Paris Original"
   C. "Brotherhood of Man"
   D. "Cinderella Darling"
   E. "A Secretary Is Not a Toy"

8. Fosse next created some dances for Sid Caesar in *Little Me* (1962) while Verdon was expecting their daughter, Nicole. Verdon was next interested in doing a musical version of *Chicago*, but was having trouble getting the rights. Fosse, meanwhile, was looking at foreign films for source material. He decided on Fellini's *Nights of Cabiria*, which he thought he could write as a one-act musical, with a second original one-act written by someone else. He quickly realized that *Sweet Charity* (1966) deserved a full-blown production. The show, with music and lyrics by Cy Coleman and Dorothy Fields and book by Neil Simon, became an enduring hit. Who was to have written the second half of Fosse's original concept?

   A. Neil Simon
   B. Moss Hart
   C. Paddy Chayefsky
   D. Elaine May
   E. George Abbott

9. Fosse directed the film version of *Sweet Charity*, but Hollywood insisted on Shirley MacLaine as the star. Gwen Verdon helped tutor MacLaine in the role she had originated. The movie was a disappointment, but only a few years later, Fosse would accomplish a feat unlikely to ever be duplicated. He won the triple crown: an Oscar, a Tony, and an Emmy for directing the film version of *Cabaret*, the stage musical *Pippin*, and the television special, *Liza with a Z*. He had also separated from Verdon after countless affairs with other women. No longer a couple, they continued to work professionally. Verdon had finally gotten the rights to *Chicago* (1975) and Fosse, John Kander, and Fred Ebb created "a musical vaudeville," with Verdon as murderess Roxie Hart. They purposely devised the songs as pastiches of styles from the vaudeville era. For example, Amos' song, "Mr. Cellophane," was modeled on the mournful "Nobody" of Bert Williams and Billy's "All I Care About" played on the style of band leader Ted Lewis. What star was the model for Roxie's "Funny Honey"?

 A. Marilyn Miller
 B. Helen Morgan
 C. Sophie Tucker
 D. Texas Guinan
 E. Sally Rand

10. Fosse had had fights with librettists over the years, so for 1978's *Dancin'*, he decided to dispense with them entirely. This "musical entertainment" was a dance revue with no script, and it ran for 1,774 performances. Verdon was his assistant and production supervisor. Fosse included in the playbill a special dedication for the number, "Sing, Sing, Sing." It read "For Gwen Verdon and _____." What was the other name?

 A. Fred Astaire
 B. Mr. Bojangles
 C. Jack Cole
 D. George M. Cohan
 E. Benny Goodman

 After *Dancin'*, Fosse would film the quasi-autobiographical *All That Jazz* and *Star 80*, and stage the flop *Big Deal* (1986). He and Verdon both worked on the Debbie Allen revival of *Sweet Charity* and were planning the film version of *Chicago* when Fosse died of a heart attack in 1987. In 1992, Richard Maltby, Jr., and former Fosse dancers Chet Walker and Ann Reinking, who had been one of Fosse's many girlfriends, devised the dance revue *Fosse*, which won the Best Musical Tony. Gwen Verdon, who was *Fosse*'s artistic adviser, died in 2000.

Answers on page 237.

Alfred Drake

Alfred Drake was one of Broadway's truly legendary leading men. A talented actor, singer, adaptor, and director, he dominated the Great White Way for decades. He didn't just play in musicals, either, getting notices at the American Shakespeare Festival as Benedick to Katharine Hepburn's Beatrice in *Much Ado About Nothing* and as Iago to

Earl Hyman's Othello. On Broadway, he was Claudius to Richard Burton's Hamlet. As one might expect from a man with such presence, he often played roles that were larger than life.

1. Early in his career, Drake performed in the chorus of some Gilbert and Sullivan revivals, which led to his being cast in Rodgers and Hart's *Babes in Arms* (1937). He had plenty of company, for the show was crowded with many stars-to-be. Who was *not* one of Drake's comrades in *Babes in Arms*?
   A. Mitzi Green
   B. Dan Dailey
   C. Joan Roberts
   D. Robert Rounseville
   E. Roy Heatherton

2. Following *Babes*, Drake appeared in several revues before being tapped as Curley in *Oklahoma!* On the original cast album, Drake sings a song not assigned to his character. What was it?

3. Drake had the lead in the 1944 folk music revue *Sing Out, Sweet Land*. He then landed the role of Macheath opposite Zero Mostel's Peachum in a musical version of John Gay's *Beggar's Opera*. This show, retitled *Beggar's Holiday* (1946), was not the Brecht-Weill adaptation that had flopped on Broadway in 1933, and would be a later success off-Broadway in the fifties. Who wrote the music for this 1946 version?
   A. Duke Ellington
   B. Sammy Fain
   C. Harold Arlen
   D. Jule Styne
   E. Sidney Lippman

4. One of Drake's best-known roles, for which he won the Donaldson as Best Actor, was that of Fred Graham, the actor-director in *Kiss Me, Kate* (1948), who is trying to put on a show and retain the services of his estranged wife and fellow star, Lilli (Patricia Morison), despite some mobsters who mistakenly think he owes their boss a ton of money. Fred may want to get back with Lilli, but that doesn't stop him from appreciating the beauty of dancer Lois (Lisa Kirk). Name the kinds of flowers that make up Lilli's wedding bouquet—the same ones Fred sends to Lois on opening night, but are delivered to Lilli, complete with a compromising card inscribed to Lois!

5. Drake was the composer's first choice for the male lead in which of the following musicals? Hint: he initially refused the part, but played it later, during the originator's vacation.
   A. *Hello, Dolly!*
   B. *The Sound of Music*
   C. *The King and I*
   D. *A Funny Thing Happened on the Way to the Forum*
   E. *Silk Stockings*

6. *Kismet*, 1953's musical *Arabian Nights* (music and lyrics by Robert Wright and George Forrest, using themes by Borodin), was another huge hit for Drake. He

played the Poet, later called Hajj, earning a Tony Award for Best Actor. The cast in this enchanting operetta was top-notch, with Joan Diener belting as Hajj's love interest, Doretta Morrow as his daughter, and Richard Kiley as the Caliph who falls for the girl. Kiley, deferring to Drake's baritone, sang as a tenor, something he would not do again. What happened on *Kismet*'s opening night?

    A. a rat in the generator caused a cancellation
    B. one of the princesses of Abubu got stuck in her basket
    C. the olive tree fell over
    D. it still had "Bored," which was later cut
    E. there was a newspaper strike, so the mostly negative reviews didn't come out until word of mouth had established the show as a hit

7. The 1950s saw a number of made-for-TV musicals featuring Broadway stars. Drake played a historical figure in one. Who?

    A. Cristoforo Columbo
    B. Benvenuto Cellini
    C. Victor Emmanuel II
    D. Marco Polo
    E. Leonardo da Vinci

8. Drake bought the rights to Jean-Paul Sartre's play about Regency actor Edmund Kean (itself based on an earlier play by Alexander Dumas), intending to play the title role. With a score by Wright and Forrest, a book by Peter Stone, and choreography by Jack Cole, *Kean* (1961) seemed a surefire hit. But though the out-of-town notices were terrific, it failed to find Broadway audiences. Drake's frequent illnesses didn't help, since there was no show without him. In desperation, the producers offered discount pricing and slashed twenty minutes, including which song?

    A. "Willow, Willow, Willow"
    B. "Domesticity"
    C. "Chime In"
    D. "Sweet Danger"
    E. "Penny Plain"

9. This 1964 show was performed in Italian, with English subtitles—translated by Drake—projected on a screen. A man better known for writing whimsical children's fantasies wrote the lyrics. The hero—or rather, antihero—winds up beheaded at the tale's end. What on earth was this show?

    A. *Rugantino*
    B. *Regina*
    C. *The Firebrand of Florence*
    D. *Theatre of the Piccolini*
    E. *The Rape of Lucretia*

10. In 1973, Lerner and Loewe attempted to transfer their hit movie *Gigi* into a stage musical, and hired Drake to play the role of Honoré, originally created by Maurice Chevalier. Which song was specifically written for Drake's character, and was *not* in the original film score?

A. "In This Wide, Wide World"
B. "I Never Want to Go Home Again"
C. "The Contract"
D. "Paris Is Paris Again"
E. "The Earth and Other Minor Things"

Answers on page 238.

Mary Martin

1. Mary Martin, who had been singing and dancing since her childhood in Texas, made her debut on Broadway at the age of twenty-four in one of the most memorable showstoppers of all time. The show was Cole Porter and Sam and Bella Spewack's 1938 hit *Leave It to Me*, and the song was "My Heart Belongs to Daddy." Clad in a fur-trimmed coat, seated on a trunk in a Russian train station, Martin wowed the crowd with the sexy number. While she sang, she was surrounded by admiring chorus boys dressed in parkas. One of them went on to capture a bit of fame himself. Who was it?
   A. Alfred Drake
   B. Gene Kelly
   C. Stanley Donen
   D. Dan Dailey, Jr.
   E. Eddie Albert

2. Following *Leave It to Me*, Hollywood called. Martin appeared in several bad films, then returned to New York, where she turned down the role of Laurey in *Oklahoma!* (now there's an interesting alternate-history musical to contemplate). Instead, she took the title role in Weill and Nash's *One Touch of Venus* (1943). Martin played the goddess Venus, who comes to life after a meek barber (Kenny Baker) slipped a ring on the finger of a statue. Venus learns about life among twentieth-century mortals and the barber develops a backbone, dumping his obnoxious fiancée. In the final scene, he meets a girl . . . who looks amazingly like the goddess. One of the show's hits was "Speak Low," which Martin performed sitting far downstage, perched on a chair. Martin had performed the number that way when she, Weill, and Nash were trying to get someone to join the *Venus* team. After seeing Martin perform the number with such stunning simplicity, that person agreed to come on board on the condition that Martin perform the number in the show exactly the same way. Who was it?
   A. Agnes de Mille, choreographer
   B. Elia Kazan, director
   C. S. J. Perelman, librettist
   D. Cheryl Crawford, producer
   E. Mainbocher, fashion designer

3. Martin's string of hits ended with 1946's *Lute Song*, with music and lyrics by Raymond Scott and Bernard Hanighen, and direction by John Houseman. Sidney Howard and

Will Irwin's book told the tale of a Chinese man (Yul Brynner, in his first important role) who journeys from his village to take the imperial civil service examinations at Beijing. After years of waiting and numerous disasters, his wife (Martin) follows after him. Judging by the reviews, *Lute Song* was a muddled mess, saving its impressive scenic design and costumes by Robert Edmond Jones. Which of the following is *not* true about *Lute Song*?

    A. it lasted only three performances
    B. all Yul Brynner's songs were cut from the cast album
    C. it was based on an ancient Chinese play
    D. it featured a lion dance and other elements of Asian theatre
    E. Martin changed the ending—in which a princess and the faithful wife shared the husband—over Houseman's protests

4. Martin's next big show was in London, Noel Coward's 1946 production of *Pacific 1860*, set, interestingly enough, in the South Pacific. Coward had invented an island called Samolo, complete with topography, history, and its own Polynesian-like language, which he used as a setting for several works. He originally wanted Irene Dunne to play the lead, an opera diva regaining her health in the tropics who falls for a much younger man, the son of a British official, and then loses him. Dunne was unavailable, so casting Martin—much closer in age to actor Graham Payn— meant rewriting the book and providing a happy ending. The creaky operetta flopped, and squabbles between Coward and Martin led to an estrangement that lasted for years. He objected to her accent and voice; she to the wigs and especially the costumes ("I'm allergic to bows," she claimed, but was forced to wear a skirt festooned with them). She also didn't like a song with naughty lyrics, though Coward noted that "My Heart Belongs to Daddy" was similarly risqué. Martin countered that *Leave It to Me* was a different sort of show and that it was out of character for an opera star to sing of prostitution, though she recognized the song's showstopping potential. Martin won that clash, and Coward wrote another number. The cut song later became a hit in his cabaret act, and was used in the Coward revues, *Oh Coward!* and *Cowardy Custard*. What was the lusty girl in the song named?

    A. Gladys
    B. Elena
    C. Alice
    D. Joyce
    E. Rita

5. Martin quickly returned to the heights after those flops, touring in a highly acclaimed production of *Annie Get Your Gun,* for which she got a special Tony for "Out-of-Town Performance." Then came the role of Nellie Forbush in Rodgers and Hammerstein's *South Pacific* (1949). She won the Tony for Best Actress and took the show to London for a lengthy run. True or false: Martin washed her hair onstage eight times a week during the course of the show.

6. Martin won another Tony playing the title role in *Peter Pan* (1954) opposite the deliciously evil Cyril Ritchard as Captain Hook. The show had a short run of only 149 performances because of a television deal with NBC that brought the boy who

wouldn't grow up into millions of living rooms. How many times did Martin play Peter for TV (I don't mean the endless reruns, but different broadcast versions)?

A. it was a one-time deal

B. two times

C. three times

D. four times

E. five times

7. Rodgers and Hammerstein's *The Sound of Music* (1959) might never have been created had it not been for Mary Martin. Director Vincent Donehue, who had worked with Martin on *The Skin of Our Teeth* (Martin as Sabina—does this sound like sensible casting to you?), had seen a German film on the Von Trapp family and wanted her as Maria. They planned it as a straight play, written by Russel Crouse and Howard Lindsay, with some Austrian folksongs added. Martin then asked her good friends Rodgers and Hammerstein to write one or two new songs. They were writing *Flower Drum Song*, but said if Martin and Donehue were willing to wait, they'd write the whole score. Though Martin was far from the right age for Maria, she played the role well, and did extensive research with Mrs. Trapp and with nuns.

Who sang "My Favorite Things" with Maria in the stage version?

A. Mother Abbess

B. Captain Von Trapp

C. the kids

D. Max

E. the lonely goatherd

8. In order to play the title role in *Jennie* (1963, with songs by Schwartz and Dietz, book by Arnold Schulmann), Martin turned down the roles of Dolly Levi and Fanny Brice. (Yes, that Fanny Brice. And you thought casting her as Sabina was odd.) *Jennie* was loosely based on the life of actress Laurette Taylor, who traveled the country in the early part of the century playing in melodramas. It staggered through eighty-two performances, with nearly everyone involved fighting with everyone else. These days, *Jennie* is best remembered for its fantastic scenic design by George Jenkins. *Jennie* featured all of the following *except:*

A. an erupting volcano

B. a pursuing grizzly bear

C. a baby about to go over a waterfall

D. a rotating torture wheel in a harem

E. a fire that destroys a theatre

9. Though Martin turned down the chance to originate the role of Dolly Levi, she did take *Hello, Dolly!* on tour, and to great notices. The tour began in Minnesota and Texas and was supposed to go to Moscow with NBC News as part of a cultural exchange program. At the last minute, the Soviets canceled the show. Producer David Merrick, never one to miss an opportunity for publicity, arranged for the tour to play to American GIs in Japan, Korea, and Vietnam. Shortly before the *Dolly!* tour, Martin turned down another role. What was it?

A. Daisy Gamble, *On a Clear Day*

B. Mame Dennis, *Mame*

C. Fraulein Schneider, *Cabaret*

D. Annie Oakley, revival of *Annie Get Your Gun*

E. Georgina Allerton, *Skyscraper*

10. Martin's final musical role on Broadway was the 1966 hit *I Do! I Do!*, produced by David Merrick with music and lyrics by Schmidt and Jones. Based on the play *The Fourposter*, it told of a fifty-year marriage between Agnes (Martin) and Michael (Robert Preston). Martin wasn't interested at first, especially since Preston was reluctant to sign, but she took a cassette tape of the score on the *Dolly!* tour which convinced her to do it. Preston came on board as well, and they worked extensively with director Gower Champion to create the first two-person musical in history. The show was so demanding, requiring the "stamina of boxers going fifteen rounds," as Martin put it, they initially played no matinees and had no understudies. Carol Lawrence and Gordon MacRae later took on matinees and covered when needed.

Which song nearly got cut, since Harvey Schmidt "hated it" and Champion was having trouble staging it? It was saved when Martin spoke up for it, suggesting a different staging and a shortened ending.

A. "I Love My Wife"

B. "Something Has Happened"

C. "Nobody's Perfect"

D. "My Cup Runneth Over"

E. "A Well-Known Fact"

Answers on page 238.

Patti LuPone

One of the great figures in modern musical theatre history, Patti LuPone is a multiple-Tony winner whose unique talents provide flair and drama to any production lucky enough to have her. There's talent in Patti's family: her great-grandmother was a renowned nineteenth-century opera singer and brother Robert is himself a Tony nominee.

1. LuPone attended Julliard, where she claims they didn't know where to put her since she didn't fit any one acting category. Afterward, she joined John Houseman's Acting Company, itself a Julliard offshoot. The Company's original folk musical, *The Robber Bridegroom* (music by Robert Waldman, book and lyrics by Alfred Uhry), played a mere fifteen performances on Broadway in 1975, but both the libretto and LuPone's Rosamund garnered Tony nominations. Who played the title role opposite her?

A. Kevin Kline

B. Barry Bostwick

C. Raul Julia

D. Tim Curry

E. Tom Wopat

2. Despite the Tony nomination, LuPone was asked to re-audition for *The Robber Bridegroom*'s second Broadway engagement. She declined, as David Merrick had tapped her to take over the title role in *The Baker's Wife* (1976), then on its lengthy, and ultimately futile, tryout. Fortunately for musical fans, LuPone, Paul Sorvino, Kurt Peterson, and Teri Ralston recorded the best songs from Stephen Schwartz' score. Merrick, not known for his musical judgment, intensely disliked one of LuPone's songs and even arranged to have the sheet music for it stolen from the musicians' stands while the show played in Washington. What was the song?

3. In 1978, LuPone appeared in the ensemble revue *Working*, inspired by Studs Turkel's oral histories of people describing their work lives. What was LuPone's occupation?
   A. call girl
   B. baker of meat pies
   C. cleaning woman
   D. housewife
   E. supermarket checker

4. Andrew Lloyd Webber and Tim Rice's *Evita* originated in London in 1978, with Elaine Paige in the title role and Hal Prince handling the incredible staging. LuPone won the Broadway spot over Meryl Streep, Raquel Welch, and Faye Dunaway. *Evita* proved to be a huge hit, running 1,587 performances and picking up Tonys for LuPone, Mandy Patinkin, Prince, score, lighting design, and Best Musical. In Rice's lyrics, Eva—herself a former actress—instructs her staff to glamorize her in the style of which famous movie star?
   A. Bette Davis
   B. Katharine Hepburn
   C. Lauren Bacall
   D. Vivian Leigh
   E. Elsa Lanchester

5. LuPone reunited with other Acting Company alumni for 1983's revival of Marc Blitzstein's *The Cradle Will Rock*. She played the dual roles of Moll and Sister Mister. Who directed this off-Broadway production?
   A. Will Geer
   B. Tim Robbins
   C. Leonard Bernstein
   D. Howard da Silva
   E. John Houseman

6. LuPone returned to the Great White Way in 1984, playing Nancy in a short-lived revival of *Oliver!* The following year, she headed to London for two shows. She first re-created her roles in *The Cradle Will Rock* and then became the first American woman to play a lead role with the Royal Shakespeare Company. The role was that of Fantine, the tragic young mother forced into prostitution to support her child, in *Les Misérables*. True or false: for her work in *Cradle* and *Les Miz*, LuPone became the first American to win an Olivier Award.

7. LuPone nabbed another Tony nomination, but no hardware, for her portrayal of Reno Sweeney in the 1987 revival of *Anything Goes*, which ran 804 performances. The highly acclaimed production featured a book revised by John Weidman and

Timothy Crouse, son of Russel Crouse, one of the original writers. Whose voice was the first heard in this production?

A. Patti LuPone

B. Ethel Merman (the original "Reno")

C. Howard McGillin ("Billy")

D. Cole Porter (the composer)

E. Jerry Zaks (the director)

8. Andrew Lloyd Webber cast LuPone in the plum role of Norma Desmond in *Sunset Boulevard* in the 1993 London production and had promised her (in her contract) that she would re-create the role on Broadway. But Lloyd Webber opted for a West Coast premiere, away from the New York critics, where Glenn Close got great notices as Norma. He then broke LuPone's contract and named Close for the Broadway cast. LuPone sued and settled for a reported million dollars. What did LuPone do with the money?

A. she took a trip around the world

B. she built a staircase like Norma's

C. she built a swimming pool at her house

D. she threw a blowout party with Faye Dunaway, who was also suing Lloyd Webber

E. she invested it in the Broadway production of *Passion*

9. LuPone wouldn't be in another Broadway musical until 2005. That doesn't mean she wasn't busy. She performed one-woman concerts, appeared in concert versions of *Pal Joey* and *Annie Get Your Gun*, starred in the television series *Life Goes On* and the Broadway plays *Master Class* and *Noises Off*. She returned to musicals in John Doyle's staging of *Sweeney Todd* as Nellie Lovett, a role she had previously played in Lonny Price's concert version at different venues. Like many in musical theatre, LuPone is passionate about the work of Stephen Sondheim and has played many Sondheim roles (even decidedly non-diva-sized ones) at the summer festival at Ravinia. Which Sondheim show has she *not* done at Ravinia?

A. *A Little Night Music*

B. *Anyone Can Whistle*

C. *Passion*

D. *Company*

E. *Sunday in the Park with George*

❧ ❧

BROADWAY BONUS: In Doyle's *Sweeney Todd*, the actors also served as the orchestra. LuPone played the tuba, an instrument she had played in high school. What was her tuba's nickname?

❧ ❧

10. LuPone won her second Tony for the iconic role of Rose in the 2008 revival of *Gypsy*, directed by Arthur Laurents. Which of the following is *not* true about this production?

A. LuPone was the oldest actress to play Rose on Broadway

B. LuPone said the *Gypsy* company was "the best company (she) ever worked with"

C. LuPone became the fourth actress to win the Best Actress Tony as Rose

D. Arthur Laurents' longtime partner, Tom Hatcher, convinced Laurents he should direct the show with LuPone

E. LuPone once interrupted "Rose's Turn" to berate someone taking photographs

Answers on page 239.

George Abbott

George Abbott's career in theatre began in 1911, when the University of Rochester's Dramatic Club staged his first play. It ended when he was 107 and worked as a consultant on the 1994 revival of *Damn Yankees*. In between, he was a Broadway actor, playwright, director, producer, and occasional show doctor. He directed over thirty original musicals and many revivals, and wrote or co-wrote a dozen. Abbott helped define musical comedies in the thirties and forties, relying on breathtaking pace, lots of dance (but not as much character development), and greater integration of plot and music than was seen in the twenties. He had an unfailing eye for spotting new talent; countless Broadway stars worked on their first shows under his guidance.

This is one of the more challenging quizzes, as much of the material comes from anecdotes culled from Abbott's long life. And what a life!

1. What particular bit of direction did Abbott define as "the Abbott touch"?

2. At the age of one hundred, Abbott got a special Tony at the 1987 Tony Award ceremony. How many did he already have?

   A. 5
   B. 6
   C. 7
   D. 8
   E. 9

3. Abbott was a no-nonsense director who maintained complete control over his shows. He later denied this story, but Gwen Verdon swore she overheard the following conversation: Method actor Stephen Douglass asked Abbott, "What's my motivation?" What was Abbott's famous reply?

4. Abbott never removed his jacket at rehearsals and frequently terrified actors with his intensity. Mary Louise Wilson called him "the Eagle" behind his back, but nearly everyone called him "Mr. Abbott" to his face. However, one performer in 1976's *Music Is* (Abbott's last original musical, a flop adaptation of *Twelfth Night*) seemed to revel in calling him "George." Who was it?

   A. Joel Higgins
   B. Christopher Hewett
   C. Daniel Ben-Zali
   D. David Brummell
   E. Laura Waterbury

5. Abbott accomplished a feat that will likely never be repeated: he directed three Broadway productions of the same show, the original and two revivals. Which show was it?

A. *On Your Toes*
B. *Damn Yankees*
C. *Pal Joey*
D. *The Pajama Game*
E. *On the Town*

6. Abbott wasn't always right. He cut a song from Cole Porter's *Out of this World* (1950) that later became a huge hit. In Abbott's defense, the actor supposed to sing it had a weak voice. What was the song?
   A. "Begin the Beguine"
   B. "Nobody's Chasing Me"
   C. "From This Moment On"
   D. "It's De-Lovely"
   E. "Down in the Depths"

7. Abbott wrote the libretto and directed 1965's *Flora, the Red Menace*, the show that brought Liza Minnelli great notices. While Abbott came to love her, he initially rejected Liza after her audition, hiring her only after his choice became unavailable. Who was it?
   A. Barbara Cook
   B. Anita Gillette
   C. Eydie Gorme
   D. Mary Tyler Moore
   E. Anna Maria Alberghetti

8. Abbott helped many young songwriters with their early efforts on Broadway. Who was *not* among them?
   A. Adler and Ross
   B. Lerner and Loewe
   C. Bernstein, Comden, and Green
   D. Bock and Harnick
   E. Kander and Ebb

9. What were two of the reasons Abbott gave for setting *New Girl in Town*, the 1957 musical based on O'Neill's *Anna Christie*, in 1900, not 1921? Remember, pick *two*.
   A. women were more emancipated in 1921; he wanted a time when they were more inferior, making Anna's problems greater
   B. he wanted to avoid the issues posed by Prohibition
   C. he didn't want Anna to be seen as a flapper
   D. he'd had enough of twenties musicals after *Billion Dollar Baby*
   E. clothes were prettier in the 1900s

10. Abbott lived to see a theatre named for him in 1965...and see it demolished in 1970. At least we still have George Abbott Way, a little stretch of West 45th Street in the heart of Broadway! What was the earlier name of the George Abbott Theatre?
    A. the Century Theatre
    B. the 44th Street Theatre
    C. the Fulton Theatre

D. the Bijou Theatre

E. the Adelphi Theatre/the 54th Street Theatre

Answers on page 240.

Barbara Cook

1. Atlanta's own Barbara Cook made a splash in her first big show, *Flahooley* (1951), at the age of twenty-three. She got the role after composer Sammy Fain heard her in a nightclub and asked her to audition. Lyricist Yip Harburg hugged her after her tryout, leading her to think all auditions went that way! She had to learn puppetry for this satire of American business. *Flahooley* was a huge hit in Philadelphia, but tanked in New York. What does "flahooley" mean?

   A. Arabian for "genie in a lamp"

   B. the noise made by a laughing puppet

   C. Irish for "flighty, whimsical"

   D. it's gibberish

   E. Peruvian for "laughing doll," as sung over an eight-octave range

2. Following *Flahooley*, Cook toured as Ado Annie in *Oklahoma!* and Carrie in *Carousel*, then got the part of Amish girl Hilda in 1955's *Plain and Fancy* (music by Albert Hague, lyrics by Arnold Horwitt, book by Joseph Stein and Will Glickman). The show concerned a New York couple visiting Pennsylvania Dutch country, and the romantic problems of the Amish. What prompts Hilda to sing "This Is All Very New to Me"?

   A. a taste of "vegetable juice" (scotch)

   B. seeing the carnival in Lancaster, which is sinful

   C. seeing a barn raised in minutes

   D. getting "hexed"

   E. her first kiss

3. The simple Amish maiden was worlds away from Cunegonde, princess of Westphalia, Cook's next major role. The show was Leonard Bernstein's *Candide* (1956), based on Voltaire's novel. Cook got rave reviews, stopping the show nearly every night with the jewel song parody, "Glitter and Be Gay." Cunegonde's materialism is a delicious contrast to commoner Candide's earthiness, as evidenced in their notions of what makes a happy marriage. What is *not* among Cunegonde's requirements?

   A. costume balls

   B. pearl necklaces

   C. silk and satin robes

   D. champagne

   E. a twenty-carat earring

4. Cook played Julie in the City Center production of *Carousel*, then got cast in the biggest hit of her life, Meredith Willson's *The Music Man* (1957). She won the Tony for her part as Marian Paroo, the librarian of River City, Iowa, who sets out to expose con man Harold Hill (Robert Preston), only to fall for his charms. Cook's

great acting skills and empathy helped the audiences believe in such a transformation, but Willson's score gave an assist. To show the unseen connection between two dissimilar characters, he gave the same melodic line to which two songs?

5. After playing Anna to Farley Granger's King in the City Center's *The King and I* in 1960, she was cast in another historical piece, Arthur Schwartz and Howard Dietz' *The Gay Life* (1960), set in 1904 Austria. She played young Liesl, who falls for her brother's best friend Anatol (Walter Chiari), a notorious ladies' man. Though the show lasted only 113 performances, one can hear the way Liesl changes from dreamy girl to mature woman, full of independence and fire, in the cast recording. Which of the following was *not* true of *The Gay Life*?
   A. it was suggested, in vain, that Cook play all four of Anatol's mistresses
   B. Herb Ross, choreographer, took over direction, but Gerald Freedman kept the billing
   C. Anita Gillette's role was cut so she could go into *Carnival*
   D. it was revised after the opening
   E. when published in 1986, it was retitled *The High Life*

6. Cook starred in yet another Continental romance, 1963's *She Loves Me*, in which she played Amalia Balash, a store clerk who doesn't know the co-worker (Daniel Massey) with whom she daily squabbles is her lonely-hearts pen pal. Jerry Bock and Sheldon Harnick wrote over twenty wonderful songs for this show that has become a beloved cult classic. One of Amalia's finest numbers is "Will He Like Me?" Which earlier number did this song replace?
   A. "Heads, I Win"
   B. "Seasonal Pleasure"
   C. "Tell Me I Look Nice"
   D. "Christmas Eve"
   E. "Hello, Love"

7. While *She Loves Me* lives on in the collective theatre consciousness, Cook's next show, 1964's *Something More!* vanished without a trace after fifteen performances, leaving no cast album. Composer Sammy Fain and lyricists Marilyn and Alan Bergman wrote the score, and Jule Styne directed this tale of a suburban family looking for "something more" in which of these locales?
   A. Italy
   B. Saudi Arabia
   C. Monte Carlo
   D. Peoria
   E. Barcelona

8. Cook starred and toured in the 1966 revival of *Show Boat*, then took on what would be her last original role on Broadway, *The Grass Harp* (1971). This show ran only half as long as *Something More!*, but has an unforgettable score (music by Claibe Richardson, book and lyrics by Kenward Elmslie). It was based on a Truman Capote story about two sisters: Dolly (Cook), who knows how to make a miracle cure for dropsy, and Verena (Ruth Ford), who wants to give the recipe to Dr. Ritz. In protest, Dolly, cousin Collin (Russ Thacker), and housekeeper Catherine (Carol Brice) take a

stand in a tree house. Well, never mind the plot—the songs are great. What does a "cat-shaped cloud" mean?

    A. it's a sign of dropsy-cure weather

    B. it means Babylove's Miracle Show is coming

    C. a storm is coming, so go hide in a tree house

    D. it means you should listen to dead people's voices singing in the Indian grass

    E. it's a warning of Southern Gothic–eccentric atmosphere

9. Since *The Grass Harp*, Cook has spent her time in concerts and cabarets as one of the leading song interpreters of our era. Stephen Sondheim requested her as Sally in the 1985 *Follies in Concert*, and she gave us classic versions of "Losing My Mind" and "In Buddy's Eyes." For the latter, Cook has said the song itself is a lie—it's Sally trying to convince herself—but she tried singing it as if she truly meant it. The concert gave Cook a chance to reunite with Elaine Stritch from her *Plain and Fancy* tour and what other person with whom she had previously worked?

    A. Herb Ross

    B. Lee Remick

    C. Phyllis Newman

    D. Carol Burnett

    E. Betty Comden

10. In 1987, Cook was back in a musical in Stratford, England, working with the Royal Shakespeare Company in a limited run. She missed serious injury when scenery collapsed on opening night, and soon after withdrew from the role, refusing to go on to Broadway. "There isn't a chance in hell that they'll be able to pull this off" was her analysis, and truer words were never spoken. What was the show and what was Cook's role?

Answers on page 240.

Harold Prince

This was one of the hardest quizzes to write, since Hal Prince is one of the greatest figures in the history of musical theatre, first as a daring young producer, then as a pioneering director. After fifty years in the field, he's still taking chances. Prince has won more Tonys than anyone else, and was awarded one for Lifetime Achievement in 2006. Since most of these questions involve specific knowledge of Prince's contributions as a producer-director or anecdotes about him, this is one of the more challenging quizzes.

1. After college, Prince worked briefly in George Abbott's office and as an assistant to Robert Griffith, Abbott's stage manager. Following his time in the army, he was assistant stage manager on *Wonderful Town* (1953), then, though only twenty-six, teamed with Griffith and Frederick Brisson to produce *The Pajama Game* (1954). Most of that team, including director Abbott, reassembled for 1955's *Damn Yankees*. Though it ended up a hit, it struggled out of town. Prince made a key decision regarding advertising that greatly helped. What was it? Hint: it had to do with Gwen Verdon.

2. Prince continued his phenomenal career as a producer with *New Girl in Town*, *West Side Story*, *Fiorello!*, and *Tenderloin*. Following the death of co-producer Griffith in 1961, Prince reorganized their company and tackled his first directing job, replacing Word Baker on *A Family Affair* (1962). Though it didn't run long, it marked the first time Prince worked with:

   A. Stephen Sondheim
   B. Jerry Bock and Sheldon Harnick
   C. James Goldman and John Kander
   D. Michael Bennett
   E. Cy Coleman

3. Prince produced *A Funny Thing Happened on the Way to the Forum*, then had the chance to direct a show from the start in *She Loves Me* (1963), which he also produced. Barbara Cook ended up the perfect Amalia, but she wasn't the original choice. Prince made the decision to go with Cook rather than wait six months for:

   A. Julie Andrews
   B. Liza Minnelli
   C. Mary Martin
   D. Inga Swenson
   E. Judy Holliday

4. Prince stayed with Bock and Harnick for their next project, *Fiddler on the Roof* (1964), which had been rejected by many other producers. He didn't direct, but his creative input was considerable. Director Jerome Robbins had staged an elaborate fantasy ballet, which Prince dissuaded him from using, noting it wasn't right for the mood of the show. Which more modest number replaced it?

   A. "Anatevka"
   B. "Matchmaker, Matchmaker"
   C. "Sunrise, Sunset"
   D. "Miracle of Miracles"
   E. "Sabbath Prayer"

5. Producer Alexander Cohen asked Prince to direct 1965's *Baker Street*, the Sherlock Holmes musical. Cohen wanted an extravaganza, while Prince thought the material required a more intimate treatment, to say nothing of a smaller theatre. He also didn't care for the score, and had Bock and Harnick interpolate some numbers. (To his credit, the show did better after moving to the smaller Martin Beck later in the run.) Prince's staging was praised, particularly the showstopping parade for Queen Victoria's Jubilee. How was it done?

6. Following the failure of *Baker Street*, Prince worked on his last show with George Abbott, *Flora, the Red Menace* (1965), followed by *It's a Bird…It's a Plane…It's Superman* (1966). He reunited with *Flora*'s Kander and Ebb for one of the most influential shows ever, 1966's *Cabaret*. The musical showcased Prince's concept of marking the parallels between the turbulent eras of Germany in the thirties and America in the sixties. Where did the idea of the Emcee originate?

   A. Peter Lorre in *The Maltese Falcon*
   B. an art catalog of paintings banned by the Nazis as "decadent"

C. David Belasco

D. an Albrecht Dürer engraving of the devil

E. a real dwarf emcee Prince has seen at a nightclub while stationed in Germany

7. Prince remained with Kander and Ebb for *Zorba* (1968), then in 1970 began a groundbreaking series of shows with Stephen Sondheim. The pair had known each other since the opening of *South Pacific* (1949) and used to meet at Walgreen's to discuss the future of the Broadway musical and their place in it (oh, to have been a fly on the wall!). Their first effort was the dazzling, innovative *Company*, followed by the landmark *Follies* (1971). *Follies* began as a conventional show, a murder mystery about former showgirls. Prince saw the possibilities for a more surreal production, blurring the lines between past and present, framed in the metaphor of show business as life. To help get his creative team in the mood, he screened a film for them. What was it?

A. Bergman's *Smiles of a Summer Night*

B. Fellini's *8 1/2*

C. Kurosawa's *Rashomon*

D. Wilder's *Sunset Boulevard*

E. Berkeley's *42nd Street*

8. Prince's tally for the rest of the seventies was nothing short of remarkable: *A Little Night Music*, *Pacific Overtures*, the American production of *Side by Side by Sondheim*, *On the Twentieth Century*, *Evita*, and *Sweeney Todd*. Prince's 1981 venture with Sondheim, *Merrily We Roll Along*, would have a rougher time. The show lasted but sixteen performances, though few today would doubt the brilliance of the score and its overall importance. *Merrily* faced numerous changes up to and including its final previews. Which of the following was *not* replaced?

A. the original Franklin Shepard

B. the original choreographer

C. the original opening number

D. the original costumes and sets

E. the original theatre

9. How many Tonys has Prince won?

A. eighteen

B. nineteen

C. twenty

D. twenty-one

E. twenty-two

In the years since *Merrily*, Prince has given us *A Doll's Life*, *Grind*, *Roza*, the first revival of *Cabaret*, *Kiss of the Spider Woman*, a revival of *Show Boat*, *Parade*, *3hree*, *Bounce*, *LoveMusik*, and the longest-running show in Broadway history, 1988's *The Phantom of the Opera*. While researching his career and trying to decide which of his many shows to include in a quiz, I was fascinated by the material that inspired him and affected his direction or design choices. Your final test will be matching items with the shows each influenced.

---

10. the paintings of Edvard Munch
11. Polonius' advice to Laertes
12. Diego Rivera's murals
13. painted masks used by disfigured WWI soldiers
14. a photo of Gloria Swanson in the rubble of the Roxy Theatre
15. a painting by Marc Chagall
16. the Industrial Revolution
17. a painting by Magritte

A. *The Phantom of the Opera*
B. *Follies*
C. *Evita*
D. *A Doll's Life*

E. *Sweeney Todd*

F. *A Little Night Music*
G. *Fiddler on the Roof*
H. *Merrily We Roll Along*

BROADWAY BONUS: Which is the only show directed by Hal Prince not to receive a cast album recording?

Answers on page 241.

Intermission

Food, Glorious Food

People sing and dance in musicals. They fall in and out of love in musicals. They also eat in musicals, as witnessed by many lyrics and plot lines involving meals and snacks. If you're not hungry, you will be at the end of this quiz.

1. Where do the frankfurters answer back?
2. What is Conrad Birdie ready to taste?
3. What do certain baseball widows cook that is deserving of praise, but ignored by their sports-obsessed spouses?
4. Name the veggies (besides radishes) grown in the gardens of two fathers.
5. What is in Fan Tan Fanny's refrigerator?
6. What does Josephus Gage eat for breakfast?
7. William Barfée is allergic to these.
8. What does Mabel Normand dish out at the deli in Flatbush?
9. The cook brings in two dishes at the dinner celebrating the engagement of Rosa Bud and Edwin. What are they?
10. Hildy brags of her ability to cook—and how! Which of her dishes allegedly induces drool?
11. What do they serve for lunch at St. Sebastian's?
12. Babe complains about the rising costs at the butcher's. What in particular is expensive?
13. How many seaweed salads are ordered by Roger, Collins, Angel, and their friends?
14. Who sells candy on MacConnachy Square?
15. Describe Bustopher Jones' meal at the Tomb.
16. Who resists the temptation of the following menu: beefsteak, pickled pig's feet, chili, turnip greens, and ice cream?
17. Algernon keeps eating them. This bothers Jack, since their romantic prospects were at that moment in dire straits. What are they?
18. What does Muñoz suggest as Stone's last meal?
19. You can buy roses and get knives ground on a London street. What else can you buy there?
20. It keeps bloodsucking fiends away—and, apparently, audiences as well.
21. In "Live and Let Live," Pistache admits to liking a certain French dish. What is it?
22. What do Ruth and Eileen eat for an entire week?
23. What do you need at a party besides that lively Grandpere to make it a success?
24. Who is fond of strawberry tarts?
25. Where can you find home-cooked navy beans?
26. Whose doors are made of gingerbread?
27. Where can you find a musical description of how to make a pot roast?

28. What does Sherlock Holmes need besides a cryptogram to attain a paradise on earth?
29. What seafood dish does Nettie describe as prepared in iron kettles?
30. Madame Armfeldt is disappointed these are no longer served.
31. Which *Titanic* passengers are partial to kidney pie?
32. What is Nellie Lovett's secret herbal ingredient?
33. Little Edie offers Big Edith a choice for dinner. What are the options?
34. What is Mr. Zero's last meal?
35. What gets thrown out the winder?
36. What food item did Jean Valjean steal?
37. What kind of sandwich do you get with coffee in a cardboard cup?
38. What does Georg bring to Amalia?
39. What company put crackers in a package?
40. In a small SoHo cafe on a Sunday, what do customers scream for?
41. What does Zorba like to chew?
42. What kinds of fruit can the sailors in the South Pacific pick right off the trees?
43. What did Irving Berlin say the hell with?
44. Maria alludes to a Viennese specialty as one of her favorite things.
45. Next to a "Bungalow in Quogue," what can one dig for?
46. Cole Porter mentions a lot of food in "You're the Top." What kind of dinner is sublime?
47. Charley's aunt is from a country noted for its nuts.
48. If there is honey in the honeycomb, what is in a squab?
49. What rare item does Herr Schultz bring Fraulein Schneider?
50. What flavor does the Piragua Guy *not* sell: mango, passion fruit, pineapple, strawberry, orange, lemon, raspberry, *mamey*. You not only need to know the lyrics for this one, but some Spanish, too!

Answers on page 242.

Cherry Pies Ought to Be You

Baked Goods

Can you bake a pie? Annie Oakley and Frank Butler lament that they can't, but plenty of folks in musicals are dab hands with baked goods. If you want a crusty loaf or a nice dessert, check out the offerings of these noted cooks or dining establishments. Match each baker or restaurant with his/her/their/its respective creations that are mentioned in lyrics or libretti.

1. Nellie Lovett	**A.** Rice Krispie treats
2. Bobo's	**B.** mincemeat pie
3. Miss Minerva	**C.** seven-layer cake
4. Louis	**D.** plum duff
5. Mrs. Juniper	**E.** meat pies
6. Lizzie Curry	**F.** birthday cake
7. Laurey Williams	**G.** sweet potato pie
8. the Baker (unnamed)	**H.** gooseberry tarts
9. Nanette	**I.** cheesecake and streusel
10. Lovey Mars	**J.** angel food cake
11. Susan	**K.** cookies
12. Mindy's Restaurant	**L.** Toledo Surprise
13. Ado Annie Carnes	**M.** pecan pie
14. Aimable	**N.** bread
15. Jeff Moss	**O.** bread, pies, sticky buns
16. Robert's friends	**P.** corn muffins
17. The Pastry Chefs	**Q.** bread, cakes, pastries
18. Polly Browne	**R.** lemon cake, buttered biscuits, and apple crumble
19. Toad	**S.** blinis
20. Mary Turner	**T.** sugar cake

BROADWAY BONUS: Assuming you haven't said good-bye to your blueberry pie (and are you as normal as one?), try to remember what two flavors of pie Marryin' Sam mentions while talking to Daisy Mae. What Sondheim/Furth character admits that she thinks Sara Lee rates higher than Eleanor Roosevelt? What is Enoch Snow's favorite dessert?

Answers on page 244.

Dark, Secluded Places

Nightclubs and Bars

Plenty of musicals have scenes set in bars, nightclubs, cabarets, hot spots, saloons, and pubs. And why not? Such places are terrific for dramatic or romantic encounters, and lend themselves to big production numbers. Try to match these joints where you can hoist a few or dance and maybe take in a show with the musicals in which they are featured.

1. The Village Vortex
2. The Upstairs Room at the Downtown Club
3. Hernando's Hideaway
4. Green Dragon Pub
5. Clancy's Lounge/Grapes of Roth
6. Cat Scratch Club
7. Diamond Eddie's Club/Congacabana Club/Slam-Bang Club
8. Three Cripples Tavern
9. Johnny-the-Priest's Saloon
10. Club Havana/Club Oasis
11. Around the Clock
12. The Green Frog
13. Bal du Paradis
14. The Red Rat
15. Club Zanzibar
16. Club Purgatory/Club Cocteau
17. The Hot Box/Cafe El Cubano
18. Club Petite
19. The Pyramid
20. Lank's Saloon
21. Paradise Club
22. Jeunnesse Dorée Club, New Orleans
23. Hotel Las Vegas
24. Hope and Anchor Bar
25. Bar-des-Inquiets
26. Paprika's Cafe, Vienna
27. The Casacabana
28. Saddleback Saloon, Leadville, CO
29. Last Chance Saloon
30. The Celestial Bar
31. Foley's Bar
32. Kit Kat Klub
33. The Bourbon Room
34. Fan-Dango Ballroom
35. Chez Joey
36. Joe Allen's
37. The Banana Club

A. *Guys and Dolls*
B. *Oliver!*
C. *Half a Sixpence*
D. *My One and Only*
E. *Flower Drum Song*
F. *The Pajama Game*
G. *Bells Are Ringing*

H. *Redhead*
I. *Do Re Mi*
J. *Jekyll and Hyde*
K. *Oh, Kay!*
L. *Juno*
M. *Wonderful Town*
N. *The Gay Life*
O. *Rock of Ages*
P. *Sweet Charity*
Q. *Kean*
R. *Seesaw*
S. *Naughty Marietta*
T. *The Unsinkable Molly Brown*
U. *Promises, Promises*
V. *The Act*
W. *Gentlemen Prefer Blondes*
X. *Applause*
Y. *On the Town*
Z. *Destry Rides Again*
AA. *New Girl in Town*
BB. *Crazy for You*
CC. *Du Barry Was a Lady*
DD. *Cabaret*
EE. *Can-Can*
FF. *Irma la Douce*
GG. *The Sweet Smell of Success*
HH. *Pal Joey*
II. *Rent*
JJ. *Avenue Q*
KK. *Merrily We Roll Along*

Answers on page 245.

Make It Another Old-Fashioned, Please

Booze

Folks in musicals really know how to knock them back! See if you can figure out these booze-related puzzlers.

1. What is Joanne's drink of choice?
2. What does the Engineer propose pouring down the drain?
3. Cunegonde doesn't object to this.
4. Herod proposes Jesus should do this.
5. Cissy describes her lengthy date with a refined fellow. What happened to the beer?
6. At Bamboo Jack's, when people drink when they do the mambo?
7. What do bachelor dandies drink?
8. For Fanny and Nick, what's the best accompaniment for macaroons?
9. If you have half a chicken and a bottle of this, maybe you can conquer the world, too.
10. It helps to make things lovely at Jason's bar mitzvah.
11. For unemployed steel workers, the future includes this.
12. For Edna and Wilbur, how much did a beer cost?
13. Champagne makes the Chaperone drowsy, but what does she mention in her rousing anthem?
14. What does one drink while dancing "Der Guten Tag Hop-Clop"?
15. Aristide is in love. What two substances does he contemplate drinking?
16. Whose job entails amusing those who drink vodka?
17. Who is the god of drama and wine?
18. Peron wants to retire and do crosswords and drink this.
19. Queenie says just of sip of this makes her Joe happy.
20. On an especially "great" day, what do you get with Benzedrine?
21. Where can you learn the students' "Drinking Song"?
22. What does Panama Hattie order?
23. What does Emma set out with the fried chicken?
24. Who drinks so much rum Congressional President Hancock revokes his privilege?
25. Where do they demand "Vodka, Vodka"?
26. Kate Monster has too many of these at the Around the Clock.
27. Who admits that God made liquor for temptation?
28. When she's drunk, she's beautiful.
29. At whose estate does champagne flow like a river?
30. What do little songbirds drink when dining?
31. Grandpa spent all of Grandma's housekeeping money on these.
32. What kind of red wine gets served at a big Italian sposalizio?
33. Hedwig and Sugar Daddy Luther discuss modern luxuries, including this type of booze.
34. Igor says he and Frederick are like which kind of drink?
35. Why are Lord Blandings and Shorty McGee eager for their ship to come in?
36. What is Champagne Charlie drinking now?
37. Mrs. Lovett gives Tobias some of this so he'll stop looking around for Senor Pirelli.

38. At Bobo's, what is Sammy full of?

39. What do Lord Brockhurst and Dulcie think about old wine?

40. Usnavi and Vanessa try to share a bottle of this.

Answers on page 246.

1776 Mini-Quiz

Since *1776* is one of my all-time favorites, I couldn't stop at just one question, but came up with a mini-quiz. Those of you less obsessed with singing and dancing Founding Fathers can move on to another part of the book. At our house, *1776* is required viewing every Fourth of July, and I have proposed doing a shadow-cast performance (as done at cult screenings of *Rocky Horror* and *Hedwig*), but only if I can play Stephen Hopkins. In a similar vein, I have created the *1776* drinking game: one player takes a shot every time a character shouts for rum and the other every time there's a dispatch from General Washington. Both players should be blotto well before "He Plays the Violin."

1. How do you make saltpetre?

2. What is General Henry Lee's nickname?

3. Why did Rex Everhart record the role of Ben Franklin for the cast album instead of Howard da Silva?

4. Where is the turkey fresh?

5. What two numbers did a White House staff member want cut before the cast performed at the White House for Richard Nixon, and what did Nixon (a huge Broadway buff) tell Virginia Vestoff about the Adams family and the East Room?

6. What do you call two useless men?

7. What was the name of Franklin's number that was cut before the opening? (Hint: its title lives on in a line of his dialogue.)

8. Where can you not find a pin?

9. What title did producer Stuart Ostrow propose calling the show?

10. What goes on in New Brunswick?

✲✲ ✲✲

SPECIAL *1776* BROADWAY BONUS: Name the seven committees Secretary Thompson lists in scene five.

✲✲ ✲✲

Answers on page 247.

A Chorus Line Mini-Quiz

Given that it's one of the most important musicals in history, *A Chorus Line* deserves a mini-quiz. Five-six-seven-eight, answer!

1. What color did Michael Bennett want for the costumes in the finale before being overruled by Theoni Aldredge and the now-iconic gold coats and top hats?
2. What happened on September 29, 1983?
3. The character Paul has the longest monologue, telling of his stint working in a seedy drag club. He describes his embarrassment the night his parents came to the club, and his surprise at what his dad tells the director. What was it?
4. What former collaborator of Bennett's did some uncredited (and unpaid!) work on the libretto while the show was still at the Public Theatre?
5. The character of Zach was created when James Kirkwood joined the production in the second workshop. What was there before Zach?
6. How far does Mike run to go to his sister's dance class?
7. What don't they have in San Juan?
8. What was Michael Bennett's real name?
9. What did Theoni Aldredge do to Carole Bishop's costume as Sheila?
10. To whom is *A Chorus Line* dedicated?

Answers on page 248.

Nine Mini-Quiz

Nine is one of those musicals people either love or hate, with no middle ground. If you're one of those who loathes it (or bears it a grudge for beating out *Dreamgirls*), feel free to move on to another part of the book. I find myself echoing Liliane La Fleur at the end of "Folies Bergere" in my appreciation of this show.

1. Fellini's agent approached this producer-director in the 1960s about a possible musical of *8 1/2*, but he turned it down. Who was he?
2. How many women auditioned for the twenty-two roles (twenty-one parts, plus the featured dancer)?
3. Why is it called *Nine* if the film was *8 1/2*?
4. How long was Lilane LaFleur's feather boa?
5. What is Contini's signature motif in his films?
6. Which number was considered too racy to be performed on network television during the Tony Awards broadcast?
7. What creative project did Maury Yeston have in common with Guido Contini (and Fellini, too, for that matter)?
8. What's in "Beatrice's" picnic basket?
9. What was Luisa's maiden name?
10. What three types of film does Guido consider for his next project, having forgotten he'd promised his producer a musical?

Answers on page 248.

Act Two: Scene One

Something to Do with Spring

Spring may be the most popular season in the land of musicals. After all, "April Showers" bring us May flowers, as Al Jolson told us in *Bombo* (1921), and flowers go with romance in a big way. And there are all those springtime show tunes, from "Younger Than" to "For Hitler." So wander down the garden path and check out these spring questions.

1. Who declares spring's arrival by noting "Winter's on the Wing"?

2. What do bluebells do down in the dell?
    A. the hokey pokey
    B. ring ring
    C. chime chime
    D. sing out
    E. curtsey gently

3. The action for three of the following four historically based musicals opens in the month of April. Which one does *not*?
    A. *Titanic*
    B. *Miss Saigon*
    C. *Parade*
    D. *Pacific Overtures*

4. The Bible says these blooms toil not, and neither do they spin, but on Broadway, they sure can sing! You'll find one in each of the following shows *except*:
    A. *On the Twentieth Century*
    B. *Peter Pan*
    C. *Show Boat*
    D. *Annie*
    E. *Kiss Me, Kate*

5. Who has to write a song for spring, but really doesn't want to?

6. It's always May at the "Honeymoon Inn." What flowers do you find there?
    A. columbine
    B. morning glories
    C. geraniums red and delphiniums blue
    D. sweet william
    E. honeysuckle

7. Where would you find "Someone in April"?

8. General Kineisias has the attitude that people should make time for love, since life is so fleeting. In fact, he thinks it goes as fast as a bit of spring. How much?

A. one minute
B. five minutes
C. an hour
D. a day
E. a week

9. After gathering lilacs in the spring, what should you do?
A. crack a rock in Sing Sing
B. build a home for two
C. walk down an English lane
D. find the heather on the hill
E. teach a lark to pray

10. What lyricist managed to include the following garden of flowers into a single song: violets, narcissus, lilies, roses, gladioli, sunflowers, heather, lilac, hibiscus, sweet peas, and trillium?
A. Ira Gershwin
B. Oscar Hammerstein
C. Lorenz Hart
D. Bob Merrill
E. Ogden Nash

BROADWAY BONUS: Mack wouldn't send them, but the Baron had them waiting at the station for Elizavetta. No other flower is mentioned in as many show tunes as the rose. And we're not just talking American Beauties, either. In the early part of the twentieth century, there were "Rose" songs from all of the following exotic locales *except:*
A. Iran
B. Seville
C. Stamboul
D. Peking
E. Kilarney

Answers on page 249.

Summertime

Summertime is often "Too Darn Hot," but there's something about warm weather that makes for good musicals. See what you know about these sizzling tunes and shows.

1. Way back in the Middle Ages, an anonymous English bard once sang of summer's arrival in "The Cuckoo's Song." What 1940s lyricist updated this number, but kept the first line virtually intact and even managed to note the medieval origins in the verse?
A. Yip Harburg
B. Johnny Mercer
C. John Latouche

D. Marc Blitzstein

E. Harold Rome

2. This summer camp musical opened during an actual heat wave in the days before air-conditioned theatres, but at least the actors kept cool in the built-in swimming pool.

3. Where do Mother, Father, and Edgar go to escape the city heat, to say nothing of all those burning fire stations?
   A. Atlantic City
   B. Coney Island
   C. Fire Island
   D. the Catskills
   E. Martha's Vineyard

4. Every character in the park scene painted by Georges Seurat (*Sunday in the Park with George*) complains about the heat. What, in particular, is vexing the soldier?
   A. he's not in the shade
   B. his helmet
   C. that monkey
   D. he's not in proportion
   E. his companion's a bore

5. *Crazy with the Heat* was a 1941 revue starring Willie Howard, Luella Gear, and Carl Randall. It was destined to fold, but somebody influential liked it well enough to revise it, promote it, and reopen it for another three month's run. Who was it?
   A. Walter Winchell
   B. Billie Burke
   C. Theodore H. Wing, Jr.
   D. Ed Sullivan
   E. Sam Harris

6. Marge and Gower Champion, in a 1950s dance revue, once performed a number celebrating summer in what scenic spot?
   A. Paris
   B. Tahiti
   C. Santa Monica
   D. Cucamonga
   E. Fairview Falls

7. All true Broadway buffs know that the members of the Continental Congress argued over the flies and the stifling heat in foul Philly. Which Founding Father actually did keep the Congress' weather records, a fact author Peter Stone worked into the libretto?
   A. John Adams
   B. Ben Franklin
   C. Thomas Jefferson
   D. Richard Henry Lee
   E. Stephen Hopkins

8. Where did Irving Berlin's "Heat Wave" originate?
  A. Martinique
  B. Haiti
  C. Cuba
  D. Puerto Rico
  E. Jamaica

9. You may think the livin' is easy, but this question isn't. What black spiritual did Dubose Heyward adapt for the lyrics of "Summertime" in *Porgy and Bess*?
  A. "Go Down, Moses"
  B. "Lonesome Road"
  C. "Deep River"
  D. "All My Trials"
  E. "Motherless Child"

For the last part of this quiz, match these musicals, which are set largely or entirely in the summer, with the year in which they are set.

10. *Seventeen*	**A.**	1921
11. *110 in the Shade*	**B.**	1933
12. *Take Me Along*	**C.**	1898
13. *The Music Man*	**D.**	1892
14. *Come Summer*	**E.**	1840
15. *St. Louis Woman*	**F.**	1936
16. *Steel Pier*	**G.**	1953
17. *Juno*	**H.**	1912
18. *Where's Charley?*	**I.**	1910
19. *The Light in the Piazza*	**J.**	1907
20. *By the Beautiful Sea*	**K.**	1907 (yes, there are two 1907s)

I'll give you a hint by naming (though not in order) the locations in which these shows are set: St. Louis, Dublin, the Connecticut River Valley, Indianapolis, Atlantic City, Oxford, Italy, Three Point (TX), River City (IO), Centerville (CT), Coney Island. And the pair set in 1907 were both huge flops.

Answers on page 250.

Shall We All Meet in the Autumn?

Fall brings us the changing colors of the leaves and the start of a new Broadway season. Check out these questions that all have to do with autumn.

1. *She Loves Me* depicted the changing of the seasons by the tried-and-true effect of showering leaves (and snowflakes) from the flies onto the stage. Ralph Williams complained it was too hokey, but was assured—by the man who had suggested it— that it would get laughs. It did, not least because the man responsible sat in the audience and helped generate chuckles. Who was it?

A. Sheldon Harnick
B. Hal Prince
C. Jerry Bock
D. Lawrence Kasha
E. Joe Masteroff

2. This show chronicles a year in a village and features an autumn dance of courtship. What was it?
   A. *Finian's Rainbow*
   B. *The Grass Harp*
   C. *Greenwillow*
   D. *Take Me Along*
   E. *The Robber Bridegroom*

3. Why can't Lancelot leave Guenevere in autumn?

4. Everyone knows you can find a "September Song" in Weill and Anderson's *Knickerbocker Holiday*, but where would you find a "November Song"?
   A. *Mack and Mabel*
   B. *Carousel*
   C. *Camelot*
   D. *Canterbury Tales*
   E. *Sugar*

5. You are performing in "The Thanksgiving Follies," but your real job is:
   A. a Ziegfeld chorus girl
   B. a detective on the Boston police force
   C. a nurse, sailor, Seabee, or Marine, stationed in the Pacific in WWII
   D. a waitress at the Double Cupp Diner or an attendant at the gas station next door
   E. a knife-thrower with Buffalo Bill's Wild West Show

6. What do Frog and Toad do in autumn?
   A. secretly rake leaves in each other's yard
   B. bake cookies
   C. fly kites
   D. harvest nuts
   E. go trick-or-treating

7. Fall brings us football season, which is clearly the sport of choice on Broadway. Football is featured in all of the following musicals *except:*
   A. *High Button Shoes*
   B. *The Best Little Whorehouse in Texas*
   C. *All American*
   D. *Good News*
   E. *Ragtime*

8. According to Kayama and Manjiro, how do leaves change color?

9. True or false? The last song played by the band on the Titanic before it sank was called "Autumn" and that's why Maury Yeston wrote a song by that name for his 1997 musical.

10. What autumnal event is celebrated in dance in both *A Tree Grows in Brooklyn* and *Meet Me In St. Louis*?

Answers on page 250.

Merry Christmas, Maggie Thatcher

Winter's a good time for curling up with a cup of cocoa and a good musical, many of which are set in the chilly season, often with scenes and songs about the holidays.

1. Where can you find a Chanukah party?
   A. *A Family Affair*
   B. *Caroline, or Change*
   C. *The Rothschilds*
   D. *Falsettos*
   E. *Minnie's Boys*

2. What kind of entertainment goes on at Consolidated Life's 19th floor Christmas party?

3. *A Christmas Carol* has been musicalized several times. The Alan Menken-Lynn Ahrens version packed Madison Square Garden's downstairs theatre from 1994 to 2003. Who among the following actors did *not* play Scrooge?
   A. Hal Linden
   B. Roger Daltrey
   C. Frank Langella
   D. F. Murray Abraham
   E. Paul Stanley

4. In *Sunset Boulevard*, after Norma professes her love for Joe, he abruptly leaves and heads for a New Year's party with folk his own age. What do the starving actors/writers/composers sing about?
   A. doing lunch
   B. their New Year's resolutions
   C. Joe's gold cigarette case
   D. Norma's old car
   E. getting a screen test or a song heard by studio bigwigs

5. You've been invited to the annual Christmas party hosted by Aunt Julia, Aunt Kate Morkan, and their niece Mary Jane. Where are you?
   A. the East Village
   B. Trenton, New Jersey
   C. San Francisco
   D. Innisfree
   E. Dublin

6. The shoppers in "Twelve Days to Christmas" hate their better-prepared friends and neighbors for all the following reasons *except*:

A. they mail their packages in August
B. they did all their shopping in time
C. they trim their trees nine days before Christmas
D. they print their names on their cards in June
E. their cards arrive on the 24th

7. What do Germans do when Germany is filled with snow?

8. In contrast to the Germans mentioned above, who longs for days of icicles and snow?
   A. the Von Trapp kids
   B. the baseball widows in *Damn Yankees*
   C. the girls in *House of Flowers*
   D. the girls in *13 Daughters*
   E. Edvard Grieg of *Song of Norway*

9. It's not Christmas without Santa! You can find fellows who wear Santa suits, agree to be a year-round Santa, or possibly could be the real Kris Kringle in all but one of the following:
   A. *The Music Man*
   B. *Assassins*
   C. *Flahooley*
   D. *I Love My Wife*
   E. *Here's Love*

10. The action in this musical runs a single year, from December 24 to December 24. What is it?

Answers on page 251.

The Show Must Go On

Shows Within Shows

Nothing lends itself to song and dance as having a backstage musical in a show, which explains why there are so many musicals that have shows-within-the-shows. Match the "show" in the left column with the musical in the right column in which you can find it either mentioned or performed or rehearsed.

1. *Robbin' Hood of the Old West*	**A.** *Babes in Arms*
2. *Pretty Lady*	**B.** *The Girl Who Came to Supper*
3. *Springtime for Hitler*	**C.** *A Broadway Musical*
4. *The Parson's Bride*	**D.** *The Producers*
5. *Sneakers*	**E.** *42nd Street*
6. *Musical Husbands*	**F.** *The Cat and the Fiddle*
7. *The Passionate Pilgrim*	**G.** *Ain't Broadway Grand*
8. *Of the People*	**H.** *Merrily We Roll Along*
9. *The Red Devil*	**I.** *Show Boat*
10. *Lee Calhoun's Follies*	**J.** *The Girl in Pink Tights*
11. *The Coconut Girl*	**K.** *Curtains*

BROADWAY BONUS: Where would you find *Rhinestones of 1932*?

Answers on page 251.

What If?

Musicals That Might Have Been

So you know musicals. But do you know about musicals that never existed, but *might have*, given other circumstances? For example, producer Gabriel Pascal offered George Bernard Shaw's *Pygmalion* to many songwriters and librettists, including Cole Porter, Noel Coward, Schwartz and Dietz, Harburg and Saidy, and Rodgers and Hammerstein. Some flatly refused it; Rodgers and Hammerstein struggled before declaring "it couldn't be done." Lerner and Loewe finally succeeded, on their second try, with the classic *My Fair Lady*. Aside from that well-known example, there have been many other cases where composers, lyricists, and librettists either failed in an attempt to create a musical (for whatever reasons), or were invited by producers to tackle a topic but refused the offer (for whatever reasons). Fortunately for us, others saw the promise in the material and persevered. But it's fascinating to think about these What Might Have Beens, isn't it?

The songwriters and librettists listed below were in some way briefly associated with the material in the opposite column. They might have started work on the show and died; they might have been fired; they might have abandoned it in frustration; they might have been unable to get the rights; or they might have turned down a producer's invitation without ever writing a note. If people worked as a team, they are listed with "and" joining the partners, as in "Kurt Weill and Maxwell Anderson." If more than one composer or team were affiliated with a show, they are listed together, but separated by a semicolon (Rodgers and Hammerstein; Lerner and Loewe). Some names will appear more than once, which means they were associated with more than one of these musicals that never saw the light of day (e.g., Frank Loesser has three entries.) The source material is listed in the opposite column, with the actual musical named in parentheses if it differed from the original. Be warned! This is probably the hardest quiz in the book, since it requires thoroughly obscure knowledge.

1. Cole Porter
2. Jerome Kern and Dorothy and Herbert Fields
3. Frank Loesser
4. Kurt Weill and Maxwell Anderson
5. Maury Yeston

6. Leonard Bernstein and Lillian Hellman
7. George and Ira Gershwin; Kurt Weill

8. Irving Berlin

9. Michel Legrand and Richard Wilbur; Stephen Sondheim
10. Rodgers and Hammerstein; Lerner and Loewe
11. Stephen Sondheim
12. Jerry Herman

13. Lerner and Loewe
14. Irving Berlin; Cole Porter; Cy Coleman and Carolyn Leigh
15. Sandy Wilson
16. Jerry Herman

17. Frank Loesser
18. Rodgers and Hammerstein; Lerner and Burton Lane
19. Dorothy, Herbert Fields, and Burton Lane; Cole Porter; Irving Berlin; Leroy Anderson and Arnold Hewitt
20. Jeff Bowen and Hunter Bell

21. Frank Loesser

Answers on page 252.

A. *Greenwillow*
B. *My Sister Eileen* (*Wonderful Town*)
C. life of Eva Peron (*Evita*)
D. *Liliom* (*Carousel*)
E. *Anna and the King of Siam* (*The King and I*)
F. Huckleberry Finn (*Big River*)
G. the life of Annie Oakley (*Annie Get Your Gun*)
H. the life of the Mizner Brothers (*Road Show*)
I. *La Cage aux Folles*

J. *The Madwoman of Chaillot* (*Dear World*)
K. *Marius, Cesar, Fanny* (*Fanny*)
L. *The Apartment* (*Promises, Promises*)
M. *9 to 5*
N. the trial of Leo Frank (*Parade*)

O. *Ninotchka* (*Silk Stockings*)
P. *La Femme du Bolanger* (*The Baker's Wife*)
Q. the life of Gypsy Rose Lee (*Gypsy*)

R. *The Producers*
S. *I Am a Camera/Berlin Stories* (*Cabaret*)

T. *Cannery Row, Sweet Thursday* (*Pipe Dream*)
U. *Li'l Abner*

Who Am I?

Biographical Musicals

Many musicals tell the life stories of real people, even though a few played fast and loose with the facts (hey, dramatic license and all that!). Most of the titles are too obvious for me to sneak them into a quiz; I mean, it's clear that Fiorello la Guardia and George M. Cohan were the subjects of *Fiorello!* and *George M.!*, respectively. The individuals listed below have all had musicals based on their lives, but I hope they'll be a little harder to identify.

1. Jackie Robinson _____
2. Mike Todd _____
3. Franz Schubert _____
4. Edith and "Little Edie" Bouvier Beale _____
5. Peter Allen _____
6. Benvenuto Cellini _____
7. Laurette Taylor (well, it's kinda sorta based on her) _____
8. Kurt Weill and Lotte Lenya _____
9. Boy George _____
10. Ed Kleban _____
11. Stew _____
12. Edvard Grieg _____
13. Addison and Wilson Mizner _____
14. Edward I Koch _____
15. Charles, Dauphin of France _____
16. Jacques Offenbach _____
17. Frederick Chopin _____
18. Fanny Brice _____
19. Henry VIII _____
20. Victoria Woodhull _____
21. Queen Victoria _____
22. the Marx Brothers and their mom _____
23. Gabrielle Chanel _____
24. Johann Strauss I and II _____
25. Ellie Greenwich _____

Answers on page 254.

It's Still Rock and Roll to Me

Jukebox Musicals

You'd have to be an *American Idiot* not to have realized how the jukebox musical has grown in popularity in the last quarter century. Broadly speaking, a jukebox musical is a show that uses previously written popular songs, often pop or rock, in a new libretto.

(One could argue that *My One and Only* and *LoveMusik* were jukebox musicals, too, but that would assume you could find a jukebox that plays Gershwin and Weill.) The libretto for a jukebox musical can either focus on the career of a particular singer, song-writer, or group, as in *Jersey Boys* (Frankie Valli and the Four Seasons), *Million Dollar Quartet* (Elvis, Cash, Perkins, and Lewis), or *Fela!* (Nigerian singer-songwriter Fela Kuti), or create a fictitious scenario in which to interpolate the songs, as in *Mamma Mia!* or *Rock of Ages*. As with other musicals, jukebox musicals have had some enormous success and some horrendous fates; we'll look at both kinds in this quiz. Love them or loathe them, jukebox musicals have become fixtures in the musical theatre world.

1. One of the earliest jukebox musicals was 1984's *Leader of the Pack*, which examined the career of singer-songwriter Ellie Greenwich. Anne Beatts' libretto followed Greenwich's life from college, where she met and married fellow composer Jeff Barry, through years of writing hits for doo-wop groups, to divorce, depression, and recovery. Greenwich played herself in the second act of the show, which debuted off-Broadway, but later transferred. It has remained popular in regional and community theatre ever since.
   Which of these groups did *not* record songs written by Ellie Greenwich?
   A. the Ronettes
   B. the Dixie Cups
   C. the Shangri-Las
   D. the Plaids
   E. the Crystals

2. 1989's *Buddy* was based on the short life of Buddy Holly. This hit, with book by Alan Janes and Rob Bettinson, ran for twelve years in the West End, and has been seen by over 20 million people in seventeen countries. Who owned the rights to the Buddy Holly song catalog and gave his blessing and assistance to producer Paul Elliot in making the musical a reality? Hint: there's a very specific connection between this man's career and Holly.
   A. Clive Davis
   B. Michael Jackson
   C. Quincy Jones
   D. Paul McCartney
   E. Michael Bolton

3. Bob Carlton first put together *Return to the Forbidden Planet* in the mid-eighties, then reworked it for a West End opening in 1989, where it won the Olivier Award for Best Musical two years in a row. This campy outer-space adventure used pop and rock songs largely from the fifties and sixties, including "Teenager in Love," "Born to Be Wild," "Who's Sorry Now?" and "Great Balls of Fire." The plot was based partly on the classic science fiction film *Forbidden Planet* and partly on one of Shakespeare's plays. What was it?
   A. *Romeo and Juliet*
   B. *Twelfth Night*
   C. *As You Like It*
   D. *King Lear*
   E. *The Tempest*

4. The behemoth among jukebox musicals is unquestionably *Mamma Mia!*, seen by over 40 million people worldwide and also made into a hit movie. Catherine Johnson wrote the book around song hits by the Swedish group ABBA (music and lyrics by Benny Andersson and Björn Ulvaeus). It opened in London in 1999 and on Broadway in 2001, where it is now the thirteenth longest-running musical. *Mamma Mia!* tells the story of Donna, a middle-aged woman once part of a singing group and now living on a Greek island, whose daughter Sophie is about to marry. Sophie has discovered that Donna was involved with three men, any of whom could be her father, and invites them to the wedding. Louise Pitre originated the role of Donna on Broadway, and it has since been played by other talented "Dancing Queens." Which of these Tony-nominated and Tony-winning actresses has *not* played Donna?

  A. Judy Kaye
  B. Carolee Carmello
  C. Beth Leavel
  D. Michele Pawk
  E. Dee Hoty

5. *Movin' Out* (2002) has a somewhat different format than other jukebox musicals. Twyla Tharp and Billy Joel created a successful dance piece around Joel's songs, many of which were stories in themselves. The dancers portrayed five young people growing up in the sixties, from high school to Vietnam and its aftermath. The lyrics were sung by the "Piano Man," who sat with the band above the action. *Movin' Out* ran for 1303 performances, a definite crowd pleaser. True or false: Twyla Tharp took home *Movin' Out*'s only Tony (for Best Choreography).

6. *The Boy from Oz* was about singer-songwriter-actor Peter Allen, responsible for many pop hits and the notorious Broadway flop *Legs Diamond*. In 1998, the stage musical version of Allen's life (book by Martin Sherman), chronicling his roots down under to his marriage to Liza Minnelli to his death from AIDS, debuted in Australia. It came to Broadway in 2003, starring Hugh Jackman, who would win the Tony for Best Actor. Jackman also hosted the Tony ceremony that year, winning an Emmy for his stint. One of the ceremony's more memorable bits was a number in which Jackman, in character as Peter Allen, plucked an actress from the audience to dance with him onstage. Who was the lucky gal?

  A. Stephanie Block
  B. Rebecca Luker
  C. Anne Hathaway
  D. Sarah Jessica Parker
  E. Cynthia Nixon

7. The only jukebox musical to win the Tony for Best Musical was 2005's *Jersey Boys*, a biographical show about Frankie Valli and the Four Seasons, and how they went from kids on the wrong side of the tracks to singing sensations. John Lloyd Young and Christian Hoff took home the acting awards, and Howell Brinkley was honored for Best Lighting Design.

  The original notion for using the songs of the Four Seasons in a musical first came to Bob Gaudio, one of the founding members of the group, after he saw one of their songs used to great effect in a movie. His first idea was to create a fictional scenario in which to use the songs, but librettists Marshall Brickman and Rick Elice realized that the Four Seasons' story was dramatic in itself. Which song gave Gaudio his inspiration? (Bonus points for knowing the award-winning movie, too.)

    A. "December 1963 (Oh, What a Night)"
    B. "Big Girls Don't Cry"
    C. "Can't Take My Eyes Off of You"
    D. "Walk Like a Man"
    E. "Stay"

8. The year 2005 was one of jukebox musicals. *Jersey Boys*, of course, was the champion, but there were lots of other shows based on popular singers or groups that didn't fare as well. Which of these did *not* have a jukebox musical about him or them in 2005?

    A. John Lennon
    B. the Beach Boys
    C. Elvis Presley
    D. Harry Chapin
    E. John Denver

9. Another jukebox musical that began in Australia is *Priscilla, Queen of the Desert*, which debuted in Sydney in 2006, and in London and Toronto in 2009. *Priscilla* is based on the 1994 cult movie of the same name, about three drag queens traveling across the outback in their giant motorcoach, Priscilla. The bus used onstage weighed six tons, is covered in LED bulbs, has a removable side panel, and is fully equipped with hydraulic lifts so it can move and turn. Stephan Elliott and Alan Scott adapted Elliott's screenplay and added an eclectic playlist. Which of the following songs is *not* used?

    A. "Thank God I'm a Country Boy"
    B. "Magic Bus"
    C. "A Fine Romance"
    D. "Follie! Delirio vano è questo! Sempre libera!"
    E. "MacArthur Park"

10. One of the most recent successful jukebox musicals is 2009's *Rock of Ages*. This playful show, directed by Kristin Hanggi with a book by Chris D'Arienzo, is set in Los Angeles in 1987. At a Sunset Strip rock club, a love story unfolds to the tunes of Journey, Styx, Pat Benatar, Whitesnake, Foreigner, and other glam-rock and metal bands of the eighties. *American Idol* star Constantine Maroulis and an onstage rock band kept audiences hopping. *Rock of Ages* thankfully does not take itself seriously (it's about eighties rock; how serious is that?) and has even helped set a Guinness world record for the most people playing air guitar.

Which of the following things does *not* happen at *Rock of Ages*?

    A. waving imitation lighters during song numbers
    B. drinks are served in-house by the ushers
    C. a sing-along
    D. guitar picks are thrown into the audience
    E. the people in the front row are given florescent-colored leg warmers

Answers on page 255.

Act Two: Scene Two

Masquerade

Characters Using False Names

Many characters in musicals use false names, travel incognito, or have secret identities. Professor Harold Hill is probably not the real name of the traveling salesman who comes to River City; indeed, his pal Marcellus calls him "Greg," but for all we know, that's another pseudonym! Listed below are the false names used by some characters. Your task is to fill in their real names. Spoiler warning: a few of these answers involve real twists in the plots of their respective shows.

1. Sweeney Todd _____

2. The Jackal _____

3. Bill Starbuck _____

4. The Scarlet Pimpernel _____

5. Joe Hardy _____

6. The Red Shadow _____

7. Flip, the Prince, Charming _____

8. The Cat_____

9. Lily Garland _____

10. "Miss Turnstiles" (for June) _____

11. "Rosabella" Esposito _____

12. Mimi, a beautiful French girl _____

13. "Ze Lady from Lourdes" (Colette Antoinette Alouette Mistinguette Alfabette) _____

14. M. Madeleine_____

15. Melisande (not the one Starbuck sings about) _____

16. M. Oscar _____

17. "Body Beautiful Beale" _____

18. Phocion, Aspasie, and Cécile _____

❧ ❧

BROADWAY BONUS: What other alias does Bill Starbuck use? And what is Sky Masterson's real first name?

❧ ❧

Answers on page 256.

I'm Looking for Something

Word Association

For this quiz, you need to match the following words or phrases with the musicals in which they can be found. Many are song titles or are adapted from titles; the ones in the final section are not. Most of these are fairly easy, and there are sixty-five of them. Go on, time yourself.

Where would you find Big...

1. -Ass Rock?
2. Black Giant?
3. Brother?
4. Bow-Wow?
5. D?
6. Spender?
7. Beat?
8. Time?
9. Trouble?

Where would you find Miss...

10. Turnstiles?
11. Marmelstein?
12. Blendo?
13. Baltimore Crabs?
14. Langley's School for Girls?

Where would you find Mister...

15. Cellophane?
16. Andrews' Vision?
17. Greed?
18. Bojangles?
19. Fezziwig's Annual Christmas Ball?
20. Monotony?
21. Goldstone?
22. Witherspoon's Friday Night?
23. Snow?

Where would you find Old...

24. Devil Moon?
25. -Fashioned Wedding?
26. Friends?
27. Deuteronomy?
28. Red Hills of Home?
29. Military Canal?

Where would you find New...

30. Deal for Christmas?
31. Ashmolean Marching Society and Students' Conservatory Band?
32. Music?
33. Ways to Dream?
34. Pair of Shoes?
35. -Fangled Preacher Man?
36. Town Is a Blue Town?

Where would you find Little...

37. Red Hat?
38. Biscuit?
39. Egypt?
40. Girl from Little Rock?
41. More Mascara?
42. Tin Box?
43. One's ABC?
44. Boy Blues?
45. Rumba Numba?
46. Do They Know?

Where would you find The...

47. Terror of the Thames?
48. Honeybunny Girl?
49. Simpson Sisters' Waxworks?
50. Opera Ghost?
51. 14th Earl of Hareford?
52. Lawd's General?
53. Red Shadow?
54. Wazir?
55. Jackal?
56. Incomparable Rosalie?
57. Inevitable Roscoe?

Where would you find the following newspapers or magazines?

58. *The Tatler*?
59. *The Manhatter*?
60. *Madame*?
61. *The Daily Planet*?
62. *Everywhere*?
63. *The Lily*? (I'll give you a hint: it's an abolitionist-feminist newspaper.)
64. *Allure*?
65. *The New York Globe*?

BROADWAY BONUS: Can you name two musicals in which the rival newspapers, *The New York Herald* and *The New York World* both were featured?

Answers on page 256.

Has Anybody Seen Our Ship?
Ships and Boats

Many musicals are set at sea. Others have song numbers or make other references to ships. Test your nautical-musical knowledge by matching the ship with the show in which it is mentioned.

1. *Coronia*		**A.** *Ben Franklin in Paris*
2. *U.S.S. Powhatan*		**B.** *Show Boat*
3. *S.S. Bernard Cohn*		**C.** *Little Me*
4. *Ile de France*		**D.** *Pacific Overtures*
5. *S.S. Paradise*		**E.** *Hit the Deck*
6. *New Caledonia*		**F.** *Sail Away*
7. *Erasmus*		**G.** *On a Clear Day You Can See Forever*
8. *Cotton Blossom*		**H.** *Sugar*
9. *S.S. Reprisal*		**I.** *Gentlemen Prefer Blondes*
10. *S.S. Gigantic*		**J.** *Miss Liberty*
11. *U.S.S. Nebraska*		**K.** *Oh Captain!*
12. *R.M.S. Aurania*		**L.** *Shogun: The Musical*
13. *S.S. American*		**M.** *Very Good Eddie*
14. *Catskill*		**N.** *Anything Goes*

BROADWAY BONUS: You don't get any credit for naming the doomed ship in *Titanic*, but can you name the two other White Star Line ships mentioned in the opening number?

Answers on page 258.

I Could Pass the Football
Sports

Sports and musicals have always gotten along well, going back to the early days of the twentieth century, when auto racing was in vogue and *The Vanderbilt Cup* (1906) had cars on treadmills and *The Auto Race* (1907) actually staged a race in the Hippodrome. Rodgers and Hart's 1926 *The Girl Friend* featured the then-popular six-day bicycle races.

College football is probably the sport portrayed most often in musicals, but the long-run champion was the award-winning *Damn Yankees*, which had the hapless Washington Senators finally winning the pennant from the Bronx Bombers.

For this quiz on sports-themed musicals, only one question actually requires any sports knowledge, so it doesn't matter if you don't know Barry Bonds from Gene Barry.

1. Where did Chuck Baxter want to take the girl of his dreams? Extra points for knowing the opponent, and a special Broadway sports trivia gold medal for knowing the final score.
   A. a New York Jets game
   B. a New York Yankees game
   C. a New York Mets game
   D. a New York Islanders game
   E. a New York Knicks game

2. *Bells Are Ringing*, *Guys and Dolls*, and *Little Johnny Jones* all feature which sport?

3. In which Sondheim show can you see a karate demonstration?

4. Lyricist David Zippel made it clear that someone was about to score in a duet filled with double entendres about which sport?
   A. hockey
   B. golf
   C. sharpshooting
   D. tennis
   E. synchronized swimming

5. Two gay men are playing racquetball onstage. Where are you?

6. Which two sports are mentioned in "My Heart Belongs to Daddy"?

7. Hub Perdue of the Boston Braves is pitching to Jack Murray of the New York Giants. Where are you?

8. Professor Fodorski uses his background in engineering to develop winning football strategy in which musical?

9. What are the soldiers playing in *Passion*?

10. Which Broadway composer wrote "Bingo, Eli Yale," a fight song still performed today at Yale University?
    A. Cole Porter
    B. Vincent Youmans
    C. Arthur Schwartz
    D. Richard Rodgers
    E. Harry Tierney

11. *Good News*, the 1927 hit about a football-mad college, helped get audiences in the mood by:
    A. handing out pompoms
    B. dressing the ushers in collegiate jerseys

C. inviting the front row to join in "The Varsity Drag" onstage

D. sticking pennants in the aisle seats

E. having cheerleaders do routines during the overture

12. Who is the only member of major league baseball's Hall of Fame to have a Broadway musical about his life?

13. Which dancer in *A Chorus Line* got a sports scholarship to college?

    A. Richie

    B. Bobby

    C. Paul

    D. Greg

    E. Mike

14. This character became famous for swimming the English Channel, but she's starring in an aquacade when she meets her true love. Who is she, and what show is this?

15. According to the chorus of *The Beautiful Game*, why did God give us feet?

16. In *The Full Monty*, the cast praises the playing style of which Hall of Famer?

    A. Magic Johnson

    B. "Broadway" Joe Namath

    C. Joe Montana

    D. Michael Jordan

    E. Wilt Chamberlain

17. In this Gershwin musical, the nine justices of the Supreme Court square off in a baseball game against members of the League of Nations to settle the matter of war debts from the Great War.

    A. *Of Thee I Sing*

    B. *Tip-Toes*

    C. *Strike Up the Band*

    D. *Pardon My English*

    E. *Let 'Em Eat Cake*

18. Where would you find Jason Alexander, Scott Ellis, and Rob Marshall on roller skates?

19. How does Linus help his baseball team?

20. Which sport is satirized in Sondheim's "Pour le Sport," written for the unproduced musical (book by Jean Kerr) *The Last Resorts* (1956)?

    A. badminton

    B. golf

    C. tennis

    D. polo

    E. mumblety-peg

Answers on page 259.

So Much in Common

Common Themes

This short quiz requires you to think about shows in a very wide sense. Each question lists musicals that seemingly have nothing in common, yet there is a link. It could be something in the song list, the staging, a character, background material, or its history. For example, most Broadway buffs would see the connection between *Sweet Charity*, *La Strata*, and *Nine:* they're all based on Fellini films. These are a little more difficult!

1. *Call Me Mister, Irma la Douce, Subways Are for Sleeping, She Loves Me, Mame*
2. *No Strings, Cabaret, Chicago, I Love My Wife*
3. *The Golden Apple, Camelot, Into the Woods, Wicked*
4. Irving Berlin, Harold Arlen, Kurt Weill, Al Jolson
5. *Of Thee I Sing, The Boy Friend, Bye Bye Birdie, Annie, The Best Little Whorehouse in Texas*
6. *Face the Music, How to Succeed in Business Without Really Trying, 70, Girls, 70, Big*
7. *Merrily We Roll Along, They're Playing Our Song, Rent, A New Brain, Curtains*
8. *The Boys from Syracuse, By Jupiter, The Happiest Girl in the World, The Frogs, Home Sweet Homer*
9. *Flahooley, Carnival, Little Shop of Horrors, The Lion King, Sweet Smell of Success, Avenue Q*
10. *Going Up, Rosalie, My One and Only, Steel Pier, The Drowsy Chaperone, Catch Me If You Can*

Answers on page 260.

Safety in Numbers

Song Titles with Numbers

From "One" (singular sensation) onward, you can do a lot of counting in show tune titles. The object here is to match the number in the first column with the item or phrase in the second column to complete a song title. Some of these will be ridiculously easy, others will be more obscure. It could be worse; I left out "Seventeen Gun Salute," *Carnival in Flanders*; "Eighteen Days Ago," *George White's Scandals of 1929*; "Twenty-one Chateaux," *Music Is*; "Twenty-nine Years Ago," *Mail*; and "Four Hundred Girls Ago," *Via Galactica*; just to name a few.

1. One
2. Two
3. Three
4. Four
5. Five
6. Six
7. Seven
8. Eight
9. Nine
10. Ten
11. Eleven
12. Twelve
13. Thirteen
14. Fourteen
15. Sixteen
16. Twenty
17. Twenty-two
18. Twenty-four
19. Forty
20. Forty-five
21. Fifty
22. Seventy ("70," to be precise)
23. Seventy-six
24. Ninety
25. One Hundred
26. Million
27. Seven Million
28. Twenty Million
29. Fifty Million
30. Hundred Million

A. Trombones
B. Cents a Dance
C. Collar
D. Zeros
E. Years
F. Minutes from Broadway
G. Easy Ways to Lose a Man
H. Day Week
I. Going on Seventeen
J. Hours of Lovin'
K. Night in Bangkok
L. Minutes for Lunch
M. Crumbs
N. Dwight Avenue, Natick, MA
O. Deadly Virtues
P. Years Ago
Q. Sunny Rooms
R. Percent
S. Again
T. People
U. Miracles
V. Jews in a Room Bitching
W. Months Out of Every Year
X. O'clock Song
Y. Dollar Bill, and Why
Z. Days to Christmas
AA. Girls, 70
BB. Ladies in de Shade of de Banana Tree
CC. People's Favorite Thing
DD. Dollar Smile

Answers on page 261.

Old Sayin's

Quotes

Broadway history is full of famous quips and quotes. Match the sayings on the left with the person who said each one.

1. "Directors are never in short supply of girlfriends."
2. (on hearing Lerner and Loewe's first songs for *My Fair Lady*): "Those dear boys have lost their talent."
3. (on Irving Berlin's talent): "It's easy to be clever. But the really clever thing is to be simple."
4. "Call me Miss Birdseye of 1950. The show is frozen!"
5. "It's not enough that I should succeed. Others should fail."
6. "Sex in a dance is in the eyes of the beholder."
7. "Satire is what closes on Saturday night."
8. (on creating musicals): "Content dictates form."
9. "I can pee a melody."
10. "They tell me now that I was part of the Golden Age of musical comedy. Hell, I didn't know I was part of a Golden Age. Half the time I was wondering where my next job would come from."

A. David Merrick
B. Richard Rodgers

C. Gwen Verdon

D. Stephen Sondheim
E. Ethel Merman

F. Barbara Cook
G. George Kaufman
H. Mary Martin
I. Bob Fosse
J. Jule Styne

Answers on page 261.

Keeping Cool with Coolidge

U.S. History

When my daughters were taking Advanced Placement U.S. history in high school, I created mix tapes for them using show tunes about historical events and themes. Aside from the obvious—learning about the creation of the Declaration of Independence from *1776* and presidential assassinations from *Assassins*, you can learn a lot about history through musicals. For example, "What a Remarkable Age This Is" from *Titanic* not only mentions the rise of business monopolies but also the concept of social Darwinism. Other songs on the tapes included "Molasses to Rum" (*1776*, triangle trade of North Atlantic slavery); "Is That Remarkable?" (*Floyd Collins*, the rise of mass media in the twenties); "Henry Ford" (*Ragtime*, importance of the assembly line and interchangeable parts); "The Farmer and the Cowman" (*Oklahoma!*, disputes in western land use between settlers and free-range cattlemen in the 1880s, though the show is set in 1907); and "Rock Island," (*The Music Man*, rise of national marketing). Who said musicals weren't educational?

All of the following questions require a knowledge of the history of musicals, but only a couple expect you to know anything about real history.

1. Franklin D. Roosevelt has been in a number of musicals. He promised us a "New Deal for Christmas" in *Annie*, was satirized in *I'd Rather Be Right*, was a puppet in *Flahooley*, was voiced by Art Carney in *Flora, the Red Menace*, and was nearly killed (offstage) in *Assassins*. Which musical included a touching eulogy of the wartime president?
   A. *Inside U.S.A.*
   B. *Miss Liberty*
   C. *Call Me Mister*
   D. *Yip Yip Yaphank*
   E. *Tars and Spars*

2. This 1989 rock opera about a notorious communist hunter closed after three previews. What was it? (No multiple choice here—the subject matter is a dead giveaway!)

3. Who wrote a musical flop that featured little-known President Rutherford B. Hayes?
   A. Richard Adler
   B. Irving Berlin
   C. Vernon Duke
   D. Leonard Bernstein
   E. Kurt Weill

4. This musical, which some regarded as too imitative of *The Sound of Music*, was set during the Civil War draft riots of 1863 in New York. What was it?
   A. *Hazel Flagg*
   B. *Maggie Flynn*
   C. *Christine*
   D. *Little Mary Sunshine*
   E. *Jane Eyre*

5. Which president has never been mentioned in a Sondheim lyric?
   A. Millard Fillmore
   B. William McKinley
   C. Herbert Hoover
   D. Abraham Lincoln
   E. Ronald Reagan

6. The novel *Uncle Tom's Cabin* by Harriet Beecher Stowe greatly helped the abolitionist cause. It was soon turned into a popular play, touring the nation well into the twentieth century. Most Broadway buffs are familiar with Jerome Robbins' innovative staging of the story in *The King and I*, but it was also the source of a 1924 musical *Topsy and Eva*. References to the iconic scene of Eliza crossing the ice can also be found in musicals as diverse as *Subways Are for Sleeping* and *Company*. Which musical, besides *The King and I*, featured an abridged performance of the story, including that scene?
   A. *A Connecticut Yankee*
   B. *Bloomer Girl*
   C. *What's Up?*
   D. *Damn Yankees*
   E. *The Civil War*

7. What horrific event during the Vietnam War was the basis for the short-lived 1975 rock opera *The Lieutenant*?

8. In the nineteenth century, "Boss" Tweed established Tammany Hall, the corrupt political machine that ran New York city for decades. Which classic song satirizes the notorious graft of Tammany Hall?
- **A.** "Guv'ment"
- **B.** "Think Big Rich"
- **C.** "Little Tin Box"
- **D.** "It's a Simple Little System"
- **E.** "Ace in the Hole"

9. What historical event provides the backdrop for *Caroline, or Change*?

10. This 1987 musical, which used the music of John Philip Sousa, featured a number set at the 1904 Republican National Convention.

11. "I Love the Ladies," sang this notable American with a roving eye in a flawed musical offering that was based on historic events. Who was it?
- **A.** Thomas Jefferson
- **B.** Bill Clinton
- **C.** Mickey Rooney
- **D.** Benjamin Franklin
- **E.** John F. Kennedy

12. This question requires searching the libretto (or the liner notes to the CD) with gun, camera, and encyclopedia. How many characters in *Ragtime* are based on historical figures? Don't include Edgar, the little boy loosely based on author E. L. Doctorow.
- **A.** 9
- **B.** 10
- **C.** 11
- **D.** 12
- **E.** 15

13. The Civil War has been the background for many musicals, including *Shenandoah* and *The Civil War*. But other significant events have provided fodder for shows. Which of the events below has *not* been featured in a musical?
- **A.** the impeachment of Andrew Johnson
- **B.** the fall of Saigon in the Vietnam War
- **C.** the women's suffrage movement of the nineteenth century
- **D.** the opening of Japan to Western trade, 1853
- **E.** Columbus' preparations to voyage to the New World

14. Peter Stuyvesant, a leading figure in the Dutch colony of New Netherland (later New York) in the seventeenth century, is a character in which musical?
- **A.** *Arms and the Girl*
- **B.** *Knickerbocker Holiday*
- **C.** *Sleepy Hollow*
- **D.** *Dearest Enemy*
- **E.** *Old Dutch*

15. Can you pass U.S. History—Show Tunes 101? Which song lyric repeatedly refers to the name given to the U.S. diplomatic policy of improving relations with Latin America?
  A. "America"
  B. "Conga!"
  C. "What's New, Buenos Aires?"
  D. "The Men Who Run the Country"
  E. "How Can You Tell an American?"
Answers on page 262.

The Doctor Is In
Physicians, Shrinks, and Dentists

Is there a doctor in the house? There are more than a few onstage in musicals! Below is a list of medical men, dentists, and head shrinkers. Your goal is to match the docs with their shows. I've excluded those with doctorates in philosophy (Dr. Dillamond of *Wicked*, Professor Henry Higgins of *My Fair Lady*, Dr. Pangloss in *Candide*) or theology (Dr. Brock of *Tenderloin*; but I should add that one of the men below held both medical *and* theology degrees!). Dr. Abner Sedgwick of *It's a Bird...It's a Plane...It's Superman* apparently held multiple degrees, but since I couldn't check his resume to see if any of them was an M.D., I've left him off, too. (One more slight for which he can plot revenge!)

And, I should note, a few of those listed below are merely masquerading as doctors.

1. Dr. Joseph Taylor, Jr.	**A.** *Dirty Rotten Scoundrels*
2. Dr. Frank N. Furter	**B.** *Passion*
3. Dr. Lyman Hall	**C.** *Grand Hotel*
4. Dr. Emil Shüffhausen III	**D.** *Amour*
5. Dr. Van Helsing	**E.** *Lady in the Dark*
6. Dr. Rocquefort	**F.** *Jekyll and Hyde*
7. Dr. Mendel (no last name given)	**G.** *Baker Street*
8. Dr. Tambourri	**H.** *Young Frankenstein*
9. Dr. Fine and Dr. Madden	**I.** *Allegro*
10. Dr. Kitchell	**J.** *Falsettos*
11. Dr. Brooks	**K.** *Promises, Promises*
12. Dr. Lucy Van Pelt	**L.** *Christine*
13. Dr. Rashil Singh	**M.** *1776*
14. Dr. J. Bowden Hapgood	**N.** *The Secret Garden*
15. Dr. Henry Jekyll	**O.** *Dracula*
16. Dr. Dreyfuss	**P.** *Little Shop of Horrors*
17. Dr. Neville Craven	**Q.** *Bells Are Ringing*
18. Dr. Carrasco	**R.** *You're a Good Man, Charlie Brown*
19. Col. Dr. Otternschlag	**S.** *Man of La Mancha*
20. Dr. Orin Bernstein	**T.** *The Rocky Horror Show*
21. Dr. Mark Bruckner	**U.** *Anyone Can Whistle*
22. Dr. Frederick Frankenstein	**V.** *On a Clear Day You Can See Forever*
23. Dr. John Watson	**X.** *Next to Normal*

Answers on page 263.

Chaucer, Rabelais, and Balzac

Literature

Rose wanted Albert to become an English teacher, but he was too busy promoting Conrad Birdie. You, however, can get a fairly good grade in English yourself just by going to musicals. Prove your knowledge of English and world literature by listing the famous works by these authors with the musicals they inspired. Many of these authors had more than one work adapted, and some individual works have been musicalized more than once. How many can you name?

1. Jane Austen: _____

2. Charlotte and Emily Brontë: _____

3. Pearl Buck: _____

4. Miguel Cervantes: _____

5. Geoffrey Chaucer: _____

6. Charles Dickens (six major productions): _____

7. T. S. Eliot: _____

8. Edna Ferber: _____

9. James Hilton: _____

10. Homer: _____

11. Victor Hugo: _____

12. Henry James: _____

13. James Joyce: _____

14. Herman Melville: _____

15. James Michener: _____

16. Marjorie Kinnan Rawlings: _____

17. John Steinbeck: _____

18. Robert Louis Stevenson: _____

19. Leo Tolstoy: _____

20. Mark Twain: _____

21. Jules Verne: _____

22. Voltaire: _____

23. Alice Walker: _____

24. Oscar Wilde: _____

25. Thomas Wolfe: _____

26. Émile Zola: _____

Knowing great literature doesn't just mean familiarity with novels and poetry. Many great (and not so great) musicals have been adapted, sometimes quite freely, from well-known plays. Sometimes those plays provided enterprising librettists with material for a whole new way of telling the story, such as in a different setting or era. Name the plays written by these masters of drama and the musicals they inspired.

27. Aristophanes: _____

28. Anton Chekhov: _____

29. Euripides: _____

30. Henrik Ibsen: _____

31. Ben Jonson: _____

32. Eugene O'Neill: _____

33. Plautus: _____

34. Edmond Rostand: _____

35. Richard Sheridan: _____

36. William Shakespeare (eight major productions, many minor): _____

37. Oscar Wilde: _____

Answers on page 264.

ANSWERS

Ah, Paris! Answers

1. False—the action in *Les Miz* (1987, music by Claude-Michel Schönberg, lyrics by Alain Boublil, Herbert Kretzmer) covers the years from 1815 to 1832. The French Revolution, as every schoolchild should know (or at least people who have seen the movie *Start the Revolution Without Me*), began in 1789. The revolution in *Les Miz* was a lesser-known, student-driven cause. See, musicals are educational!

2. Panisse is the aging sailmaker in *Fanny* (1954, songs by Harold Rome).

3. On the island of La Grande Jatte, c. 1884, people would go strolling—at least on Sundays—and Georges Seurat would sketch them. Some of them conducted affairs, had picnics, got drunk, or tried to pick up a date. See *Sunday in the Park with George* (1984, songs by Stephen Sondheim) for further details.

4. *Irma la Douce* (1960, music by Marguerite Monnot, lyrics by Alexandre Breffort) charges one thousand francs, which includes the tax.

5. M. Fermin and M. Andre succeeded M. Lefevre at the Paris Opera House, but *The Phantom of the Opera* (music by Andrew Lloyd Webber, lyrics by Charles Hart and Richard Stilgoe) soon drives them to distraction as well.

6. Madame Dubonnet's Finishing School is in Nice, as seen in *The Boy Friend* (1954, songs by Sandy Wilson). As we learned in the 1970 revival, it's much nicer there.

7. Cunegonde says she's in Paris during "Glitter and Be Gay."

8. The woman is French novelist Colette, and the show is *Colette Collage: Two Musicals About Colette* by Harvey Schmidt and Tom Jones, who have been working on variations of this show for decades.

9. You find the inmates of the insane asylum of Du Temps, now roaming freely about the town. The show is *King of Hearts* (1978, music by Peter Link, lyrics by Jacob Brackman; based on the cult movie).

10. Boublil and Schönberg's *Martin Guerre* first debuted in England in 1996. A revised version failed on the road in America in 2000. If you want an example of outstanding orchestrations, track down a copy of the original 1996 cast recording. It has a full orchestra playing beautiful Jonathan Tunick orchestrations. Tunick can make even a less than stellar score sound great.

11. Georges and Albin's nightclub, *La Cage aux Folles* (1983, songs by Jerry Herman), is in St. Tropez.

12. Maud, Bobo, and Henry are the leads in *Oh Captain!* (1958, music by Jay Livingston, lyrics by Ray Evans).

13. Champion's fabled ballet in the department store was called "The Sale," and the show was *Make a Wish* (songs by Hugh Martin).

14. Villon becomes *The Vagabond King* in this classic operetta by Rudolf Friml and Brian Hooker (1925).

15. The taunting French knights in *Monty Python's Spamalot* (2005, music by John DuPrez, lyrics by Eric Idle) say, "Fetchez la vache!," which they then catapult at King Arthur and his men. Someday I hope to write the definitive study of cows in

musicals, and while there have been many dancing ones, this ranks as the only catapulted one.

16. Ben Franklin (Robert Preston) and his lady love, Diane (Ulla Sallert), sing the charming ballad, "To Be Alone with You" while in a balloon. The show was *Ben Franklin in Paris* (1964, music by Mark Sandrich, Jr., book and lyrics by Sidney Michaels—although it's widely known that this ballad was a Jerry Herman interpolation).

17. The departing GIs in New York harbor gave Sherwood the idea for *Miss Liberty* (1949, songs by Irving Berlin), about newspaper rivalry in 1880s America and the creation of the Statue of Liberty, a gift from the French.

18. D—Peter takes his tourists to all those sights except Du Barry's bedroom. You need to see a different Porter show for that.

19. Pistache, in *Can-Can* (1953, songs by Cole Porter), knows that Paris sizzles in the summer. She loves it anyway.

20. M. Passepartout helps the poor in *Amour* (2002, music by Michel Legrand, English lyrics by Jeremy Sams).

21. You can find all those ladies in the songs of *Jacques Brel Is Alive and Well and Living in Paris* (1968, 1972).

22. Jo Mielziner's last sets were for the little village of Concorde, the scene of Stephen Schwartz' *The Baker's Wife* (1976).

23. The three Russian agents sent to decadent Paris in *Silk Stockings* (1955, songs by Cole Porter) can't wait to go to the Folies Bergère.

24. *Dear World* (1969, songs by Jerry Herman) sets the song "Garbage" in the sewers. Porter had seven French musicals, but Herman hasn't done badly, with *Dear World*, *La Cage aux Folles*, and *The Grand Tour*.

25. *Coco*, also known as Gabrielle Chanel, reveals her childhood desire for a red communion dress (1969, music by Andre Previn, lyrics by Alan Jay Lerner).

26. The leads in *No Strings* (1962, songs by Richard Rodgers) travel all over France.

27. The original source material is Rostand's *Cyrano de Bergerac*. The fourth attempt to make it into a musical, *Cyrano* (music by Michael J. Lewis, book and lyrics by Anthony Burgess), got to Broadway in 1973 and Christopher Plummer earned a Tony. He had previously played Cyrano in Burgess' nonmusical version. Weirdly enough, another attempt to do a Cyrano musical, *A Song for Cyrano*, played summer stock also in 1973, similarly with a lead actor famous for playing the role in the nonmusical version. Jose Ferrer, who portrayed the dashing swordsman/poet in the film version, produced, directed, and starred in this version with songs by Wright and Forrest. The Dutch brought a Cyrano musical to Broadway for 137 performances in 1993, and Frank Wildhorn and Leslie Bricusse have a current version. Their demo, featuring Douglas Sills, appeared in 1996, but plans for an English premiere fell through. It debuted in Tokyo in the spring of 2009 in Japanese, followed by a Spanish version in Madrid in the fall.

28. *Roberta* (1933, music by Jerome Kern, lyrics by Otto Harbach) is set in the Parisian dress shop and is based on the novel *Gowns by Roberta*.

29. Aunt Alicia, in the stage version of Lerner and Loewe's *Gigi* (1973) wants seven rooms in the home Gaston will provide for Gigi. And a northern view is definitely out.

30. Bert Lahr was Louis XV in Cole Porter's 1939 hit, *Du Barry Was a Lady*.

31. The girls of "Maxim's" are found in Franz Lehár and Adrian Ross' *The Merry Widow* (1907), which, despite its Viennese origins, is set in Paris.

32. Ann Reinking was Joan, Joel Grey the Dauphin in *Goodtime Charley* (1975, music by Larry Grossman, lyrics by Hal Hackady).

33. You can either translate *La Plume de Ma Tante* or you could have gone to see it in 1958 (music by Gerard Calvi, French lyrics by Francis Blanche, English lyrics by Ross Parker). Just so people wouldn't be confused (much of the show was in pantomime), they put a sign on the door which read: "English Spoken Here."

34. *Ambassador* (1972, Grossman and Hackady again) did not have the staying power of the original James novel.

35. Freddy Benson, one of those *Dirty Rotten Scoundrels* (songs by David Yazbek), is looking to pull off con jobs on the French Riviera, specifically, the fictional town of Beaumont-sur-Mer. But I give you credit if you just said the Riviera.

36. Maury Yeston did a musical of Gaston Leroux's *The Phantom of the Opera*, which he called *Phantom* (first produced in Houston, 1991). He began work on it in 1983, after completing *Nine*, but Lloyd Webber beat him to the finish line.

37. During WW II, Polish Colonel Stjerbinsky (Ron Holgate) must travel through Nazi-occupied France to meet the man with the flower in his lapel, who will give him the papers needed to get to England, where the Polish government was in exile. Along the way on *The Grand Tour* (1979, songs by Jerry Herman), he is accompanied by a Jewish refugee, S. I. Jacobowsky (Joel Grey).

38. Marguerite St. Just, before she became Lady Percival Blakeney, performed at the Comédie Française. (*The Scarlet Pimpernel*, 1997, music by Frank Wildhorn, lyrics by Nan Knighton).

39. Toddy, in *Victor Victoria* (1995, music by Henry Mancini, lyrics by Leslie Bricusse), enjoys "Paris by Night."

40. Porter's first French musical (billed as a "musicomedy" in the program) was 1928's *Paris*. It introduced the hit song "Let's Do It, Let's Fall in Love."

41. She's not a character in *Gentlemen Prefer Blondes* (1949, music by Jule Styne, lyrics by Leo Robin), but everyone has a great time singing about how "Mamie Is Mimi." Do any of you find yourself thinking of the "Saga of Jenny," who couldn't say no in a multitude of languages when you hear the verse about how Mamie, now Mimi, could only say "oui"?

42. Porter's 1938 hit about Americans in Paris and then Russia was *Leave It to Me*, best remembered today for Mary Martin's debut, singing "My Heart Belongs to Daddy."

43. The imperial Russian refugees, now in service in a wealthy American's Parisian home, can be found in 1963's *Tovarich* (music by Lee Pockriss, lyrics by Anne Croswell).

44. Ahrens and Flaherty's early work off-Broadway, *Lucky Stiff* (1988), was based on the novel *The Man Who Broke the Bank at Monte Carlo*.

45. *Mata Hari* (1967, songs by Edward Thomas and Martin Charnin) was the storied flop based on the life of the notorious French spy.

46. In "Be Our Guest," the show-stopping production number in *Beauty and the Beast* (1994, music by Alan Menken, lyrics by Howard Ashman and Tim Rice), Lumiere tells Belle that their spirit of hospitality comes from the fact that they're in France. Of course they act like that. And there's a baker in the opening number calling for his wife to get the baguettes. All that's missing is the concertina. Yet the show never specifies which era—the costumes (enchanted objects aside) seem to dwell in some undefined fairy tale era, as seen in the concept that the Beast is really a prince. A prince? Of which royal house? See, this is what happens when a historian starts analyzing the background of a musical based on a *cartoon*.

47. The answer is *Marguerite*, which played at the Haymarket in 2008.

48. *The Unsinkable Molly Brown* (songs by Meredith Willson) goes from rags to riches, and from Leadville to Paris, and learns some French, too ("Bon Jour").

49. The vampire Lestat in Anne Rice's novels is immortal, but at thirty-nine performances in 2006, the musical *Lestat* (book by Linda Woolverton, music by Elton John, lyrics by Bernie Taupin) wasn't.

50. Dickens' *A Tale of Two Cities*, set during the French Revolution, has been musicalized at least three times, including a sixty-performance Broadway run in 2008 (book and songs by Jill Santoriello).

~~ ~~

BROADWAY BONUS: Porter wrote seven musicals with French settings. 1938's *You Never Know* had a short run, compared to the six shows (*Paris*, *Fifty Million Frenchmen*, *Leave It to Me*, *Du Barry Was a Lady*, *Can-Can*, and *Silk Stockings*) mentioned in this quiz. The fact that Porter suffered his crippling horse-riding accident while working on this show might have something to do with its overall quality and how he remembered it. Still, a show that gives us such a great number as "At Long Last Love" can't be that bad.

~~ ~~

How Are Things in Glocca Morra? Answers

1. Lichtenburg—*Call Me Madam*

2. Rumson, California—*Paint Your Wagon*

3. The Kingdom of Romanza—*Rosalie*

4. The Jungle of Nool—*Seussical*

5. Bali Hai—*South Pacific*

6. Bottleneck—*Destry Rides Again*

7. Concorde, France—*The Baker's Wife*

8. Czechogovia—*Sally*

9. Dogpatch, U.S.A.—*Li'l Abner*

10. Rainbow Valley, Missitucky—*Finian's Rainbow*. And Glocca Morra's not real, either.

11. Sweet Apple, Ohio—*Bye Bye Birdie*

12. Steeltown, U.S.A.—*The Cradle Will Rock*

13. Custerville, Arizona—*Girl Crazy*

14. Ruritania—*Princess Flavia*, but you also get full credit if you said *Zenda*, the 1963 Edwin Lester show by Duke and Charnin that starred Alfred Drake and Chita Rivera and never got to Broadway. In fact, you are a Broadway mythical geography expert if you named both shows, and you clearly need to get out of the house more often.

15. Bird-in-Hand, Pennsylvania—*Plain and Fancy*. Have you ever noticed weird similarities between the road directions for getting to Bird-in-Hand and the subway directions in *Subways Are for Sleeping*?

16. Mira—*Carnival*. I've always assumed that Mira got bombed out of existence by the Germans and Lili is suffering from post-traumatic stress disorder, and that's why she's messed up and talking to puppets. And Paul's clearly suffering from his own ghastly war experiences. So they (and Carrot Top) can help heal each other, since psychoanalysis in postwar France was not easy to find.

17. Never-Never Land—*Peter Pan*. Did you know it's simply "Neverland" in Barrie's book?

18. D'hum—*Hot Spot*

19. Brunswick, Iowa—*State Fair*

20. Rodney, Mississippi Territory—*The Robber Bridegroom*

21. Katwyk-ann-Zee, Holland—*The Red Mill*

22. River City, Iowa—*The Music Man*. Oh, come on. Did I really need to write the answer for this one?

23. Marsovia—*The Merry Widow*. The show is set in Vienna, but characters include the prince and the ambassador from Marsovia, which I'm guessing is somewhere near Czechogovia.

24. Angel's Roost and Rhododendron, Washington—*The Golden Apple*

25. Joy City—*The Grass Harp*

26. Stoneyhead, Vermont—*Hazel Flagg*

27. St. Pierre, Quebec—*The Happy Time*. I felt sure there must be a real St. Pierre somewhere in Quebec, but while there is a lake, there's no town by that name.

28. Carpathia is a mythical Balkan state in *The Girl Who Came to Supper*. The Carpathian Mountains are real, but there is no Carpathia outside of Noel Coward's imagination.

29. Three Point, Texas, is the town suffering from heat that's *110 in the Shade*.

30. Samolo is another Coward creation, a fictional British colony in the South Seas that was the setting for *Pacific 1860*.

I couldn't include *It's a Bird...It's a Plane...It's Superman* because there are several towns named Metropolis in the United States, and one even hosts an annual Superman convention. (Thanks to my good friend and fellow Broadway buff Len Wein, creator of the character Wolverine and writer for the *Superman* comic, for that fact.) And there are no fewer than nine Putnam Counties, so *The 25th Annual Putnam County Spelling Bee* was out.

Large, Monopolizing Corporations Answers

1. Harriman Munitions—*Hooray for What!*
2. Sleep-Tite Pajamas—*The Pajama Game*
3. Horace J. Fletcher Chocolate Works—*Strike Up the Band*
4. Henry Ford's Factory—*Ragtime*

5. a parachute factory in the South—*Carmen Jones*
6. World Wide Wickets Company—*How to Succeed in Business Without Really Trying*
7. B. G. Bigelow, Inc.—*Flahooley*
8. Apex Modes Inc.—*I Can Get It for You Wholesale*
9. Consolidated Life—*Promises, Promises*
10. the U.G.C. (Urine Good Company)—*Urinetown*
11. Sincere Trust Insurance Company—*Thoroughly Modern Millie*
12. World Wide Pictures—*What Makes Sammy Run?*
13. Shalford's Drapery Emporium—*Half a Sixpence*
14. F.F.F. Studios—*Fade Out—Fade In*

Typically English Answers

1. E—Richard O'Brien did not direct *The Rocky Horror Show*. That honor went to Jim Sharman, fresh off his record-breaking success with the British production of *Jesus Christ Superstar*.

2. A—the concept was David Kernan's. He was then performing in a production of *A Little Night Music* when asked by Cleo Laine if he could come up with a Sunday concert of Sondheim songs. He approached Martin and McKenzie, who were performing next door to *A Little Night Music* in *The Norman Conquests*, when their two casts met for tea on matinee days. They readily came on board. And in case you were wondering, the Book of Kells was an illuminated manuscript of the Gospels created by Irish monks around 800 C.E. A beautiful facsimile edition had been published not long before the creation of *Side by Side by Sondheim*, so maybe the composer had it on his mind. It's really quite beautiful, even if you don't know Latin.

BROADWAY BONUS : Young Mackintosh saw Julian Slade's *Salad Days* and vowed to work in the theatre when he grew up.

3. The dance was "The Lambeth Walk."

4. D—9.2 million people saw *Les Misérables* during its original Broadway run. Over 50 million have seen it worldwide, and it has grossed over $2 billion.

5. E—Warsaw is not mentioned in the lyrics to *Chess*.

6. A—Bob Avian, another of Bennett's protégés, choreographed *Miss Saigon*.

7. A—David and Shaun Cassidy, who are half-brothers and the sons of Tony winner Jack Cassidy, played the doomed twins in *Blood Brothers*. And yes, answer E was a joke, so Sutton Foster fans need not write indignant letters. I really wanted to list Murray and Anthony Head, which would have been brilliant casting had the musical been written about fifteen years earlier.

8. C—*Diamond in the Rough* is the name of the film within the show. "Love's Never Easy" and "The Journey Home" are two song titles, and *Slumdog Millionaire* won the Oscar.

9. B—Stiles and Drewe wrote the score for *Just So*, Mackintosh's production of Rudyard Kipling's stories. The show was first staged in 1989, with Julia McKenzie directing,

and has undergone many rewrites since. Stiles and Drewe feel the latest (2004) version may be the best and final draft. They are also responsible for adapting Hans Christian Andersen's *The Ugly Duckling* into the award-winning musical *Honk!*

10. Trent Kowalik was the Billy who performed the "Angry Dance" at the Tonys. The most ever co-nominees for a Tony Award were Lauri Peters (Liesl) and the six Von Trapp kids from *The Sound of Music*, but they lost to Sandra Church in Gypsy. The entire cast of *La Plume de ma Tante* won a special Tony.

Groundhog! Groundhog! Answers

1. O—Tait College—*Good News*
2. N—Knickerbocker University—*On Your Toes*
3. G—Southern Baptist Institute of Technology—*All American*
4. D—Harrison University—*The Day Before Spring*
5. A—University of Heidelberg—*The Student Prince*
6. J—Pottawattomie College—*Too Many Girls*
7. H—Santa Rosa Junior College—*Smile*
8. K—Texas A&M—*The Best Little Whorehouse in Texas* (which should have been a dead giveaway!)
9. B—Rutgers University—*High Button Shoes*
10. I—St. Olde's College, Oxford—*Where's Charley?*
11. L—Haverhill College—*Roberta*
12. E—University of Minnesota (Alpha Cholera Fraternity)—*Barefoot Boy with Cheek*
13. M—Metropolis Institute of Technology (MIT)—*It's a Bird…It's a Plane…It's Superman*
14. P—Harvard University—*Legally Blonde*
15. F—Atwater College—*Leave It to Jane*
16. C—Shiz University—*Wicked*
17. The kids in *Grease* attend Rydell High.
18. East High School (imaginative name, that) is the setting for *High School Musical*. And before any purists scream at me, there is a stage version of the incredibly popular Disney TV movie, and it's being performed everywhere.
19. The teens in *Sarafina!* go to Morris Isaacson High.
20. Patterson Park High, a real Baltimore high school, is where you can find Tracy and her pals from *Hairspray*.

BROADWAY BONUS: Wreck of *Wonderful Town* attended Trenton Tech. Miss Marmelstein (*I Can Get It for You Wholesale*) was an English major at CCNY. Tait College's arch rival was Colton College in *Good News*. Atwater College's dire foe was Bingham, as seen in *Leave It to Jane*. The yucky school colors of the unnamed college of Joseph Taylor, Jr. (*Allegro*) are purple and brown. George and Ira Gershwin, while out in Hollywood writing movie musicals, revised "Strike Up the Band" with special lyrics for UCLA (my alma mater! Go, Bruins!). And you graduate summa cum laude if you knew that Liza Elliott, the *Lady in the Dark*, went to Mapleton High.

Be Italian Answers

1. Guido and Luisa stay at Fontana di Luna (*Nine*).
2. Venice, Verona, Cremona, Parma, Mantua, and Padua are the towns visited by those players in *Kiss Me, Kate*.
3. Giorgio and Clara fall in love in a park in Milan (*Passion*).
4. Leona stays at the Pensione Fioria (*Do I Hear a Waltz?*).
5. Fabrizio's shop is next to the Arno River (*The Light in the Piazza*).
6. Benvenuto Cellini was *The Firebrand of Florence*.
7. *Rugatino* was the only Broadway musical entirely performed in Italian with English supra-titles.
8. Giulietta's studio is in Venice.
9. *Bravo, Giovanni* centered on the rival Roman restaurants.
10. *Carmelina*, set in San Forino, has a plot quite similar to that of the later show, *Mamma Mia!*, and the earlier movie, *Buona Sera, Mrs. Campbell*, although Alan Jay Lerner vehemently denied any resemblance.
11. *The Glorious Ones* was the title of Ahrens and Flaherty's off-Broadway commedia musical.
12. This show was *Portofino*, one of the greatest Broadway disasters of all time.
13. *A Funny Thing Happened on the Way to the Forum* was adapted from elements in the ancient Roman plays of Plautus. (Plautus himself freely borrowed stuff from the Greeks.)
14. Barbara Cook's flop Italian musical was *Something More*. One would think anyone involved with Broadway would have run screaming from the word "Portofino."
15. *Ankles Aweigh* was set in Sicily and in the Mediterranean, or was it a sea of red ink?
16. Valentine, one of the *Two Gentlemen from Verona*, wants to go to Milan.

The Only Lobby I Know Is the Martin Beck Answers

1. O—the Alvin Theatre became the Neil Simon Theatre.
2. K—the Guild Theatre/the ANTA (American National Theatre and Academy)/the Virginia Theatre became the August Wilson Theatre.
3. I—the 46th Street Theatre became the Richard Rodgers Theatre.
4. L—the National Theatre/the Billy Rose Theatre became the Nederlander Theatre.
5. U—the Uris Theatre became the George Gershwin Theatre.
6. A—the Forrest Theatre/the Coronet Theatre became the Eugene O'Neill Theatre.
7. F—the Richard Mansfield Theatre became the Brooks Atkinson Theatre.
8. B—the Selwyn Theatre became the American Airlines Theatre.
9. N—the Globe Theatre became the Lunt-Fontanne Theatre.
10. J—the Little Theatre became the Helen Hayes Theatre, the second of that name. The original historic Helen Hayes was demolished in 1982 to make room for the Marriott Hotel.
11. S—the Ritz Theatre/the RFK Children's Theatre became the Walter Kerr Theatre.
12. R—the Martin Beck Theatre became the Al Hirschfeld Theatre.

13. H—the Theatre Masque became the John Golden Theatre.
14. C—Erlanger's Theatre became the St. James Theatre.
15. T—the Colony Theatre became the Broadway Theatre.
16. G—the Stuyvesant Theatre became the Belasco Theatre, the second of that name.
17. D—the Republic Theatre/the Belasco Theatre (first)/Minsky's/the Victory Theatre became the New Victory Theatre.
18. Q—the Plymouth Theatre became the Gerald Schoenfeld Theatre.
19. E—the Golden Theatre/CBS Radio Theatre/the Royale Theatre became the Bernard Jacobs Theatre.
20. M—Henry Miller's Theatre became the Stephen Sondheim Theatre on March 22, 2010, on Sondheim's eightieth birthday.
21. P—the Gallo Opera House/the New Yorker Theatre/the Palladium Theatre/the Federal Music Theatre/CBS Studio became Studio 54. Aside from previously housing the Studio 54 disco, it housed Billy Rose's nightclub, the Casino de Paris, in the 1930s.

BROADWAY BONUS: Portions of the Lyric and the Apollo were preserved and restored in 1998 and used to create the Ford Center, which is now the Hilton Theatre. The Mark Hellinger is now the Times Square Church.

On the Street Where You Live Answers

1. W—Henry Higgins of *My Fair Lady* lives at 27-A Wimpole Street.
2. J—the Sherwood sisters of *Wonderful Town* live on Christopher Street. In the original stories, they lived on Delancey, but the show pointedly notes that interesting people live on Christopher Street.
3. M—Marcel Dusoleil of *Amour* lives at 23 Rue St. Vincent, in the 17th Arrondissement in Paris. If you're not familiar with *Amour*, buy the cast album now. It's a fantasy about an ordinary guy who develops the ability to walk through walls. It boasts a charming score by Michel Legrand, and starred Malcolm Gets, Melissa Errico, and a top-notch comic ensemble. It ran for a handful of weeks back in 2002 and deserved a better fate.
4. T—Judge Turpin and his ward Johanna (*Sweeney Todd*) live in Kearney's Lane, London.
5. V—the Banks family and their new nanny, Mary Poppins, live at 17 Cherry Tree Lane in London.
6. K—Ida, Harry, Gert, Eunice, and the rest of the seniors in *70, Girls, 70* live at the Sussex Arms Hotel.
7. S—Sherlock Holmes lives at 221-B *Baker Street*.
8. L—Mother, Father, Younger Brother, Edgar, and Grandfather live at Broadview Avenue in New Rochelle, as told in *Ragtime*.
9. O—Porgy and Bess and their friends live at Catfish Row, Charleston, South Carolina. According to *Porgy and Bess* author DuBose Heyward, it was really called "Cabbage Row."

10. C—Mame Dennis (and her nephew Patrick) live at 3 Beekman Place.

11. I—the Smith family of *Meet Me in St. Louis* live at 5135 Kensington Avenue.

12. R—Daddy Warbucks and his Annie live in that 5th Avenue mansion.

13. D—Noble Eggleston of *Little Me* lives at Quality Hill, Hackensack, New Jersey.

14. P—Rita and Hal of *Mr. Wonderful* live at 1617 Broadway.

15. F—Mrs. Johnstone and Mickey were thrilled to move to 65 Skelmersdale Lane, but there's no escaping fate for *Blood Brothers*.

16. E—Rita Racine longs to stop dancing on the *Steel Pier* and go back to 12 Ocean Drive.

17. A—Alvin and Cleo in *I Love My Wife* live in an apartment on 7 Elm St., Trenton, New Jersey.

18. G—Clara and her mother live at 125 East Lake Street, Winston-Salem, North Carolina, but Clara is moving to Firenze, where she can enjoy *The Light in the Piazza*.

19. B—Archibald and Colin Craven live at Misselthwaite Manor in Yorkshire, where the late Mrs. Craven had a lovely *Secret Garden*.

20. U—the Perons live at the Casa Rosada (*Evita*).

21. N—Chuck Baxter (*Promises, Promises*) has his apartment at 9 West 67th Street, but all those senior executives keep using it.

22. H—Fanny Brice, that *Funny Girl*, lived with her mom at 24 Henry Street until she married Mr. Arnstein.

❧ ❧

BROADWAY BONUS: Peggy Sawyer (*42nd Street*) and Rose Grant (*Bye Bye Birdie*) both hail from Allentown, Pennsylvania. Yes, I said, Allentown. Kringelein is at first refused a room, but the Baron pressures the staff into giving him Room 418.

❧ ❧

The 1900s Answers

1. E—"That was no lady. That was my wife," or, to do it properly in Weber and Fields' "Dutch" dialect: "Dot vass no lady. Dot vass my vife." "The Belt in the Back," or "the Tailor Sketch," was popularized by Eddie Cantor. "Slowly I Turn. . . ." is attributed variously to early vaudeville stars Joe Fay, Harry Steppe, and Samuel Goldman, but was immortalized by Abbott and Costello, the Three Stooges, and the *I Love Lucy* show. "Half of Everything I Own Is Yours" belongs to Burns and Allen. "Waiter, There's a Fly in My Soup" first saw print in 1872, but I suspect it's even older than that.

2. D—Florodora was the name of the island and its perfume.

3. B—Imogene, the dancing cow, one of a long line of bovine Terpsichoreans, accompanied Dorothy in the 1903 musical. Those familiar with the Baum novels will recognize Billina, the talking chicken; the odious Button Bright, whose answer to most questions is "Don't know!"; Polychrome, the Rainbow's daughter; and one of my favorites, the nine tiny piglets.

4. B—"Go to Sleep, Slumber Deep" was another of the hits from *Babes in Toyland*. "Moonbeams" and "The Streets of New York" were from *The Red Mill*. "Tramp! Tramp! Tramp!" and "Ah, Sweet Mystery of Life" were from *Naughty Marietta*.

∿∿ ∿∿

BROADWAY BONUS: Victor Herbert was a founding member of ASCAP and let his musical *Sweethearts* (1913) be used as the test case in the Supreme Court regarding public performances. Herbert had entered a restaurant where the orchestra was playing songs from *Sweethearts* and helped set the case in motion. Justice Oliver Wendell Holmes ruled in favor of ASCAP, allowing songwriters to receive royalties for public performances of their works. So, thank you, Victor Herbert!

∿∿ ∿∿

5. C—Paul Laurence Dunbar, one of the first black poets to gain national acclaim, was the lyricist for *In Dahomey*. The others were all part of the Harlem Renaissance and date to a later period. Langston Hughes' work made it to Broadway in Kurt Weill's *Street Scene*.

6. E—during the actors' strike, Cohan vowed he would *operate an elevator* (not drive a taxi) rather than stay in show biz. Whereupon Eddie Cantor quipped he'd have to join a union to do that.

7. True—the giant red mill was the first moving, electric sign on the Great White Way.

8. B—Frederick Loewe's father, Edmund Loewe, was a renowned tenor, the original Prince Danilo. Kurt Weill's dad was a cantor. Arthur Schwartz' father was a lawyer, who wanted his son to follow in his footsteps. Vernon Duke was born in Russia, the son of an engineer. Frank Loesser's father was a German piano teacher.

9. A—The *Follies* girls, as far as I know, didn't wear dinosaur headdresses, though it's cool to imagine them doing so. The "Age of Reptiles" murals date from the 1940s, which might have given some of you a clue that this was the right answer. In 1909, they did dress as mosquitoes in a number about a tunnel from Manhattan to New Jersey—no, really, could I make that up? It referred to the bugs in the Jersey marshes. They also wore the battleship headdresses that year. In 1907, they dressed as jurors, mocking the legal woes of Enrico Caruso, who had gotten in hot water pinching a girl at the Central Park monkey house. And they dressed as taxi cabs in the 1908 version.

   In later productions, the girls would appear as salad items, bottles of soda pop and fruit juice during Prohibition, as classical melodies, and as members of Washington's Continental Army.

10. E—*Arms and the Man* was the basis for *The Chocolate Soldier*. *The Chocolate Soldier* so irked Shaw that when producers tried getting the musical rights to *The Devil's Disciple*, Shaw said it was to be an opera or nothing else. There was an attempt in London, in 1983, to turn *The Admirable Bashville* into a musical (*Bashville*). *The Man of Destiny* and *Captain Brasshound's Conversion* remain unconverted to musical form, but smart fans will know that besides *Pygmalion* (*My Fair Lady*), Shaw's *Caesar and Cleopatra* became *Her First Roman*.

   Useless Operetta Fact of the Day: both *The Merry Widow* and *The Chocolate Soldier* have characters named Popoff.

The 1910s Answers

1. E—Nijinsky—the skit spoofed *Sheherazade*, with Williams playing Nijinsky and Brice doing the commentary on the side.

2. Oscar Hammerstein had just closed his Manhattan Opera House after coming to an agreement with the Metropolitan Opera House (this town ain't big enough for the both of us, said the Met, so here's a million dollars to make you go away), and was looking to use his opera stars, so he cast them in *Naughty Marietta* to great success. More than he'd had with them at the Manhattan.

3. B—Will Rogers never appeared in a *Passing Show*, but the others all did. Miller, Wynn, and Allen all moved to the Follies, and the Astaires began appearing in book shows.

4. D—the parrot kept squawking, "Oh! Oh! Delphine!" but the show also boasted the randy commanding officer and the elephant named Toodle-Doo, who only semaphores in my fevered imagination. Delphine makes a big entrance on Toodle-Doo's back and warns that the beast will stomp anyone who sings flat.

5. D—"It's a Long, Long Way to Tipperary" was the hit song from *Chin-Chin*. Irving Berlin wrote "Alexander's Ragtime Band" independent of any show, but performed it at a Friars' Club benefit in 1911. However, the slaves of the lamp in *Chin-Chin* do sing about "Ragtime Bells" after hearing bells ringing at a Chinese temple. Well, that makes as much sense as Aladdin falling in love with an American girl. "A Little Girl at Home" was from Victor Herbert's 1912 show, *The Lady of the Slipper*, and all you Jerome Kern addicts out there should have recognized "They Didn't Believe Me" from 1914's *The Girl from Utah*.

   As far as I know, "Oh! Oh! Delphine!" didn't become a national catch phrase, but Stone played a ventriloquist in *Chin-Chin* whose dummy constantly quipped, "Very good, Eddie!" This, of course, became the title (minus the comma) of the 1915 Princess show, *Very Good Eddie* one year after *Chin-Chin*.

6. A—Trentini's refusal to perform the encore so enraged Herbert, he vowed to never work with her again. Trentini did end up having an affair with Friml, but after the show had begun production.

7. False—this is one of those Broadway legends. *Maytime* was popular, but not popular enough to warrant two theatres at once. I suspect the story began after the Shuberts revived *Blossom Time*, in May 1923, for a very brief time at two venues, the Shubert and the 44th Street theatres.

8. E—the Tickle Toe was the dance from *Going Up*. The Gaby Glide debuted in the 1911 Al Jolson vehicle, *Vera Violetta* (with a young Mae West in the chorus!), while the Monkey Doodle Doo was from Berlin's *The Cocoanuts*, and the Syncopated Walk was from Berlin's *Watch Your Step* (1914). The Toddle, which later became hugely popular with flappers (especially in Chicago, which is why it's a "toddlin' town"), arose out of fox-trots.

9. C—"I Want to See a Minstrel Show" was a Berlin song written for the famous *Ziegfeld Follies of 1919* and was performed by Eddie Cantor and Bert Williams. The other songs were all introduced by Jolson: "Where Did Robinson Crusoe Go with Friday on Saturday Night?" came from *Robinson Crusoe, Junior* (1916); Gershwin

and Irving Caesar wrote "Swanee" and Caesar and Walter Donaldson wrote "My Mammy" for *Sinbad* (1918); "Sister Susie's Sewing Shirts for Soldiers" came from *Dancing Around* (1914), one of the Shuberts' Winter Garden revues. Jolson turned "Sister Susie" into a hit by making it a sing-along with the audience. It's interesting that although the Great War had only been raging for a few months by the time of *Dancing Around*'s debut in November 1914, Broadway was showing its colors for the Allies. The quintessential WWI song, "It's a Long, Long Way to Tipperary," was interpolated in this show as well, but didn't stick. It would show up a few weeks later in *Chin-Chin*.

10. A—Alice Roosevelt Longfellow once wore a dress of a particular shade of blue that became known as "Alice Blue." Alice Paul helped get women the vote, even enduring forced feedings while attempting a hunger strike in prison. The heroine of *Alice in Wonderland* is often depicted wearing blue, but not "Alice Blue." Alice B. Toklas was Gertrude Stein's friend and famous for her brownies. And Alice J. Shaw was apparently the greatest, most versatile professional whistler the world has ever known. Her heyday was in the late 1880s and early 1890s.

The 1920s Answers

1. D—Jack builds mobile homes in Kansas. Cole Porter wrote of shooting-boxes in Scotland; the bungalows in Quogue are from *Leave It to Jane*; the Edies sing about cottages in Cape Cod in "Peas in a Pod" in *Grey Gardens*; and flats in Flatbush are alliterative.

2. A—she ends up a Ziegfeld girl and married to a millionaire. Shades of the *Florodora* sextette! Miller plays a circus performer in *Sunny*, and in *Rosalie* is engaged to the Romanzan prince but ends up married to the aviator; and Gertie Lawrence was married to the English aristocratic bootlegger in 1926's *Oh, Kay!*

3. A—Jules Bledsoe did not appear in the cast of *Shuffle Along*.

4. C—Kitzi, Fritzi, and Mitzi were the trio from *Blossom Time*, with Mitzi as Schubert's love. The original Austrian play that was the basis for the musical (*Das Dreimäderlhaus*) gave us Hannerl, Heiderl, and Hederl. The French version, *Chanson d'Amour*, had Annette, Jeanette, and Nanette. Sally, Irene, and Mary all had musicals named after them in this period, including a successful show called *Sally, Irene, and Mary* written to cash in on the popularity of the earlier musicals. Betty, Winnie, and Flora are the trio from *No, No, Nanette*.

5. E—Ethel Shutta played Cantor's nurse. She will also be remembered as the original Hattie from *Follies* (Sondheim's, not Ziegfeld's). Frances Upton was the romantic lead and Ruth Etting played the movie star in *Whoopee*. Mary Eaton and six-foot-three Jobyna Howard played opposite Cantor in *Kid Boots*.

6. C—the forty-five girls were dressed as totem poles in costumes that cost an astronomical $2,400.

7. D—Billy was not among Rosie's playmates.

8. C—"The Charleston" was introduced in *Runnin' Wild*. "The Birth of the Blues" and "The Black Bottom" came from the 1926 *Scandals*; Gershwin's "Blue Monday Blues" from the 1922 edition, and "Somebody Loves Me" from the 1924 edition.

9. B—Pierre's alter ego was the Red Shadow. The Scarlet Pimpernel has his own musical in which he saves French nobles from the excesses of the Revolution. Rudolph Valentino was the Sheik and Danny Kaye (in *The Court Jester*) was the Black Fox. The Kinkajou was the bandit in *Rio Rita*.

10. E—blue skies don't cost anything, but they belong to Irving Berlin.

The 1930s Answers

1. B—as one might have guessed from the title, *Flying High* was about a mechanic who sets an aviation record since he doesn't know how to land the plane. The other answers describe characters played by other great comics of the period: Ed Wynn played the daydreaming paper vendor in *Simple Simon* (1931); W. C. Fields was the flimflam man in *Ballyhoo* (1930); Jimmy Durante was the convict longing for jail in *Red, Hot and Blue* (1936); and William Williams played the son of the Grand Eunuch in *Chee-Chee* (1928).

2. B—William Gaxton didn't appear in *The Band Wagon*. It only seems as if he shows up in the cast lists of every major 1930s musical.

3. A—the 46'-tall dinosaur, which appeared with a girl in its mouth, was the talk of Broadway. You can find the students' barricade in *Les Misérables*, the live ostrich in *Ziegfeld Follies of 1927*, the heroine on the movie crane in *Mack and Mabel*, and the swimming pool in *Wish You Were Here*.

4. C—*The Cat and the Fiddle* was the 1931 Kern-Harbach operetta. *Music in the Air* was also an integrated show set in Europe, but was written with Oscar Hammerstein, who also authored *Very Warm for May*, situated in Long Island. Harbach and Kern did collaborate on *Roberta*, but the plot concerned a Parisian dress shop, not the music profession. And *On Your Toes*, while addressing the conflict between the popular and classical, albeit in dance, was by Rodgers and Hart. But you already knew that, right?

5. A—the iconic "Brother, Can You Spare a Dime?" was the big hit from *Americana*. "Let's Have Another Cup of Coffee" was from Irving Berlin's *Face the Music* (1932); "I've Got Five Dollars" was from Rodgers and Hart's *America's Sweetheart* (1931); Dubin and Warren's "We're in the Money" was from the movie *Gold Diggers of 1933*, later used in the 1980 stage version of *42nd Street*; and "We'd Like to Thank You, Herbert Hoover" was from Strouse and Charnin's *Annie* (1977).

6. E—Moss Hart, not known for lush operettas, wrote the libretto to *The Great Waltz*.

7. B—Hope and Arden sang "I Can't Get Started with You" in the short-lived *Follies of 1936*. Hope introduced all the other songs: "It's De-Lovely" in *Red, Hot and Blue* (1936); "You're Devastating" in *Roberta* (1933); "Don't Tell Me It's Bad" in the 1934 flop *Say When*; and the song that became his theme, "Thanks for the Memory" in the film *The Big Broadcast of 1938*. And it's "memory," not "memories."

8. A—while FDR's attempt to pack the Supreme Court with pro–New Deal justices was big news in 1937, it's not mentioned in the lyrics to "Sing Me a Song of Social Significance."

9. E—Jackie Gleason, not Eddie Cantor, headed the national tour of *Hellzapoppin*.

10. E—the second-act ballet in *I Married an Angel* was set at Roxy Music Hall. You can find the other New York settings elsewhere. *I Can Get It for You Wholesale* (1962) was set in the garment district in 1937; "Let's Have Another Cup of Coffee" was set at the Automat in *Face the Music* (1932); *I'd Rather Be Right* (1937) was set in Central Park; and the ballet "Forty Minutes for Lunch" at the Radio City Arcade was from *One Touch of Venus* (1943)—another show about a nonhuman facing the modern, human world.

The 1940s Answers

1. C—"Taking a Chance on Love" was originally penned by Duke and Fetter. Broadway Bonus for knowing the original title was "Fooling Around with Love." "Happiness Is (Just) a Thing Called Joe" was written for the film version of *Cabin in the Sky* by Harold Arlen and Yip Harburg.

2. A—Gene Kelly, who had previously worked with Rodgers and Abbott in *Pal Joey*, was the dance director for *Best Foot Forward*. Stanley Donen and Danny Daniels were both in the chorus of *BFF*; Agnes de Mille was still doing ballets; and Robert Alton was in *Pal Joey*.

3. E—"Stan' Up and Fight (Until You Hear de Bell)" was Hammerstein's adaptation of Bizet's "Toreador Song," not the "Gypsy Song." *Carmen*'s toreador Escamillo thus became a prize fighter, Husky Miller, in Hammerstein's modernization.

4. False! There were cast albums, in various forms, going back to 1900's *Florodora*. The British, in fact, were far ahead of Americans in producing cast albums. But it is true that *Oklahoma!*'s was a bestseller, and set the fashion for cast albums to follow.

5. B—Kitty Carlisle (Mrs. Moss Hart) did Petina's role in the cast album of *Song of Norway*. If the other ladies sounded vaguely familiar, they were all leads in revivals of operettas roughly contemporary with *Song of Norway*: Ruby Mercer—*New Moon*, Barbara Scully—*Blossom Time*, Marta Eggerth—*The Merry Widow*, and Ann Andre—*The Red Mill* (also the chorus of *Song of Norway*). And I should note that Marta Eggerth's husband was a performer as well—Polish tenor Jan Kiepura, who performed with his wife all over Europe and America, sang at the Metropolitan Opera, and played opposite her in that revival of *The Merry Widow*.

6. E—Gleason ejaculated, "What the hell!," repeatedly throughout *Follow the Girls*. George Jean Nathan gives an account of the action with numerous "What the hells!" included. There is a female spy uncovered in the flimsy plot and Gleason does impersonate a W.A.V.E. to sneak into the club. "Oh! Oh! Delphine!" is from the 1917 show of that name, and you should check out the 1910s quiz for more on that catchphrase. Very good, Eddie.

7. D—Walker played the brassy taxicab driver, Hildy, in *On the Town*, while lyricist/ actress Betty Comden played Claire de Loone. Walker's role as the Blind Date was from Best Foot Forward; Yetta Samovar, student radical, was from *Barefoot Boy with Cheek*; Lily Malloy, the brewery heiress with a passion for ballet, was from *Look, Ma! I'm Dancin'*; and the sketch roles as the perfume clerk and poison victim (among others) were from the revue *Along Fifth Avenue*.

8. A—"The Red Ball Express" refers to the truckers—mostly black—who supplied the Allied forces in the Normandy campaign (hence the reference to French farmers in the lyrics). This song of tribute to their courage and hard work was paired with a

sketch of postwar truck drivers trying to get jobs. The whites were hired, but the black was turned away because of his race.

9. B—Leonard Bernstein was the only major participant from the creative team of *On the Town* who did not work on *Billion Dollar Baby*. Morton Gould supplied the music. These days, the show is best remembered for Robbins' inventive "Mack Sennett Ballet."

10. D—Clark played the first First Husband in *As the Girls Go*. His comic contemporaries who created the other goofy characters were as follows: Bert Lahr played the washroom attendant who gets knocked out in *Du Barry Was a Lady*; Ed Wynn was the crazy scientist who concocts a poison gas in *Hooray for What!*; Eddie Cantor gets tips straight from the horses' mouths while he sleeps in *Banjo Eyes*; and Danny Kaye played the effeminate photographer in 1941's *Lady in the Dark*, showing off his fast-talking skills and knowledge of Russian composers.

The 1950s Answers

1. A—a trip to the moon, is, of course, "Just One of Those Things."

2. C—*The Threepenny Opera* ran at the Theatre de Lys. The Sullivan was where *The Fantasticks* resided for decades; the Phoenix gave us *The Golden Apple* and *Once Upon a Mattress* before their transfers to Broadway; *You're a Good Man, Charlie Brown* got its start at the Theatre 80 St. Marks; and the Cherry Lane Theatre gave us *Godspell*.

3. D—Tony poses as a delivery boy.

4. D—traveling salesman Paris arrives in a balloon. Let me add my favorite example of Latouche's genius. In the *Odyssey*, Ulysses tells the Cyclops his name is "No One." After Ulysses wounds the Cyclops, the monster yells, "No One is hurting me!" So the other cyclopses ignore his cries, allowing Ulysses to escape. In a single lyric for *The Golden Apple*, Latouche gives Ulysses the last name of "Spelvin." In theatre lore, "George Spelvin" is the name given to an actor in a playbill when a production does not want the audience to know who is playing the role (as, for example, if someone important in act one is in disguise in act two). "Spelvin" is the perfect theatrical counterpart to Homer's use of "No One." But you need to know both your Homer and your theatre history to understand the joke.

5. C—Robbins staged "Seven and a Half Cents" and "There Once Was a Man." Anyone who answered "Steam Heat" deserves to have a fist punched through his or her derby hat.

6. True—Elvis was strongly considered for Li'l Abner. So were Dick Shawn and Andy Griffith. The producers spotted Peter Palmer on *The Ed Sullivan Show* and decided they'd druther have him.

7. A—the boys are supposed to think about Beethoven's "Minuet in G."

8. D—the king will speak again when the mouse (his weak-willed son) will devour (stand up to) the hawk (the domineering queen).

9. A—"Nine O'clock." Georg will meet his Dear Friend "Tonight at Eight"; the chorus will go into their dance on *42nd Street* at "About a Quarter to Nine"; orphan kids know when the sun comes out "Tomorrow"; and I had to find a way to stick Porter's

"Sunday Morning, Breakfast Time" (*Jubilee*) into a quiz because it's one of my favorite show tunes.

10. C—*Little Mary Sunshine* was set in the Colorado Rockies, with direct parallels to the Canadian Northwest of *Rose-Marie*, its closest model.

The 1960s Answers

1. B—the circus has come "Direct from Vienna." They want to get to Paris (the big time). Strolling players go to Padua, stewardesses go to Barcelona, and people interested in complex wills involving $6 million go to Monte Carlo.

2. B—Rodgers had hoped to cast Carroll as an Asian in *Flower Drum Song*, but the makeup was a disaster. Juanita Hall, another black, did play an Asian in the show, as she had in the earlier Rodgers show *South Pacific*.

3. D—Elliott Gould (who married Streisand after the show closed) had the lead. Lawrence Harvey was considered, but had disputes with producer David Merrick. Robert Morse was then playing a more likable rogue in *How to Succeed*; Larry Kert had just closed in a story about another Jewish clan in *A Family Affair*; and Bob Fosse had just played another antihero in the revival of *Pal Joey* the year before.

4. C—a "bajour" was a swindle or a confidence game in Romany, the Gypsy language. I wasn't going to include a *Bajour* question, but I knew there would be people out there who would say, "How can you write about over 700 musicals and *not* include *Bajour*?" And they'd be right.

5. Hapgood divides them into "Group One" and "Group A," but doesn't elaborate any further on distinctions between the two.

BROADWAY BONUS: The real name of the "Cookie Jar" in *Anyone Can Whistle* is Dr. Detmold's Sanitarium for the Socially Pressured.

6. E—The Dutch are not on Fioria's list of past or future guests. You could also add the Spanish, the Greeks, the Swedes, and the Russians to the list if you're familiar with the song "Last Week, Americans," which was cut from the original run.

7. E—the coin is Kipps' love token to Ann.

8. B—Michael Redgrave was originally named as the lead, but it went to Kiley. The others all played the role throughout its long run. Ferrer and Kiley were among those who dreamed impossible dreams on the lengthy national tour, and Michell played the part in London as well.

9. D—William Shakespeare's words comprise lyrics in "What a Piece of Work Is Man" and "Eyes Look Your Last." The former is taken from *Hamlet*, and the latter from *Romeo and Juliet*, with the concluding line "the rest is silence" taken from *Hamlet* as well. (There were also bits from *Hamlet* in the cut song, "Mess o' Dirt.") MacDermot did put the Gettysburg Address to music for the movie, but "Fourscore" was cut.

10. Due to the Tony rules, names listed below the title were not considered eligible for the Tony for Best Actor. Daniels was nominated for Best Featured Actor, but rightly

complained that Adams was a lead role. (The character is onstage for all but two scenes in the entire show!) Richard Holgate, who played Richard Henry Lee, was also nominated for Featured Actor and won.

The 1970s Answers

1. Both *Two by Two* and *Coco* were allegedly family shows, yet both had their stars say, "Shit!" Apparently, someone suggested to Katharine Hepburn that Coco could say "Merde!" but she replied that not everyone in the audience could speak French. On tour, Ginger Rogers did say "Merde!" as she felt the other was too coarse. I suppose, given the portrayal of Noah and his family as New York Jews, that Kaye could have used Yiddish. Makes about as much sense as anything else in *Two by Two*.

2. D—Ossie Davis was the original playwright for both *Purlie Victorious* and *Purlie*, as well as originating the role. Roscoe Lee Browne did play a singing minister in *My One and Only*, and Emmett "Babe" Wallace played Arvide Abernathy in the 1976 *Guys and Dolls*.

3. A—Proteus does not pack his quiver and bow, though you may remember that Count Carl-Magnus told his wife to pack his.

4. D—Bobby Rydell is not mentioned in the lyrics to "Look at Me, I'm Sandra Dee," but does get his tribute as the kids in *Grease* attend Rydell High.

5. B—Ken Harper bought TV and R & B radio ads and plugged "Ease on Down the Road" to boost sales. *Pippin* had earlier shown the benefits of such ads. The producers of *Purlie* targeted black church groups in their marketing. Dorothy's costume was changed from jeans to the white dress, but that was done even before the Philly tryouts. And you could find winged monkeys singing parody lyrics to Cole Porter in *Forbidden Broadway: Rude Awakening*.

❧ ❧

BROADWAY BONUS: Butterfly McQueen, most famous for *Gone with the Wind*, was cast in the role of the Queen of the Mice, a role that was cut.

❧ ❧

6. B—Martha was the name of the dead wife in *Shenandoah*. Jenny was the daughter and Anne the daughter-in-law. Evelina was the *Bloomer Girl*, and Sarah can be found in *The Civil War*. Right era, but different gals.

7. A—$1.00 was what each gypsy was paid for contributing to the original thirty hours of tape recordings. Joseph Papp paid each $100 per week through the workshops and $650 per week was their pay after the opening. $88.00 is what Rose wants from her dad.

   When *A Chorus Line* moved to Broadway, Bennett worked out a new contract with the original gypsies and others involved in the show's development, dividing around a tenth of his royalties and about a third of his rights income among them. This contract applied to the fifteen-year run and to subsidiary rights, but not to later Broadway productions or national tours. In 2008, a group of the original dancers successfully sued Michael Bennett's estate, gaining a financial interest in the 2006 revival and subsequent "first-class" productions.

8. Local 802's contract with the Longacre Theatre demanded more musicians than would have played in a typical jazz band of Fats Waller's time. So they hired the extras and paid them to goof off each show, rather than have the music sound inauthentic.

9. E—King wrote a *Playboy* article about the Chicken Ranch, and since it evolved into a Broadway show, this is proof that at least some people buy the magazine for the articles.

10. C—Judy Kaye was the first choice for Sonia. Stockard Channing came in as a later replacement.

The 1980s Answers

1. A—Roy Rogers. There were cowboy boots in the "Famous Feet" number, but they belonged to Tom Mix. "Tom" was written on one, "Mix" on the other, just so the audience would know which movie cowpoke was being honored.

2. When the show reached Washington, Hines was fired for speaking out against the revisions that were made in Philadelphia, but then was hastily rehired when the understudy did not know the revised changes and the cast threatened to walk out. It took a frantic manhunt to track him down.

3. A—Tom Eyen was the *Dreamgirls* director when it was in the workshop stages. Michael Bennett, of course, ended up as director; Michael Peters was Bennett's co-choreographer; Bob Avian was a co-producer, along with Bennett, the Shuberts, and David Geffen; and Tom Stevens directed the touring revival in 1997.

4. B—Jonathan Tunick was *Nine*'s orchestrator. He has also orchestrated most of Sondheim's shows, and I freely confess to being a rabid fan of his work, so I had to make him the subject of a quiz question.

5. E—Nathan Lane, funny man par excellence, is not an alumnus of *Forbidden Broadway*.

6. E— "Sweet and Low Down" was from *Tip-Toes*, not *Funny Face*. However, "How Long Has This Been Going On?" (which I did not include among your choices) was used in *My One and Only*; it was a song cut from *Funny Face*, only to be used seven weeks later in *Rosalie*.

7. D—"Patterns" was the cut song from *Baby* that was later restored. Beth Fowler sings it beautifully on the cast album.

8. C—the Nonesuch cannot smoke a cigarette. That's a reference to "Hand for the Hog."

9. C—Princess Puffer runs an opium den.

10. A—the late, great Cyd Charisse made her Broadway debut as a replacement for Grushinskaya. Rita Moreno debuted as a kid in 1945's *Skydrift*, but her first musical was *Gantry* in 1970. Taina Elg debuted in Look to the Lilies, and was in the 1974 revival of *Where's Charley* and the original company of *Nine*. Leslie Caron has never been on Broadway, although she was considered for the lead in *Her First Roman* and played Grushinskaya in the Berlin cast of *Grand Hotel*. Debbie Reynolds, as good Broadway fans should know, had the lead in 1973's *Irene*.

The 1990s Answers

1. C—the amazing Daisy Eagan was eleven when she won her Tony. Frankie Michaels was ten when he won Best Featured Actor for playing Young Patrick in *Mame* (1966), the youngest Tony winner ever.
2. C—Kristin Chenoweth did not play Belle on Broadway.
3. E—Frank Loesser's work was used in the revue *Perfectly Frank*, but back in 1980. Louis Jordan's songs were used in *Five Guys Named Moe* (1992), the only one of these revues to be a success. Johnny Burke was highlighted in *Swingin' on a Star* (1995), Johnny Mercer in *Dream* (1997), and the Gershwins in *The Gershwins' Fascinatin' Rhythm* (1999). Does anyone else besides me think of the Loesser revue (*Perfectly Frank*) when Mary in "Opening Doors" from *Merrily We Roll Along* (1981) suggests the name "Frankly Frank" as the title of their revue? And why doesn't Charley complain that Frank is getting all the billing when he did the lyrics and, presumably, many of the sketches? Ah, the things Sondheads ponder at odd moments during the day....
4. C—The Magna Carta, that landmark document from the early thirteenth century, is not mentioned in *Rent*, but I bet if Larson has put his mind to it, he could have squeezed it in somewhere to great effect. After all, it's the foundation of our political and civil liberties! The German philosopher Heidegger is mentioned in "Santa Fe"; the movie characters Thelma and Louise in "Today 4 You"; newsman Ted Koppel is noted in "On the Street"; and Larson's hero, Sondheim, is listed among the many cultural icons in "La Vie Boheme."
5. E—Adam Guettel wrote the music and most of the lyrics to *Floyd Collins*, which Stephen Sondheim described as his "favorite new musical," and also said that "The Riddle Song" was one of the fifty songs he wishes he had written.
6. A—Kevin Gray was not in the opening night cast of *Titanic*, but played shipbuilder Andrews on the national tour.
7. D—Percy learns the truth about his beloved Marguerite at the footbridge in the garden. And you thought that was where lovers in River City, Iowa, liked to spoon.
8. A—Daisy is alone during "Private Conversation," which takes place in (Jeff McCarthy) Terry's mind.
9. Disney helped refurbish the classic New Amsterdam Theatre to its glory days when it was the home of the *Ziegfeld Follies* and hits like *Sally*, *Rosalie*, and *The Band Wagon*.
10. A—Daisy Prince was in a show called *The Petrified Prince* (1994, songs by Michael John LaChiusa), based on a Bergman film—hey, it worked with *A Little Night Music*—why hasn't somebody taken a whack at *The Seventh Seal*? I want to see the numbo for the chess game with Death!) on which Jason Robert Brown was the music director and her dad, Hal, was the director. So connections between the three went back a few years. Then in 1996, Daisy directed Brown's song cycle, *Songs for a New World*. After Stephen Sondheim turned down *Parade*, Daisy suggested that Hal approach Brown. Among the wrong answers: Alfred Uhry wrote the libretto; Evan Pappas was in *Parade*'s workshops; Carolee Carmello starred as Leo Frank's wife; and Andrew Lippa did the book and music for *john and jen* in 1995, which starred Carmello and for which Brown did the orchestrations.

The 2000s Answers

1. B—12. *The Producers* won the maximum possible, barring any ties, since there were a few acting categories in which the show had cast members (as in Lane over Broderick) competing against each other.
2. C—Little Becky Two Shoes sings about people going to Urinetown, but she doesn't go there.
3. B—Peter Maxx' artwork, while colorful, dates from several years after *Hairspray*'s early 1960s setting. Of course, so did the Lite Brite toy, but that didn't stop them from using the effect of glowing circles. John Waters took the design crew on a tour of Baltimore, which gave them ideas. The "Formstone" exteriors were used in Baltimore's architecture of that era, and the muted colors reminded them of the powdery pastels of Necco wafers. Aronson's design for 1961's *Do Re Mi* were the inspiration for the set of *The Corny Collins Show*.

⚡ ⚡

BROADWAY BONUS: Tracy sings about rats on the sidewalk, so they tried putting actors in dancing rat suits. It didn't work. Hal Prince tried putting animatronic rats in the bowels of the Paris Opera House, but they looked too artificial. Apparently, he took one look and declared, "Cut those rats!" However, there *are* rats in *Phantom:* the opera's ballet dancers were known as "petit rats." Broadway's first glimpse of a chorus line of guys dressed as tap-dancing rats came in 2008's *Shrek*.

⚡ ⚡

4. Rod mentions *Pal Joey* and *High Button Shoes*.
5. E—Douglas Sills was slated to play Galahad the handsome. I want my readers to know I did painstaking, exhaustive research for this book. I had to spend *hours* considering Broadway hunks as potential answers for this question. I had to concentrate very hard about adding Hugh Jackman, even though that would have been much too easy an answer. Still, it required plenty of thought. Seriously. Then I had to contemplate the relative merits of Patrick Wilson and Matthew Morrison and Nathan Gunn and Robert Sean Leonard and Norm Lewis and Anthony Crivello and James Barbour and Taye Diggs and Christopher Innvar and countless others. Relentless toil, let me tell you!
6. C—Fabrizio wants to be like Van Johnson.
7. During *The Drowsy Chaperone*'s tryout in Los Angeles, Foster fell and broke her wrist. Oddly enough, she fell during "An Accident Waiting to Happen," not "Show Off." When she had recovered, she wanted to keep the cartwheel in "Show Off," and worked on doing it one-handed. Even after the cast came off her wrist, she kept on doing it one-handed. Weird trivia of the day: Foster's cast members autographed her cast, and after it was removed, it was placed among the objects in Man in Chair's apartment.
8. D—"Goin' Places" was added for Broadway, replacing "Better Fall Out of Love." It's interesting comparing the two numbers if you're a confirmed *GG* nut to see which better illustrates the potential rifts in Little Edie and Joe's relationship.
9. D—Mayer says the audience members onstage represent community. In the original Frank Wedekind play, Melchior is stopped from killing himself not by a visit from

the ghosts of his dead lover and best friend, but by a mysterious masked man in black who is supposed to represent the "spirit of life." Adult authority is represented in the musical by the two older performers, one male and one female, who play all the characters not in their teens. *Hairspray*, perhaps the camp inverse of *Spring Awakening*, uses a similar effect—two actors play a variety of roles, from the prison guard to the gym teacher, under the umbrella titles of "Male Authority Figure" and "Female Authority Figure."

BONUS BROADWAY BONUS: Good lord, you people have dirty minds. Here's the truth: Gallagher brought his hand mike up to his mouth with such force on opening night that he chipped his front teeth.

10. B—Nina is a student at Stanford.

Richard Rodgers and Oscar Hammerstein II Answers

1. C—the rams and ewes are in *Carousel*'s "June Is Busting Out All Over." The other beasties are in the following *Oklahoma!* songs: the hawk, "Oklahoma!"; the lark, "The Surrey with the Fringe on Top"; the field mouse, "Lonely Room"; the maverick, "Oh, What a Beautiful Mornin'." Be honest, now. How many of you guessed the lark because you thought of the one learning to pray in "The Sound of Music" instead of the one waking up in the meadow?

2. E—the Starkeeper previously was Mr. God, stuck in the parlor with Mrs. God, which led to one of my favorite Broadway quotes, when Rodgers exclaimed, "We've got to get God out of that parlor!" Thank heavens they did.

3. A—young Stephen Sondheim, a close friend of the Hammerstein family, worked as a "gofer" on *Allegro*. Who can say what kind of ideas evolved from that experience?

4. B—Cable hands over his grandfather's watch (the one that saw his ancestor safely through the Spanish-American war; you knew he was doomed as soon as he gave that up. Survival 101—do not lose lucky family heirlooms!), but Bloody Mary stomps on it. Luther covets the boar's tooth necklace; Bloody Mary's skin is as tender as DiMaggio's glove and she charges "fo' dolla'" for her goods; and Nellie is as normal as blueberry pie. Not that you would find blueberries on a South Pacific island.

5. C—Rex Harrison did play the King of Siam, but in the earlier, nonmusical movie version. He was asked to play the singing monarch, but turned it down. Granger, McGavin, and Phillips all played in revivals of the musical, while Alfred Drake (who, like Harrison, was courted for the role, but refused it because of the pay) filled in while Brynner took a vacation during the original run. Noel Coward, lifelong chum and acting partner of Gertie Lawrence, also refused the part.

6. D—the actors and crew of the play-within-a-play in *Me and Juliet* regard the audience as "the Big Black Giant."

7. A—the Bear Flag Cafe was "the Happiest House on the Block."

8. Gene Kelly was the director of *Flower Drum Song*.

9. D—"Edelweiss" was the last lyric Hammerstein wrote.
10. E—the two songs recycled in *State Fair* were cut from *Oklahoma!*

Jerry Bock and Sheldon Harnick Answers

1. C—Alice Ghostley introduced "Boston Beguine" in *New Faces of 1952*.
2. A—Chita Rivera also appeared in *Mr. Wonderful*.
3. E—*The Body Beautiful* was about boxing.
4. D—Bock and Harnick wrote the first three songs for *Fiorello!* without knowing it was about Fiorello. Jerome Weidman had written a few scenes, which original director Penn felt weren't dark enough. George Abbott took over as director, and Bock and Harnick were asked to write some songs on trial, using only the era (early-twentieth-century New York) and Weidman's initial scenes (one of which became "Politics and Poker"). The subject matter was kept secret. When their first songs were approved, they got the job and learned what the show was about.
5. C—Tommy relates in "The Picture of Happiness" how lobster (and sparkling wine) set one woman down the delightful road to ruin. "Artificial Flowers" was the hit from *Tenderloin*, but you can find a kiss on the hand, educated fleas, and rahadlakum in *Gentlemen Prefer Blondes*, *Barnum*, and *Kismet*, respectively.
6. According to Arpad, the nose must find the perfume's scent attractive, it must be invisible, and it must be functional. (Like the musical candy box, one assumes.)
7. A—"Dear, Sweet Sewing Machine" was a second-act lullaby for Motel and Tzeitel.
8. B—neither Bock nor Harnick worked on *A Family Affair*. The duo provided four uncredited songs for Hal Prince's troubled *Baker Street*, three of which were used, and three uncredited songs for *Her First Roman*. Harnick provided additional lyrics for *Shangri-la* and *Portofino*, not that those are shows one proudly displayed on a resume.
9. C—Mike Nichols directed *The Apple Tree*, his first musical. Gower Champion was slated to direct Nichols' 1962 *The Worlds of Jules Feiffer*, which included *Passionella* with Sondheim songs, but the show was unproduced.
10. C—Keene Curtis played multiple roles in *The Rothschilds* and earned a Tony. Chris Sarandon and Paul Hecht were also in the show, playing two of the sons. Hecht had come over from *1776*, where William Daniels was still playing; the producers must have concluded that Hecht looked good in late-eighteenth-century garb. And Len Cariou was busy earning *Applause*.

Frank Loesser and Burton Lane Answers

1. A—Bobby was Cy Feuer's son. Feuer describes the incident in his memoirs.
2. A—Mindy's Restaurant plays a role in *Guys and Dolls* (which of their desserts is selling better, the cheesecake or the strudel?), but not as a potential site for the crap game.

3. They were all names of members of the cast and crew, including "Sullivan" (Jo, soon to be the second Mrs. Loesser), "Johnson" (Susan), and "Herbie Greene" (the musical director).
4. E—Pert Kelton went from playing Mrs. Paroo in *The Music Man* to Gramma Briggs in *Greenwillow*.

~ ~

BROADWAY BONUS: The cow's name was Buttercup Hyacinth Bertram III and she left cow flops onstage in Philadelphia. Apparently, everyone was so glum about the show's troubles that no one even laughed. You get one bonus point for each of the cow's names you knew, but only a half point for knowing she pooped. I mean, that's easy to guess. What else do cows do, when they're not tap dancing?

~ ~

5. E—kazoos were used to mimic the sound of electric razors as the men's chorus sang while shaving in the executive washroom.
6. B—Stephen Sondheim was not part of the Frank Music catalog.
7. A—Al Jolson's last show was *Hold On to Your Hats*.
8. Rainbow Valley was near Fort Knox, and he hoped that gold would then sprout out of the ground.
9. C—Melinda was Daisy's previous incarnation in *On a Clear Day You Can See Forever*.
10. E—Paul Sorvino took Siepi's role on the cast recording of *Carmelina*.

Lynn Ahrens and Stephen Flaherty Answers

1. B—Harry Witherspoon of *Lucky Stiff* is a shoe salesman.
2. C—Papa Gé of *Once on This Island* is Death.
3. D—Andrea Martin, playing the Imogene Coca–like actress/writer on the *King Kaiser Show* was the sole Tony winner from *My Favorite Year*. In 2007, Ahrens and Flaherty revised *My Favorite Year*, lightening the dark second act, and this version is the one available for licensing.
4. A—*A Christmas Carol* played at Madison Square Garden's downstairs theatre.
5. B—Baron Ashkenazy is the name Tateh adopts when he gains financial success with his moving pictures. He is a fictional character, but the others listed were historical.
6. B—JoJo and the other Whos in Whoville shout, "Yopp!," and make themselves known.
7. E—Alfie wants to stage Wilde's *Salome*, but the subject matter causes controversy.
8. A—Dessa Rose and Ruth are a runaway slave and an abandoned white farmwife, who form an uneasy alliance that leads to a deep friendship. The Wicked Witch of the East is Nessarose, but you knew that already, right?
9. B—Flaherty's *Loving Repeating* is based on the life and work of Gertrude Stein, especially material from her 1934 lecture tour and her relationship with Alice B. Toklas.
10. E—"I Was Here" is destined to become a classic number, poignantly defining why actors act. It has been performed in concert by Patti LuPone, Brian Stokes Mitchell, Philip Quast, Marin Mazzie, and Jason Danieley.

Leonard Bernstein and Marc Blitzstein Answers

1. B—Hershy Kay, who later would do the fantastic orchestrations for *Candide*, did the symphonic numbers in *On the Town*.
2. Bernstein wrote five songs and two pirates' choruses for the 1950 play *Peter Pan*. Not long after, the Disney animated musical debuted, followed by the Charnap/Leigh/Styne/Comden/Green stage vehicle starring Mary Martin.
3. C—the replacement song was "One Hundred Ways to Lose a Man."
4. D—although portions of *Candide* take place in Lisbon, the Old Lady does not speak Portuguese in "I Am Easily Assimilated."

~ ~

BROADWAY BONUS: Bernstein's wife, Felicia Montealegre, who was born in Chile, helped her husband with the Spanish lyrics for the song.

~ ~

5. E—"Gee, Officer Krupke" was based on a discarded song from *Candide*.
6. The revised and shortened version of *1600 Pennsylvania Avenue* is called *A White House Cantata*.
7. D—Blitzstein died in 1964, beaten to death outside a bar in Martinique. The lyricist on the unfinished *A Pray by Blecht* was Stephen Sondheim.
8. C—Bertolt Brecht told Blitzstein to expand his prostitute sketch into a full musical.
9. C—*Regina* was based on Hellman's *The Little Foxes*. *Toys in the Attic* was produced in 1960, eleven years after *Regina*, but Blitzstein did do the incidental music for it.
10. E—Johnny Boyle's dance in *Juno* was called a "haunt." Captain Boyle won't find a steady job because he has "pains in the legs," which somehow don't prevent him from going to the pub.

One more connection between Bernstein and Blitzstein, in case you haven't had enough: *West Side Story* vacated the Winter Garden Theatre for *Juno*. After *Juno* closed in a fortnight, the Jets and Sharks moved back.

Alan Jay Lerner and Frederick Loewe Answers

1. E—though accounts vary somewhat, it is generally agreed that Lerner and Loewe met at the Lambs Club. Loewe was older than Lerner, and was not at Harvard with him when he worked on the *Hasty Pudding* shows, nor did he work at the radio station where Lerner wrote for *Your Hit Parade*. They met in 1942, before the opening of *Oklahoma!*
2. C—Lerner and Loewe's first Broadway show was *What's Up*. *The Life of the Party*, based on a play called *The Patsy*, was a show that Loewe had been working on when he met Lerner. Lerner helped rewrite the book and some songs for the show, which closed in Detroit. *Great Lady* was the title of an operetta by Loewe from 1938 that ran for two weeks. *Here's Love* was Meredith Willson's 1963 flop.
3. A—*The Day Before Spring* concerns a married couple at their college reunion, where the wife meets the man she nearly eloped with, who is now a famous writer. His

best-selling novel imagines what would have happened had the elopement taken place. At the reunion, the events of a decade ago begin to repeat. The angel and the football team musical was 1946's *Toplitsky of Notre Dame*, which lasted three weeks. The Kosciuszko bio-musical was *Polonaise*, a flop from 1945, using themes from Chopin. The Indian stuck in a girls' school was Lerner and Loewe's earlier offering, *What's Up*. And the one about the guy hit on the head who dreams he's Goya was 1946's *The Duchess Misbehaves*, which managed five performances. It might have lasted longer if lead Jackie Gleason had stayed, but he left with a "sprain." Smart move.

4. B—you'll have to catch your own fish in Brigadoon, for there's "nae" to be had at the market.

5. E—Nanette Fabray, a great talent who, like her contemporary Nancy Walker, kept ending up in flops, starred in *Love Life*.

6. As described in the song "They Call the Wind Maria," Maria is the wind, Tess is the rain, and the fire is Joe. I have no idea where Tess and Joe came from, but I can enlighten you on the origins of Maria. In 1941, writer George R. Stewart published a novel called *Storm* in which the protagonist was a huge Pacific storm called Maria. This popular novel led to the National Weather Service adopting the practice of naming hurricanes and to Lerner's using "Maria" for the wind in his lyric.

7. A—Lerner stood up for Freddy's solo, "On the Street Where You Live," and it stayed in the final score.

8. D—Cecil Beaton, who designed the costumes for *My Fair Lady*, did not do the costumes for *Camelot*. Noted designer Adrian began the work, but died of a heart attack, another of the troubles to plague the show. Tony Duquette finished the designs.

9. A—Mark suggests many modes of transportation, but not a stagecoach.

10. B—Danielle Darrieux, though a talented actress and a much better singer than Hepburn, did not have the box office magic of the movie star.

George and Ira Gershwin Answers

1. Ira's pseudonym, "Arthur Francis," was derived from the names of the other Gershwin siblings, brother Arthur and sister Frances.

2. D—"Fascinating Rhythm" developed out of the earlier "Syncopated City."

3. E—Ira used P. G. Wodehouse as his inspiration for the lyrics to *Tip-Toes*, having long admired "Plum's" work. W. S. Gilbert's influence on Ira is more noticeable in *Of Thee I Sing*. Woolcott and Hart both publicly admired Ira's lyrics for *Tip-Toes*.

4. E—Gertie was holding a rag doll that George bought for her in a Philadelphia toy store while *Oh, Kay!* was on tryout. There is a reference to a lamb in the lyrics and she was dressed as a maid, though not holding a feather duster or a scarf.

5. The Alvin Theatre got its name from the first syllables of the first names of owners/producers Alex Aarons and Vinton Freedley, who backed many Gershwin shows.

6. C—Sigmund Romberg wrote the other half of *Rosalie*'s score, with most of the lyrics to his melodies by P. G. Wodehouse. There were two Gershwin songs and one Romberg number on which Ira and Wodehouse collaborated.

7. E—Bunny Berigan wasn't in the pit for *Girl Crazy*, but in addition to the big band and swing giants-to-be that I mentioned (Krupa, Goodman, Dorsey, and Miller), the orchestra also boasted Red Nichols and Jack Teagarden.

✧ ✧

BROADWAY BONUS: Gershwin veteran Fred Astaire staged the dance for "Embraceable You" for Ginger Rogers, later to be his partner in Hollywood.

✧ ✧

8. D—"The Man I Love" was not restored, but proved to be one of those songs that became a standard without ever latching on to a show. George and Ira first wrote it for *Lady, Be Good!* in 1924, but it was cut. They tried putting it in the 1927 version of *Strike Up the Band*, but it was cut. They tried putting it in *Rosalie* (1928), but it was cut. It had been published, however, and turned into a smash both in America and in Britain.

9. A—Ira does not mention escargot among the Frenchified mishmash he created for the French honor guard.

10. E—*Blue Monday Blues* predates DeBose Heyward's novel *Porgy* (1925) by three years. George wanted to do a musical version of the novel as soon as he read it during a bout of insomnia in 1926, even before Heyward had adapted it into a straight play.

Charles Strouse and Lee Adams Answers

1. Conrad Birdie was based on Conway Twitty.
2. E—Mel Brooks wrote *All American*, and presumably used this background for the screenplay of *The Producers* a few years later. Robert Lewis Taylor wrote the novel *Professor Fodorski*, upon which Brooks based the libretto. Larry Gelbart, Samuel Taylor, and Jerome Weidman were all busy around this time writing *A Funny Thing Happened on the Way to the Forum*, *No Strings*, and *I Can Get It for You Wholesale*.
3. C—no overture, but boxers in the gym with percussion matching their every blow.
4. C—apparently the Nobel committee hasn't gotten around to kryptonite analysis yet.
5. A—Diane McAfee was the original Eve. Dilys Watling had just closed in *Georgy* and Susan Browning was about to open in *Company*.
6. E—Oxydent, an imaginary product when *Annie* was written in 1977, sponsored "The Hour of Smiles." (Today, there is a dental whitening gel called "Oxydent." I don't know if this counts as product placement or not.) In real life, Ovaltine sponsored "Little Orphan Annie" on the radio from 1931 to 1940. Beau Brummel is mentioned in the lyrics to "You're Never Fully Dressed Without a Smile." Pepsodent is what Bloody Mary doesn't use.
7. Algernon was a white mouse. In the story, doctors perform an operation on Charlie, who is mentally deficient, to improve his IQ. A similar surgery is performed on Algernon, with tragic results.
8. A—the music came from the London production of *Golden Boy*.
9. B—Sophie Tucker performs in *Rags*. Carnegie is mentioned in the lyrics of "Yankee Boy." The characters Rebecca and David got to see a Yiddish production of *Hamlet*;

Jacob Adler was a star in Yiddish theatre, but was best known for his King Lear and Shylock. Fanny Brice and Fiorello got musicals of their own.

10. A—the 1968 film *The Night They Raided Minsky's* was the original inspiration for Strouse's latest musical, *Minsky's*. Did I fool you by listing *Bonnie and Clyde*? Strouse did the film score, but there are two new musicals about the gangsters making the rounds, one by Frank Wildhorn and Don Black (debuted in La Jolla, late 2009) and one by Hunter Foster and Rick Crom (2008).

Harvey Schmidt and Tom Jones Answers

1. C—the original off-Broadway run of *The Fantasticks* lasted 17,162 performances. If the other numbers looked vaguely familiar: there were 5,683 women traveling daily on the subways in *On the Town*; *Cats* ran for 7,485 performances; Princess Winifred counted 37,428 sheep trying to sleep in *Once Upon a Mattress*; and there are 525,600 minutes in those "Seasons of Love" in *Rent*.

2. C—Tom Jones used the name Thomas Bruce when acting in *The Fantasticks*. Jay Hampton was also in that original cast, playing the soon-to-be-cut role of the Handyman. Edmond Rostand wrote *Les Romanesques*, the play upon which the show was based. George Spelvin and Walter Plinge are pseudonyms used by actors who want (for whatever reason) to conceal their identities.

3. E—Joel Grey was not in the Sullivan Street *Fantasticks*, but he was in the 1995 movie version, which somehow squeezed all the warmth and magic out of the piece.

4. B—"Evenin' Star" was the cut song restored to the 2007 revival of *110 in the Shade*.

5. E—Agnes and Michael's pillow read "God Is Love."

6. C—James J. Ratfink was not a character in *Celebration*. However, he was the central figure in the 1961 unproduced show *Ratfink*, which Schmidt and Jones later revised into *Celebration*. The villain in *Celebration*, Edgar Allen Rich, was apparently based on David Merrick.

7. A—Dorothy Loudon didn't play Colette, but I bet she would have been great in the part.

8. C—Mary Martin, believe it or not, was Schmidt and Jones' choice for the Stage Manager in *Grover's Corners*, but her failing health caused her to withdraw.

9. E—*Mirette* is a little girl who helps a tightrope walker regain his nerve. The original picture book was only 800 words, so Jones greatly expanded the storyline, adding many new characters.

10. D—*Roadside* and *Oklahoma!* are both based on plays by Lynn Riggs.

John Kander and Fred Ebb Answers

1. According to Flora, happiness comes in on tip-toe.

2. D—it came to Fred Ebb in a dream.

3. B—David Wayne got the rave reviews in *The Happy Time*.

4. *Zorba* opens in a "bouzouki circle"…which is entirely invented by Prince. There is no such thing.

5. E—Roxie wore silver shoes with rhinestone buckles at her trial.
6. C—Mamie. The other girls' names were characters in *A Family Affair*.
7. D—Fred Ebb. Tune doctored the show for $25K and 1%; Coco was a good pal of Bacall's; Moore directed.
8. A—Balanciaga scarf. The Lavin perfume and lilac water appear elsewhere in *Kiss of the Spider Woman* lyrics.
9. B—Kristin Chenoweth played Precious McGuire in *Steel Pier*.
10. E—Rupert Holmes, whose previous Broadway title was also a mystery (*The Mystery of Edwin Drood*), helped Kander complete *Curtains*.

∿∿∿∿∿∿∿∿∿∿∿∿∿∿∿∿∿∿∿∿∿∿∿∿∿∿∿∿∿∿∿∿∿∿

BROADWAY BONUS: *Who Killed David Merrick?* was the original title for *Curtains*.

∿∿∿∿∿∿∿∿∿∿∿∿∿∿∿∿∿∿∿∿∿∿∿∿∿∿∿∿∿∿∿∿∿∿

Betty Comden and Adolph Green Answers

1. They played Claire de Loone, the anthropologist who gets "carried away," and Ozzie, the sailor always on the make.
2. D—Ivy is the name of Gaby's love interest in *On the Town*, but the other gals all had flings with Joe in "If You Hadn't."
3. E—Ruth has been reading *Moby Dick*, although later in the show she does want to know what the Brazilian sailors think of Steinbeck's prose.
4. Cyril Ritchard won *two* Donaldsons: Best Actor for playing Captain Hook and Best Supporting Actor for Mr. Darling.
5. C—"(It's) Better than a Dream" was the late addition to the stage version. "Do It Yourself" was written directly for the movie version.
6. D—Fatso, Stein, and Brains are the retired gangsters. The other trios include the horses in "Fugue for Tinhorns," potential swains mentioned in *Kiss Me, Kate*, three Marx Brothers, and three Guys from *Guys and Dolls*.
7. A—Emmelina Sue gave "Cousin Willie" mint juleps.
8. Despite covering a large number of years, the lead characters in both shows did not age!
9. Anne Baxter succeeded Bacall as Margo Channing, but she had played Eve in the classic movie version.
10. E—Knowing Oscar's ways, Lily signed "Peter Rabbit." Mrs. Primrose was the one urging us to "Repent!" Mildred Plotka was Lily's real name; Veronique was the role that shot her to stardom; and Babette was the society lush she decided to play for Max instead of being Mary Magdelene for Oscar.

Richard Rodgers and Lorenz Hart Answers

1. A—George Washington. Adams, of course, can be found in *1776*. If you remember your U.S. history, you know Peter Stuyvesant predates the Revolution and Theodore Roosevelt postdates it. Stuyvesant is the star of Weill's *Knickerbocker Holiday*, but

there is an amusing song ("Sweet Peter") about him in *Dearest Enemy*. Theodore Roosevelt is the lead in the musical *Teddy and Alice*. Paul Revere's Broadway connections include *Call Me Mister*, *Hellzapoppin*, and "Fugue for Tinhorns."

❀ ❀

BROADWAY BONUS: She was wearing a barrel. Her character had been swimming in the river when her clothes were stolen.

❀ ❀

2. E—the cut "Hollywood Dream" comes from *Lady in the Dark*, a show with certain similarities to *Peggy-Ann*, including the opening without music.

3. D—bow and arrow. But Morgan used all the other methods and more. She's the role model for the merry murderesses in *Chicago*!

4. E—Big Rosie was the elephant that played Jumbo. Billy Rose was the producer; Durante and Hannaford were in the cast; and Rose allegedly got the money for the show from "Jock" Whitney. *Jumbo* was the last show to play at the Hippodrome before its demolition in 1939. (Do you find you can't read the word "Hippodrome" without hearing Nancy Walker bellowing "The Hippodrome!" from *On the Town* in your head? Me too.)

5. C—"Three Blind Mice" is used for the three cops' entrance. Rodgers loved playing musical jokes, as when he included a selection from Tschaikowsky's "The Nutcracker" in *Chee-Chee*, which concerned a young man who didn't want to become a eunuch.

6. D—the banquet of sandwiches and beans is in the "Mountain Greenery" (*Garrick Gaieties of 1926*). The guy with limited range is, of course, "Johnny One-Note"; the performing seals are in "I Wish I Were in Love Again"; there's a character named Valentine; and the lady who is a tramp prefers the bleachers.

7. B—Kaufman and Hart. Abbott, Fields, and Hecht and MacArthur wrote the books for other Rodgers and Hart shows. Bolton never did.

8. Hart's younger brother Teddy, who was an actor, was frequently mistaken for another actor, Jimmy Savo. This gave Hart the notion to cast them as the comic slave twins, the Dromios. Ever counted how many times they yell "Let Antipholus in!" on the Encores cast album of *The Boys from Syracuse*? Twenty-seven. Hey, I could have made that a quiz question.

9. "Zip" is about Gypsy Rose Lee. June Havoc, who played Gladys, was the stripper's sister, as all good Broadway buffs know. And you thought I was going to ask you, "Who the hell is Sally Rand?"

10. A—Bolger went to entertain the troops.

Jerry Herman Answers

1. D—Charles Nelson Reilly was in both *Nightcap* and *Parade*. Phyllis Newman had been a pal of Herman's since childhood and choreographed *Nightcap*. There were some talented young folks hanging around that place: Dom DeLuise was the bartender, who also did magic acts, with Ruth Buzzi as his assistant.

2. A—Sol Horowitz becomes Clara's second husband. Hymie Weiss was the first; S. I. Jacobowsky was the little refugee in *The Grand Tour*, and Ephraim Levi was Dolly's

dead husband in *Hello, Dolly!*; and Phil Arkin was Robert Weede's character in *Milk and Honey*.

3. E—"Come and Be My Butterfly" was replaced by "Polka Contest" after the opening. *Hello, Dolly!* had no overture on Broadway; there was an orchestrated medley placed on the cast album, but it was not used. "Love, Look in My Window" and "World, Take Me Back" were added especially for Ethel Merman. "You're a Damned Exasperating Woman" was cut before the opening, along with "Penny in My Pocket."

4. D—There is no pousse café in *Mame*, though there is one in a lyric in *Dear World* (as well as a flop musical by that title). The mint julep, of course, is in "Mame"; the recent bubbly vintage is in "Open a New Window"; the Scotch is in "It's Today"; and Patrick demonstrates how much he's learned from his auntie by mixing Mr. Babcock a perfect martini.

5. A—Aurelia is looking for a nine-foot-long feather boa, which is twenty-six feet shorter than Liliane LaFleur's. The Madwoman of Montmartre, Gabrielle, has the imaginary dog named Dickie; the Madwoman of the Flea Market, Constance, believes pearls equal memories; the Sewerman reveals to Aurelia how the gargoyle trap door works; and the villains are involved with the radioactive water, hoping to blow up the bistro to get to the oil under Paris.

6. Champion wanted the number changed because he feared comparisons with Jerome Robbins' classic Keystone Kops dance, the "Mack Sennett Ballet," from *High Button Shoes*. Despite the changes, people still compared the numbers.

∾ ∾

BROADWAY BONUS: The earliest version for this number was "Call a Kop."

∾ ∾

7. E—Tommy Tune was the show doctor for *The Grand Tour* in San Francisco.

8. B—"Nelson" parodied Nelson Eddy and Jeanette MacDonald and the famous "Indian Love Call."

9. A—the "Song on the Sand" refers to a romantic walk in September.

10. E—Leslie Uggams was in both versions of *Jerry's Girls*, as was ensemble member Ellyn Arons. The production seemed plagued: Chita Rivera was the one in the car accident; Carol Channing broke her arm three days before previews and had severe laryngitis during the tour; Andrea McArdle had an emergency appendectomy and missed a month; and Dorothy Loudon broke two toes.

Kurt Weill Answers

1. D—Elia Kazan did not direct; he played a private. Lee Strasberg directed. Kazan would later direct *Venus* and *Love Life*.

2. E—Burgess Meredith, who was in the cast of Weill's 1933 Broadway show *The Threepenny Opera*, quit *Knickerbocker Holiday* after conceiving the show. His 1950 flop was *Happy as Larry*.

3. C—*Les Misérables*. An extra point if you knew they also read *A Tale of Two Cities*. Characters from *Romeo and Juliet*, Arthurian romances, and *The Divine Comedy* are mentioned in "Oh, Fabulous One," and "Kubla Khan" is mentioned in "This Is New."

4. A—the North Pole, though the other locales are all cited in the show.
5. A—*Much Ado About Love* was the title in Boston. It had earlier been dubbed *It Happened in Florence* and *Make Way for Love*. *The Dagger and the Rose* was a failed 1928 musical on the same subject. "Life, Love and Laughter" was a song from the show.
6. D—Broadway. The primrose path and the castle in Spain are mentioned in "What Good Will the Moon Be?"; the lilac bushes are in "Don't Forget the Lilacs"; and a character graduated from the high school.
7. B—Michael Kidd choreographed "Punch and Judy Get a Divorce."
8. E—*Lost in the Stars* is set in apartheid South Africa.
9. E—Howard Dietz, though an accomplished translator, wasn't asked about adapting *The Threepenny Opera*. He did write the lyrics for Weill's anti-Hitler ditty, "Schickelgruber," for the *Lunchtime Follies*.
10. A—"Alabama Song." A thank-you here from me and my daughter Rebecca, the theatre studies major, for Mr. Prince's audacity in conceiving *LoveMusik*. In current Broadway's wilderness of relentless camp, cartoons, and regurgitated movies, Prince and his stellar cast dared to give us something different and worth thinking about. We've spent more time discussing *LoveMusik*'s pros and cons than many other shows we've seen lately. And another thank-you to Kurt Deutsch and Joel Moss of Ghostlight Records for the *LoveMusik* cast album, preserving those performances.

Cole Porter Answers

1. C—Irving Berlin took out the paid ad praising *Fifty Million Frenchmen*.
2. C—Astaire wanted "Night and Day" cut. Thankfully, Porter overruled him. Astaire sings the difficult song beautifully. I'm sure all good Porter fans out there noticed that "The Physician" was not even in *The Gay Divorce* but *The New Yorkers* and later in *Nymph Errant*.
3. A—John Donne is not mentioned in "You're the Top."

~~ ~~

BROADWAY BONUS: Porter had a reference to flying with Lindbergh, which he altered after the tragic kidnapping and murder of the Lindberghs' baby son.

~~ ~~

4. A, B, and D—Noel Coward, Elsa Maxwell, and Johnny Weismuller are all parodied in *Jubilee*. Revivalist preacher Aimee Semple McPherson may have contributed a bit to the character of Reno Sweeney in *Anything Goes* and Alexander Woollcott was the basis for Sheridan Whiteside in Hart and Kaufman's *The Man Who Came to Dinner*. Under the name "Noel Porter," Porter wrote a song for that show's own imitation Noel Coward.
5. C—Betty Grable was in *Du Barry Was a Lady*, but the other gals were all in Porter shows. Mary Martin debuted in *Leave It to Me*; Eve Arden was in *Let's Face It*; Betty Hutton was in *Panama Hattie*; and Betty Garrett was in *Something for the Boys*.
6. The phrase was "I Love You" and the song was in *Mexican Hayride*.
7. The gangsters made reference to fourteen Shakespearean plays: *Othello, Anthony and Cleopatra, Much Ado About Nothing, Troilus and Cressida, As You Like It, Coriolanus,*

Hamlet, Measure for Measure, The Merchant of Venice, All's Well That Ends Well, A Midsummer Night's Dream, Twelfth Night, Macbeth, and *The Taming of the Shrew.*

8. D—"Nobody's Chasing Me" was Greenwood's showstopper.

9. The French titles are "Allez-vous-en" and "C'est Magnifique."

10. E—the Soviet expert on sex is Kamichev, who claims it's all due to chemicals.

Stephen Sondheim Answers

1. D—"Comedy Tonight" replaced "Love Is in the Air," which had replaced "Invocation," which later ended up in *The Frogs*.

2. Aronson's set included two elevators. It took fifteen seconds for the actors to get from the upper level of the set down to center stage, which Sondheim and Bennett wrote into the music and staging. Integration of set design, score, and choreography, all in one.

3. C—"One More Kiss" is in the style of operetta composers Friml and Romberg.

4. F—"The Story of Lucy and Jessie" is a pastiche of Cole Porter.

5. E—"Losing My Mind" conjures up Gershwin, with a Dorothy Fields lyric.

6. A—"Beautiful Girls" parallels Irving Berlin's classic *Ziegfeld Follies* number "A Pretty Girl Is Like a Melody."

7. D—"Broadway Baby" is in the style of DeSylva, Brown, and Henderson.

8. B—"You're Gonna Love Tomorrow"/"Love Will See Us Through" evokes Jerome Kern.

9. B—Madame Armfeldt may have gotten pearls from one of her former lovers, but she doesn't cite them in the song. There are pearls mentioned in "The Miller's Tale" and Anne frets about her earrings in "Soon."

10. A—Patti LuPone was not in *The Frogs* and did not attend Yale. Though if Ravinia ever stages *The Frogs*, don't be surprised if Patti shows up as Charon, guiding Dionysus across the Styx.

11. C—in the original Broadway production of *Pacific Overtures*, Commodore Perry was depicted as a Kabuki lion and performed the classic Lion Dance. A *kurombo* was one of the stagehands dressed in black. Perry's ships were described as "Four Black Dragons." The Meiji emperor was shown as a puppet until the show's end.

12. Mrs. Lovett says Sweeney is a relative from Birmingham.

13. While Sondheim was in London, he saw a production of Christopher Bond's straight play about the demon barber, and thought it would make a great musical. Sondheim rarely originates the idea for his musicals; *Sweeney* is one of the exceptions.

14. Hal Prince cut Judge Turpin's version of "Johanna," during which he whips himself into a sexual frenzy while secretly watching his young ward. The show was running long, and he felt the Judge's villainy was already well established and did not need a number that made many (including Prince) uncomfortable. The cast album has preserved Edmund Lyndeck's creepy solo, and it has been reinstated in most productions since. Also on the album are the full versions of "The Contest" and "Parlor Songs," both of which were trimmed of verses, though not cut entirely.

15. Ash has fine textures, is rare, and looks quite fair, while flaxen is cheaper.

16. *Sweeney* did not play out-of-town previews because it was impossible to transport its set. Designer Eugene Lee reassembled an entire iron foundry from Rhode Island on the stage of the Uris Theatre, which fit in with Prince's concept that the dehumanizing effects of the Industrial Revolution played a role in creating the horrors of the libretto.

17. There are twelve bells in the Tower of Bray.
18. George Hearn and Dorothy Loudon took over from Cariou and Lansbury.
19. In "Poor Thing," the Beggar Woman's theme is played as a minuet at the Judge's gathering where he rapes Sweeney's wife—a musical clue to her identity.
20. In the final line of "My Friends," Sweeney sings that his right arm is once more complete, now that he has his razor back. But Cariou was left-handed.
21. Eugene Lee constructed Pirelli's wagon out of some old wood he found (either part of a barn or in a junkyard), which turned out to be full of wood lice. They got all over the stage and into the costumes.
22. B—Kaufman and Hart wrote the original *Merrily We Roll Along*.
23. E—blue is the dominant color in *Sunday*, followed by red, green, yellow, and purple.
24. B—Rumpelstiltskin was an early cut from *Into the Woods*. So were the Three Little Pigs, but they ended up making a cameo appearance in the 2002 revival.
25. Anarchist Emma Goldman appears in both *Assassins* and *Ragtime*.
26. C—Ludovic's wife and child live in Dalmatia.
27. E—*Sentimental Guy* was, in fact, the proposed title for a musical based on the Mizner brothers...by Irving Berlin. Berlin, who was a friend of Wilson's and an investor in Addison's Florida developments, wrote several songs for the proposed show in the mid-fifties, but nothing ever came of it.

Irving Berlin Answers

1. Berlin performed "Oh, How I Hate to Get Up in the Morning," a soldier's lament at hearing reveille.

~ ~

BROADWAY BONUS: Berlin cut "God Bless America" from *Yip Yip Yaphank* because it was too solemn for the lighthearted revue. He hauled it out again twenty years later, when tensions in Europe were growing, and revised the lyrics. Berlin donated all royalties from the song to the Boy Scouts and Girl Scouts of America.

~ ~

2. A—"How Ya Gonna Keep 'Em Down on the Farm (After They've Seen Paree)?" was not written by Berlin, but by Sam Lewis and Walter Donaldson.
3. E—the inspiration for the song was a 1928 cartoon in the *New Yorker* by Carl Rose. One number in *Face the Music* was set in an Automat.
4. A—there were no classified ads in *As Thousands Cheer*, but there were numbers based on all those other features, as well as news items about the Hoovers leaving the White House, Noel Coward visiting the States, Gandhi, and Rockefeller.
5. True—Sgt. Berlin again performed "Oh, How I Hate to Get Up in the Morning," and for the stage version, several other soldiers who were original "Yaphankers" accompanied him. I don't know if they toured abroad. Berlin's performance was filmed for the movie version of *This Is the Army*, so it's preserved for all time.

6. A.—Frank Butler can go back to Texas, where he can meet Annie's uncle, who can't sign his name, but he'd better stay away from those other places.

7. C—Emma Lazarus' "The New Colossus," which is inscribed on a plaque on the Statue of Liberty ("Give me your tired, your poor, your huddled masses..."), provided the lyrics for *Miss Liberty*'s finale.

8. D—Elaine Stritch was Merman's standby and later toured as Sally Adams. Fanatical fan points to you if you also knew that Nancy Andrews was a standby, though she didn't tour.

9. D—the younger set dance to "The Washington Twist." Some of you probably recognized the "Washington Square Dance" from *Call Me Madam*.

10. Berlin's last hit song was "An Old-Fashioned Wedding."

Cy Coleman Answers

1. B—N. Richard Nash wrote the *Wildcat* libretto.

2. Nancy Andrews and Virginia Martin played Belle.

3. E—"Charlie" is tattooed on Charity's arm.

4. A—Eleanor Roosevelt was the First Lady in question. You can find Dolly Madison in *1600 Pennsylvania Avenue*, Abigail Adams in *1776*, and Rachel Jackson in 2008's *Bloody Bloody Andrew Jackson*, a rock musical about Old Hickory. To the best of my knowledge, nobody's done a musical about Edith Wilson, but someone should, given the dramatic possibilities in her secretly running the government after Woodrow had a stroke.

5. False. *I Love My Wife* was based on a French play called *Viens Chez Moi, J'habite Chez une Copine* by Luis Pego.

6. D—Mildred Natwick found Mrs. Primrose's solo too scandalous to sing. Ethel Merman reportedly had one of the filthiest mouths on Broadway, but she allegedly bowed out of Howard Dietz' *Sadie Thompson* because of dirty lyrics (or because she realized the show would tank?). And I'm sure after singing naughty Porter lyrics in *Silk Stockings*, Gretchen Wyler wouldn't have objected to the things Mrs. Primrose does.

7. D—Sophie the seal was in Rodgers and Hart's *Jumbo*, but not *Barnum*.

8. E—both B and C were used as titles: *Death Is for Suckers* and *Double Exposure*. "Double Talk" was a number in the show.

9. A—Gregory Peck provided the voice of the great Ziegfeld.

10. D—it took seven years (and $7 million) to get *The Life* to Broadway.

Andrew Lloyd Webber Answers

1. B—turquoise is not one of the colors described in Joseph's coat, which nearly wasn't Technicolor. MGM, which owned the Technicolor trademark, contacted Lloyd Webber and Rice after the show began gaining popularity and threatened a suit unless they used the U.S. spelling (it's "Technicolour" in British usage) and the trademark logo. Whereupon the creators said they would retitle the show *Joseph and the Amazing Eastmancolo(u)r Dreamcoat*. MGM gave up.

2. D—Ian Gillian of Deep Purple was Jesus on the concept album.
3. Eva goes to Spain, Italy, and France on the Rainbow Tour, but not England.
4. B—Betty Buckley, the original U.S. Grizabella, played Emma at the end of the Broadway run, but all the other ladies had A.L.W. connections. Melissa Manchester toured as Emma in 1987; Marti Webb was the original U.K. Emma; Elaine Paige was the original U.K. Grizabella; and Loni Ackerman played Evita on Broadway and on tour.
5. D—Trevor Nunn wrote "Memory" after finding an Eliot poem, "Rhapsody on a Windy Night," suitable for adapting. They initially had asked Tim Rice for help, but he wasn't interested. Meanwhile, Judi Dench, the original Grizabella, tore her Achilles tendon and was replaced by Elaine Paige. Since Paige was Rice's girlfriend, he changed his mind about the song, but "Memory" was already in the works.
6. A—Diesel is the name of the nasty engine in the *Thomas the Tank Engine* series of books. That series, as well as inspiring *Starlight Express*, gave Lloyd Webber the name for his production company, the Really Useful Group. One of the engines, James, was constantly described as a Really Useful engine.
7. C—Lloyd Webber asked Alan Jay Lerner, not Lionel Bart, to collaborate on *Phantom*, and he worked on one song, "Masquerade" (not the same one that ended up in the show), but was too ill to continue.
8. B—Roger Moore was the original choice for Uncle George.
9. A—"Blind Windows" is the name of the script. "Bases Loaded" is the title of the outline Joe shows Sheldrake. "Salome" is the name of Norma's Biblical epic. The other possible answers are song titles.
10. D—The mysterious woman in white is, in fact, a girl trapped in an asylum by the villain. The way she appears and hastily vanishes causes some to think she's a ghost. Count Fosco's mouse may not even be female, but is notable as the second rodent to appear onstage with Michael Crawford; the first being Algernon in *Flowers for Algernon*. That must be some kind of a record.

William Finn Answers

1. Chip Zien played Marvin in 1979's *In Trousers*, but would later play Mendel. Stephen Bogardus played Marvin in the 1985 production, having played Whizzer in 1981's *March of the Falsettos* (and would again play him in *Falsettoland* and *Falsettos*.) Official William Finn-atic Award to those who know that Finn himself played Marvin in *In Trousers'* original workshop.
2. C—"I'm Breaking Down," Trina's big number, was added to *March of the Falsettos*.
3. D—Orpheus and Eurydice's tale is the basis for *Tango Apasionado*.
4. B—everyone hates his parents.
5. E—Bock and Finn's aborted show was based on the U.S. tax code.
6. D—Adam Guettel provided the incidental music, working with jazz composer/saxophonist Chico Freeman.
7. A—the waitress brings the fish of the day, calamari, even though squid really aren't fish.

8. E—Wendy Wasserstein, whose weekend baby-sitter, Sara Saltzberg, was in the original cast of *C-R-E-P-U-S-C-U-L-E*, went to see the show and immediately thought it was good material for Finn.

\~\~ \~\~ \~\~ \~\~ \~\~ \~\~ \~\~ \~\~ \~\~ \~\~ \~\~ \~\~ \~\~ \~\~ \~\~ \~\~ \~\~ \~\~ \~\~

BROADWAY BONUS: The Putnam Valley Middle School team fights as the Piranhas. Speller Julie Andrews was eliminated on the word "supercalifragilisticexpialidocious."

\~\~ \~\~ \~\~ \~\~ \~\~ \~\~ \~\~ \~\~ \~\~ \~\~ \~\~ \~\~ \~\~ \~\~ \~\~ \~\~ \~\~ \~\~ \~\~

9. A—one of the songs in *Elegies* remembers Joseph Papp, at whose Public Theatre Finn worked on *Romance in Hard Times*.
10. E—alas, it seems that because of the Kaufman estate, we will never see Finn's *The Royal Family of Broadway*.

Jerome Kern Answers

1. D—Charles Frohman produced many of Kern's early shows.

\~\~ \~\~ \~\~ \~\~ \~\~ \~\~ \~\~ \~\~ \~\~ \~\~ \~\~ \~\~ \~\~ \~\~ \~\~ \~\~ \~\~ \~\~ \~\~

BROADWAY BONUS: Frohman died on the *Lusitania* in 1915. Kern always claimed he had a ticket, but overslept. His wife denied the story.

\~\~ \~\~ \~\~ \~\~ \~\~ \~\~ \~\~ \~\~ \~\~ \~\~ \~\~ \~\~ \~\~ \~\~ \~\~ \~\~ \~\~ \~\~ \~\~

2. B—"They Didn't Believe Me" appeared in *The Girl from Utah* (1914). But to give you an idea of what was popular in the early twentieth century, Kern also wrote songs for *The Sunshine Girl*, *The Doll Girl*, *The Riviera Girl*, *A Girl of Today*, and *The Cabaret Girl*.
3. C—*Leave It to Jane* was a "Princess" show that played at the larger Longacre Theatre.
4. D—Bud DeSylva was the lyricist for "Look for the Silver Lining" and "Whip-poor-will." When Ziegfeld hired Clifford Grey to work on *Sally*'s score, P. G. Wodehouse threatened to withdraw *his* lyrics. Two of Grey's lyrics remained.
5. E—"Who?" was the smash hit from *Sunny*.
6. Alexander Woolcott introduced Kern and Ferber.
7. D—Paul Robeson, though much associated with the role of Joe and the song "Ol' Man River," was not in the original cast of *Show Boat*—though they tried to get him. Jules Bledsoe played Joe when the show opened.
8. B—a Nantucket songbird gave Kern the melody for "I've Told Ev'ry Little Star." The brook is mentioned in the lyric; the Bavarian linnet inspires the melody in the libretto; the green finch is in *Sweeney Todd*; and I have no idea if Dorothy Hammerstein owned a canary.
9. A—"Lovely to Look At" (lyrics by Dorothy Fields) was written for the 1935 film version of *Roberta*, which starred Fred Astaire and Ginger Rogers. The film cut a number of the stage songs and added "Lovely" and "I Won't Dance," which both became hits. These songs were kept when the film was remade in 1952 as *Lovely to Look At*. "Smoke Gets in Your Eyes" was such a huge hit for the original production that producer Max Gordon advertised *Roberta* as "the 'Smoke Gets in Your Eyes' musical."

10. Irving Berlin took over the musical based on Annie Oakley, which, of course, was *Annie Get Your Gun*. Haven't you ever wondered what it would have sounded like with a Kern-Fields score?

Jule Styne Answers

1. C—Dorothy Fields never wrote a lyric to a Jule Styne song, more's the pity.
2. C—Nanette Fabray played Mama Longstreet.
3. E—Henry Spofford comes from a wealthy Philadelphia family, so Dorothy imagines life at Rittenhouse Square.
4. D—Jeff calls Ella "Mom."
5. A—Robert Morse's character in *Say, Darling* was based on young Hal Prince, who had produced *The Pajama Game*, the source material for *Say, Darling*.
6. E—"You'll Never Get Away from Me" used the same melody as "I'm in Pursuit of Happiness" from the TV musical, *Ruggles of Red Gap*. Styne did not tell Sondheim the music had been used before.
7. D—believe it or not, Kanin wanted "People" cut.
8. B—"Smaxie" was the name of the seal that was the logo for the movie studio, as Leo the Lion was the emblem for MGM.
9. Styne and lyricists Comden and Green and librettist Arthur Laurents created *Hallelujah, Baby!*, which won Tonys for Best Musical and Best Composer and Lyricist for 1967.
10. C—"Tear the Town Apart" wowed audiences with the machine-gun tapping of Steve Condos as gangster Spats Palazzo. Styne reportedly still disliked the number, though he couldn't argue with its success.

Noel Coward Answers

1. A—Fred Astaire, then performing in London, helped Coward learn tap dancing and helped choreograph some of the numbers. They were both attending classes at the Guildhall School of Music at the time, since neither had had much formal music training and thought it would be useful in their careers. His sister Adele married Lord Charles Cavendish.
2. C—*This Year of Grace* opened in 1928. "Don't Let's Be Beastly to the Germans" was written during World War II, though it was banned by the BBC after its initial airing since some people misunderstood the satire and thought it was a pro-German piece.
3. E—Carl in *Bitter Sweet* was Sarah's music teacher.
4. D—Coward's 1931 spectacle was *Cavalcade*. Its film version would win the Oscar for Best Picture, but few people these days have seen it, as it's one of just two Best Picture winners never to appear on DVD.
5. A—Valentino is not mentioned in "Mad About the Boy."
6. B—Coward wrote *Conversation Piece* with Yvonne Printemps in mind, and when she left to do a French film, they couldn't find a suitable replacement. Printemps knew little English, learned her role phonetically, and forced the entire cast to speak to her in French.

7. A—George IV used the lavatory mentioned in "The Stately Homes of England."
8. E—Coward wrote many different (mostly naughty) lyrics to "Let's Do It" over the years, including the ones used in his Vegas act. He also wrote lyrics to Porter's "Let's Fly Away," "You're the Top," "Thank You So Much, Mrs. Lowsborough-Goodby," "Fresh as a Daisy," and "Siberia." Of the songs listed as possible answers, "What Am I to Do?" was the Coward-like song Porter wrote for the Coward-like character in *The Man Who Came to Dinner* (and was, in fact, published as "by Noel Porter"). "Eric Dare" in Porter's *Jubilee* was another character based on Coward.
9. A—Mimi says the wrong people drink dry martinis in Greece. But you can find lyric references in *Sail Away* to all the other beverages except ouzo.

❦ ❦

BROADWAY BONUS: Gottlieb got $100,000 from Cunard Lines and American Express. In exchange, the ship was named the *Coronia* (one of Cunard's ships was the *Caronia*); the crew members wore Cunard uniforms; there was a lyric referring to American Express and a character described as "the man from American Express." Product placement is nothing new to Broadway.

❦ ❦

10. C—Jose Ferrer played the Prince Regent from Carpathia in *The Girl Who Came to Supper*. Coward had hoped for Harrison or Plummer, and Redgrave played the role in the original straight play, *The Sleeping Prince*.

Stephen Schwartz Answers

1. E—Karl Marx, who said religion was the opium of the masses, is not cited in the "Prologue" from *Godspell*.
2. E—Pippin is not concerned about a leaky moat.
3. D—Doug Henning sawed Barbara Walters in half. She got better.
4. C—Pompom is the name of the baker's cat. Asparagus is the theatre cat in *Cats*; Meowrice is the villainous cat in the animated film *Gay Purree* (with the voice talents of Judy Garland, Robert Goulet, and Red Buttons—and some truly psychedelic scenes that may have warped my children for life); Minou is the most common cat name in France.
5. C—Walt Whitman's poem "I Hear America Singing" was adapted for the opening number of *Working*.
6. E—The cast of *Rags* protested its closing by marching down Broadway to Duffy Square.
7. A—God is called "Father" in *Children of Eden*.
8. C—Schwartz wrote the lyrics for Alan Menken's music in the Disney films *Pocahontas* and *The Hunchback of Notre Dame* (adapted for the stage in Germany), and teamed up with him more recently for the film *Enchanted*. He won Oscars for *Pocahontas* and his own score for *Prince of Egypt*.
9. B—Dr. Dillamond is a goat. Elphaba has the monkeys; the pushmi-pullyu comes from *Dr. Dolittle*; and the highly-magnified Wogglebug is a character from the Oz books, but not, alas, *Wicked*.

10. C—Ezra Jack Keats wrote *The Trip*, the basis for *Captain Louie*. But did you know that Bernadette Peters, John Lithgow, Julie Andrews, and Stephen Schwartz himself have all written children's books? Yes, it's true. And very good they are. Broadway buffs can have special fun recognizing the real-life analogues of the stage mice in Andrews' *The Great American Mousical*.

Harold Arlen Answers

1. B—"Get Happy" (lyrics by Ted Koehler) was Arlen's first big hit in 1929.
2. A—*George White's Scandals* saw Arlen playing in the orchestra.
3. E—Oscar Hammerstein II never collaborated with Arlen.
4. C—Ethel Waters. Of the cast members of *Life Begins at 8:40*, Ray Bolger was Arlen's roommate and Frances Williams was his girlfriend when he first came to New York.
5. C—Chuckles. Frankenstein builds a monster; Parker is the scientist in *Bat Boy*; Sedgwick is the evil scientist in *It's a Bird...It's a Plane...It's Superman*; and I picked Smiley to confuse you because it's similar to Chuckles.
6. Arlen, who was a fine singer, performs "Man for Sale" on the *Bloomer Girl* cast album.
7. Lena Horne objected to the material in *St. Louis Woman*.
8. E—Rose cannot be found in the *House of Flowers*.
9. A—Jack Cole, whose work seems under-appreciated when compared to other choreographers who went on to become high-powered directors, did the choreography for *Jamaica*.
10. E—"Gettin' a Man" was composed by Mercer, not Arlen.

Go into Your Dance Answers

1. H—Rob Ashford, "Forget About the Boy," *Thoroughly Modern Millie*
2. R—George Balanchine, "Slaughter on 10th Avenue," *On Your Toes*
3. O—Michael Bennett, "Who's That Woman?" *Follies* (o)
4. X—Patricia Birch, "We Go Together," *Grease* (o)
5. Q—Gower Champion, "The Waiters' Gallop," *Hello, Dolly!* (o)
6. Z—Wayne Cilento, "One Short Day," *Wicked*
7. W—Jack Cole, "Not Since Nineveh," *Kismet*
8. D—Graciela Daniele, "We Dance," *Once on This Island*
9. A—Agnes de Mille, "Laurey Makes Up Her Mind," *Oklahoma!* (o)
10. J—Ron Field, "But Alive," *Applause*
11. M—Bob Fosse, "Magic to Do," *Pippin*
12. B—Peter Gennaro, "Gentleman Jimmy," *Fiorello!*
13. E—Hanya Holm, "Too Darn Hot," *Kiss Me, Kate* (o)
14. P—Bill T. Jones, "The Bitch of Living," *Spring Awakening*
15. F—Michael Kidd, "The Garden of Eden Ballet," *Can-Can* (o)
16. K—Joe Layton, "Love Makes the World Go," *No Strings*
17. T—Gillian Lynne, "The Jellicle Ball," *Cats*

18. N—Kathleen Marshall, "Conga!" *Wonderful Town* (r)
19. L—Jerry Mitchell, "Let It Go," *The Full Monty*
20. S—Casey Nicholaw, "Fisch Schlapping Dance," *Monty Python's Spamalot*
21. V—Jerome Robbins, "Mack Sennett Ballet," *High Button Shoes*
22. U—Herb Ross, "The Cookie Chase," *Anyone Can Whistle*
23. Y—Susan Strohman, "Along Came Bialy," *The Producers*
24. I—Lee (Becker) Theodore, "The Tree of Life Ballet," *Flora, the Red Menace*
25. G—Tommy Tune, "We'll Take a Glass Together," *Grand Hotel*
26. C—Onna White, "Marian the Librarian," *The Music Man* (o)

⁓ ⁓

BROADWAY BONUS: Hanya Holm's ballet for *Camelot* was set in the Enchanted Forest, in which Morgan le Fay and Mordred trapped Arthur, and featured magical animals.

⁓ ⁓

Backstage Babble Answers

1. Harry is on the spotlight for *Robbin' Hood*—an unseen character in *Curtains*.
2. Bob is the jealous electrician in *Me and Juliet*.
3. Duane Fox is Margo's hairdresser in *Applause*.
4. Joseph Buquet is the chief of the flies in *The Phantom of the Opera*.
5. Shirley Markowitz is Roger de Bris' lighting designer in *The Producers*.
6. Harry, the bald doorman at the Weismann Theatre in *Follies*, is mentioned only in lyrics.
7. Hog Eye works the spotlight on Norma Desmond in *Sunset Blvd.*
8. Hattie is Lilli's dresser/maid in *Kiss Me, Kate*.
9. Zach's assistant is Larry. Ever notice how Larry is the only character in *A Chorus Line* who has *no* story, excluding the dancers who get cut right away? Don't you wonder what Larry has to say? Does he like working for Zach or does he see him as a Robbins-like tyrant? Does he think Zach is casting the show correctly ("I can't believe he cast his ex-girlfriend")? Obviously, Larry's backstory is one of the great unanswered mysteries of Broadway.

Ensemble Number Answers

1. In the original *Cabaret*, the Kit Kat Klub girls included Rosie, Lulu, Frenchie, Texas, Fritzie, Marlene, Maria, and Hulda. In the revival, Maria and Marlene vanished and Hulda became Helga. The original boys were Bobby, Victor, and Felix. In the revival, Felix departed (with Marlene and Maria?) and was replaced by Hans and Herman. Don't you ever wonder where these characters go when there are revisions like this? Some kind of offstage eternal limbo?
2. Annie's buddies at Miss Hannigan's were Molly, Pepper, Duffy, July, Tessie, and Kate.
3. Sir Dinadan, Sir Lionel, and Sir Sagramore wanted to take the Queen to various venues in *Camelot* (until "You Can Take Me to the Fair" got cut in the original run). Sir Dinadan was killed by Lance in the tournament, but got revived.

4. Tevye's daughters in *Fiddler on the Roof* were Tzeitel, Hodel, Chavah, and the ones you had trouble remembering were Shprintze and Bielke.
5. The merry murderesses in *Chicago* sharing the pen with Velma and Roxie were Liz, Annie, June, Hunyak, and Mona.
6. Competing with the Dreamettes at the Apollo in *Dreamgirls* were the Stepp Sisters, Tiny Joe Dixon, and Little Albert and the Tru-tones.
7. The girls in *Little Shop of Horrors* were Ronette, Chiffon, and Crystal (all names of girl groups in the sixties).
8. *The Rothschilds'* boys were Amshel, Solomon, Nathan, Jacob, and Kalman. Amshel goes to Prussia, Solomon goes to Vienna, Nathan goes to London, Jacob goes to Prague, and Kalman is at first sent to bed, then to Hamburg, which is just about as safe.
9. Oscar Jaffe's put-upon assistants in *On the Twentieth Century* were Owen O'Malley and Oliver Webb.
10. In *Grease*, the Pink Ladies were Rizzo, Frenchie, Jan, and Marty. The Burger Palace Boys were Kenickie, Doody, Roger, and Sonny.
11. The girls at Madame DuBonnet's school (*The Boy Friend*) include Nancy, Maisie, Fay, and Dulcie, in addition to Polly, the lead.
12. The other kids who are Corny Collins' Council Members are Brad, Tammy, Fender, Brenda, Sketch, Shelley, I. Q., and Lou Ann (*Hairspray*).
13. Charlie Anderson's six sons in *Shenandoah* are Jacob, James, John, Nathan, Henry, and Robert (usually called "the Boy").

〰 〰

BROADWAY BONUS: Wiggins, Duckbellows, Nipper, Perkins, and Macipper are Sherlock Holmes' *Baker Street* Irregulars.

〰 〰

Ethel Merman Answers

1. D—according to Merman herself, she held the note for sixteen bars. I've seen it in print from anywhere from sixteen to thirty-two, but let's leave it to the diva's own words. During the opening night, producer Alex Aarons thought a shot had gone off in the theatre while Merman held that note.
2. B—it wasn't Bert Lahr, but Fernando Lamas, Merman's unhappy co-star in *Happy Hunting*, who complained about her kissing on the *Mike Wallace Show*. He would also wipe them off while onstage, much to the audience's amusement and Merman's fury.
3. C—William Gaxton introduced "All Through the Night," which was itself a replacement for "Easy to Love," which Gaxton found too hard to sing. Strangely enough, Jimmy Stewart, not known for his singing, managed his way through "Easy to Love," which Porter recycled a few years later in the film Born to Dance.
4. B—Cole Porter had the notion to alternate Merman and Durante's names in a criss-cross for the posters of *Red, Hot and Blue.*
5. C—Grable introduced "Give Him the Oo-La-La" in Boston, but Merman's character had it in New York. There's no evidence that Merman herself demanded it, or if it

was jointly decided that such a strong song had to go to the big star. Grable ended up doing all right for herself.

6. A—the poodle's name was Serutan, which was a popular health tonic. The product's ads always stated that Serutan was "nature's" spelled backwards.

7. E—Chief Sitting Bull advises Annie, whom he regards as a daughter, to throw the match in order to win Frank.

8. C—both Perle Mesta and the character Mrs. Sally Adams got their family fortune from Oklahoma oil fields.

9. B—the wedding of Grace Kelly and Prince Rainier was the inspiration for *Happy Hunting*. The Molnár play was adapted into 1951's *Make a Wish*; Dreiser's story became the off-Broadway musical about men digging tunnels for subways, *Sandhog* (1954); and the Kober play became *Wish You Were Here* (1952). Wallis and Edward's tale became a London musical, *Always*, in 1997, and Madonna apparently wants to do a film musical about Wallis.

10. Oscar Hammerstein, Sondheim's mentor, convinced him to do the lyrics for *Gypsy*, even though he wanted to prove himself as a composer, not just a lyricist. Hammerstein noted that writing lyrics for a big star like Merman was a different kind of writing and would be good experience. One more reason to be grateful for Mr. Hammerstein! As it turned out, Sondheim and Merman did not get along, but musical theatre fans will eternally appreciate what they created together despite their differences.

_{❧ ❧}

BROADWAY BONUS: *Jenny Get Your Gun* was the original title of *Something for the Boys*. The title is a pun on an enlisting slogan, "Johnny, Get Your Gun," which was used in the late nineteenth and early twentieth centuries. George M. Cohan used the phrase in his World War I song, "Over There." *While Jenny Get Your Gun* was abandoned as a title, *Annie Get Your Gun* lives on.

_{❧ ❧}

David Merrick Answers

1. D—he chose Merrick because it rhymed with Garrick, as in the famous actor.

2. B—Merrick did not have bellhops and hotel operators page "Mademoiselle Fanny" to promote the musical. He did, however, have "Mr. Clutterbuck" paged in order to gain attention to a straight play he produced in 1949 called *Clutterbuck*. The *Fanny* publicity campaign included other things I didn't list in the answers, including Merrick's placing ads in foreign and out-of-state newspapers urging those intending to visit New York to see the show, and a strange attempt to use a high-powered projector to shine the *Fanny* logo on a billboard that featured a real waterfall. Merrick rented a hotel room directly across from the waterfall billboard, but the hotel staff would not let him use their facility for his illicit advertisement.

3. C—Dolores Gray really wanted to be part of the "Whip Dance," which led to a serious feud with Michael Kidd, culminating in a physical, face-slapping fight. Merrick loved every minute. The story about the mikes picking up actors in the toilet is most

often associated with Anna Maria Alberghetti, who wore a body mike in Merrick's *Carnival* (and with whom he had a tremendous feud), but may be a myth. Alberghetti did admit to stealing a plaque honoring Merrick and hanging it above her own toilet.

4. False—Merrick did have men in French attire with sandwich boards, but they weren't carrying rubber chickens. They had portable urinals (*pissoirs*) attached to the boards. Go figure.

5. Merrick had to wait until theatre critic Brooks Atkinson retired, since there was only one person with that name.

6. A—the astronauts saw *Stop the World, I Want to Get Off*, which is kind of funny when you remember they *had* gotten off the earth and were actually in orbit.

7. D—Merrick used a full complement of orphans in *Oliver!*

8. C—those of you who are big Jerry Herman buffs will know the story of the out-of-town origin of "Before the Parade Passes By." Still, it's damn impressive that Herman could churn out four songs in three days and have three be so good they made the final version of the show.

9. D—Edward Albee, not a name usually associated with musicals, wrote the new libretto for *Breakfast at Tiffany's*. If George Axelrod's name sounded familiar, it's because he wrote the screenplay.

10. In 1987, Merrick moved the start time of *42nd Street* by fifteen minutes to lure people who couldn't get tickets to *The Phantom of the Opera*, then playing to packed houses right across the street.

Carol Channing and Jerry Orbach Answers

1. E—"The Gladiola Girl" made fun of twenties' musical comedies.

2. E—Channing has reported that costume designer Miles White was inspired by the image of the Pope on the balcony at the Vatican, waving to crowds, for his design for "Diamonds Are a Girl's Best Friend."

3. D—Flora, the country girl in Hollywood, played Delilah.

4. D—she was listening to Herman play "Before the Parade Passes By," the song he'd just written under tremendous pressure. She learned the song on the spot, then she and Herman woke up Champion. Channing performed the song, and Champion went wild, immediately conjuring up new staging.

5. A—"Bye, Bye Baby" was in both *Gentlemen Prefer Blondes* and *Lorelei*, along with ten other numbers (though not the other four listed in the answers).

6. The role of the Handyman in *The Fantasticks* vanished in 1961, never to return.

7. D—Jacquot was Paul's assistant, not one of the puppets.

8. Orbach crumpled up his raincoat and used it as a basketball for the number.

9. D—Orbach had been told that Fosse was self-conscious about his lack of education. While few things intimidated him, large vocabularies did. When no one could get Fosse to budge on the sleazy staging for "Razzle Dazzle," Orbach carefully crafted his approach. He pretended that Fosse had been using Brechtian techniques in the number and ever so casually remarked that the simulated sex was hindering the desired effect. Fosse, not understanding, mumbled in agreement and soon after announced that the "stuff on the stairs" was out.

10. "Musical comedy," of course! How could anyone in her right mind go back to Allentown and give that up?

Bob Fosse and Gwen Verdon Answers

1. A—Abbott hated "Steam Heat" and wanted to cut it because it was a showstopper. He felt numbers that stopped the show did so literally: they prevented the plot from progressing. But audiences adored "Steam Heat," and Robbins convinced Abbott to keep it.
2. D—"Apache Dance" and the "Garden of Eden Ballet" both stopped the show, earning raves for Verdon, but it was after the "Apache Dance" that she had to be dragged back onstage in her robe. Plenty of books misidentify this as the "Garden of Eden Ballet," perhaps because Verdon wasn't wearing much in that number, but both the critical reviews and Cy Feuer's autobiography confirm it as the "Apache Dance."
3. B—the original ending of the book *The Year the Yankees Lost the Pennant* had the umpire calling Old Joe safe at home over Applegate's protests. But not even the devil can overrule an umpire. By the opening, Lola had regained her beauty, the baseball ballet was cut, and "Two Lost Souls" had more of a swing beat. "Not Meg" would be cut just after opening to save time.
4. The number in question was "The Red Light Ballet" (a.k.a. "The Whorehouse Ballet"). In it, the character of Anna looks back on her days as a prostitute. The number was extraordinarily graphic for its time, and Abbott and Prince felt it glamorized something that Anna was supposed to regard as loathsome.
5. D—"'Erbie Fitch's Twitch" was the number Verdon performed in male drag and derby—iconic Fosse-wear, one might say.
6. C—Fosse was awarded six cents in damages.

~ ~

BROADWAY BONUS: Larry Gelbart reportedly said while on *The Conquering Hero*'s disastrous tryout, "If Hitler is alive, I hope he's out of town with a musical."

~ ~

7. E—"A Secretary Is Not a Toy" became an enchanting soft-shoe for much of the company, thanks to the determined Fosse, who had also rehearsed "Coffee Break" in secret. In fact, he asked Gwen Verdon to keep the temperamental Loesser away from the stage, until his work on "Coffee Break" was done. Shame on you if you guessed "Cinderella Darling" or "Paris Original," since I can't imagine any possible reworking of the script to have Rudy Vallee singing those numbers.
8. D—Elaine May was supposed to have written the second one-act musical before *Sweet Charity* grew into a full-length show. Moss Hart had died in 1961 and Abbott never worked with Fosse again after the fights during *New Girl in Town*.
9. B—Helen Morgan's torch songs, including her traditional pose on top of the piano, provided the inspiration for Roxie's "Funny Honey." Sophie Tucker's "Got to See Mama" was the model for Mama Morton's "When You're Good to Mama;" Texas Guinan ("Hello, suckers!") influenced the character of Velma; Sally Rand's fan dance

was featured in "All I Care About;" and the optimistic lyrics of "Look for the Silver Lining," made popular by Marilyn Miller, were paralleled in "Little Bit of Good," though the character of Mary Sunshine more closely resembled drag star Julian Eltinge, coupled with the vaudeville offerings of opera divas like Rosa Ponselle. *Chicago* is a deliciously complicated show.

10. C—"Sing, Sing, Sing" was dedicated to "Gwen Verdon and Jack Cole, and the latter would have hated it." The number itself was a tribute to big-band leader Benny Goodman, but not specifically dedicated to him.

Alfred Drake Answers

1. C—Joan Roberts was not one of the *Babes in Arms*.
2. Drake sang "Lonely Room" on the cast album of *Oklahoma!*, which, as all good fans of Rodgers and Hammerstein know, was Jud's song.
3. A—Duke Ellington wrote the music for *Beggar's Holiday*.
4. Lilli's wedding bouquet—and the flowers meant for Lois—included snowdrops, pansies, and rosemary.
5. C—Rodgers wanted Drake for the King in *The King and I*, but he wanted more money. He later was a replacement when Yul Brynner went on vacation.
6. E—the newspaper strike greatly helped *Kismet*'s chances by withholding the bad reviews.
7. D—Drake played Marco Polo in a television musical. Doretta Morrow from *Kismet* joined him.
8. B—"Domesticity" was a late cut in *Kean*.
9. A—*Rugantino* was Drake's Italian-language experiment on Broadway. Edward Eager, who wrote some classic children's fantasies, translated the lyrics, while Drake translated the libretto for the subtitles. Eager had done the lyrics for Drake's television musical, *Marco Polo*.
10. D—Honoré revels in the fact that "Paris Is Paris Again."

Mary Martin Answers

1. B—Gene Kelly was one of those smiling chorus boys listening to Mary Martin sing of her fine finnan haddie.
2. E—Fashion designer Mainbocher wasn't sure if he wanted to design *Venus* until Martin sat on a chair and sang "Speak Low" right at him. He had earlier done costumes for *Blithe Spirit*, and would do shows through the forties and fifties, including those for the leading ladies of *Wonderful Town*, *Call Me Madam*, and *The Sound of Music*.
3. A—*Lute Song* lasted 142 performances. Even if you didn't know much about the show, you probably could have figured this one out, since Martin was a big enough star to command advance sales of more than three performances.
4. C—"Alice (Is at It Again)" has lived on far longer than the show for which it was written.

5. True—Martin washed her hair onstage for every performance of *South Pacific*, and the gimmick was her idea, too. Of course, she found that the repeated washing onstage, at home, and at the salon played hell on her short locks.

6. C—Martin played Peter for television three times. The first live broadcast was in March 1955 and was seen by 70 million people. It was again broadcast live, but in color, in January 1956, and then it was videotaped for posterity (and multiple reruns) in December 1960. Each broadcast featured most of the original Broadway cast. Mia Farrow played Peter for NBC's Hallmark Hall of Fame in 1976 in a different musical version, with a score by Anthony Newley and Leslie Briccuse.

7. A—Maria sings "My Favorite Things" with the Mother Abbess very early in the stage version. If you're conditioned by the movie, this may seem odd to you.

8. A—There was no volcano in *Jennie*, though it had plenty of everything else. However, Noel Coward's island of Samolo has a volcano and Bali Ha'i has two. Even more obscure fact: the sultan's "torture wheel" in the harem scene was actually a spinning exercise device from Martin's home. Apparently, she didn't mind singing while upside down and spinning.

9. B—Martin turned down *Mame*, though Jerry Herman had traveled all the way to her ranch in the middle of the Amazon jungle to ask her. He describes spending the night in her guest bungalow with many, many bats.

10. D—Martin's campaigning saved "My Cup Runneth Over," which became the big hit from *I Do! I Do!* As Irving Berlin once told Cole Porter, "Never hate a song that's sold a half million copies." Harvey Schmidt no longer hates "My Cup Runneth Over."

Patti LuPone Answers

1. A—LuPone's robber bridegroom was Kevin Kline, her one-time boyfriend. Barry Bostwick played the role in the Center Theatre Group production and the later 1976 Broadway run, earning a Tony. Raul Julia had the part in the original workshop version. Tom Wopat played it in Washington, D.C.

2. The song David Merrick tried to cut from *The Baker's Wife* was "Meadowlark," which he nastily called "Dickie Bird." You knew that, right?

3. A—LuPone played a call girl in *Working*. Bonus points if you knew she also played an editor in one scene.

4. C—Eva wants to be like Lauren Bacall.

5. E—John Houseman directed, produced, and performed a prologue relating the fascinating history of the original *The Cradle Will Rock*. Will Geer was a performer in that original show; Leonard Bernstein arranged and conducted a 1939 performance at Harvard; Howard Da Silva, another original cast member, directed revivals in 1947, 1960, and 1964; and Tim Robbins directed the movie *Cradle Will Rock* about the show's creation.

6. True—LuPone was the first American to win an Olivier Award. She was honored for her performances in both *Cradle* and *Les Misérables*.

7. D—the first voice heard in the 1987 revival of *Anything Goes* was that of composer Cole Porter, singing the title song. At the end, a giant portrait of Porter descended from the flies.

8. C—LuPone built a swimming pool, dubbed the "Andrew Lloyd Webber Memorial Pool," with the damages from the suit. Given the importance of Norma's pool in *Sunset Boulevard*, this has a kind of delicious twist.

9. D—LuPone has not done *Company* at Ravinia, but she did all the other Sondheim titles listed in the question, as well as *Sweeney Todd*.

❀ ❀

BROADWAY BONUS: Patti's tuba was named Irene. After each show, she would put it back in its case and say, "Good night, Irene."

❀ ❀

10. C—LuPone is the third, not the fourth, woman to win the Tony for Best Actress with the demanding role of Rose in *Gypsy*. Angela Lansbury (1975) and Tyne Daly (1990) both won Tonys. In 1960, the original Rose—Ethel Merman—lost to Mary Martin's Maria ("Ya can't buck a nun!") and Bernadette Peters lost in 2003 to Marissa Jaret Winokur in *Hairspray*.

George Abbott Answers

1. The Abbott touch: "I make them [actors] say their final syllables."
2. B—Abbott already had six Tonys, including one for Lifetime Achievement, when he was given a special Tony on his centennial.
3. Abbott's alleged response: "Your paycheck."
4. A—Joel Higgins called him George to his face and apparently lived.
5. A—*On Your Toes* was the show Abbott directed three different times on Broadway: 1936, 1954, 1983. He directed the originals of all the other shows listed there and the 1973 revival of *The Pajama Game*.
6. C—"From This Moment On" was the song Abbott cut from *Out of This World*, but it soon resurfaced in the film version of *Kiss Me, Kate*, becoming a big hit. Now it is usually added to *Kiss Me, Kate* stagings.
7. C—Eydie Gorme was Abbott's initial choice for Flora.
8. B—Abbott helped all those songwriters get started except Lerner and Loewe.
9. A and E—Abbott felt there were more dramatic possibilities setting the show in 1900, when a woman's place was more inferior, and he felt the clothes were prettier than in 1921.
10. E—the Adelphi/54th Street Theatre was the short-lived George Abbott Theatre. All the other theatres listed for this question have been razed.

Barbara Cook Answers

1. C—the word "flahooley" is Irish for "flighty, whimsical."
2. E—Hilda sings "This Is All Very New to Me" after getting her first kiss.
3. E—the twenty-carat earring is mentioned in "Glitter and Be Gay," but all the other trappings of a good marriage are listed by Cunegonde in "Oh Happy We."

4. Fans of *The Music Man* know that Willson used the same melodic line in Marian's "Goodnight, My Someone" and Harold's "Seventy-six Trombones." In fact, after the characters realize they're both in love, they sing verses of the other's key song. Now that's true love, in Broadway musical terms! Willson also wrote two other paired song sets: "Will I Ever Tell You" and "Lida Rose," and "The Sadder-but-Wiser Girl" and "My White Knight."

5. C—Anita Gillette was in *Carnival* as Anna Maria Allberghetti's understudy and left it to go into *The Gay Life*. She next starred in the similarly ill-fated *All American*.

6. C—the song "Tell Me I Look Nice" was replaced by "Will He Like Me?" "Heads, I Win" was added to the London production for Ilona, not Amalia.

7. A—the family in *Something More!* moves to Portofino, Italy. The novel that was its basis was called *Portofino, P.T.A.*, which was to be the musical's title. They changed it because it called to mind the infamous musical flop *Portofino*. It didn't help.

8. A—a cat-shaped cloud means dropsy-cure weather.

9. A—*Follies in Concert* gave Cook a chance to work again with director Herb Ross from *The Gay Life*.

10. Cook's role was Mrs. White and the show was *Carrie*. Betty Buckley would (briefly!) play the role on Broadway.

Harold Prince Answers

1. The original ads for *Damn Yankees* showed Gwen Verdon in a baseball uniform. Prince changed the picture to one of "Lola" in barely anything at all—and sales improved!

2. C—Prince worked with James Goldman and John Kander for the first time on *A Family Affair*.

3. A—Julie Andrews was making a film, but Prince chose to go ahead with Barbara Cook as Amalia, rather than wait half a year.

4. A—"Anatevka" replaced the far more elaborate fantasy ballet Robbins had devised. Prince felt the show's mood was harmed by an extravagant eleven o'clock number.

5. Prince staged the Queen's Jubilee using the Bil Baird Puppets, including a carriage from which a white hanky (presumably the queen's) waved to the crowds.

6. E—while in Germany, Prince went to a nightclub hosted by a creepy dwarf who apparently made a lasting impression. Some people have said that Grey's portrayal did remind them of Belasco, Lorre, or the devil.

7. B—Prince screened Fellini's *8 1/2* to his *Follies* colleagues. Interestingly enough, Fellini had once inquired about Prince's adapting the film into a musical, but he declined.

8. E—*Merrily* kept its original theatre, the Alvin. *Annie* moved to accommodate it.

9. D—Hal Prince has twenty-one Tonys: eight for directing, eight for producing, two as producer of the Best Musical, and three special Tonys, including one for Lifetime Achievement.

10. Munch paintings—D—*A Doll's Life*
11. Polonius' advice—H—*Merrily We Roll Along*
12. Diego Rivera murals—C—*Evita*

13. WWI soldiers' masks—A—*The Phantom of the Opera*
14. Swanson in rubble photo—B—*Follies*
15. Chagall painting—G—*Fiddler on the Roof*
16. Industrial Revolution—E—*Sweeney Todd*
17. Magritte painting—F—*A Little Night Music*

꙳ ꙳

BROADWAY BONUS: *Roza* (1987) is the only show directed by Prince not to have a cast album recording.

꙳ ꙳

Food, Glorious Food Answers

1. The frankfurters can answer back in "NYC" (*Annie*).
2. Conrad Birdie is all set to eat steaks, preferably the sizzling variety ("Lot of Livin' to Do," *Bye Bye Birdie*).
3. Those baseball widows prepared goulash, but their hubbies like Willie Mays better ("Six Months Out of Every Year," *Damn Yankees*).
4. The two fathers in *The Fantasticks* grow radishes, turnips, carrots, Brussels sprouts, beans, and cabbages, as described in "Plant a Radish," and clearly they have plums and kumquats, too ("This Plum Is Too Ripe"), but those aren't veggies.
5. "Fan Tan Fanny" (*Flower Drum Song*) has leftover moo goo gai pan in her fridge.
6. Josephus Gage eats bran for breakfast, which gives him lots of roughage ("I'm A-Tingle, I'm A-Glow," *Gentlemen Prefer Blondes*).
7. During *The 25th Annual Putnam County Spelling Bee*, William reveals his allergy to peanuts.
8. Mabel serves BLTs down, pickles, bagels, knishes, corned beef, and salami at that deli "(Look What Happened to Mabel," *Mack and Mabel*).
9. The cook serves oysters on the half shell and the roast, though the company appears ready to carve each other ("No Good Can Come from Bad," *The Mystery of Edwin Drood*).
10. Hildy's lamb chops apparently can cause people to drool ("I Can Cook, Too," *On the Town*).
11. The students at St. Sebastian's eat country cheese with buttered bread for lunch ("The Bells of St. Sebastian's," *Nine*).
12. Babe complains about the cost of ham ("Small Talk," *The Pajama Game*).
13. The gang from *Rent* orders four seaweed salads ("La Vie Boheme").
14. Sandy sells the candy "Down on MacConnachy Square" (*Brigadoon*), and hopes he'll sell out, since eating his own product is making him ill.
15. "Bustopher Jones" (*Cats*) eats cabbage and rice pudding and mutton at the Tomb.
16. Sheriff File, though tempted by the Curry men's description of picnic goodies ("Poker Polka," *110 in the Shade*), declines their invitation.
17. Algernon eats muffins, despite women trouble ("The Muffin Song," *Earnest in Love*).
18. Muñoz suggests a gas-inducing meal of tacos and beans for Stone ("All You Have to Do Is Wait," *City of Angels*).

19. As orphan Oliver discovers, you can buy milk and ripe strawberries on the street ("Who Will Buy?").
20. "Garlic," as seen in *Dance of the Vampires*, will keep vampires and audiences away.
21. Pistache likes bouillabaisse ("Live and Let Live," *Can-Can*).
22. Ruth and Eileen eat spaghetti and meat balls all week (*Wonderful Town*).
23. Besides that "Life of the Party" Grandpere, you need caviar and chocolate soufflé at your party (*The Happy Time*).
24. Eliza Doolittle likes strawberry tarts, but is irked when Higgins feeds the last one to his bird (*My Fair Lady*).
25. You can get those navy beans at the Seaman's Home ("Chess and Checkers," *New Girl in Town*).
26. Morgan Le Fey's doors are made of gingerbread (*Camelot*).
27. There's a description of how to make a pot roast in "The Grass Is Always Greener" (*Woman of the Year*).
28. Sherlock Holmes needs a loaf of bread to chew on besides that cryptogram ("Cold Clear World," *Baker Street*).
29. At that "Real Nice Clambake" (*Carousel*), the codfish chowder comes in iron kettles.
30. Madame Armfeldt bemoans that you can't get proper food during "Liaisons" (*A Little Night Music*) any more, including figs.
31. The Wideners of Pennsylvania dined on kidney pie while aboard the *Titanic* ("What a Remarkable Age This Is!").
32. Mrs. Lovett adds coriander to her gravy ("God, That's Good," *Sweeney Todd*).
33. Little Edie offers Big Edith a choice of soups at the finale of *Grey Gardens:* bisque or tomato.
34. Mr. Zero's final meal is "Ham and Eggs" (*The Adding Machine*).
35. That can o' beans gets chucked out the winder ("Hand Me Down that Can o' Beans," *Paint Your Wagon*).
36. Jean Valjean is arrested for stealing a loaf of bread (*Les Misérables*).
37. You can have a BLT on rye with that "Coffee in a Cardboard Cup" (*70, Girls, 70*).
38. George brings Amalia "Vanilla Ice Cream" (*She Loves Me*).
39. The Uneeda Biscuit Company first packaged crackers, leading to the demise of the cracker barrel, as the traveling salesmen relate in "Rock Island" (*The Music Man*).
40. The customers on that "Sunday" scream for toast (*tick, tick… BOOM!*).
41. Zorba likes to chew mutton ("The First Time," *Zorba*).
42. Those sailors stationed in the *South Pacific* can pick mangoes and bananas ("There Is Nothing Like a Dame").
43. Irving Berlin wrote, "I Say It's Spinach and I Say the Hell with It" (*Face the Music*).
44. Maria likes (Weiner) schnitzel mit noodles ("My Favorite Things," *The Sound of Music*).
45. You can dig for asparagus next to your "Bungalow in Quogue" (*The Riviera Girl*).
46. A turkey dinner is sublime ("You're the Top," *Anything Goes*).
47. Charley's aunt claims to be from Brazil, land fabled for its nuts (*Where's Charley?*).
48. There is "Honey in the Honeycomb" and you will find stuffing in a squab (*Cabin in the Sky*).
49. Herr Schultz, who owns a produce store, brings a pineapple to Fraulein Schneider ("It Couldn't Please Me More," *Cabaret*).

50. The Piragua Guy ("Piragua," *In the Heights*) sells mango, passion fruit (*parcha*), pineapple (*piña*), strawberry (*fresa*), orange (*china*), lemon (*limon*), and in the opening number, just for that day, he has *mamey*, a tropical fruit sometimes described as being similar to pumpkin, chocolate, and mangoes. (*Mamey* is sometimes called *sapote*.) He does not sell raspberry (*frambuesa*).

Cherry Pies Ought to Be You Answers

1. E—Nellie Lovett makes meat pies with a bad reputation in *Sweeney Todd*.
2. M—"Bobo's" (*The Act*) is the home of pecan pie for fifty cents a slice.
3. C—Miss Minerva bakes a seven-layer cake to tempt Paris in *The Golden Apple*, but in vain.
4. Q—Louis, the baker in *Sunday in the Park with George*, makes bread and cakes, according to Dot, but we also see the American tourists enjoying his gooey pastries.
5. J—Mrs. Juniper's angel food cake fails to win the competition in *The Golden Apple*.
6. R—Lizzie Curry bakes her lemon cake with Sheriff File in mind in *110 in the Shade*, and her brother, Noah, praises her buttered biscuits and apple crumble in song.
7. H—Laurey Williams' gooseberry tarts in *Oklahoma!* must be pretty damn good, given what Curly pays at the box social.
8. O—the unnamed Baker in *Into the Woods* bakes bread, pies, and sticky buns, or at least that's what Red Riding Hood orders from him.
9. T—Nanette will bake a sugar cake that her Jimmy will take for all the boys to see ("Tea for Two," *No, No, Nanette*).
10. B—Lovey Mars and her mincemeat pie win Paris' heart and stomach in *The Golden Apple*.
11. A—Susan in [*title of show*] baked Rice Krispie Treats for the church bazaar in Ohio when she was eight, and one judge felt it was better than the red velvet cake.
12. I—Mindy's Restaurant, in *Guys and Dolls*, is the subject of much speculation over whether their cheesecake or their streusel is selling better.
13. G—Ado Annie Carnes makes sweet-potato pie in *Oklahoma!*, which apparently is hazardous to the digestion.
14. N—Aimable, the baker in *The Baker's Wife*, bakes the only bread in Concorde, and the village despairs when he stops baking because of his marital woes.
15. S—Jeff Moss, showing off how "Independent" he is in *Bells Are Ringing*, declares he doesn't need anyone's help to mix martinis, roast wienies, or bake blinis. Everyone says "blinis," but the plural is really "blini." And while Russian tradition says one bakes blini, most folks (including Russians) make them in a frying pan.
16. F—Robert's friends have made him a birthday cake in *Company*. Or possibly they bought it at that pastry shop, Mahler's, the one Elaine Stritch mentions in *Elaine Stritch at Liberty*.
17. L—the Pastry Chefs, with Mr. Feldzieg's help, display how to create the sugary yum-yum that is a Toledo Surprise in *The Drowsy Chaperone*.
18. D—Polly Browne, while daydreaming of a cozy future, promises someday to make a plum duff for her Tony (*The Boy Friend*).
19. K—Toad makes the tastiest cookies in *A Year with Frog and Toad*.

20. P—Mary Turner's corn muffins are worthy of intense political discussion in *Of Thee I Sing*.

꙳ ꙳

BROADWAY BONUS: In "I'm Past My Prime," Marryin' Sam mentions huckleberry and peach pies. Sarah in *Company*, bemoaning her diet, praises Sara Lee to the skies. Mr. Snow of *Carousel* is partial to Boston cream pie.

꙳ ꙳

Dark, Secluded Places Answers

1. M—The Village Vortex—*Wonderful Town*
2. KK—The Upstairs Room at the Downtown Club—*Merrily We Roll Along*
3. F—Hernando's Hideaway—*The Pajama Game*
4. H—Green Dragon Pub—*Redhead*
5. U—Clancy's Lounge/Grapes of Roth—*Promises, Promises*
6. II—Cat Scratch Club—*Rent*
7. Y—Diamond Eddies Club/Congacabana Club/Slam-Bang Club—*On the Town*
8. B—Three Cripples Tavern—*Oliver!*
9. AA—Johnny-the-Priest's Saloon—*New Girl in Town*
10. D—Club Havana/Club Oasis—*My One and Only*
11. JJ—Around the Clock—*Avenue Q*
12. Q—the Green Frog—*Kean*
13. EE—Bal du Paradis—*Can-Can*
14. J—The Red Rat—*Jekyll and Hyde*
15. GG—Club Zanzibar—*The Sweet Smell of Success*
16. W—Club Purgatory/Club Cocteau—*Gentlemen Prefer Blondes*
17. A—The Hot Box/Cafe El Cubano—*Guys and Dolls*
18. CC—Club Petite—*Du Barry Was a Lady*
19. G—The Pyramid—*Bells Are Ringing*
20. BB—Lank's Saloon—*Crazy for You*
21. K—Paradise Club—*Oh, Kay!*
22. S—Jeunnesse Dorée Club, New Orleans—*Naughty Marietta*
23. V—Hotel Las Vegas—*The Act*
24. C—Hope and Anchor Bar—*Half a Sixpence*
25. FF—Bar-des-Inquiets—*Irma la Douce*
26. N—Paprika's Cafe—*The Gay Life*
27. I—The Casacabana—*Do Re Mi*
28. T—Saddleback Saloon—*The Unsinkable Molly Brown*
29. Z—Last Chance Saloon—*Destry Rides Again*
30. E—The Celestial Bar—*Flower Drum Song*
31. L—Foley's Bar—*Juno*
32. DD—Kit Kat Klub—*Cabaret*
33. O—The Bourbon Room—*Rock of Ages*
34. P—Fan-Dango Ballroom—*Sweet Charity*

35. HH—Chez Joey—*Pal Joey*
36. X—Joe Allen's—*Applause*
37. R—The Banana Club—*Seesaw*

Make It Another Old-Fashioned, Please Answers

1. Joanne in *Company* is partial to vodka stingers.
2. The Engineer proposes pouring the Schlitz down the drain. Good idea, says I. ("American Dream," *Miss Saigon*)
3. Cunegonde doesn't object to champagne ("Glitter and Be Gay," *Candide*).
4. Herod asks Jesus to turn water into wine ("King Herod's Song," *Jesus Christ Superstar*).
5. The beer got flat on Cissy's date ("He Had Refinement," *A Tree Grows in Brooklyn*).
6. People doing the mambo at Bamboo Jack's drink Golden Cadillacs ("See What I Wanna See," *See What I Wanna See*).
7. Bachelor dandies drink brandies ("Sixteen Going on Seventeen," *The Sound of Music*).
8. Fanny and Nick think light beer goes with macaroons ("I Want to Be Seen with You Tonight," *Funny Girl*).
9. You need a half a chicken and a bottle of bourbon to conquer the world ("Look at Me Now," *The Wild Party*).
10. Champagne helps things get lovely at Jason's bar mitzvah (*Falsettos*).
11. For the out-of-work steelworkers in *The Full Monty*, the future includes beer ("Scrap").
12. Edna and Wilbur reminisce about when beer cost a quarter ("Timeless to Me," *Hairspray*).
13. *The Drowsy Chaperone*'s title character is fond of highballs ("As We Stumble Along").
14. You drink schnapps while dancing "Der Guten Tag Hop-Clop" (*The Producers*).
15. Aristide ponders cyanide and champagne ("I Am in Love," *Can-Can*).
16. "The Hostess with the Mostess on the Ball," Mrs. Sally Adams, amuses the vodka drinkers (*Call Me Madam*).
17. Dionysus (*The Frogs*) is the god of drama and wine. The latter helps one get through the former.
18. Peron, in retirement, wants to drink cocktails, but Eva has other plans ("A New Argentina," *Evita*).
19. A sip of gin makes Queenie's Joe happy ("Can't Help Lovin' Dat Man," *Show Boat*).
20. You get beer and Benzedrine on that "Great Come and Get It Day" (*Finian's Rainbow*).
21. You can learn the students' "Drinking Song" at the Inn of the Three Golden Apples, but I'll give credit just for listing the University of Heidelberg (*The Student Prince*).
22. The title character in *Panama Hattie* drinks old-fashioneds ("Make It Another Old-Fashioned, Please").
23. Emma serves a bottle of Chablis with the fried chicken ("Second Letter Home," *Song and Dance*).
24. Representative Stephen Hopkins of Rhode Island gets his access to the Continental Congress' rum revoked, but it's restored (*1776*).

25. The call for "Vodka, Vodka" rings out at the Café Czarina (*Anya*).
26. Kate Monster drinks too many Long Island Iced Teas at the Around the Clock (*Avenue Q*).
27. Alfred P. Doolittle notes that God made liquor to tempt man ("With a Little Bit of Luck," *My Fair Lady*).
28. *Prettybelle* is beautiful when she's drunk, but she still closed in Boston.
29. Lily Garland's estate has champagne flowing like rivers ("I've Got It All," *On the Twentieth Century*).
30. Little songbirds drink their wine of choice while dining ("Sing for Your Supper," *The Boys from Syracuse*).
31. Grandpa spent the housekeeping cash on whiskey and beer ("Grandma's Song," *Billy Elliot*).
32. Malaga is served at a big "Sposalizio" (*The Most Happy Fella*).
33. Among Hedwig's modern luxuries is whiskey ("Sugar Daddy," *Hedwig and the Angry Inch*).
34. Igor says he and Frederick are like Coke and Baccardi ("Together Again," *Young Frankenstein*).
35. Lord Blandings and Shorty McGee are bootleggers in Long Island during Prohibition and the ship is full of gin ("When Our Ship Comes Sailing In," *Oh, Kay!*).
36. Champagne Charlie (from a popular nineteenth-century British song) is drinking gin now, according to Lorenz Hart ("Give It Back to the Indians," *Too Many Girls*).
37. Mrs. Lovett gives Tobias gin (*Sweeney Todd*).
38. Sammy is full of Bud(weiser) at "Bobo's" (*The Act*).
39. Lord Brockhurst and Dulcie agree that old wine tastes nicer than new wine ("It's Never Too Late to Fall in Love," *The Boy Friend*).
40. Usnavi and Vanessa try to share a bottle of cold champagne ("Champagne," *In the Heights*).

1776 Mini-Quiz Answers

1. You make salt petre by treating sodium nitrate with potassium chloride. Of course.
2. Harry Lee's nickname is "Lighthorse," but Sherman Edwards made two historical goofs in this lyric. Harry Lee was still a captain at the time of the show's action (spring, 1776), nor had he acquired his nickname. He earned that as a major, leading "Lee's Legion," a mixed division of cavalry and infantry, against the British in 1778–1779. He became a general in 1798, and his son was Robert E. Lee. But, hey, it's a great song, and we'll forgive Richard Henry for bragging about his relatives.
3. Howard da Silva suffered a heart attack and his understudy, Rex Everhart, sang Franklin's part for the cast recording. Fortunately, we can see (and hear) da Silva in the movie.
4. The turkey is fresh at the Bunch o' Grapes.
5. According to producer Stuart Ostrow, a woman on Nixon's staff wanted "Cool, Cool, Considerate Men" (which made the right look less attractive) and "Momma, Look Sharp" (which made war look unattractive) cut, but the cast said they would perform the show in its entirety or not at all. (Ostrow also says "Molasses to Rum"

was on this woman's list, too.) Nixon's speechwriter, William Safire, who previously worked for the League of New York Theatres, defended the show's integrity, although many versions of this anecdote cast him as the villain.

This marked the first time a complete Broadway show had been staged at the White House. Nixon greatly enjoyed the production, and told Vestoff (Abigail Adams) that Abigail used to do the wash in the East Room, where the actors had performed. "You can hang your laundry here any day," he joked.

6. Two useless men make up a law firm.
7. Franklin's number was in the New Brunswick scene, cut out of town. It was called "Increase and Multiply," and in it, he ponders population growth in the new nation. And, naturally, how one gets population growth, a subject dear to old Ben.
8. There are no pins anywhere from Framingham to Boston.
9. Ostrow suggested calling the show *Fireworks!*, a suggestion that was met with a deadly silence from Edwards and Stone
10. Whoring and drinking—and desertion, too—go on in New Brunswick.

⚜ ⚜

Special *1776* BROADWAY BONUS: Secretary Thompson lists seven congressional committees in scene five: the Yeast Committee, the Spies Committee, the Drum and Fife Committee, the Congressional Correspondence Committee, the Counterfeit Money Committee, the Military Defeat Committee, and the Secrets Committee.

⚜ ⚜

A Chorus Line Mini-Quiz Answers

1. Bennett wanted red for the finale's costumes, as had been used in "The Story of Lucy and Jessie" in *Follies*.
2. On September 29, 1983, *A Chorus Line* passed *Grease* as the longest-running show in history. There was a gala celebration with 350 players, including most of the original cast, directed by Bennett.
3. Paul's dad tells the director to take good care of his son.
4. Neil Simon did uncredited work on the libretto before it moved to Broadway.
5. Before there was Zach, there was a Godlike "Voice."
6. Mike runs seven blocks to his sister's dance class.
7. They don't have bobsleds in San Juan.
8. Bennett's birth name was Michael DiFiglia.
9. Aldredge deliberately made Sheila's leotard too small, the better to show the inner conflict of the character.
10. *A Chorus Line* is dedicated "to anyone who has ever danced in a chorus or marched in step . . . anywhere."

Nine Mini-Quiz Answers

1. Fellini's agent approached Hal Prince about a possible *8 1/2* musical in the sixties.
2. One thousand women auditioned for the twenty-two roles.

3. Despite his apparent interest in a sixties musical of his film, by the eighties, Fellini did not care to have a direct connection between his work and the Yeston-Kopit musical, so he said it could not have the same title.
4. The feather boa was thirty-five feet long.
5. Guido Contini's signature motif is a train.
6. "A Call from the Vatican" was too racy for network TV, so instead they aired "Be Italian," which featured a prostitute singing to four little boys. Go figure.
7. The character Guido Contini, composer Maury Yeston, and filmmaker Frederico Fellini have all tried their hands at works about fabled lover Casanova.
8. "Beatrice's" basket holds prosciutto, olives, and white wine.
9. Luisa's maiden name was del Forno.
10. Guido considers making a Western, a biblical epic, and a documentary.

Something to Do with Spring Answers

1. Dickon in *The Secret Garden* heralds spring's arrival with "Winter's on the Wing."
2. B—As Cole Porter tells us in "Let's Do It," the fabled ode to the mating season, bluebells down in the dell ring ring.
3. D—*Pacific Overtures* opens in July 1853, as the Reciter tells us in "The Advantages of Floating in the Middle of the Sea." *Titanic* opens in April 1912. *Parade* opens in April 1913. *Miss Saigon* opens in April 1975. And if Jerry Bock and William Finn ever finished their musical about Form 1040, I'm sure it would open on April 15. Ah, the cruelest month!
4. C—*Show Boat* has a Magnolia, but no Lily, Lili, or Lilly.
5. Gordon Schwinn, in *A New Brain*, has to write a spring song for Mr. Bungee, but isn't enthusiastic about writing for frogs.
6. E—"The Honeymoon Inn" by Jerome Kern and P. G. Wodehouse was a hit for *Have a Heart* in 1917 and was interpolated in the 1975 revival of *Very Good Eddie*. It's allegedly covered in honeysuckle, though the woman character singing it admits she's never seen it.
7. The mother in Lerner and Lane's flop *Carmelina* wonders which of three someones left her pregnant in April many years before.
8. B—the general sings of "Five Minutes of Spring" in *The Happiest Girl in the World*.
9. C—in Ivor Novello's "We'll Gather Lilacs," the lovers sing of walking down an English lane afterward (sometimes this lyric reads "endless," in case you're not in England). The song debuted in the London musical *Perchance to Dream* (1945), and given its theme of lovers reuniting in the spring, became a huge wartime hit.
10. C—Lorenz Hart combined all those blooms in "The Flower Garden of My Heart" in *Pal Joey* (1940).

BROADWAY BONUS: D—somehow, there was no "Rose of Peking" in those early rose tunes, though there was a short-lived 1925 musical called *China Rose*.

Summertime Answers

1. C—John Latouche updated the thirteenth-century "Cuckoo Song" ("Sumer is icumen in, Lhude sing cuccu!") into "Summer Is a-Comin' In," with music by Vernon Duke, for the 1942 flop *The Lady Comes Across*. But Nat King Cole made the song a hit, even if the show tanked.
2. *Wish You Were Here*, Harold Rome's 1952 hit, was the first musical with a swimming pool onstage.
3. A—Mother, Father and Edgar of *Ragtime* go to Atlantic City to escape the heat.
4. B—the soldier's helmet is bothering him.
5. D—Ed Sullivan revised and resuscitated *Crazy with the Heat*.
6. E—the Champions danced their way through "Summer in Fairview Falls."
7. C—Thomas Jefferson kept the weather records for Congress.
8. A—Berlin's "Heat Wave" (*As Thousands Cheer*) came up from Martinique.
9. D—"All My Trials" gave Heyward lyrical cues for "Summertime."
10. J or K—*Seventeen*, a flop from 1951, is set in the summer of 1907 in Indianapolis.
11. F—*110 in the Shade* is set in July 1936 in Three Point, Texas.
12. I—*Take Me Along* takes place around July 4, 1910, in Centerville, Connecticut, and was originally titled *Connecticut Summer*.
13. H—*The Music Man* is set in River City, Iowa, in the summer of 1912.
14. E—*Come Summer* is set in the Connecticut River Valley, from late spring to early fall in 1840, and lasted but seven performances in 1969.
15. C—*St. Louis Woman* is set in August 1898 in St. Louis. The 1946 show may not have lasted long, but those Arlen-Mercer songs will endure—"Come Rain or Come Shine."
16. B—*Steel Pier* is set in Atlantic City during August 1933.
17. A—*Juno* is set in the turbulent summer of 1921 in Dublin.
18. D—*Where's Charley?* is set in Oxford during the summer of 1892.
19. G—*The Light in the Piazza* is set in Italy during the summer of 1953.
20. J or K—*By the Beautiful Sea* is set at Coney Island in the summer of 1907.

Shall We All Meet in the Autumn? Answers

1. B—Hal Prince had the idea for the falling leaves. According to Williams, the line barely got chuckles on nights when Prince wasn't in the house.
2. C—*Greenwillow* had the autumn courtship dance.
3. In *Camelot*, Lance can't leave because Guenevere sparkles in that nippy fall air. And we all know how Frenchmen love sparkles.
4. E—*Sugar* has a "November Song." However, *Carousel* has June, which is busting out all over; *Camelot* celebrates "The Lusty Month of May;" *The Canterbury Tales* has an "April Song;" and *Mack and Mabel* bounces around the calendar in "Time Heals Everything."
5. C—the nurses and the boys stationed on that island in WWII put on "The Thanksgiving Follies" in *South Pacific*. But I'd bet Lt. Cioffi would have loved to audition.

6. A—Frog and Toad rake leaves in autumn (*A Year with Frog and Toad*).
7. E—*Ragtime*'s "What a Game!" is about baseball, not football.
8. As described in *Pacific Overtures*' "Poems," the leaves' colors change from green to pink to gold.
9. True! It's an urban legend that the band played "Nearer My God to Thee."
10. Both *A Tree Grows in Brooklyn* and *Meet Me in St. Louis* have Halloween ballets.

Merry Christmas, Maggie Thatcher Answers

1. B—*Caroline, or Change* has a Chanukah party.
2. The "Turkey Lurkey Time" dance, what else? (*Promises, Promises*)
3. E—Paul Stanley, best known for his years with the rock band KISS, did not play Scrooge, but he has played the Phantom of the Opera.
4. B—the young Hollywood hopefuls make their New Year's resolutions.
5. E—Dublin, around the turn of the twentieth century (*James Joyce's The Dead*).
6. C—they (apparently) haven't trimmed their trees nine days before Christmas (*She Loves Me*).
7. The German go to Italian spas to take the waters with the daughters of Italian counts, according to "The Germans at the Spa" in *Nine*.
8. B—the baseball widows in *Damn Yankees* are longing for cold weather days.
9. A—*The Music Man* has no Santa and is set in the summer.
10. *Rent* runs from December 24 to December 24.

The Show Must Go On Answers

1. K—*Robbin' Hood of the Old West* is the *Oklahoma!* spoof from *Curtains*.
2. E—director Julian Marsh tries to stage *Pretty Lady* in *42nd Street*.
3. D—Leo and Max think *Springtime for Hitler* is the perfect flop musical in *The Producers*.
4. I—Cap'n Andy's players perform *The Parson's Bride* in *Show Boat*.
5. C—*Sneakers* is the musical in the short-lived (one performance!) *A Broadway Musical*.
6. H—though the name is not mentioned often, real Sondheim fans know that Frank and Charley are working on *Musical Husbands* in *Merrily We Roll Along*. But how many know that their political show, the one Josephson didn't want to produce, was called *Take a Left*?
7. F—*The Passionate Pilgrim* is an operetta (and a major source of contention) in *The Cat and the Fiddle*.
8. G—*Of the People* is the show within *Ain't Broadway Grand*.
9. J—*The Red Devil* is a thinly disguised version of *The Black Crook* in *The Girl in Pink Tights*.
10. A—those *Babes in Arms* are trying to put together *Lee Calhoun's Follies*.
11. B—*The Coconut Girl* is Florence Henderson's show from *The Girl Who Came to Supper*.

BROADWAY BONUS: *Rhinestones of 1932* was the show in Irving Berlin's *Face the Music*. Isn't that just a perfect title for a thirties musical?

What If? Answers

1. E—Gertrude Lawrence wanted Cole Porter to adapt *Anna and the King of Siam* for her, but Porter turned it down. When Rodgers and Hammerstein took it on, Rodgers asked Lawrence's lifelong friend and acting partner Noel Coward to play the King, but he refused, though tempted by the offer.

2. G—Jerome Kern, Herbert, and Dorothy Fields began work on the musical version of Annie Oakley's life (*Annie Get Your Gun*), but Kern suddenly died. Rodgers and Hammerstein, the producers, talked Irving Berlin into doing the score. Dorothy Fields withdrew as lyricist, since Berlin always wrote his own lyrics.

3. O or P or T—Frank Loesser was going to do a musical version of the film *Ninotchka*, with book by George Kaufman and direction by Jerome Robbins, but he was too busy with *The Most Happy Fella*, and Robbins was working on *Peter Pan*. Loesser was going to adapt the French film *La Femme du Bolanger* for Cy Feuer and Ernest Martin in 1952, with book by Abe Burrows and starring Burt Lahr, but it fell though. Feuer and Martin offered John Steinbeck's *Cannery Row* to Loesser, and Steinbeck, a great friend of Loesser's, was to write the libretto. At the same time, Steinbeck was writing a new novel, *Sweet Thursday*, using the same characters. The delays involved led to the project being passed to Rodgers and Hammerstein, who agreed to give Feuer and Martin a cut of the profits. (There weren't any.) The resulting musical, *Pipe Dream*, had a libretto by Oscar Hammerstein that was based on *Sweet Thursday* as Steinbeck wrote it, chapter by chapter, week by week. This, along with Rodgers' health, may have contributed to it being a flop.

4. F—Kurt Weill and Maxwell Anderson began their adaptation of *Huckleberry Finn*, but Weill died in 1950, too damn soon.

5. I—Maury Yeston was going to write the score for an adaptation of the French play and film *La Cage aux Folles*. Producer Allan Carr had named Mike Nichols as director, Tommy Tune as choreographer, and Jay Presson Allen as librettist, with the show relocated to New Orleans and renamed *The Queen of Basin Street*. Then Fritz Holt and Barry Brown came on as executive producers and fired everyone Carr had hired, eventually signing the team of Laurents, Herman, and Fierstein. Lawsuits ensued, and Yeston won some royalties.

6. C—Leonard Bernstein and Lillian Hellman were fascinated by the life of Eva Peron, and considered making her the subject of an opera in the early fifties.

7. D—George Gershwin wanted to do a musical of *Liliom*, but playwright Ferenc Molnár refused him, saying he wanted the work to remain his own. (He apparently also turned down Puccini.) Kurt Weill attempted to get the rights in early 1937, but failed. Molnár changed his mind after seeing *Oklahoma!* and decided a musical of his work might not be a bad thing.

8. H—Irving Berlin was a friend of Wilson Mizner and a substantial investor in Addison Mizner's Boca Raton resort. He worked for many years on *Sentimental Guy*, a musical about the brothers' lives, completing several songs and the libretto for the first act.

9. J—the team of Michel Legrand and Richard Wilbur had the rights to *The Madwoman of Chaillot*, and Maurice Valency was to write the book, but they had no producer. Stephen Sondheim made an attempt in 1955.

10. K—after David Merrick's relentless persistence got him the rights to *Marius*, *Fanny*, and *Cesar*, he asked Rodgers and Hammerstein if they would do the score. They were interested, but wanted to produce as well, since Merrick was then a novice. Merrick intended to produce on his own, and asked Lerner and Loewe, who also refused him. Finally, Merrick ended up with one of Harold Rome's loveliest scores.

11. N—Stephen Sondheim was offered the musical based on the trial and lynching of Leo Frank by director Hal Prince and librettist Alfred Uhry, but turned it down.

12. L or R—David Merrick offered *The Apartment* to Jerry Herman, who refused it. Producer David Geffen, the man who initially fought for the musical version of *The Producers*, wanted Herman for that project. But Herman knew the right man for *The Producers*, and invited Mel Brooks to his home, where he played a medley of Brooks' own songs from over the years and convinced him he was the only one who could do justice to the piece.

13. A—Lerner and Loewe were offered *Greenwillow*, possibly because of their work on another odd little village musical, but refused it.

14. Q—Irving Berlin and Cole Porter both turned down the memoirs of Gypsy Rose Lee. Cy Coleman and Carolyn Leigh auditioned with a few songs, but were rejected. True Broadway fans will know that David Merrick intended to go with Stephen Sondheim as composer and lyricist, but Ethel Merman, just coming off a bad time with novice songwriters in *Happy Hunting*, demanded someone more experienced. Veteran Jule Styne came on as composer.

15. S—Sandy Wilson was working on *Goodbye to Berlin*, a musical version of Isherwood's *I Am a Camera/Berlin Stories* at the same time Hal Prince was getting interested in the material. Wilson was working with producer David Black, who held the rights, but when they lapsed, Prince got them. Prince had Joe Masteroff working on the libretto, and he and Masteroff listened to Wilson's score. They felt it wasn't dark enough for the Berlin they had in mind and hired Kander and Ebb.

16. L or R—see answer #12 for details of these Jerry Herman musicals that never happened.

17. O or P or T—see answer #3 for details of these Frank Loesser musicals that never happened.

18. U—*Li'l Abner* was a cultural phenomenon in the forties and fifties, so it's not surprising it generated talk as a musical property. In 1947, Rodgers and Hammerstein turned it down due to other projects. Alan Jay Lerner and Burton Lane worked on it in the early fifties, with Herman Levin as producer. (Lerner also worked on it for a while with Arthur Schwartz, as a possible film.) Lerner and Lane's material apparently was passed to Melvin Frank and Norman Panama, who jettisoned it all, and came up with their own Dogpatch tale.

19. B—there are a lot of possible alternate musical *My Sister Eileens*! Producer Leland Hayward wanted either Cole Porter or Irving Berlin to write it. Didn't happen. Producer Max Gordon had a creative team assembled of librettist George Kaufman, lyricists Herbert and Dorothy Fields, and composer Burton Lane. Also didn't happen. Finally, producer Robert Fryer looked as if he'd mount a production with a score by Leroy Anderson and Arnold Hewitt. Accounts vary as to the reasons, but the score and the songwriters were gone—with five weeks to opening. Five critical weeks, because if they delayed longer, they lost their star, Rosalind Russell. Bernstein, Comden, and Green came in, creating *Wonderful Town* in about a month.

20. M—those talented nobodies in New York, Jeff Bowen and Hunter Bell, wrote an unproduced musical based on the film *9 to 5* before they came up with *[title of show]*. And wouldn't you like to compare that with Dolly Parton's, just for kicks?

21. O or P or T—see answer #3 for details of these Frank Loesser musicals that never happened.

Who Am I? Answers

1. Jackie Robinson—*The First*
2. Mike Todd—*Ain't Broadway Grand*
3. Franz Schubert—*Blossom Time*
4. Edith and "Little Edie" Bouvier Beale—*Grey Gardens*
5. Peter Allen—*The Boy from Oz*
6. Benvenuto Cellini—*The Firebrand of Florence*
7. Laurette Taylor—*Jennie*
8. Weill and Lenya—*LoveMusik*
9. Boy George—*Taboo*
10. Ed Kleban—*A Class Act*
11. Stew—*Passing Strange*
12. Edvard Grieg—*Song of Norway*
13. Addison and Wilson Mizner—*Road Show*
14. Edward Koch—*Mayor*
15. Charles, Dauphin of France—*Goodtime Charley*
16. Jacques Offenbach—*The Love Song*
17. Frederick Chopin—*White Lilacs*
18. Fanny Brice—*Funny Girl*
19. Henry VIII—*Rex*
20. Victoria Woodhull—*Onward, Victoria*
21. Queen Victoria—*I and Albert*
22. the Marx Brothers and their mom—*Minnie's Boys*
23. Gabrielle Chanel—*Coco*
24. Johann Strauss I and II—*The Great Waltz*
25. Ellie Greenwich—*Leader of the Pack*

It's Still Rock and Roll to Me Answers

1. D—Ellie Greenwich did not write for the Plaids, a fictional band in Stuart Ross' 1990 off-Broadway jukebox musical, *Forever Plaid*. The Plaids were a close-harmony group who are finally on their way to record an album in 1964, when they are killed in an accident with a bus of schoolgirls going to see the Beatles on *The Ed Sullivan Show*. In *Forever Plaid*, they return from heaven to sing their songs once more.

2. D—Paul McCartney always regarded Buddy Holly as one of his greatest influences. The Beatles (originally Beetles) were named in tribute to Holly's band, the Crickets. McCartney bought Holly's song catalog in 1976, but was so annoyed by errors in the 1978 Gary Busey film, *The Buddy Holly Story*, that he created a documentary, *The Real Buddy Holly Story*, in 1985. He helped producer Paul Elliott get the musical *Buddy* off the ground, in part because he knew the librettists had their facts straight.

3. E—*Return to the Forbidden Planet* is partly based on *The Tempest*, as is the original film, *Forbidden Planet*. However, *All Shook Up* is a jukebox musical inspired by *Twelfth Night*.

4. A—Judy Kaye did not play Donna; she played Donna's pal Rosie.

5. False—Billy Joel and Stuart Malina won for Best Orchestrations.

6. D—Hugh Jackman pulled Sarah Jessica Parker from the audience to dance with him in "The Boy Next Door." Ms. Parker, fearing a wardrobe malfunction, did not join in with as much verve as one might have hoped, but Hugh was shaking enough for any dozen people. Anne Hathaway came up from the audience to dance with Jackman at the 2009 Oscars.

7. C—"Can't Take My Eyes Off of You" was used to great effect in 1978's *The Deer Hunter*, and helped inspire Gaudio to create *Jersey Boys*. The other songs listed also appeared in films: "December 1963" in *Forrest Gump*; "Big Girls Don't Cry" in *The Hard Way*; "Stay" in *Dirty Dancing*; and "Walk Like a Man" in a television movie, *Dear America: Letters from Vietnam*.

8. D—Harry Chapin helped turn his own songs into an early jukebox musical, 1975's *The Night That Made America Famous*, 47 performances. The other shows date from 2005: *Lennon* (John Lennon, 49 performances), *Good Vibrations* (the Beach Boys, 94 performances), *All Shook Up* (Elvis Presley, 213 performances), and *Almost Heaven* (John Denver, in an off-Broadway show that lasted two months). There was also a 2005 jukebox musical about the 1980s Spanish pop band Mecano, *Hoy no me puedo levantar*, that ran for four years in Spain and has played in Mexico.

9. B—"Magic Bus" by the Who seems like a natural for *Priscilla, Queen of the Desert*, but it's not among the show's songs.

10. E—although the show's Web site encourages people to come to *Rock of Ages* dressed in eighties-style clothes, including leg warmers, they do not actually give them away. They do hand out LED lighters to mimic the effect of lighters at concerts, but without the fire danger.

Masquerade Answers

1. Sweeney Todd is Benjamin Barker.
2. The Jackal is the nom de crime of Christine Colgate (*Dirty Rotten Scoundrels*).
3. Bill Starbuck's real name is Bill Smith (*110 in the Shade*).
4. The Scarlet Pimpernel is Sir Percy Blakeney in disguise.
5. Joe Hardy is the name old Joe Boyd takes when Mr. Applegate turns him into a young, talented baseball player (*Damn Yankees*).
6. The Red Shadow is the heroic identity of Pierre Birabeau (*The Desert Song*).
7. Flip, the Prince, Charming is really George L. Brown, as Passionella discovers (*The Apple Tree*).
8. "The Cat" is the nickname given to that sly jewel thief, Alice van Guilder (*Drat! The Cat!*).
9. Lily Garland, world-famous actress, was once known as Mildred Plotka (*On the Twentieth Century*).
10. "Miss Turnstiles" (for the month of June) on the New York subways is one Ivy Smith, and poor Gaby loses his heart over her picture (*On the Town*).
11. "Rosabella" is the name Tony Esposito gives to the waitress he falls for and marries, not knowing her real name is Amy (*The Most Happy Fella*).
12. Mimi, a beautiful French girl, is the persona adopted by Janet Vandergraff when she sees Percy, her groom-to-be, approaching her, wearing a blindfold and roller skates (*The Drowsy Chaperone*).
13. "Ze Lady from Lourdes" sent to investigate the miracle in Cora Hoover Hooper's town is actually Nurse Fay Apple (*Anyone Can Whistle*).
14. M. Madeleine, factory owner, mayor, and respectable citizen, is actually ex-convict and parole breaker Jean Valjean (*Les Misérables*).
15. Melisande is the name Ella Peterson uses since she doesn't want Jeff to know she's the girl at his answering service (*Bells Are Ringing*).
16. M. Oscar is the name used by Nestor-le-Fripé when visiting *Irma la Douce*.
17. "Body Beautiful Beale" was the soubriquet for Little Edie Bouvier Beale (*Grey Gardens*).
18. Phocion, Aspasie, and Cécile are all personae created by the clever Princess Léonide of Sparta as she schemes to win the heart of Agis (*Triumph of Love*).

BROADWAY BONUS ANSWERS: Starbuck's other alias is Tornado Johnson, and Sky Masterson's real first name is Obediah.

I'm Looking for Something Answers

1. "Big-Ass Rock," *The Full Monty*
2. "The Big Black Giant," *Me and Juliet*
3. "Big Brother," *The Boys From Syracuse*
4. "Big Bow-Wow," *Snoopy*

5. "Big D," *The Most Happy Fella*
6. "Big Spender," *Sweet Charity*
7. "The Big Beat," *Over Here*
8. "The Big Time," *The Will Rogers Follies*; or "Big Time," *Mr. Wonderful*; or "Big Time," *Mack and Mabel*. You get extra credit for your encyclopedic mind if you came up with all of them.
9. "Big Trouble," *How Now, Dow Jones*
10. "Miss Turnstiles," *On the Town*
11. "Miss Marmelstein," *I Can Get It for You Wholesale*
12. "Meet Miss Blendo," *Top Banana*
13. "Miss Baltimore Crabs," *Hairspray*
14. "Miss Langley's School for Girls," *What's Up?*
15. "Mister Cellophane," *Chicago*
16. "Mr. Andrews' Vision," *Titanic*
17. "Mister Greed," *The Life*
18. "Mr. Bojangles," *Dancin'* or *Fosse* or the Sammy Davis, Jr., revue, *Sammy*
19. "Mr. Fezziwig's Annual Christmas Ball," *A Christmas Carol*
20. "Mr. Monotony" was first performed in *Jerome Robbins' Broadway*. But it was originally written for Berlin's film *Easter Parade* (as "Mrs. Monotony") and was cut from both *Miss Liberty* and *Call Me Madam*. You get an official Irving Berlin trivia nut award if you knew that.
21. "Mr. Goldstone," *Gypsy*
22. "Mr. Witherspoon's Friday Night," *Lucky Stiff*
23. "Mister Snow," *Carousel*
24. "Old Devil Moon," *Finian's Rainbow*
25. "An Old-Fashioned Wedding," *Annie Get Your Gun*
26. "Old Friends," *Merrily We Roll Along*
27. "Old Deuteronomy," *Cats*
28. "Old Red Hills of Home," *Parade*
29. "The Old Military Canal," *Half a Sixpence*
30. "A New Deal for Christmas," *Annie*
31. "The New Ashmolean Marching Society and Students' Conservatory Band," *Where's Charley?*
32. "New Music," *Ragtime*
33. "New Ways to Dream," *Sunset Boulevard*
34. "New Pair of Shoes," *What Makes Sammy Run?*
35. "New-Fangled Preacher Man," *Purlie*
36. "A New Town Is a Blue Town," *The Pajama Game*
37. "Little Red Hat," *110 in the Shade*
38. "Little Biscuit," *Jamaica*
39. "Little Egypt," *Smokey Joe's Cafe*
40. "Little Girl from Little Rock," *Gentlemen Prefer Blondes*
41. "A Little More Mascara," *La Cage aux Folles*
42. "Little Tin Box," *Fiorello!*
43. "The Little One's ABC," *Sail Away*
44. "Little Boy Blues," *Look, Ma, I'm Dancin'*

45. "A Little Rumba Numba," *Let's Face It*
46. "Little Do They Know," *The Act*
47. "The Terror of the Thames" was the, what do you call it, sobriquet of Growltiger, the pirate cat ably portrayed by Gus, the theatre cat, in *Cats*.
48. "The Honeybunny Girl" was played by Elsie in *The Vamp*.
49. "The Simpson Sisters' Waxworks" was the site of much of the action in *Redhead*.
50. "The Opera Ghost," or "O.G.," was the way *The Phantom of the Opera* signed his notes. Very few people knew his name was Erik.
51. "The 14th Earl of Hareford" was the title Bill Snibson discovered he had inherited in *Me and My Girl*.
52. "The Lawd's General" was the good guy fighting for the soul of Joe in *Cabin in the Sky*.
53. "The Red Shadow" was the alter ego of Pierre Birabeau in *The Desert Song*.
54. "The Wazir" was the baddie in *Kismet*.
55. "The Jackal" was the name of the con artist moving in on Lawrence's territory in the French Riviera in *Dirty Rotten Scoundrels*.
56. "The Incomparable Rosalie" was the long-suffering partner of Marco the Magnificent in *Carnival*.
57. "The Inevitable Roscoe" was how Dmitri Weismann introduced the big-voiced fellow who always brought on the girls in *Follies*.
58. *The Tatler* was the paper in *Tenderloin*.
59. *The Manhatter* was the thinly disguised *New Yorker* that Ruth Sherwood hoped to write for in *Wonderful Town*.
60. *Madame* magazine was writer Angie's employer in *Subways Are for Sleeping*.
61. Lots of people (Clark, Lois, Max, etc.) in *It's a Bird...It's a Plane...It's Superman* worked at *The Daily Planet*.
62. *Everywhere* magazine was featured in *Hazel Flagg*.
63. *The Lily* was the feminist-abolitionist newspaper in *Bloomer Girl*.
64. Liza Elliott, the *Lady in the Dark*, was editor at *Allure*.
65. J. J. Hunsecker's gossip column in the *New York Globe* is crucial to the action in *Sweet Smell of Success*. There had been earlier, real-life versions of the *Globe*: it was a black newspaper in the 1880s, then resurfaced as a daily in the teens (in which "Ripley's Believe It or Not" first appeared); then was bought by the *Sun* in 1923. By the fifties, the era of *Sweet Smell*, there no longer was a real *Globe*.

❧ ❧

BROADWAY BONUS: The late-nineteenth-century rivalry between Joseph Pulitzer's *World* and James Gordon Bennett's *Herald* provided a backdrop for *Miss Liberty* and *Nellie Bly*.

❧ ❧

Has Anybody Seen Our Ship? Answers

1. F—*Coronia*—*Sail Away*
2. D—U.S.S. *Powhatan*—*Pacific Overtures*. If you knew this one, you are either a rabid Sondhead or have studied a lot of nineteenth-century history.

3. G—S.S. *Bernard Cohn*—*On a Clear Day You Can See Forever*
4. I—*Ile de France*—*Gentlemen Prefer Blondes*
5. K—S.S. *Paradise*—*Oh Captain!*
6. H—*New Caledonia*—*Sugar*
7. L—*Erasmus*—*Shogun: The Musical*. Now be honest: did you know this one because you're familiar with this flop, or because you read James Clavell's best-selling novel?
8. B—*Cotton Blossom*—*Show Boat*. If you got this one wrong, you really missed the boat.
9. A—S.S. *Reprisal*—*Ben Franklin in Paris*. Okay, this was a toughie, even if you are familiar enough with the score to sing "We Sail the Seas."
10. C—S.S. *Gigantic*—*Little Me*
11. E—U.S.S. *Nebraska*—*Hit the Deck*
12. J—R.M.S. *Aurania*—*Miss Liberty*
13. N—S.S. *American*—*Anything Goes*
14. M—*Catskill*—*Very Good Eddie*

BROADWAY BONUS: The other White Star ships cited in *Titanic* were the *Baltic*, on which Barrett had been stoker, and the *Majestic*, on which Fleet had been lookout. Both ships remained in service many years after their sister vessel hit that iceberg.

I Could Pass the Football Answers

1. E—Chuck in *Promises, Promises*, hopes to take the girl of his dreams, a basketball fan, to the Knicks-Celtics game. She doesn't show, and while waiting for her outside Madison Square Garden, he misses a 129–128 loss for the Knicks in double over-time.
2. *Bells Are Ringing*, *Guys and Dolls*, and *Little Johnny Jones* all feature horse racing.
3. In *Company*, Sarah shows Harry her progress in her karate lessons.
4. D—"The Tennis Song" in *City of Angels* is one of the naughtiest songs ever.
5. If there are two gay men playing racquetball onstage, it's probably Marvin and Whizzer, and you're at a production of *Falsettos*.
6. Golf and football are mentioned in the lyrics to "My Heart Belongs to Daddy."
7. You get full credit for this question if you answered either the Polo Grounds or Braves Field, c. 1911–1914, but the correct answer is *Ragtime* ("What a Game!"). Hub Perdue's name is spelled incorrectly in the liner notes to the cast album. His nickname was "the Gallatin Squash," but somehow Lynn Ahrens couldn't work that little tidbit into the lyrics.
8. Professor Fodorski (Ray Bolger) mixes engineering and football in 1962's *All American*, but the show was sacked for a huge loss.
9. The soldiers in *Passion* are playing pool.
10. A—Cole Porter wrote "Bingo, Eli Yale" and several other Yale fight songs still used today.
11. B—the ushers at *Good News* were dressed in collegiate jerseys.

12. Jackie Robinson, who broke baseball's color barrier, was the subject of the musical *The First* (1981).
13. A—Richie got a sports scholarship to college in *A Chorus Line*. It's not specified which sport, but I'm guessing basketball from the lyrics.
14. Edith Herbert, a famous long-distance swimmer, in *My One and Only* is performing in an aquacade when she meets aviator Billy Buck Chandler.
15. God gave us feet to play football. Soccer, that is.
16. D—the boys in *The Full Monty* develop their striptease choreography by thinking of the moves of basketball great Michael Jordan.
17. E—in *Let 'Em Eat Cake*, the Supreme Court justices and the League of Nations play baseball. Vice President Throttlebottom is the umpire, with dangerous results.
18. Please tell me you didn't answer *Starlight Express*. The correct answer, of course, is *The Rink* (1984).
19. In "T.E.A.M." from *You're a Good Man, Charlie Brown*, Charlie Brown describes how Linus, leaning out of a third-story window, caught fly balls with his blanket.
20. B—"Pour le Sport" satirizes golf.

So Much in Common Answers

1. All these shows had songs with a Christmas theme: "Yuletide, Park Avenue," *Call Me Mister*; "Christmas Child," *Irma la Douce*; "Be a Santa," *Subways Are for Sleeping*; "Twelve Days to Christmas," *She Loves Me*; "We Need a Little Christmas," *Mame*.
2. The original productions of *No Strings, Cabaret, Chicago*, and *I Love My Wife* had the orchestra or band onstage.
3. *The Golden Apple, Camelot, Into the Woods*, and *Wicked* all had witches or sorceresses.
4. Irving Berlin, Harold Arlen, Kurt Weill, and Al Jolson were all sons of cantors.
5. *Of Thee I Sing, The Boy Friend, Bye Bye Birdie, Annie*, and *The Best Little Whorehouse in Texas* all had sequels, none of which were successful. (*Let 'Em Eat Cake, Divorce Me, Darling, Bring Back Birdie, Annie II* and *Annie Warbucks*, and The Best Little Whorehouse Goes Public, respectively.)
6. All these shows had songs about coffee: "Let's Have Another Cup of Coffee," *Face the Music*; "Coffee Break," *How to Succeed*; "Coffee in a Cardboard Cup," *70, Girls, 70*; "Coffee, Black," *Big*.
7. *Merrily We Roll Along, They're Playing Our Song, Rent, A New Brain*, and *Curtains* all have composers as characters.
8. *The Boys from Syracuse, By Jupiter, The Happiest Girl in the World, The Frogs*, and *Home Sweet Homer* are all set in ancient Greece. Well, technically, *The Happiest Girl in the World* is set in Pontus, land of the ancient Amazons, located in what is now Turkey, but back then it was Asia Minor and plenty of Greeks lived in that region. And there are Greeks and Greek gods in the show.
9. *Flahooley, Carnival, Little Shop of Horrors, The Lion King, Sweet Smell of Success*, and *Avenue Q* all have puppets.
10. *Going Up, Rosalie, My One and Only, Steel Pier, The Drowsy Chaperone*, and *Catch Me If You Can* all feature characters who are aviators. I could have added *Flying High*, but I think that would have made things too obvious.

Safety in Numbers Answers

1. K—"One Night in Bangkok," *Chess*
2. BB—"Two Ladies in de Shade of de Banana Tree," *House of Flowers*
3. Q—"Three Sunny Rooms," *Rags*
4. V—"Four Jews in a Room Bitching," *Falsettos*
5. D—"Five Zeros," *On the Twentieth Century*
6. W—"Six Months Out of Every Year," *Damn Yankees*
7. O—"Seven Deadly Virtues," *Camelot*
8. H—"Eight Day Week," *Don't Play Us Cheap*
9. CC—"Nine People's Favorite Thing," *[title of show]*
10. B—"Ten Cents a Dance," *Simple Simon*
11. X—"Eleven O'clock Song," *Ankles Aweigh*
12. Z—"Twelve Days to Christmas," *She Loves Me*
13. C—"Thirteen Collar," *Very Good Eddie*
14. N—"Fourteen Dwight Avenue, Natick, MA," *Elegies: A Song Cycle*
15. I—"Sixteen Going on Seventeen," *The Sound of Music*
16. Y—"Twenty Dollar Bill, and Why," *Caroline, or Change*
17. E—"Twenty-two Years," *Grand Hotel*
18. J—"Twenty-four Hours of Lovin'," *The Best Little Whorehouse in Texas*
19. L—"Forty Minutes for Lunch," *One Touch of Venus*
20. F—"Forty-five Minutes from Broadway," *Forty-five Minutes from Broadway*
21. R—"Fifty Percent," *Ballroom*
22. AA—"70, Girls, 70," *70, Girls, 70*
23. A—"Seventy-six Trombones," *The Music Man*
24. S—"Ninety Again," *Two by Two*
25. G—"One Hundred Easy Ways to Lose a Man," *Wonderful Town*
26. DD—"Million Dollar Smile," *Billion Dollar Baby*
27. M—"Seven Million Crumbs," *The Most Happy Fella*
28. T—"Twenty Million People," *My Favorite Year*
29. P—"Fifty Million Years Ago," *Celebration*
30. U—"A Hundred Million Miracles," *Flower Drum Song*

Old Sayin's Answers

1. I—Bob Fosse, "Directors are never in short supply of girlfriends."
2. H—Mary Martin, on hearing Lerner and Loewe's first songs for *My Fair Lady*, "Those dear boys have lost their talent."
3. K—Jule Styne, evaluating Irving Berlin's talent, "It's easy to be clever. But the really clever thing is to be simple."
4. E—Ethel Merman, "Call me Miss Birdseye of 1950. The show is frozen!" This comment, one of the most famous in musical history, came when Irving Berlin brought her a finished lyric to replace the dummy lyric she'd been singing in *Call Me Madam*. (This is my tribute to Broadway historian Ethan Mordden, who manages to sneak this quote into nearly all his books.)

5. A—David Merrick, "It's not enough that I should succeed. Others should fail." So said the Abominable Showman.
6. C—Gwen Verdon, "Sex in a dance is in the eye of the beholder." And then Verdon continued, "I never thought my dances sexy. I suppose that's because I see myself with my face washed and I look like a rabbit."
7. G—George Kaufman, who knew a thing or two about satire, famously proclaimed, "Satire is what closes on Saturday night."
8. D—Stephen Sondheim, on creating musicals, "Content dictates form." This dictum explains why no two Sondheim musicals resemble each other.
9. B—Richard Rodgers, "I can pee a melody." But it's kind of hard to write lyrics that way.
10. F—Barbara Cook, "I didn't know I was part of a Golden Age." She might not have known, but she certainly helped make it golden.

Keeping Cool with Coolidge Answers

1. C—"The Face on the Dime" in *Call Me Mister* honored FDR.
2. The 1989 rock opera *Senator Joe*, about Commie-chasing Joseph McCarthy, closed after three previews.
3. D—Leonard Bernstein and Alan Jay Lerner's *1600 Pennsylvania Avenue* looked at a century of presidents, including Hayes, all played by Ken Howard (who trained for the role by playing Jefferson in *1776*).
4. B—*Maggie Flynn* was set in 1863 New York during the draft riots, and starred Jack Cassidy and Shirley Jones.
5. E—Ronald Reagan, whose quips are quoted in Jerome Weidman's *Assassins* libretto, is not mentioned in a Sondheim lyric. Did you pick Hoover? Hoover is mentioned in *Assassins*' "How I Saved Roosevelt" and in "Montana Chem," from *Saturday Night*. As for the others, Fillmore and his successor Pierce are cited in "Please Hello" from *Pacific Overtures* and Lincoln and McKinley are featured in *Assassins*' "The Ballad of Booth" and "The Ballad of Csolgosz."
6. B—the characters in *Bloomer Girl* attend a production of *Uncle Tom's Cabin*.
7. The massacre at My Lai was the basis for the flop rock opera *The Lieutenant*.
8. C—"Little Tin Box" from *Fiorello!* satirized the corruption of Tammany Hall.
9. The assassination of John F. Kennedy on November 22, 1963, provides the backdrop for *Caroline, or Change*.
10. If you know your history, you know who was at the 1904 Republican National Convention, and could guess that the musical was *Teddy and Alice*, about Theodore Roosevelt and his lively daughter Alice. If you don't know your U.S. history, but do know your Broadway history, you could have gone over the 1987 season in your mind (I know, that's painful) and come to the same conclusion.
11. D—Benjamin Franklin, as played by Robert Preston in *Ben Franklin in Paris*, sang "I Love the Ladies." This 1964 musical by Sidney Michaels and Mark Sandrich was based on the trip Franklin took to France to get backing for the United States' war against the British.
12. D—there are twelve historical figures in *Ragtime:* Booker T. Washington, Houdini and his mother, J. P. Morgan, Henry Ford, Emma Goldman, Evelyn Nesbit, Stanford

White, Harry Thaw, Admiral Peary, Matthew Henson, and probably the least known of the lot, Charles S. Whitman, who was the district attorney of Manhattan and later the governor of the state of New York.

13. A—Andrew Johnson's impeachment has never been the subject of a musical. However, there is a rock musical called *Bloody Bloody Andrew Jackson* (premiered in Los Angeles, 2008), which depicts the seventh president in rock star fashion. You can find the fall of Saigon in *Miss Saigon*, the women's suffrage movement in *Bloomer Girl*, the opening of Japan in *Pacific Overtures*, and Columbus' preparations for his voyage in the closed-out-of-town *1491*.

14. B—Peter Stuyvesant appears in *Knickerbocker Holiday*, but there's a song about him in *Dearest Enemy*.

15. B—the policy of improving U.S. relations with Latin America was called "the Good Neighbor policy." Given that Ruth in the "Conga!" number from *Wonderful Town* is singing with a bunch of Brazilian cadets, it makes sense for her to mention this. But the song is chock-full of things to learn about in thirties America, ranging from various New Deal organizations (the N.R.A. and the T.V.A.) to Charles G. Dawes (v.p. under Coolidge and creator of the Dawes plan to assist bankrupt Germany with its reparation payments) to author John Steinbeck and tennis star Helen Wills.

The Doctor Is In Answers

1. I—Dr. Joseph Taylor, Jr.—*Allegro*. I refrained from adding Joseph's dad and various other partners mentioned in the show. Too many docs spoil the trivia quiz.

2. T—Dr. Frank N. Furter—*The Rocky Horror Show*

3. M—Dr. Lyman Hall—*1776*. Dr. Hall is the gentleman with degrees in both medicine and theology. One of his co-signers of the Declaration was also a doctor, Josiah Bartlett of New Hampshire, but Hall has the larger role in the show.

4. A—"Dr. Emil Shüffhausen III"—*Dirty Rotten Scoundrels*

5. O—Dr. Van Helsing—*Dracula*

6. D—Dr. Rocquefort of *Amour* treats Dusoleil.

7. J—Dr. Mendel—*Falsettos*. No wonder Mendel ends up on such familiar terms with Marvin and then Trina. He's always been on a first-name basis with them.

8. B—Dr. Tambourri—*Passion*. I concede that Fosca is around the bend, but don't you think Dr. Tambourri deserves an awful lot of the blame for what happens in *Passion*?

9. X—Dr. Fine and Dr. Madden are the medicos treating Diana in *Next to Normal*.

10. Q—Dr. Kitchell—*Bells Are Ringing*. One of the two dentists on our list.

11. E—Dr. Brooks—*Lady in the Dark*

12. R—Dr. Lucy Van Pelt—*You're a Good Man, Charlie Brown*. I'm not exactly sure how a five-year-old wound up with a degree in psychiatry, but clearly she was practicing.

13. L—Dr. Rashil Singh—*Christine*. The only show in Broadway history with a hymn to the joys (and pains) of vaccination.

14. U—"Dr. J. Bowen Hapgood"—*Anyone Can Whistle*

15. F—Dr. Henry Jekyll—*Jekyll and Hyde*. Was this too easy? I considered adding Dr. Downer from *Hazel Flagg*, but figured that was too obscure.

16. **K**—Dr. Dreyfuss—*Promises, Promises.* I confess I entirely forgot this character's name until squinting through my bifocals at the tiny type of playbills, searching for doctors.

17. **N**—Dr. Neville Craven—*The Secret Garden.* The authors of the show added this character, who is not found in the classic children's novel, but making him the boy's uncle and burdening him with an unrequited love for his own sister-in-law made for great dramatic theatre. Not to mention a rattle-the-rafters number for Robert Westenburg and Mandy Patinkin.

18. **S**—Dr. Carrasco—*Man of La Mancha*

19. **C**—Col. Dr. Otternschlag—*Grand Hotel.* Nobody remembers his name, but if you remembered there was a doctor (shooting up in the lobby) in *Grand Hotel* and looked through the list of obvious Germanic names (besides Frankenstein and Dr. Shüffhausen of Vienna), you could guess this was the right answer.

20. **P**—Dr. Orin Bernstein—*Little Shop of Horrors.* Our other dentist. This character is a good musical reminder to brush and floss regularly.

21. **V**—Dr. Mark Bruckner—*On a Clear Day You Can See Forever*

22. **H**—Dr. Frederick Frankenstein—*Young Frankenstein.* I suppose I could have added Frederick's grandfather, Victor, who appeared in the short-lived musical, *Frankenstein,* but that might have gotten a little confusing. Unless I listed them phonetically: Fran-ken-*steen* and Frank-en-*styne.*

23. **G**—Dr. John Watson—*Baker Street.* Actually, Dr. Watson's Christian name is not given in the playbill, but all good Holmesians know it.

Chaucer, Rabelais, and Balzac Answers

The answers in this section are as detailed as I could possibly make them. As such, many refer to particularly obscure or little-known productions. Unless you're obsessed or a grad student in musical theatre studies who specializes in literary adaptations, no one expects you to know all of these.

1. Jane Austen's *Pride and Prejudice* became the 1959 musical *First Impressions* (book by Abe Burrows, songs by Robert Goldman, Glenn Paxton, and George Weiss). Another version, *Jane Austen's Pride and Prejudice: The Musical Play* (book by Lindsay Warren Baker, Amanda Jacobs, and Jeffrey Hatcher, songs by Baker and Jacobs), had hopes of reaching Broadway in 2009, but plans fell through. Austen's *Emma* (book, music, lyrics by Joel Adlen) was an entry at the 2007 New York Musical Theatre Festival.

2. Charlotte Brontë's *Jane Eyre* became a musical in 2000 (book by John Caird, songs by Paul Gordon). *Wuthering Heights,* by Charlotte's sister Emily, became the musical *Heathcliff,* through the efforts of musician-singer Cliff Richard, who played the lead. The production, with music by John Farrar and lyrics by Tim Rice, debuted in 1996 and toured the U.K., also placing several songs on the pop charts.

3. Pearl Buck's *My Indian Family* became the musical *Christine* (1960, book by Buck and Charles Peck, Jr., music by Sammy Fain, lyrics by Paul Francis Webster).

4. Miguel Cervantes' *Don Quixote* was turned into *Man of La Mancha* in 1965 by librettist Dale Wasserman, with music by Mitch Leigh and lyrics by Joe Darion.

5. Geoffrey Chaucer's *The Canterbury Tales* became a musical in London in 1968, and ran for 2,080 performances (book by Martin Starkie and Neville Coghill, lyrics by Coghill, music by John Hawkins and Richard Hill). The Broadway production in 1969 managed just 121 showings and suffered from high expenses.

6. The prolific Charles Dickens is one of the champions of adapted musicals. The biggest success was *Oliver!*, Lionel Bart's creation from 1960 that enjoyed a long run in London, followed by the David Merrick production on Broadway in 1963 (774 performances). Following hard on *Oliver!*'s heels was the flop *Pickwick*, which also originated in London, then briefly transferred to Broadway in 1965 (book by Wolf Markowitz, music by Cyril Ornadel, lyrics by Leslie Bricusse). *David Copperfield* became the musical *Copperfield* in 1981 (created by Al Kasha and Joel Hirschhorn), but, again, didn't fare well.

   The Mystery of Edwin Drood (title shortened later in the run to *Drood*) did far better in 1985. *Drood* was the brainchild of Rupert Holmes, who handled book, music, lyrics, and orchestrations and, since Dickens died before finishing the mystery, cleverly devised multiple endings. The audience voted on the outcome of the plot each night. *Drood* ran for 608 performances, a highlight in the dismal eighties.

   A Christmas Carol has seen several adaptations, including the one that ran from 1994 to 2003 at Madison Square Garden, with lyrics by Lynn Ahrens and music by Alan Menken, and *Comin' Uptown* (1979), with Gregory Hines as Scrooge, a slumlord in Harlem. (I confess my favorite is still the television musical *Mr. Magoo's Christmas Carol*, with songs by Jule Styne and Bob Merrill).

   A Tale of Two Cities has had at least three different musical versions, the latest and largest created by Jill Santoriello in 2008 (sixty performances, hurt badly by the economy).

   You get a big Dickensisan bonus if you could also name: *My Gentleman Pip*, an English production of *Great Expectations* from 1968; the 1975–1976 production of *Great Expectations* that ran in England and Canada but never caught on; or the English production *Nickleby and Me* (1975), based on *Nicholas Nickleby*.

7. T. S. Eliot's *Old Possum's Book of Practical Cats* became Andrew Lloyd Webber and Trevor Nunn's *Cats* in London in 1981. I'm still waiting for the musical adaptation of "The Love Song of J. Alfred Prufrock."

8. Edna Ferber's mammoth novel *Show Boat* became the 1927 classic by Jerome Kern and Oscar Hammerstein II. *Show Boat* ran for 572 performances, has been revived and filmed many times, and included many songs that became standards. None of that applies to *Saratoga*, the 1959 musical based on *The Saratoga Trunk* (book by Morton da Costa, music by Harold Arlen, lyrics by Johnny Mercer). *Saratoga* limped along for eighty performances before packing its trunks.

9. With Jerome Lawrence and Robert E. Lee, James Hilton wrote the lyrics and book for *Shangri-la*, the short-lived musical based on his novel *Lost Horizon*. Harry Warren handled the music, but today the show is largely remembered for the giant Lucite cubes that were supposed to be mountains.

10. Homer's ancient Greek poems, *The Iliad* and *The Odyssey*, were used as the basis for two very different musicals. *The Golden Apple* (1954), with music by Jerome Moross and lyrics by John Latouche, updated the action to Washington State, just after the Spanish-American War. The unusual piece was a success off-Broadway, but didn't do

well after transferring. Years later, in 1976, *Home, Sweet Homer* opened and closed on the same night. This work (book by Albert Marre and Roland Kibbee, music by Mitch Leigh, lyrics by Charles Burr and Forman Brown) followed Homer's original plot more closely, with Yul Brynner as Odysseus, but even his commanding presence couldn't save it.

11. Victor Hugo's classic novel *Les Misérables* was turned into one of the most successful musicals of all time by Frenchmen Alain Boublil and Claude-Michel Schönberg in 1985. Hugo's *The Hunchback of Notre Dame* has had multiple productions, though far from that kind of success. Hugo himself wrote the book for an opera based on it back in 1836. Bryon Janis and Hal Hackady had an off-Broadway production in 1993, and Riccardo Cocciante and Luc Plamondon had a French production in 1998 that has toured the world in different languages. Disney had a successful animated film version, with songs by Broadway veterans Alan Menken and Steven Schwartz, which was adapted for the stage in Berlin by James Lapine as *Der Glöckner der Notre-Dame*. C. Rainey Lewis has created a rock *Hunchback*, which debuted in Seattle in 1998, and former member of the rock group Styx, Dennis DeYoung, debuted his *The Hunchback of Notre-Dame* in Chicago in 2008.

12. Henry James' *The Ambassadors* became the flop musical *Ambassador* (1972), with music and lyrics by Don Gohman and Hal Hackady, and book by Don Ettlinger and Anna Marie Barlow. James' *The Turn of the Screw* became a popular opera by Britten in 1954, which may have scared anyone away from trying to make it into a musical.

13. James Joyce's work would not seem a likely candidate for musicalizations, but in 1999, Richard Nelson and Shaun Davey turned Joyce's short story "The Dead" into *James Joyce's The Dead*. It was a quiet, thoughtful piece, with excellent Irish music, but audiences never took to it.

14. Herman Melville's *Billy Budd* became the 1969 musical *Billy*, but only for one evening. Stephen Glassman wrote the book, while Ron Dante and Gene Allan created the songs. Melville's greatest work, *Moby Dick*, is the basis for a show-within-a-show in the British musical *Moby Dick: A Whale of a Tale*. The work, created by Robert Longden, was first produced by Cameron Mackintosh in 1992, but has seen revisions and regional productions since then. The setting is a girls' school, rather like St. Trinian's, where the students intend to put on their own musical version of *Moby Dick* to raise money to save the school. Ahab is portrayed by the headmistress, who, in best British pantomime tradition, is always played by a man.

15. James Michener's *Tales of the South Pacific* won the Pulitzer Prize for the novel. Richard Rodgers, Oscar Hammerstein, and Joshua Logan's 1949 adaptation, *South Pacific*, won the Pulitzer Prize for drama.

16. Marjorie Kinnan Rawlings' *The Yearling* also won the Pulitzer for the novel and was made into a successful film. But its musical version (book by Herbert Martin and Lore Noto, music by Michael Leonard, and lyrics by Martin) only stayed on the boards for three performances in 1965.

17. John Steinbeck's *East of Eden* became the 1968 musical *Here's Where I Belong*, which opened and closed on the same night. Alex Gordon wrote the book (Terrence McNally requested the removal of his writing credit); Robert Waldman did the music; and the lyrics were by Alfred Uhry. Steinbeck was involved in the creation of the other musical based on his work. He was supposed to write a libretto based on

Cannery Row, but ended up using characters from that novel and writing a new novel, *Sweet Thursday*, at the same time as he sent chapters of it to Oscar Hammerstein, who wrote the libretto in pieces. This convoluted history may help explain why the result, 1955's *Pipe Dream*, wasn't a success for Rodgers and Hammerstein.

18. Robert Louis Stevenson's novella *The Strange Case of Dr. Jekyll and Mr. Hyde* became the long-running (1,543 performances) but still too costly musical *Jekyll and Hyde*, with book and lyrics by Leslie Bricusse and a pop score by Frank Wildhorn. Stevenson's classic adventure tale *Treasure Island* was the basis for one of Jule Styne's last musicals, *Pieces of Eight*, with book by Michael Stewart and Mark Bramble, and lyrics by Susan Birkenhead. It premiered in Edmonton, Alberta, in 1985, but has not been produced since. I, for one, would have liked to have seen George Hearn as Long John Silver.

19. Leo Tolstoy wrote in *Anna Karenina* that every unhappy family is unhappy in its own way. Judging by the forty-six performances of the 1992 musical based on the novel, one could say every unhappy musical is unhappy in its own way. Ann Crumb starred as the doomed Russian, while Peter Kellogg wrote the book and the lyrics for Daniel Levine's music.

20. Mark Twain is well represented in musical form, providing fodder for several hits. In 1927, Rodgers and Hart and librettist Herbert Fields adapted *A Connecticut Yankee in King Arthur's Court* into *A Connecticut Yankee*, which ran for 421 performances—a smash for the twenties. Bock and Harnick used Twain's short piece "The Diary of Adam and Eve" for the first act of their 1966 hit, *The Apple Tree*. Librettist William Hauptman and country music legend Roger Miller created 1985's *Big River* from *The Adventures of Huckleberry Finn*. It ran over one thousand performances. All three of these shows have had popular revivals.

    Tom Sawyer in 2001 was not so fortunate. Ken Ludwig adapted Twain's novel, and Don Schlitz wrote the songs for the short-lived show. A British librettist-composer, Tom Boyd, created a version that played in London and in British regional theatre in 1960–1961.

    The latest Twain musical was Neil Berg's off-Broadway production of *The Prince and the Pauper*, which ran for over a year in 2002–2003.

21. Jules Verne's *Around the World in 80 Days* was turned into a costly extravaganza in 1946 by Orson Welles, with songs by Cole Porter, but was not very faithful to Verne's story. It sank in a sea of red ink. Mike Todd had been one of the show's producers, but bailed out, leaving Welles holding the bag. Todd would get the movie rights, and the resulting film, which cut all the songs, won five Oscars, including Best Picture.

    In 1988, director Des McAnuff staged a different version of the tale, called *80 Days*, with book by Snoo Wilson and songs by Ray Davies of the Kinks. The production premiered in San Diego.

    So far there have been no musical versions of *20,000 Leagues Under the Sea*, but if they can spend millions to make Spider-Man swoop on his web above a stage, I don't see why a giant singing squid is so difficult.

22. Voltaire has had but one work turned into a musical, the cult classic *Candide* (1956, music by Leonard Bernstein, book by Lillian Hellman, lyrics by Hellman, Bernstein, Richard Wilbur, John Latouche, and Dorothy Parker).

23. Alice Walker's novel *The Color Purple* won the Pulitzer Prize for fiction. The musical adaptation by Marsha Norman, with songs by Allee Willis, Brenda Russell, and Stephen Brice, debuted in 2005 and had a successful run of 910 performances. LaChanze, in the lead role of Celie, won the Best Actress Tony.

24. Oscar Wilde's novel *The Picture of Dorian Gray* has been musicalized three times, but none of them lasted long. They include: *Dorian* (1990), with songs by Michael Rubell and Nan Barcan; *Dorian Gray* (1996), with music by Gary David Levinson, book and lyrics by Allan Rieser; and *Dorian* (2000) at the Goodspeed Theatre, created by Richard Gleaves and directed by Gabriel Barre.

25. In 1958, playwright Ketti Frings adapted Thomas Wolfe's *Look Homeward, Angel* into a play, winning the Pulitzer Prize for drama. The play had a run of over 500 performances, but Frings and Peter Udell's 1978 musical, *Angel* (music by Gary Geld, lyrics by Udell), hung on for barely a week.

26. Émile Zola's 1867 novel, *Thérèse Racquin*, became the 2001 musical *Thou Shalt Not*, staged by Susan Strohman, with a book by David Thompson and songs by Harry Connick, Jr. The cast included Kate Levering, Debra Monk, Craig Bierko, and Norbert Leo Butz. Thompson updated the action to late-forties New Orleans, and Connick provided a jazzy score, but the show's previews and run were hurt by the September 11 disaster.

27. Aristophanes was the leading comic playwright in ancient Athens. Two of his works have become musicals. *Lysistrata*, in which the women of Athens attempt to stop an ongoing war by withholding sex, became the 1961 flop *The Happiest Girl in the World*. Fred Saidy and Henry Mayer wrote the libretto, and Yip Harburg penned sassy lyrics to the music of Jacques Offenbach.

The Frogs was first adapted in 1974 by Burt Shevelove, with songs by Stephen Sondheim, and performed in the Yale University swimming pool. (The play takes place in the underworld, and the pool represented the river Styx.) Twenty years later, Nathan Lane expanded the brief piece and played the lead role, Dionysus, on Broadway.

28. Anton Chekhov has had only one of his plays turned into a musical—well, sort of. The 1980 spoof *A Day in Hollywood/A Night in the Ukraine* (book and lyrics by Dick Vosburgh, music by Frank Lazarus) featured as its second act a musical version of *The Bear*—as performed by the Marx Brothers. Patricia Lopez earned a Beat Featured Actress Tony for her Harpo Marx.

29. The ancient Greek tragedies of Euripides haven't fared well as musicals. *Medea*, in which the vengeful princess takes bloody revenge on the husband who betrays her, became 1999's *Marie Christine*. Michael John LaChiusa updated the action to late-1890s New Orleans and Chicago, and Audra McDonald played the terrifying title role. Perhaps the material was too grim for audiences to bear, but the score is unquestionably powerful.

Medea was the basis for a parody in 1955's *Ben Bagley's Shoestring Revue*.

Euripides' *The Trojan Women* has recently (2008) been updated into a musical, *Trojan Women 2.1* for Wilmington, North Carolina's Guerilla Theatre. The work, by Gareth Hides and Gavin Thatcher, moves the action to 1920s America.

30. Henrik Ibsen hasn't really had any of his works turned into musicals. Somehow, *Hedda Gabler: The Musical* just hasn't caught any producer's eye. Yet Ibsen's *A Doll*

House provided the characters for the brief run of 1982's *A Doll's Life* (book and lyrics by Betty Comden and Adolph Green, music by Larry Grossman). The show imagined Nora's life after she walks out at the end of *A Doll House*.

Roger McGuinn of the Byrds has apparently been working on a country-rock version of Ibsen's *Peer Gynt* since 1969. Some songs have appeared on Bryds' albums.

31. Ben Jonson's *Volpone* became the 1964 flop musical *Foxy*. Ring Lardner, Jr., and Ian McLellan Hunter wrote the libretto; Johnny Mercer penned the lyrics to Robert Emmett Dolan's music; and Bert Lahr and Larry Blyden starred. The action was updated to the 1890s Klondike gold rush.

32. Eugene O'Neill has had two Broadway musicals created from his work, and oddly enough, Bob Merrill did the songs for both. O'Neill's Pulitzer winner, *Anna Christie*, became 1957's *New Girl in Town*, with direction and book by George Abbott. Gwen Verdon starred as former prostitute Anna, with choreography by Bob Fosse. Two years later, Jackie Gleason starred in *Take Me Along*, adapted from *Ah, Wilderness!*, one of O'Neill's few comedies. Joseph Stein and Robert Russell handled the libretto about a Connecticut family in 1910. Both shows ran for over four hundred performances.

33. Plautus was a Roman comic playwright whose works *Pseudolus* and *Miles Gloriosus* provided the basis for *A Funny Thing Happened on the Way to the Forum*, the 1962 hit by Larry Gelbart and Burt Shevelove, with songs by Stephen Sondheim. *Forum* starred Zero Mostel as the sly slave Pseudolus, and ran for 964 performances, winning the Best Musical Tony.

34. Edmond Rostand's beloved romantic play *Cyrano* has been musicalized at least seven times, as is discussed in the Ah, Paris! quiz.

35. Richard Sheridan's *The Rivals* became the 1961 off-Broadway musical *All in Love*. Librettist-lyricist Bruce Geller and composer Jack Urbont created a delightful score from Sheridan's comedy of manners.

36. William Shakespeare is the unquestioned king of musical adaptations. *The Comedy of Errors* has been turned into two Broadway musicals: the hit *The Boys from Syracuse* (1938, Abbott and Rodgers and Hart) and the flop *Oh, Brother!* (1981, book and lyrics by Donald Driver and music by Michael Valenti).

The Taming of the Shrew became Cole Porter's most enduring hit, 1948's *Kiss Me, Kate*, with libretto by Sam and Bella Spewack, running over a thousand performances and winning the Best Musical Tony.

Romeo and Juliet provided the inspiration for another classic, *West Side Story* (1957, book by Arthur Laurents, music by Leonard Bernstein, lyrics by Stephen Sondheim). The creators took Shakespeare's star-crossed lovers and transplanted them to rival gangs in a gritty New York slum. In St. Paul (1999), Terrence Mann and Jerome Korman debuted a more traditional *Romeo and Juliet*, using a pop-rock score.

Twelfth Night has been adapted into musical form six times. *Your Own Thing* (1968, book by Donald Driver, songs by Hal Hester and Danny Apolinar) ran for 933 performances off-Broadway and toured overseas. The show used a rock score, updating the action to the present. In direct competition with it was *Love and Let Love* (music by Stanley Garber, book and lyrics by Don Christopher and John Lollos). But 1968 off-Broadway was only big enough for one musical *Twelfth Night*, and *Your Own Thing* was it.

George Abbott was unaware of *Your Own Thing*, or he might not have tackled *Music Is*, his last original show, in 1976. With music by Richard Adler and lyrics by Will Holt, the show lasted just over a week on Broadway. The 1997 adaptation, *Play On!*, which used the music of Duke Ellington and set the piece in "the magical Kingdom of Harlem in the Swinging Forties," also flopped. More recently, *Illyria* (book, music, and lyrics by Peter Mills) premiered in 2002, providing a more traditional take on the story with a contemporary musical theatre score. *Illyria* ran off-Broadway in 2008 to good notices. The 2005 jukebox musical *All Shook Up* also used *Twelfth Night* as its inspiration.

Two Gentlemen of Verona, like *Kiss Me, Kate*, won the Best Musical Tony. The 1971 crowd-pleaser by Galt MacDermot, John Guare, and Mel Shapiro had a rock score and a playful air. Clifton Davis and Raul Julia starred as the Gentlemen.

Rockabye Hamlet (book, music, and lyrics by Cliff Jones) also had a rock score, but lasted only a week in 1976. *Hamlet* has been the basis of a parody, the off-Broadway *The Melancholy Dane—Hamlet! The Musical* by Michael Bouson, Joe Correll, Jamey Green, and Kathy Shepard—the same people responsible for 2002's *McBeth! The Musical Comedy!* And lest anyone forget, it's really the story behind *The Lion King*, after dilution through the Japanese anime series *Kimba, the White Lion*. Nor should we forget Max Bialystock's *Funny Boy*.

There have been sundry attempts to turn *A Midsummer Night's Dream* into a musical, none of which succeeded, including 1939's *Swingin' the Dream*, which set the work in 1890s Louisiana. Louis Armstrong played Bottom and Butterfly McQueen was Puck, but only for two weeks. Jimmy van Heusen supplied a lively score. Arthur Perlman and Jeffrey Lunden's *Another Midsummer Night*, a kind of modern riff on the original, premiered in Chicago in 1995.

As You Like It became the award-winning musical *Like You Like It*, set in a 1985 high school, where everyone discovers that "All the world's a mall." Librettist-lyricist Sammy Buck and composer Daniel S. Acquisto's effort has been popular in regional theatre.

Catch My Soul, a 1967 modernization of *Othello*, was set in a hippie commune with a rock score by composers Roy Pohlman and Emil Dean Zoghby, and librettist-lyricist Jack Good. Jerry Lee Lewis played Iago in the Los Angeles production, and the rock band Gass, led by Robert Tench, performed in the U.K. edition.

The Merry Wives of Windsor became 1988's *Lone Star Love: The Merry Wives of Windsor, Texas*, updating the play to post–Civil War Texas. It debuted in Houston, but later had an acclaimed off-Broadway run and a 2004 cast album. Plans to go to Broadway with Randy Quaid as "Colonel John Falstaff" fell through.

Another adaptation set in the old West was 2004's *Desperate Measures*, which used *Measure for Measure* as its basis. Peter Kellogg handled the book and lyrics, while David Friedman wrote the music. The show appeared in the New York Musical Theatre Festival in 2006.

Venus and Adonis recently had a musical adaptation in Australia. The 2008 effort by Andree Greenwell debuted in Melbourne and later traveled to New Zealand.

The Boys Are Coming Home was originally commissioned by the National Arts Center of Canada and debuted in 2006. This adaptation of *Much Ado About Nothing* updates the plot to America in 1945, with the soldiers returning from the war. Berni

Stapleton wrote the libretto and Leslie Arden provided the songs. A revised book by Rebecca Gilman was slated for a 2008 summer run at Chicago's Goodman Theatre, but differences between Arden and Gilman canceled the production.

The lengthy histories of *Henry IV* may seem highly unlikely material for a musical, but Matt Sax created *Clay* in 2008, with characters modeled after Prince Hal and Falstaff. "Sir John" is an older rapper who takes Clifford "Clay" Keys under his musical wing and trains him in hip-hop. The show debuted at the Edinburgh Fringe Festival, and later played at New York's Lincoln Center.

The Tempest was the inspiration for the science fiction film *Forbidden Planet* and the 1980s British jukebox musical *Return to the Forbidden Planet*, which is discussed further in the jukebox musical quiz. There was also *The Tempest*, which played off-Broadway in 2006, created by Daniel Neiden and Ryan Knowles from a concept by Thomas Meehan.

Finally, while there is no musical version of *Cymbeline*, the character Shakespeare in *The Frogs* sings the speech, "Fear no more," to the music of Stephen Sondheim.

37. Oscar Wilde hasn't had much success in musical adaptations, despite many people taking shots at Jack and Algernon. The best known try at *The Importance of Being Earnest* was the 1960 off-Broadway *Earnest in Love* (music by Lee Pockriss, book and lyrics by Anne Crosswell), which didn't last long, but did leave a cast album with certain charms. Playwright Arnold Sundgaard, lyricist Ethan Ayer, and composer Alec Wilder created 1973's *Nobody's Earnest*. John Hugh Dean's *The Importance* played in London in 1984, and there was an *Ernest* in 2000, with music by Vance Lehmkuhl and book and lyrics by Gayden Wren.

Lady Windermere's Fan was given a musical makeover by Noel Coward in 1952's *After the Ball*, but unfortunately British audiences panned it.